Lecture Notes
in Business Information Processing   350

Series Editors

Wil van der Aalst
   RWTH Aachen University, Aachen, Germany
John Mylopoulos
   University of Trento, Trento, Italy
Michael Rosemann
   Queensland University of Technology, Brisbane, QLD, Australia
Michael J. Shaw
   University of Illinois, Urbana-Champaign, IL, USA
Clemens Szyperski
   Microsoft Research, Redmond, WA, USA

More information about this series at http://www.springer.com/series/7911

Cinzia Cappiello · Marcela Ruiz (Eds.)

Information Systems Engineering in Responsible Information Systems

CAiSE Forum 2019
Rome, Italy, June 3–7, 2019
Proceedings

Springer

Editors
Cinzia Cappiello 🅐
Politecnico di Milano
Milan, Italy

Marcela Ruiz 🅐
Universiteit Utrecht
Utrecht, The Netherlands

ISSN 1865-1348   ISSN 1865-1356   (electronic)
Lecture Notes in Business Information Processing
ISBN 978-3-030-21296-4   ISBN 978-3-030-21297-1   (eBook)
https://doi.org/10.1007/978-3-030-21297-1

This Springer imprint is published by the registered company Springer Nature Switzerland AG
The registered company address is: Gewerbestrasse 11, 6330 Cham, Switzerland

Preface

The objective of the CAiSE conferences is to provide a platform for the exchange of experience, research results, ideas, and prototypes between the research community and industry in the field of information systems engineering. Over almost three decades, the conference has become the yearly worldwide meeting point for the information system engineering community. This year, the 31st edition of the CAiSE conference was held in Rome, Italy, during June 5–7, 2019.

The CAiSE Forum is one of the traditional tracks of the CAiSE conference. Intended to serve as an interactive platform, the CAiSE Forum aims to present emerging new topics and controversial positions, as well as a demonstration of innovative systems, tools, and applications. The CAiSE Forum sessions facilitate the interaction, discussion, and exchange of ideas among presenters and participants. In accordance, two types of submissions have been called to the forum:

- Visionary papers presenting innovative research projects, which are still at a relatively early stage and do not necessarily include a full-scale validation. Visionary papers are presented as posters in the forum.
- Demo papers describe innovative tools and prototypes that implement the results of research efforts. The tools and prototypes are presented as demos in the forum.

Each submission to the CAiSE 2019 Forum was reviewed by three Program Committee members. Only those submissions for which there was an agreement on their relevance, novelty, and rigor were accepted for presentation in the forum. Additionally, some papers were invited to the forum as a result of the evaluation process in the CAiSE main conference. All in all, 22 papers were accepted for presentation. The presenters gave a 1-minute elevator pitch and were available to discuss their work through a poster and/or system demonstration in a dedicated session.

The papers describing the works are collected in these proceedings. We would like to thank everyone who contributed to CAiSE 2019 Forum. First, to our excellent Program Committee members who provided thorough evaluations of the papers and contributed to the promotion of the event. We thank all the authors who submitted to and presented papers at the forum for having shared their work with the community. Last, we would like to thank the CAiSE 2019 Program Committee and general chairs as well as the local Organizing Committee for their support.

June 2019

Cinzia Cappiello
Marcela Ruiz

Organization

General Chairs

Massimo Mecella   Sapienza Universitá di Roma, Italy
Barbara Pernici   Politecnico di Milano, Italy

Organization Chair

Andrea Marrella   Sapienza Universitá di Roma, Italy

Program Committee Chairs

Cinzia Cappiello   Politecnico di Milano, Italy
Marcela Ruiz   Utrecht University, The Netherlands

Program Committee

Raian Ali   University of Bournemouth, UK
Said Assar   Institut Mines-Télécom, France
Fatma Başak Aydemir   Boğaziçi University, Turkey
Saimir Bala   WU Vienna, Austria
Jan Claes   University of Ghent, Belgium
Marco Comuzzi   Ulsan National Institute of Science and Technology,
                                   South Korea
Dirk Fahland   Eindhoven University of Technology, The Netherlands
Luciano García-Bañuelos   University of Tartu, Estonia
Christos Kalloniatis   University of the Aegean, Greece
Dimka Karastoyanova   University of Groningen, The Netherlands
Daniel Lübke   Leibniz Universität Hannover, Germany
Selmin Nurcan   Université de Paris 1 Panthéon-Sorbonne, France
Michalis Pavlidis   University of Brighton, UK
Luise Pufahl   Hasso Plattner Institute, University of Potsdam,
                                   Germany
Jolita Ralyté   University of Geneva, Switzerland
David Rosado   Universidad de Castilla-La Mancha, Spain
Stefan Schönig   University of Bayreuth, Germany
Arik Senderovich   University of Toronto, Canada
Dolors Costal   Universitat Politècnica de Catalunya, Spain
Arnon Sturm   Ben-Gurion University of the Negev, Israel
Lucinéia Thom   Federal University of Rio Grande do Sul, Brazil

Gianluigi Viscusi	École Polytechnique Fédérale de Lausanne, Switzerland
Monica Vitali	Politecnico di Milano, Italy
Samuel Fricker	FHNW, Switzerland
Moe Wynn	Queensland University of Technology, Australia
Jose Luis de la Vara	Universidad de Castilla-La Mancha, Spain
Renata Guizzardi	Universidade Federal do Espírito Santo (UFES), Brazil

Contents

UBBA: Unity Based BPMN Animator

Basit Mubeen Abdul, Flavio Corradini, Barbara Re, Lorenzo Rossi$^{(\boxtimes)}$,
and Francesco Tiezzi

School of Science and Technology, University of Camerino, Camerino, Italy
basitmubeen.abdul@studenti.unicam.it,
{flavio.corradini,barbara.re,lorenzo.rossi,
francesco.tiezzi}@unicam.it

Abstract. In the last years BPMN became the most prominent notation for representing business processes, thanks to its wide usage in academic and industrial contexts. Despite BPMN is very intuitive, it's way
of representing activities with static flow charts may result effective just
for the BPM experts. Stakeholders who are not too much aware of the
BPMN notation could misread the behavior of the business process. To
this aim, BPMN animation tools can help model comprehension. However they are mainly based on 2D diagrams, just few works investigate
the use of a 3D world as an environment for closely portray the reality
of the business process. In this paper, we propose our tool UBBA, which
creates a custom 3D virtual world from an input *.bpmn* file. Besides
this 3-dimensional view of the diagram, we also integrate into UBBA the
semantics of the BPMN elements in order to enable the animation.

Keywords: BPMN · Collaboration · 3D visualization · Animation

1 Introduction

Business Process Model and Notation (BPMN) [14] is a well-established standard
for describing organization activities in a very intuitive way. BPMN allows to
easily represent single organization workflows and their compositions by means
of *process* and *collaboration* diagrams. Therefore, process stakeholders can communicate and reason about their processes in a standard manner. Business processes in the BPMN graphical notation are represented by means of static 2D
flow charts, where the graphics of the elements embeds their semantic categories
(e.g., rectangles for activities, diamonds for choices, circles for events, etc.). This
graphical representation is very straightforward for experts, but it results difficult
to understand for stakeholders [6] who have to know the syntax and semantics
of BPMN. Furthermore, when models become very large it is difficult to follow
their execution semantics [7] and the use of 2D instead of 3D representations
limits the amount of information the user can perceive [16].

In this regard, recent works foster new techniques for modeling and visualizing organization processes capable to bridge the gap between business people

© Springer Nature Switzerland AG 2019
C. Cappiello and M. Ruiz (Eds.): CAiSE Forum 2019, LNBIP 350, pp. 1–9, 2019.
https://doi.org/10.1007/978-3-030-21297-1_1

and BPMN. On the one hand, a virtual world representing a business process can enhance the communication activities, thus facilitating interactions between businessmen and stakeholders [11]. On the other hand, the animation of business processes can increase their understanding [4, 10, 13] and also the possibility to debug them [8].

The literature proposes several tool prototypes that follow such principles. Indeed, in [6] an implementation of a 3D virtual BPMN editor that embeds process models into a 3D world is presented. Similarly, in [5] and [17] the representation of

Table 1. Literature comparison

	[6]	[5]	[12]	[1]	[15]	[3]	[2]	[9]	UBBA
Collaboration	✗	✗	✗	✗	✗	✗	✓	✓	✓
Visualization	3D	3D	3D	▲	✗	2D	2D	2D	3D
Animation	✗	✗	✗	▲	3D	2D	2D	2D	3D
Custom graphics	✗	✗	✗	✗	✗	✗	✗	▲	✓
Standard input	✗	✓	✓	✗	✗	✓	✓	✓	✓

✓: fully, ▲: partially, ✗: not supported

Petri net-based business process models is enriched with the third dimension. Virtual worlds have also been used in the context of Workflow Management Systems (WfMSs). In [12] the authors have implemented an agent-based simulation architecture that can be used as a simulation component for any WfMS. It is also worth mentioning the BPM simulation game *Innov8* by IBM [1]. It gives to both IT and business players an excellent introduction to BPM, useful for learning the anatomy of a model. Another example is *Be a Token* [15], a javascript tool based on the A-Frame framework. This tool represents sequence flows as hallways to cross, and tasks as rooms with a door in the wall for each incoming/outgoing sequence flow. For what concerns the business process animation there are works attempting to show the processes execution, which however just provide a 2D visualization. These contributions use token flow or elements highlighting to indicate the current execution state of the process models. In [3], business processes are animated by means of a token game within the Signavio modeler, where users can step through the process element-by-element. Visual Paradigm [2] provides an animator that supports also collaboration diagrams. Finally, [9] provides an animator of BPMN collaborations enriched with data and multiple instances, which is based on token flow animation. However, the above solutions suffer from three main limitations. Firstly, works recreating a 3D world do not provide any animation of the business process, but just visualization. This means that they statically show a 3D version of the model without supporting a representation of its execution. Moreover, these projects are not very customizable, but instead are limited to describing a particular setting without the possibility of using custom 3D models. On the other hand, works providing animation of business processes use only 2D environments. Table 1 summarizes the features provided by the tools available in the literature and by our work. We compare the tools on their capability to: deal with BPMN *collaboration* models, *visualize* and *animate* in 2D or 3D the models execution, insert *custom graphical elements*, and parse model files compliant with the *standard format*.

To overcome the above limitations, in this paper we propose the prototype tool UBBA. Taken in input a BPMN collaboration diagram with standard XML format, UBBA recreates a custom virtual world where to visualize and to animate the input diagram decorated with 3D graphics chosen by the user. The user can follow the execution of its model looking at the animation on the newly created virtual world. As far as we know, UBBA is the first tool that can be exploited for representing and animating any kind of business scenario (e.g., order fulfillments, retrieval of healthcare data, bureaucratic procedures), thanks to its capability of loading standard BPMN XML files and custom 3D graphics. UBBA is conceived to support its users, i.e. business process designers, in *(i)* validating their diagrams and, possibly in collaboration with domain experts who help in choosing effective 3D graphics, *(ii)* creating appealing 3D animations for stakeholders, who are the final audience for the products of the tool.

The rest of the paper is organized as follows. Section 2 provides an overview of the UBBA development and features. Section 3 introduces the case study we used to test our solution and describe the tool functioning. Finally, Sect. 4 closes the paper with UBBA links and information.

2   UBBA

In this section we present our tool UBBA (Unity Based BPMN Animator). UBBA is a cross-platform and stand-alone tool that has been realized in Unity (unity3d.com), a game engine for creating 2D/3D video-games or other interactive contents, such as architectural visualizations or animations in real time. More in detail, UBBA aims at reproducing the setting described in a BPMN collaboration diagram and animating its execution, by means of token flow [14, p. 27]. Indeed, the BPMN elements are transformed into 3D graphics and visualized in a virtual space. Then, one or more tokens cross the diagram following the semantics of the BPMN elements they met. Figure 1 depicts the UBBA workflow functioning. In the following, we introduce the tool focusing on the visualization and then on the animation features.

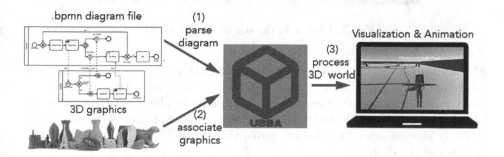

Fig. 1. UBBA functioning

3D Process Visualization. The first characteristic of UBBA is the rendering of a BPMN model into a 3D space. To this aim, UBBA provides three main features: (i) read a standard *.bpmn* file; (ii) associate a graphic to each diagram element; (iii) show the resulting 3D scene.

To read a BPMN file we resort to our parser, which takes in input a *.bpmn* file and produces a custom data structure. From the parsed model, UBBA collects the information regarding the elements contained in the diagram, such as the id, the name, the type (i.e., activity, gateway, event, etc.), the position in the 2D plane, and the list of nodes reachable from it. The tool exploits this information to set the 3D space. For each discovered element the tool allows to associate a 3D graphic; the designer can choose whether to load them from his/her PC or choose the ones already present in UBBA. External graphics have to be *.fbx* files[1], available online for free or to pay. Even the tokens can be customized: the user can specify a personal graphic representing tokens generated by each pool in the diagram. The chosen graphics for elements and tokens are then embedded by the tool in a 3D space. Those graphics are positioned following the spacial information of the *.bpmn* file and connected by lines that represent sequence flows. Then a view from above of the model is shown, and the user can start to navigate it (see Fig. 2).

Fig. 2. View from the top of the 3D world

3D Animation. The already created custom 3D world let us introduce the animation feature of UBBA. It supports the diagram execution by means of token movements so that the user can continuously check their distribution. This facility results particularly useful for understanding not only the role of the token as process actor but also the semantics of the BPMN elements and the meaning of the diagram.

The animation can be triggered by the user by clicking the *Play* button depicted on the top right side of the interface. In turn, from each start event the chosen 3D graphic, representing the token, starts to cross the diagram following the path indicated by sequence flows. The animation terminates once

---

[1] Filmbox (*.fbx*) is a file format for geometry definition widely adopted by 3D graphical application vendors, storing 2D, 3D, motion, audio, and video data.

no more token moves are allowed. A token can behave differently depending on the type of the node it is going to cross. UBBA implements the semantics of a core set of BPMN elements. Clearly, this collection is not the full list of BPMN elements, but it is enough to captures several semantic concepts. More in detail, UBBA considers BPMN collaboration or process models with the following elements: *Task, Send Task, Receive Task, Exclusive Gateway, Parallel Gateway, Event-Based Gateway, Start Event, Start Message Event, End Event, Intermediate Catch Event*, and *Intermediate Throw Event*. The semantics of such elements is implemented in UBBA leaving the possibility of adding other element behaviors just extending a project class.

During the animation, different points of views on the 3D environment are available for the user, who is free to switch from a camera to another one using the buttons on the right side of the interface. UBBA has a point of view for each active token (see Fig. 3), plus another that covers the whole collaboration.

Fig. 3. Token point of view

3   UBBA in Action

This section provides the validation of our tool throughout the implementation of a case study. Firstly, we present the BPMN collaboration diagram we used as an example, and then we show how to use it in UBBA.

Pizza Order Collaboration. To better show the tool functionalities we rely on the BPMN collaboration diagram depicted in Fig. 4. The diagram concerns an order placement in a pizzeria that involves two participants: a *Customer* and the *Pizzeria* itself. It is a collaboration diagram, composed of two pools communicating with each other. The whole collaboration aims at illustrating the procedure the customer has to follow in order to get a pizza. The customer plays the first move choosing the desired pizza and placing the order through a message. The message arrival in the pizzeria pool triggers the start of its internal process that immediately retrieves the *order* message. Then, the pizzeria decides to accept or reject the order advising the customer that, in turn, reacts on the acceptance/rejection via an event-based gateway. If the order is rejected the collaboration ends, otherwise the pizzeria prepares the order and sends it to the customer that eats the pizza. Lastly, if the customer is still hungry, he can decide to place another order, otherwise he pays, thus ending the collaboration.

Using UBBA. A double click on the tool executable file starts UBBA, which provides the first interaction interface where to load the collaboration diagram, (see Fig. 5(a) and (b)). For the sake of presentation, the tool provides a pre-loaded diagram (i.e. the case study in Fig. 4), but of course a *.bpmn* file can be chosen from the file system. Subsequently, UBBA asks for the element graphics to be selected from the tool assets or directly from the file system (see Fig. 5(c)). To recreate the setting described in the *Pizza Order* diagram the designer needs to use graphics capable to embody together the element type and the specific meaning it has in the diagram. For instance, a mailbox is suitable for symbolizing a receive task in general, but in our case study it may results less effective if used in place of the *Eat Pizza* receive task. The user has to consider the specific meaning of the element (the customer receives and eats the requested pizza), hence a 3D table with a pizza on it better clarify this setting.

The choice of the 3D graphics for the tokens is crucial, as well as a meaningful 3D graphic is essential to carry additional information on the diagram meaning. Tokens should represent the characters who perform the activities in the pool (see Fig. 5(d)). Alternatively, tokens describing more abstract actors, for instance, processes representing software components, can be depicted with a sphere. In our case study, we associate a *man* and a *pizza chef* respectively to the tokens of *Customer* and *Pizzeria* pools.

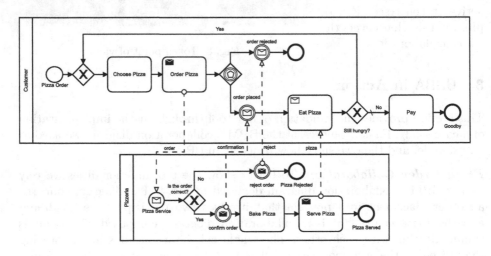

Fig. 4. Pizza order collaboration

Once the association of graphics is finished, UBBA generates the 3D model ready to be animated. A token, depicted with the *man*, is placed on the *Pizza Order* start event, which is represented by a three dimensional model of a pizzeria building. Starting the animation, it is possible to appreciate the UBBA capability to represent the reality. The *man* (the token of *Customer*) crosses the building graphic, meaning that the customer is entering in the pizzeria. In this fashion, the *man* goes ahead following the sequence flows until it reaches a 3D model of a menu that stands for the *Choose Pizza* task. Then, the *man* performs the

Order Pizza send task, played by a pizzeria cash desk graphic, which produces a message token instantiating the *Pizzeria* process and routing the *man* to the event-based gateway.

Having a new token in the collaboration, UBBA adds in the interface a new button identifying the *Pizzeria* instance just created (see Fig. 5(e)). The button switches from the current view (i.e. whole collaboration or man perspective) to that of the *pizza chef* token. It starts its execution crossing the start event until it reaches the XOR split gateway. The choice of the path to follow is made by the user; indeed he/she has to click on one of the 3D arrows depicted over the outgoing sequence flows (see Fig. 5(f)). Following the *No* path the *pizza chef* reaches a *red cross* graphic symbolizing the order rejection. Consequently, a message is sent to the *man* and the collaboration terminates. Otherwise, the *pizza chef* reaches a *green tick* symbolizing the confirmation of the order.

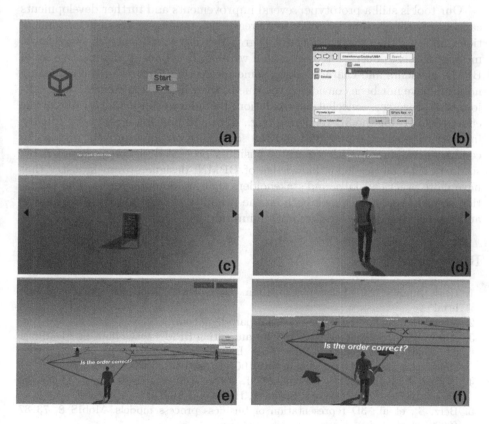

Fig. 5. UBBA in action

Therefore, the *pizza chef* goes ahead to the *Bake Pizza* task, rendered as a pizza oven, and then to the *Serve Pizza* send task, which shows a pizza into its box. The *man* instead waits for the pizza at the *Eat Pizza* task depicted as

a restaurant table with a pizza on it. Once the pizza arrives, the *man* decides
to either loop back and ask for another pizza or pay the bill. The *Pay* task is
indeed represented as a cash register. The collaboration ends with the *Customer*
crossing the *Pizzeria* building.

4   Conclusions

Visualization and animation of BPMN collaborations in a 3D virtual world can
improve the communication between business analysts and stakeholders. In this
regard, UBBA can effectively help people in sharing business knowledge. UBBA,
as well as its source code, binaries, guide, and a short demonstration video are
available at http://pros.unicam.it/ubba/. UBBA can be redistributed and/or
modified under the terms of the MIT License.

Our tool is still a prototype, several improvements and further developments
can be carried. By now, we plan to increase the number of possible customiza-
tions, allowing the user to associate 3D graphics also to sequence/message flows,
message tokens, pools. Moreover, even if we already support a significative set of
BPMN elements and characteristics, some interesting features of the modelling
notation have not been considered yet, due to their intricate semantics (e.g., OR-
join, sub-processes, cancellation/escalation, boundary events) and/or due to the
effort required for the 3D rendering (e.g., data and multiple instances). Finally,
in order to assess the potential and the scalability of the approach, we plan to
conduct a validation with groups of business process designers, composed by:
students with an academic knowledge of BPMN; designers from industry that
have more practical skills; and stakeholders that are domain expert. The validation should provide feedback both on the usability of UBBA and on the quality
and the benefits of the produced 3D animation.

References

1. IBM Innov8 2.0. http://www-01.ibm.com/software/solutions/soa/innov8/full.
   html
2. Visual Paradigm. https://www.visual-paradigm.com/
3. Allweyer, T., Schweitzer, S.: A tool for animating BPMN token flow. In: Mendling,
   J., Weidlich, M. (eds.) BPMN 2012. LNBIP, vol. 125, pp. 98–106. Springer,
   Heidelberg (2012). https://doi.org/10.1007/978-3-642-33155-8_8
4. Becker, J., Kugeler, M., Rosemann, M.: Process Management: A Guide for the
   Design of Business Processes. Springer, Heidelberg (2013)
5. Betz, S., et al.: 3D representation of business process models. MobIS **8**, 73–87
   (2008)
6. Brown, R.A.: Conceptual modelling in 3D virtual worlds for process communication. In: APCCM, pp. 25–32. Australian Computer Society, Inc. (2010)
7. Corradini, F., et al.: A guidelines framework for understandable BPMN models.
   Data Knowl. Eng. **113**, 129–154 (2017)

8. Corradini, F., Muzi, C., Re, B., Rossi, L., Tiezzi, F.: Animating multiple instances in BPMN collaborations: from formal semantics to tool support. In: Weske, M., Montali, M., Weber, I., vom Brocke, J. (eds.) BPM 2018. LNCS, vol. 11080, pp. 83–101. Springer, Cham (2018). https://doi.org/10.1007/978-3-319-98648-7_6

9. Corradini, F., Muzi, C., Re, B., Tiezzi, F., Rossi, L.: MIDA: multiple instances and data animator. In: Dissertation Award, Demonstration, and Industrial Track at BPM 2018. CEUR Workshop Proceedings, vol. 2196, pp. 86–90 (2018)

10. Desel, J.: Teaching system modeling, simulation and validation. In: WSC, pp. 1669–1675 (2000)

11. Guo, H., Brown, R., Rasmussen, R.: Virtual worlds as a model-view approach to the communication of business processes models. In: CAiSE Forum 2012. Citeseer (2012)

12. Guo, H., Brown, R., Rasmussen, R.: Human resource behaviour simulation in business processes. In: Pooley, R., Coady, J., Schneider, C., Linger, H., Barry, C., Lang, M. (eds.) Information Systems Development. Springer, New York (2013). https://doi.org/10.1007/978-1-4614-4951-5_14

13. Hermann, A., et al.: Collaborative business process management - a literature-based analysis of methods for supporting model understandability. In: WI (2017)

14. OMG: Business Process Model and Notation (BPMN V 2.0) (2011)

15. Stamm, S.: Creating a 3D Renderer for BPMN (2018). https://blog.camunda.com/post/2018/02/creating-a-3d-renderer

16. Ware, C., Franck, G.: Viewing a graph in a virtual reality display is three times as good as 2D diagram. In: VL (1994)

17. Wynn, M.T., et al.: ProcessProfiler3D: a visualisation framework for log-based process performance comparison. Decis. Support Syst. **100**, 93–108 (2017)

Achieving GDPR Compliance
of BPMN Process Models

Simone Agostinelli[1], Fabrizio Maria Maggi[2], Andrea Marrella[1(✉)],
and Francesco Sapio[1]

[1] DIAG, Sapienza University of Rome, Rome, Italy
{agostinelli,marrella,sapio}@diag.uniroma1.it
[2] University of Tartu, Tartu, Estonia
f.m.maggi@ut.ee

Abstract. In an increasingly digital world, where processing and exchange of personal data are key parts of everyday enterprise business processes (BPs), the right to data privacy is regulated and actively enforced in the Europe Union (EU) through the recently introduced General Data Protection Regulation (GDPR), whose aim is to protect EU citizens from privacy breaches. In this direction, GDPR is highly influencing the way organizations must approach data privacy, forcing them to rethink and upgrade their BPs in order to become GDPR compliant. For many organizations, this can be a daunting task, since little has been done so far to easily identify privacy issues in BPs. To tackle this challenge, in this paper, we provide an analysis of the main privacy constraints in GDPR and propose a set of design patterns to capturing and integrating such constraints in BP models. Using BPMN (Business Process Modeling Notation) as modeling notation, our approach allows us to achieve full transparency of privacy constraints in BPs making it possible to ensure their compliance with GDPR.

Keywords: Data privacy · GDPR · Process models · BPMN

1 Introduction

Nowadays, the advances in the amount of storage and processing power have made it possible to store and process virtually all the information that might be of interest for an organization to rapidly deliver digital and physical services to their customers (e.g., the creation of a new bank account, the management of a purchase order, etc.). On the other hand, the seemingly never ending collection of customers' data by large corporations such as Google and Facebook has raised public awareness on *privacy* concerns [12].

Since May 2018, in the European Union (EU), the *right to privacy* of personal data has been tackled by the General Data Protection Regulation (GDPR) [5]. The aim of GDPR is to protect EU citizens from privacy breaches on their personal data. In summary, GDPR changes the way in which organizations handle

C. Cappiello and M. Ruiz (Eds.): CAiSE Forum 2019, LNBIP 350, pp. 10–22, 2019.
https://doi.org/10.1007/978-3-030-21297-1_2

personal information of their customers, and gives individuals enhanced rights of protection when it comes to their personal data. Since organizations that are not compliant with GDPR must face heavy fines, they are required to implement correctly the GDPR data management policies and take appropriate actions on data when requested by their customers.

To achieve compliance with GDPR, among a list of technical and non-technical challenges to be tackled [3], the regulation enforces organizations to reshape the way they approach the management of personal data stored and exchanged during the execution of their everyday business processes (BPs). Although BP modeling is well-suited for expressing stakeholder collaboration and the data flow exchanged between BP activities and participants, little has been done so far to identify potential privacy breaches in BP models [13].

Conversely, the common practice to address privacy breaches in a BP is to implement ad-hoc countermeasures during the automation stage of the BP life-cycle, when the BP model is configured by a system engineer (SE) for its execution with a dedicated BP Management System (BPMS). The SE can then implement a strategy (e.g., in the form of a piece of software) directly using the BPMS at hand, in order to deal with all potential violations of privacy constraints at run-time. However, this approach requires that the SE knows exactly where potential privacy breaches can manifest in the BP, and this information, if not explicitly documented in the BP model, may lead to a defective implementation of compensatory strategies from privacy breaches.

In this paper, we advocate that privacy should be considered as a *first-class citizen* in BP models and should be introduced *by design* and not as an afterthought. In this direction, we provide an analysis of the main privacy constraints in GDPR encountered when modeling BPs with ISO/IEC 19510:2013 BPMN (Business Process Modeling and Notation). Based on this analysis, we propose a set of design patterns to integrate privacy enhancing features in a BPMN model according to GDPR. The aim of this work is to emphasize awareness of privacy-concerns in BPs at design-time, when a proper analysis of the involved data allows a BP designer to identify (possible) violations of privacy constraints and their impact. The feasibility of our approach is illustrated using a concrete case of a phone company.

The rest of the paper is organized as follows. Section 2 introduces a case in which privacy aspects of a BP for acquiring a new customer by a phone company need to be modeled. Section 3 introduces the main constraints of GDPR considered in the paper. Section 4 presents a set of design patterns to capturing and integrating GDPR constraints in BP models. Finally, Sect. 5 illustrates the relevant literature related to privacy in BPs and concludes the paper.

2   The Case of a Phone Company

With the increase of systems able to collect data automatically, privacy has been at the center of many discussions between designers who want to use such data to provide services to the users, and these last ones who want to get the services by sharing as little information as possible. In fact, users care about any data that can identify them, and this has many consequences in the corpus of laws in all countries, although different countries have different boundaries of what can be considered private information.

Let us take as an example a phone company in the process of acquiring a new customer. The phone company requests the new client's data (e.g., name, surname, address, etc.). Once the client has provided this data, the phone company goes through a verification process to determine if the data given by the new customer is correct. If not, a clear up procedure starts and the process ends. The next steps involve asking the future customer if she wants to *port* her old phone number into the new phone plan she is about to subscribe. If the answer is positive, then the phone company asks the new client the old number, and the portability procedure to the *previous phone company*. In case the procedure can not be completed or the answer is negative, the process is interrupted. Otherwise, the customer signs the contract, which only describes how the phone company will provide the service, but which does not provide any information on how the phone company will use the data of the client. After this, the phone company in parallel stores the data of the new client, requests the payment to the client, and, once the payment has been received, sends the SIM card to the client. Once these activities have been completed, the company can activate the SIM card and successfully conclude the procedure of acquiring the new customer. If the procedure takes for some reasons more than 30 days to complete, then the process is interrupted.

The BPMN model representing the scenario described above is shown in Fig. 1. It is worth noting that the procedure does not yet take into account the potential risk to get a data breach and does not provide mechanisms to protect the customer's privacy.

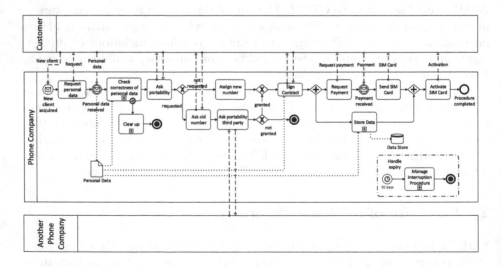

Fig. 1. BPMN model of the case of the phone company

3   Background on GDPR

GDPR has introduced changes to the privacy and data protection regulation, thus having significant consequences for who needs to design BPs. GDPR requires *privacy-by-design*, which means that data protection is not an addition to the process, but rather integral part of it, and the process should comply to GDPR since the design stage. Therefore, already at this stage, a BP designer needs to take into consideration privacy and data protection issues.

Entities involved. In order to identify who is responsible of what in a BP where data is handled, GDPR defines four entities:

- *Data Subject*: is the person the data is about.
- *Data Controller*: is the entity that collects and stores data from the Data Subject and that determines the purposes of processing such data.
- *Data Processor*: is the entity that processes data from the Data Subject on the behalf of the Data Controller.
- *Data Protection Officer (DPO)*: is the entity that performs systematic monitoring on the Data Controller and Data Processor to ensure that they comply with the GDPR constraints on the data collected from the Data Subject.

Personal Data. In the context of GDPR, *Personal data* is defined as any information related to a person (Data Subject) who can be identified, directly or indirectly, through that information (e.g., a name, an identification number, location data, online identifiers, etc.). Therefore, online identifiers, including IP address and cookies, will now be regarded as personal data if they can be linked back to the Data Subject. GDPR distinguishes three types of personal data,[1] each with a different level of protection:

- *Personal Data*: any piece of information that can identify a person.
- *Sensible Data*: is a special type of *Personal Data* that requires a higher level of security, i.e., health, genetic, physical, physiological, mental, economic, cultural, social identity and biometric data.
- *Criminal Records*: is a subset of *Sensible Data* including information to identify past crimes committed by the Data Subject.

Obligations of the Data Controller. This paper focuses on the obligations of the Data Controller. This implies a list of constraints that must be fulfilled by the Data Controller to be complaint with GDPR. These obligations are:

- *Data Breach*: in case of a data breach, the Data Controller has to communicate it within 72 h to the National Authority as well as to the Data Subject. This constraint is not subject to any *de minimis* standard, thus any data breach, it does not matter how small, needs to be always communicated in a simple way along with the actions that will be performed to limit the damage.

---

[1] The only exception is National Security Data that does not follow GDPR regulation, but is left to the jurisdiction of each State.

The only exception is the case in which the stolen data is not usable (e.g., encrypted). However, also in this case, the National Authority can force the Data Controller to communicate the breach to the Data Subject.

- *Consent to Use the Data*: when retrieving personal data, the Data Controller needs to ask the Data Subject for consent and to provide the Data Subject with information about the intentions on how to use and/or process the data.
- *Right to Access and Rectify*: at any moment, the Data Subject has the right to *access* and *rectify* the personal data associated to her. As a result, the Data Controller has the obligation to satisfy these requests.
- *Right of Portability*: at any moment, the Data Subject has the right to ask for the portability of the data associated to her to third parties and the Data Controller has the obligation to satisfy this request.
- *Right to Withdraw*: at any moment, the Data Subject can withdraw the consent to use the data associated to her and the Data Controller has to stop using such data.
- *The Right to be Forgotten*: if the Data Subject wants her data to be deleted, the Data Controller has the obligation to satisfy this request.

4   Implementing GDPR-Aware Patterns in BPMN

In this section, we introduce a list of seven privacy patterns for BPMN, which represent effective design-time solutions to tackle GDPR constraints in BP models. Notably, we developed such patterns in a way that no additional BPMN symbol is required to integrate them into a non-GDPR compliant BP model.

4.1   Data Breach

In case of a Data Breach, the Data Controller has to retrieve the breached data. From this data, the Data Controller needs to extract a list of Data Subjects who had their data breached. Then, in parallel, the Data Controller needs to limit the data loss and send a notification to the National Authority. For each breached Data Subject, the Data Controller evaluates if the stolen data is usable or not. If not, and if the Data Controller is proven to manage data using high security standards, this is communicated to the National Authority who decides whether the breach should be communicated to the Data Subject or not. Otherwise, the Data Controller needs to notify the Data Subject directly. The design pattern in Fig. 2 implements the privacy constraint *Data Breach*. It is worthwhile noting that, during any process involving personal data, a data breach can occur, and the Data Controller must promptly handle the problem within 72 h.

In the example of the phone company, a data breach can happen at any time after the personal data has been acquired. Thus, implementing the *Data Breach* pattern can help the process to be reactive in case of data breach, so to properly provide a recovery procedure and communicate the data breach to both the Data Subject and the National Authority. Notice that if the 72 h limit is not respected and the Data Controller is not able to provide a reasonable justification, the penalties amount to 20 millions Euro, or 4% of the company's global revenue, whichever is higher.

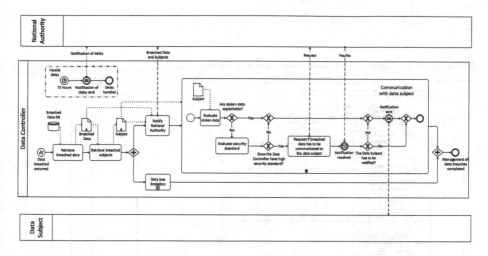

Fig. 2. BPMN model for pattern *Data Breach*

4.2 Consent to Use the Data

Before retrieving any kind of personal data from the Data Subject, the Data
Controller has to ask the Data Subject for consent. In particular, the Data
Controller needs to collect a list of aspects the Data Subject should be aware of
before giving her data to the Data Controller. This list should contain:

- in case the data has not been directly obtained from the Data Subject, from
  which source the personal data originates;
- the existence of the right to lodge a complaint to a supervisory authority;
- the existence of the right to withdraw the consent at any time;
- the existence of the right to data portability;
- the existence of the right to delete the personal data;
- the existence of the right to access the personal data;
- the existence of the right to rectify the personal data;
- the period for which the personal data will be stored, or if this is not possible,
  the criteria used to determine this period;
- the existence of any profiling and meaningful information about the envisaged
  consequences of processing the personal data;
- if the personal data can be transferred internationally;
- who are the recipients or categories of recipients of the personal data;
- which are the interests pursued by the Data Controller or by third parties;
- the legal basis of the processing;
- the purposes for which the personal data will be processed;
- the identity and the contact details of the Data Controller and of the DPO.

Then, the consent to use the data is requested to the Data Subject. If the consent
is given, the data is collected. The design pattern in Fig. 3 implements the privacy
constraint *Consent to Use the Data*.

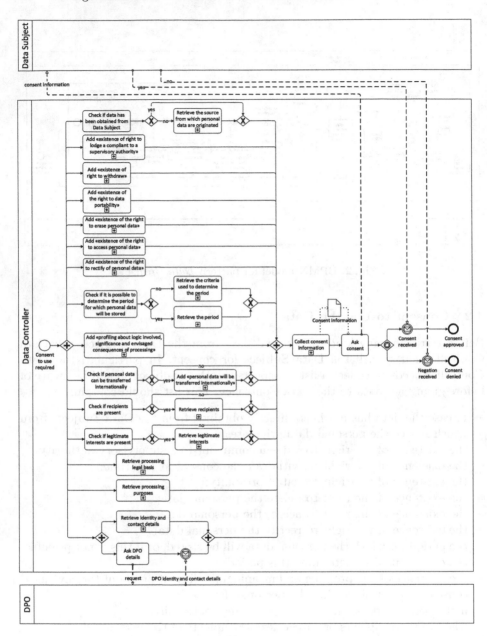

Fig. 3. BPMN model for pattern *Consent to Use the Data*

In the example of the phone company, this pattern can be added as a sub-process just before asking for the actual data to the potential new customer, at the start of the process. This guarantees that the company is transparent with the customer and asks for the explicit consent of any possible usage of the data.

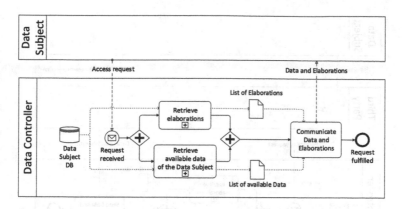

Fig. 4. BPMN model for pattern *Right to Access*

4.3 Right to Access

When the Data Subject sends a request availing the right to access, the Data Controller has to *(i)* retrieve all the data associated with the Data Subject, and *(ii)* retrieve any processing on the data that has been made. Then, they are both sent to the Data Subject. The design pattern in Fig. 4 implements the privacy constraint *Right to Access*.

In the example of the phone company, this pattern can be implemented as an asynchronous request from the Data Subject that can be received at any point in time after that any personal data has been retained. In BPMN, this pattern can be used as an event sub-process that handles the request.[2] In the example of the phone company, the customer can request to access her personal data even before the process is completed (potentially even before the customer signs the contract), and the phone company has to handle this request by providing any personal data it possesses.

4.4 Right of Portability

When the Data Subject sends a request availing the right of portability, she needs to specify the third party at hand. The third party contacts the Data Controller which has to *(i)* retrieve all the data associated with the Data Subject, and *(ii)* retrieve any processing on the data that has been made. Then, they are both sent to the third party. Finally, the third party communicates to the Data Subject that the portability happened successfully. The design pattern in Fig. 5 implements the privacy constraint *Right of Portability*.

In the example of the phone company, the company needs to have a procedure to handle portability when requested by a third party company. However, in the process of acquiring a new client, even though the user requests the portability,

---

[2] Event sub-processes are used in BPMN to capture exceptions (and define recovery procedures) that may affect an entire BP.

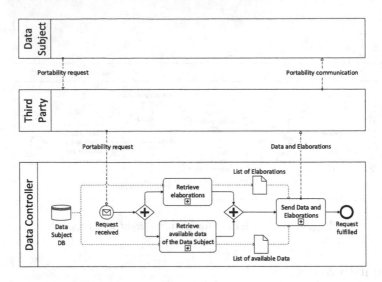

Fig. 5. BPMN model for pattern *Right of Portability*

Another Phone Company (and not the phone company of the case study) should be able to implement this pattern.

4.5 Right to Withdraw

When the Data Subject sends a request availing the right to withdraw, the Data Controller has to stop using the data associated to the Data Subject, and communicate back to the Data Subject that her data is not used anymore. The design pattern in Fig. 6 implements the privacy constraint *Right to Withdraw*.

In the example of the phone company, this asynchronous request from the client can happen at any time, thus the phone company might implement this pattern in BPMN as an event sub-process. If, at any time during the procedure of acquiring a new customer, the customer withdraws the consent to use the data, the phone company has to evaluate if that data is needed to continue the process. If this is the case, the process will terminate, since the phone company is not able to complete the procedure.

4.6 Right to Rectify

When the Data Subject sends a request availing the right to rectify, the Data Controller has to rectify the data as requested by the Data Subject, and communicate back to the Data Subject that her data has been rectified. The design pattern in Fig. 7 implements the privacy constraint *Right to Rectify*.

In the example of the phone company, the customer should be able to rectify the data at any time. For instance, if before signing the contract the customer

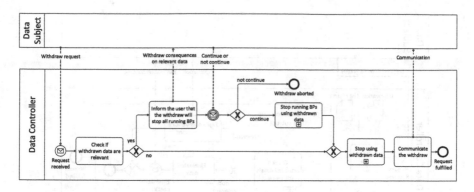

Fig. 6. BPMN model for pattern *Right to Withdraw*

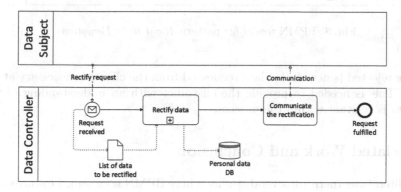

Fig. 7. BPMN model for pattern *Right to Rectify*

changes address, or simply notices incorrect information, she should be able to rectify such information. This asynchronous request could be satisfied in BPMN using an event sub-process.

4.7 Right to be Forgotten

When the Data Subject sends a request availing the right to be forgotten, the Data Controller has to retrieve the data related to the request and check if this data is relevant. If not, the Data Controller eliminates such data and communicates this to the Data Subject. Otherwise, the Data Controller communicates to the Data Subject why the data is relevant. The design pattern in Fig. 8 implements the privacy constraint *Right to be Forgotten*. This is, once again, an asynchronous request from the Data Subject, which in BPMN can be implemented as an event sub-process.

In the example of the phone company, this pattern can be implemented during the process of acquiring a new customer even though the request will be

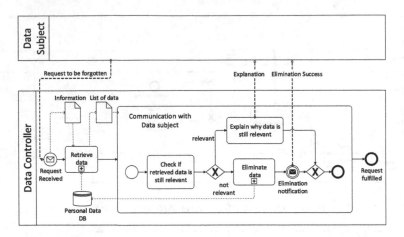

Fig. 8. BPMN model for pattern *Right to be Forgotten*

for sure rejected (since all the data requested from the clients is necessary at this stage). This is needed to provide the customer with an understanding of why the data is relevant within the process.

5   Related Work and Conclusion

In the literature, there are several studies where BPMN is extended towards security and privacy aspects. BPMN security extensions for healthcare processes are presented in [15,17]. Menzel et al. introduce security elements for BPMN to evaluate the trustworthiness of participants based on a rating of enterprise assets and to express security intentions such as confidentiality or integrity on an abstract level [11]. In [6], BPMN is enriched with information assurance and security modeling capabilities. In [1], BPMN is aligned to the domain model of security risk management. In [13], Privacy Enhancing Technologies (PETs) are applied to enforce privacy requirements and support the analysis of private data leakage. In [16], Salnitri et al. propose the SecBPMN-Q query language for representing security policies and a query engine that enables checking SecBPMN-Q policies against SecBPMN-ml specifications.

Some works are specifically related to the definition of extensions of BPMN to represent cyber security requirements [7,10]. In [9], the authors investigate a new approach to modeling security and propose a solution to include all concepts potentially modelable in BPMN related to cyber security. In [2], the BPMN choreography models are used to detail message exchange and identity contract negotiation. In [4], BPMN is extended with access control, separation of duty, binding of duty and need to know principles. Similarly to [4], in [8] privacy concerns are captured by annotating the BPMN model with access control, separation of tasks, binding of tasks, user consent and necessity to know icons.

Differently from the above studies, our work is focused on GDPR. Specifically, we have provided an analysis of the main privacy constraints in GDPR and a set of design patterns to capturing and integrating such constraints in BP models represented in BPMN. Recent works concerning GDPR have been also presented in [14,18]. In [14], the authors propose a method to support the design of GDPR compliant systems, based on a socio-technical approach composed of a modeling language and a reasoning framework. In [18], the authors present a model of GDPR that provides a visual overview of the associations between entities defined in the legislation and their constraints. If compared with [14,18], the originality of our approach lies in considering awareness of GDPR constraints at design-time, during BP modeling, and not as a run-time issue.

Our work can be extended in many aspects. For example, an extensive validation of the patterns against larger case studies is crucial to test the effectiveness of the overall approach. Nonetheless, we consider this work as an important first step towards a thorough understanding of how to build GDPR-aware processes.

References

1. Altuhhova, O., Matulevicius, R., Ahmed, N.: An extension of business process model and notation for security risk management. Int. J. Inf. Syst. Model. Design **4**(4), 93–113 (2013)
2. Ayed, G.B., Ghernaouti-Helie, S.: Processes view modeling of identity-related privacy business interoperability: considering user-supremacy federated identity technical model and identity contract negotiation. In: ASONAM 2012 (2012)
3. Basin, D., Debois, S., Hildebrandt, T.: On purpose and by necessity: compliance under the GDPR. In: Proceedings Financial Cryptography and Data Security, vol. 18 (2018)
4. Brucker, A.D.: Integrating security aspects into business process models. Inf. Technol. **55**(6), 239–246 (2013)
5. Carey, P.: Data Protection: A Practical Guide to UK and EU Law. Oxford University Press Inc., Oxford (2018)
6. Cherdantseva, Y., Hilton, J., Rana, O.: Towards secureBPMN - aligning BPMN with the information assurance and security domain. In: Mendling, J., Weidlich, M. (eds.) BPMN 2012. LNBIP, vol. 125, pp. 107–115. Springer, Heidelberg (2012). https://doi.org/10.1007/978-3-642-33155-8_9
7. Chergui, M.E.A., Benslimane, S.M.: A valid BPMN extension for supporting security requirements based on cyber security ontology. In: Abdelwahed, E.H., Bellatreche, L., Golfarelli, M., Méry, D., Ordonez, C. (eds.) MEDI 2018. LNCS, vol. 11163, pp. 219–232. Springer, Cham (2018). https://doi.org/10.1007/978-3-030-00856-7_14
8. Labda, W., Mehandjiev, N., Sampaio, P.: Modeling of privacy-aware business processes in BPMN to protect personal data. In: SAC 2014, pp. 1399–1405 (2014)
9. Maines, C.L., Zhou, B., Tang, S., Shi, Q.: Adding a third dimension to BPMN as a means of representing cyber security requirements. In: DeSE 2016 (2016)
10. Maines, C.L., Llewellyn-Jones, D., Tang, S., Zhou, B.: A cyber security ontology for BPMN-security extensions. In: CIT 2015 (2015)
11. Menzel, M., Thomas, I., Meinel, C.: Security requirements specification in service-oriented business process management. In: ARES 2009 (2009)

12. Petersen, S.A., Mannhardt, F., Oliveira, M., Torvatn, H.: A framework to navigate the privacy trade-offs for human-centred manufacturing. In: Camarinha-Matos, L.M., Afsarmanesh, H., Rezgui, Y. (eds.) PRO-VE 2018. IAICT, vol. 534, pp. 85–97. Springer, Cham (2018). https://doi.org/10.1007/978-3-319-99127-6_8

13. Pullonen, P., Matulevičius, R., Bogdanov, D.: PE-BPMN: privacy-enhanced business process model and notation. In: Carmona, J., Engels, G., Kumar, A. (eds.) BPM 2017. LNCS, vol. 10445, pp. 40–56. Springer, Cham (2017). https://doi.org/10.1007/978-3-319-65000-5_3

14. Robol, M., Salnitri, M., Giorgini, P.: Toward GDPR-compliant socio-technical systems: modeling language and reasoning framework. In: Poels, G., Gailly, F., Serral Asensio, E., Snoeck, M. (eds.) PoEM 2017. LNBIP, vol. 305, pp. 236–250. Springer, Cham (2017). https://doi.org/10.1007/978-3-319-70241-4_16

15. Rodríguez, A., Fernández-Medina, E., Piattini, M.: A BPMN extension for the modeling of security requirements in business processes. IEICE Trans. Inf. Syst. 90(4), 745–752 (2007)

16. Salnitri, M., Dalpiaz, F., Giorgini, P.: Designing secure business processes with SecBPMN. Softw. Syst. Model. 16(3), 737–757 (2017)

17. Sang, K.S., Zhou, B.: BPMN security extensions for healthcare process. In: CIT 2015 (2015)

18. Tom, J., Sing, E., Matulevičius, R.: Conceptual representation of the GDPR: model and application directions. In: Zdravkovic, J., Grabis, J., Nurcan, S., Stirna, J. (eds.) BIR 2018. LNBIP, vol. 330, pp. 18–28. Springer, Cham (2018). https://doi.org/10.1007/978-3-319-99951-7_2

How Could Systems Analysis Use the Idea of "Responsible Information System"?

Steven Alter(✉)

University of San Francisco, San Francisco, CA 94117, USA
alter@usfca.edu

Abstract. "Responsible Information Systems," the theme of CAISE 2019, is an intriguing idea that has not been explored in the readily available literature. After defining the term information system (IS), this paper applies an initial five-part framework to many examples of problematic IS to explore what the idea of responsible information system (RIS) might mean and how it might be useful. That initial exploration leads to focusing on how the concept of responsibility applies to IS in a way that is useful for systems analysis and design (SA&D). This paper addresses that question by using a new set of ideas related to facets of work system capabilities. Its application of those ideas to an EMR case study imply that they could be applied in identifying ways in which an IS might be more responsible. Overall, this paper illustrates that focusing on responsibilities related to facets of capabilities is more valuable than trying to characterize information systems as responsible or not.

Keywords: Responsible information system ·
Definition of information system · Work system · Information system impacts

1 What Responsibilities Can Be Engineered into an Information System?

The Call for Papers of CAISE 2019 emphasizes the conference theme of Responsible Information Systems: "This year, the conference theme acknowledges the need for designing information systems that are not only flexible enough for digital transformation, but are also responsible by considering privacy, security, and ethical concerns and providing trustworthiness".

People are often characterized as having responsibilities or being responsible, but one might wonder whether the term responsible applies to IS in a way that is both meaningful and useful. A great deal has been written about privacy, security, and other ethical and legal issues related to IS, but a Google scholar search on "responsible information system" (RIS) found only 23 hits, several of which mentioned responsible IS developer, manager, or user, and none of which defined RIS or used it in a significant way. Whether an IS qualifies as an RIS should hinge on more than its treatment of privacy, security, ethical concerns, and trustworthiness, but it is not obvious what other issues should be considered and how to organize those issues to make them valuable and readily accessible for IS engineering.

© Springer Nature Switzerland AG 2019
C. Cappiello and M. Ruiz (Eds.): CAiSE Forum 2019, LNBIP 350, pp. 23–35, 2019.
https://doi.org/10.1007/978-3-030-21297-1_3

Goal and Organization. This paper treats the CAISE 2019 conference theme as a challenge. Its goal is to explain how the concept of responsibility applies to IS in a way that is useful for SA&D. This paper's pursuit of this goal treats an IS as a sociotechnical or totally automated work system most of whose activities are devoted to processing information. This paper focuses on how responsibility applies to IS rather than people. It does not discuss how people are responsible for artificial systems [1].

Given the lack of prior work related to RIS per se (rather than privacy, security, and other widely studied topics), this research began by exploring the topic. An initial five-part framework (stakeholders, agency, impacts, evolution, and evaluation) for determining whether an IS qualifies as an RIS was applied to examples of IS-related mishaps, misuse, or malfeasance. Finding many types of direct and indirect impacts and many conflicts between different stakeholder interests led to concluding that an abstract definition of RIS covering many diverse examples would be too general to be useful. In contrast, a way to identify and organize typical responsibility-related issues could be quite useful in SA&D if it could help analysts, designers, and users visualize areas where an IS might need to be more responsible.

This paper summarizes how an IS can be viewed as a work system whose activities are devoted to processing information. It uses the format of a work system snapshot [2, 3] to organize minimum criteria for qualifying as an RIS and presents an initial five-part framework for deciding whether an IS qualifies as an RIS. It summarizes many selected cases that were used to test the possible effectiveness of that framework. An initial conclusion that the framework is not very useful leads to the more valuable goal of developing a useful way to apply the concept of IS responsibility to SA&D. This paper addresses that goal by using a new set of ideas related to facets of work system capabilities [4] and showing how those ideas could be applied in identifying ways in which an IS might be more responsible.

2   Thinking of Systems in Organizations as "Work Systems"

Based on work system theory (WST), an IS is a work system (WS) most of whose activities are devoted to processing information. A WS is a system in which human participants and/or machines perform processes and activities using information, technology, and other resources to produce product/services for internal and/or external customers. [2, 3] Processes and activities, participants, information, and technologies are viewed as completely within the WS. Processes and activities fall along a dimension from unstructured to structured. Customers and product/services may be partially inside and partially outside because customers often participate in work systems. A WS operates within an environment that matters (e.g., national and organizational culture, policies, history, competitive situation, demographics, technological change, other stakeholders, and so on). WSs rely on human, informational, and technical infrastructure that is shared with other WSs. They should be aligned with enterprise and departmental strategies. Hence, a basic understanding of a WS (or an IS, which is a type of WS) needs to include the nine elements of the work system framework [2, 3], customers, product/services, processes and activities, participants, information, technologies, environment, infrastructure, and strategies.

The *and/or* in the definition of WS implies that a WS can be sociotechnical (with human participants) or totally automated. That idea diverges from assumptions that "the system" is a configuration of hardware and software that is used by users. Notice, for example that accountants producing financial statements can be viewed as participants in a sociotechnical IS in which they perform work using accounting software.

An IS and related WSs can overlap in a variety of ways. In a situation with no overlap, an IS can provide information for a separate WS. With partial overlap, some of the activities within an IS are also activities within one or more WSs that it supports. In other situations, an IS is an integral component of a WS.

3 Initial Framework for Evaluating Whether an IS is an RIS

As a starting point for exploring what RIS might mean, and given that an IS is a type of WS, the format of a work system snapshot (from the work system method – [2, 3]) was used to produce Table 1, which summarizes what might viewed as a first cut at a minimum criteria for qualifying as an RIS.

Table 1. First cut at minimum criteria to qualify as a responsible information system

Customers	Product/Services
• IS provides benefits and does not harm customers. • IS provides product/services only to legitimate customers.	• Product/services are legal, beneficial, and do not harm customers. • Product/services do not include harmful byproducts or lead to harmful results.
Major Processes and Activities	
• Processes and activities are legal and use resources appropriately. • Processes and activities do not interfere unnecessarily with other activities. • Processes and activities are appropriate for people who perform the work.	

Participants	Information	Technologies
• Participants have a healthy work environment and are not harmed.	• Information is appropriate • Information is protected • Information is legal.	• Technology is appropriate • Technology operates correctly. • Technology does not interfere with other technology

• <u>Environment</u>: The work system's operation and product/services that it produces do not cause harm to the surrounding environment or society at large. • <u>Infrastructure</u>: The work system does not use enterprise infrastructure in a way that has negative effects on other parts of the enterprise. • <u>Strategies</u>: The work system operates consistent with enterprise strategies.	

Trying to produce a more nuanced view of RIS led to a simple five-part framework for evaluating whether a set of IS examples qualified as RISs. The five parts are based on typical who, what, and how questions of types that are used in systems analysis and design efforts:

- **function and scope.** (What is the relevant IS and what can it do?)
- **stakeholders** (who cares about this IS or its impacts?)
- **impacts** (what does this IS affect and in what ways?)
- **evolution** (how can this IS change over time?)
- **evaluation** (what criteria determine whether this IS qualifies as responsible?).

4 Applying the Five-Part Framework to Examples that Illustrate Different Aspects of Whether RIS Might Mean

It is easy to find examples that illustrate IS-related mishaps, misuse, or malfeasance that might demonstrate how a specific IS did not qualify as RIS. Many examples can be found through Wikipedia or through Google searches on "computer fiascos" or "computer glitches". The following (abbreviated) list of examples starts with general categories of responsibility-related problems of types that have been publicized many times. It also includes specific examples that were useful for thinking about what RIS might mean. The examples cover a wide range of situations including operational failures, theft and fraud, impacts on individuals, and impacts on society.

- Intrusion into computerized systems has led to thefts of personal customer data and corporate data at a large number of business and governmental organizations (e.g., list of such thefts in the Wikipedia page called "Data Breaches").
- IS-related problems have caused operational disruptions including grounding of numerous flights at American Airlines, Delta, and United.
- IS-related problems locked customers out of their accounts at major banks including Barclays, Royal Bank of Scotland, TSB, and Wells Fargo.
- Various kinds of malware including spyware, ransomware, viruses, and worms have sabotaged many computerized systems (Wikipedia article on "malware").
- Accidents in self-driving cars have occurred, including several involving fatalities.
- Cockpit automation in airplanes has advantages but also brings dangers including degraded manual and cognitive flying skills, disengagement, and excessive attention to alerts and other aspects of the technology.
- Bitcoins worth billions of dollars have been lost, but not hacked or stolen [5].
- An IS embedded in Volkswagen engines turned on pollution controls during pollution testing, but then turned them off while the automobile was on the road, thereby generating excessive pollution [6].
- The title of [7] asked "you want my password or a dead patient?" The article identified workarounds used by medical staff in busy, high stress medical environments to minimize the amount of time absorbed by repeated logins.
- Wells Fargo Bank "clawed back" $75 million of stock options from two former executives who were in charge when excessive sales quotas pressured employees to sell unwanted products and in some cases to open unauthorized accounts [8].

- Use of Facebook to spread hate speech against the Muslim Rohinga minority in the Buddhist majority country Myanmar has been reported widely [9].
- The SWIFT interbank messaging platform that is used for inter-bank money transfers has been used for fraudulent transfers [10].
- "Traders, bankers, and money managers [use] ["encrypted messaging services such as WhatsApp and Signal"] … to circumvent compliance, get around the human resources police, and keep bosses in the dark" [11].
- Texting on smart phones is linked to a substantial percentage of car crashes [12].
- The social scientist Sherry Turkle "found that children now compete with their parents' devices for attention, resulting in a generation afraid of the spontaneity of a phone call or face-to-face interaction" [13].
- "Surveillance capitalism" [14] involves systems with two types of beneficiaries, recipients of whatever the system produces as its nominal purpose and others who use information generated by or about the system's customers and/or participants.
- Many people are surrounded by things that are supposedly smart, but many of those things may make everyday life more complicated and less convenient [15].

In combination, the examples above led to questioning the practicality of using the five-part framework as a basis for determining whether an IS qualifies as an RIS.

- **Function and scope.** The IS in many examples above would be considered an RIS at first glance because they seemed to operate as designed and served many useful purposes. On the other hand, many brought operational failures, harmful impacts on work system participants, and harm through flawed product/services.
- **Stakeholders.** Evaluating whether an IS qualifies as an RIS is difficult when different stakeholders have conflicting goals, interests, sensibilities, and value criteria.
- **Impacts.** It is difficult to combine the positive and negative impacts of an IS in a way that meaningfully determines that it is or is not an RIS.
- **Evolution.** It is difficult to identify potentialities for evolution over time that imply than IS is or is not an RIS. For example, the ability to do workarounds is viewed as beneficial in some situations and in detrimental or harmful in others [16, 17].
- **Evaluation.** Conflicting goals of different stakeholders make it is difficult to identify criteria for determining whether an IS is or is not an RIS. Whether or not an IS qualifies an RIS should not depend on selection of which observers to consult.

Trying to describe the examples above in relation to Table 1 (first cut at minimum criteria to qualify as an RIS) and the five-part framework led to the conclusion that a yes/no definition of RIS probably would not be useful. Many IS whose everyday use seems unproblematic and uncontroversial can be implicated in some level of harm to owners, participants, customers, other stakeholders, or society (e.g., an IS that tracks the sale of cancer-causing cigarettes). Instead of pursuing a binary yes/no question (RIS or not), it is more useful to think of IS responsibility as an issue for SA&D. With that issue, the question at hand is finding a way to help IS analysts and designers make information systems more responsible.

5   Looking at IS Responsibility in Relation to Analysis and Design

Seeing IS responsibility in relation to analysis and design led to returning to seeing an IS as a sociotechnical or totally automated work system whose activities are devoted primarily to processing information. That led to two groups of responsibilities:

- responsibilities mostly related to processing information, which can be subdivided into seven types of activities: capturing, transmitting, storing, retrieving, manipulating, displaying, and deleting information [2, 3]
- responsibilities largely related to impacts on work system participants, customers, activities in work systems, other stakeholders, or society. This group of responsibilities calls for looking at many types of work system activities that are not fundamentally about processing information. [4] identifies 16 facets of capabilities, only one of which is processing information.

Facets of Capabilities. This paper cannot provide complete background on the rationale for developing the idea of facets of capabilities, which is the topic of a complete paper [4]. That paper includes background about aspects of four independent topics: (1) making more knowledge visible in IS practice, (2) different purposes of modeling, (3) views of the concept of capabilities, and (4) views of the concept of facets. For current purposes, it suffices to summarize the underlying ideas as follows:

- A *capability* is a situation-specific ability to perform an activity or set of activities (e.g., hiring employees at company X or painting cars at company Y) that might be grouped as a process and might extend across a business ecosystem.
- The concept of capability can be used without specifying how capabilities are enacted or how well. Other levels of description and analysis can specify those details when needed. That view of capabilities is much more informal than the view of capabilities in capability-driven development (e.g., [18, 19]).
- Capabilities have multiple facets, although a given facet may not apply significantly to some capabilities. Facets are types of activity that occur when enacting capabilities. Thus, goals, technologies, and actors are not facets. Every facet brings vocabulary and knowledge not typically associated with other facets. Most facets bring or imply facet-related success factors and design trade-offs.
- *Facet* is generic whereas *capability* is situation-specific. Facets of specific capabilities may overlap in some situations, as when decision making in a situation involves processing information and communicating.
- The 16 facets in [4] were chosen because they are easily understood, widely applicable, and associated with specific vocabulary and knowledge related to business situations. That set of facets could be improved or extended in the future based on exposure, discussion, and application.

The remainder of this paper relies on the concept of facets proposed in [4]. It does not use the concept of capability, which is important in [4] but is not important here.

Identifying Generic IS Responsibilities Related to (Generic) Facets. Tables 2 and 3 extend ideas in [4] by assuming that generic IS responsibilities can be identified for each (generic) facet. Table 2 covers processing information, the facet most directly related to IS since IS is defined as a work system most of whose activities are devoted to processing information. Instead of looking at information processing in general, Table 2 looks at each of seven sub-facets of information processing [4] and identifies typical IS responsibilities related to each sub-facet. It treats each sub-facet separately because an IS that processes information may perform some of the sub-facets but not others. The responsibilities listed for each sub-facet suffice for illustrative purposes even though each could surely be expanded based on further discussion and careful application to many specific examples. For example, Table 2 does not mention non-functional issues such as efficiency or speed, both of which could apply in every case. It also mentions legality only by implication.

Table 2. Generic responsibilities related to 7 sub-facets of information processing

Sub-facet	Generic responsibilities related to sub-facets of information processing
Capturing information	An IS that captures information should capture only information that is appropriate to capture and should not distort that information
Transmitting information	An IS that transmits information should transmit it only to human or automated recipients with the right to receive that information and should not distort the information during transmission
Storing information	An IS that stores information should store information only if storage is appropriate and only if storage is in an appropriate location
Retrieving information	An IS that retrieves information should retrieve only information that is appropriate to retrieve and only from locations that it has permission to access
Manipulating information	An IS that manipulates information should ensure that sources of its information are appropriate, that changes to information are justified, that calculations are performed correctly, and that manipulations combining information items are appropriate with regard to source, units of measure, and other aspects of the data items manipulated
Displaying information	An IS that displays information should ensure that information is displayed in a way that is not distorted or misleading. It should display information consistent with the access rights of users
Deleting information	An IS that deletes information should ensure that it is appropriate to delete that information

Table 3 identifies generic responsibilities related to the 15 facets other than information processing. Notice that many of those facets overlap to some extent. For example, decision-making often calls for communicating, thinking, and representing reality. While there is some overlap, the fact that each facet brings its own vocabulary and knowledge makes it appropriate to consider all of them, at least in a checklist form, when thinking about how to make an IS more responsible. Also notice that none of the responsibilities related to the facets are associated in a generic way with the widely mentioned idea of "social responsibility," such as maintaining security, privacy, or mutual respect. Topics such as those apply to all facets and therefore are not mentioned repeatedly. The goal of Tables 2 and 3 is to identify facet- or sub-facet-related responsibilities that might be overlooked even though they could be useful to consider in an attempt to make an IS more responsible.

Table 3. Generic responsibilities related to 15 facets other than information processing

Facet	Generic responsibilities related to 15 facets other than information processing
Making decisions	Supporting decision making should not interfere with any aspect of that process and should support one or more sub-facets of decision making, such as defining the problem, gathering information, defining alternatives, and selecting among alternatives
Communicating	Supporting communicating should not interfere with any aspect of communicating and should support one or more sub-facets of communicating such as formulating the message, conveying the message, and verifying receipt and comprehension of the message
Thinking	Supporting thinking should encourage conditions that are conducive to thinking, such as providing appropriate information, not overwhelming people with too much information, and not structuring work so tightly that thinking is discouraged
Representing reality	An IS that represents reality should assure that representations are complete and unbiased, do not overlook important aspects of reality, and do not exaggerate or underplay the importance of other aspects of reality
Providing information	An IS for providing information should support informational needs of users, and should do so in a way that is convenient and does not interfere with their other activities
Planning	An IS that supports planning should provide appropriate status and history information in a way that is useful for planning and/or should support useful techniques for recording and comparing alternative plans and finalizing plans
Controlling execution	An IS that supports execution control should provide information that is sufficient for controlling operations and should not perform excessive surveillance that interferes with doing work or making work system participants feel watched too closely
Improvising	There are many real-world situations where improvisation is necessary, even when highly structured software is used (e.g., [20, 21] An IS that supports improvisation should conform with the sociotechnical principle of minimum critical specification [22] and should allow appropriate interpretive flexibility
Coordinating	An IS that supports coordinating ideally should provide whatever information, communication, and record-keeping capabilities are needed by both sides of the coordination. It might support different forms of coordination as well (e.g., [23])
Performing physical work	An IS that supports performing physical work should provide information that facilitates performing that work. In some instances it should provide links to automated devices that perform that work

(*continued*)

Table 3. (*continued*)

Facet	Generic responsibilities related to 15 facets other than information processing
Performing support work	Support work is the work that facilitates other work that may be defined formally, e.g., documented as steps in a business process (e.g., [24, 25]). An IS that facilitates support work should help people who play support roles
Interacting socially	This involves conditions that encourage people to interact with each other and avoids interfering with social interaction and social relationships
Providing service	Supporting service helps in performing activities for the benefit of others. This implies focusing on fulfilling customer needs rather than on pursuing other purposes
Creating value	An IS that supports value creation helps in producing product/services that customers want and doing work in ways that also create value for providers
Co-creating value	An IS that supports value co-creation facilitates collaboration between providers and customers to produce mutual value, which often requires mutual visibility and easy exchange of information

6 Identifying Opportunities to Make an IS More Responsible

A longer version of this paper (available from the author) shows how a two-dimensional checklist based on Tables 2 and 3 can be used to identify opportunities to make an IS more responsible. The vertical dimension consists of all 22 items in Tables 2 and 3. The horizontal dimension is five groups of stakeholders: owners, participants, customers, others, and society. The longer version shows that categories in the two-dimensional checklist were clear enough for coding (classifying) responsibility-related points in an article called "The Update: Why Doctors Hate Their Computers" [26]. Due to space limitations it is only possible here to summarize the article and identify themes that became apparent from the coding of comments in the article.

An article called "The Update: Why Doctors Hate Their Computers" [26] discusses many topics related to whether an important electronic medical record (EMR) qualifies as an RIS. The author of [26] is a famous surgeon and author who experienced the $1.6 billion implementation of the EPIC EMR system in Partners HealthCare, which has 70,000 employees, 12 hospitals, and hundreds of clinics in the New England area of the USA. Under $100 million was for the software. Most of the rest was for "lost patient revenues and all the tech-support personnel and other people needed during the implementation phase." After three years, the author said: "I've come to feel that a system that promised to increase my mastery over my work has, instead, increased my work's mastery over me. ...A 2016 study found that physicians spent about two hours doing computer work for every hour spent face-to-face with the patient - whatever the brand of medical software. ... [A study] found the average workday for family physicians had grown to 11 ½ h. The result has been epidemic levels of burnout among clinicians." ... "One of the strongest predictors of burnout was how much time an individual spent tied up doing computer documentation."

Was this EMR an RIS? Ideally, an RIS should not have significant negative impacts on work system participants. Regardless of whether this IS is an RIS, different observers likely would see its scope quite differently. The software developers might focus on the software (which is not an IS from a work system perspective because it cannot perform processes and activities by itself.) In practice, the vendor's implementation support teams devote part of their effort to sociotechnical aspects, such as physicians' resentment at having to use computers while attending to patients. The reality of this IS goes further, however, including some physicians' use of "scribes" who accompany them into examining rooms or of medically trained "virtual scribes" who live and work in India but have become part of an IS in the United States.

The EPIC software surely was not developed under the assumption that scribes and virtual scribes would use the technology directly so that physicians could pay more attention to patients. However, if the system at hand is a work system that processes information, then the scribes should be viewed as system participants. Another system issue is whether unique practices of different medical sub-disciplines are reflected adequately in EPIC. The author of [26] is a surgeon who spends most of his time in the operating room and a relatively low percentage of his time in dealing with EPIC. One of his very frustrated interviewees was a primary care physician who spends much more time entering and retrieving data.

Using the 2-dimensional checklist to code aspects of the article led to identifying a series of themes that are related to IS responsibility.

Maintaining Control. The chief clinical officer supervised the software upgrade and remained focused on long-term concerns such as maintaining control and quality. He was happy to have change control processes and execution controls that would help the hospitals avoid unsafe medical practices that could not be found in the paper-based world, such as nonstandard treatments of congestive heart failure.

Feelings of Being Overconstrained. The author of the article believed that a system that promised to increase his mastery of his work instead increased his work's mastery over him. He believed that artisanship had been throttled along with a professional capacity to identify and solve problems through ground-level experimentation. In the craft-based practice of medicine there was room for individuals to do things differently, but no good way to weed out bad ideas. With computerization, the smallest changes require a committee decision plus weeks of testing.

Impacts on Interactions With Patients. Time spent dealing with a computer was time not spent looking at patients. By some reports, physicians devoted half of their patient time facing the screen to do electronic tasks. A doctor supported by an in-room human scribe was able to pay full attention to patients but still had to check that the scribe had not introduced errors. A study of scribes for emergency physicians found a 36% reduction in doctors' computer documentation time and a similar increase time directly spent with patients. Their workload did not diminish, however because they simply saw more patients.

Availability of Useful Information. The author could remotely check the vital signs of patients recovering from surgery and could look up their results from other institutions that used EPIC. The ability to provide records from all hospitals that use the same software led to improvements in care. A doctor using EPIC could manage a large number of addiction patients by seeing how they were doing as a group, which would have been impossible with the paper system. The EMR provides new ways to identify patients who have been on opioids for more than three months or who have no recent treatment for high-risk diseases. Now patients can use the EMR themselves to find lab results, read notes from doctors, and to obtain other medical information.

Decrease in Information Quality. Despite the promise of better information, some information is worse. In primary care it was more difficult to find important things in a patient's history. It had been easier to go through paper records. Doctors' handwritten notes were brief and to the point. Now, everyone could modify each patient's "problem list" of active medical issues, making the problem list useless for one physician. For example, an orthopedist might list a generic symptom such as "pain in leg," which is sufficient for billing, but not useful for colleagues who need to know the specific diagnosis. Also, inboxes were overwhelming, with messages from patients, colleagues, labs, administrators, and alarms. Many messages were deleted unread.

Personal Frustration and Inefficiency. The promise of "We'd be greener, faster, better" was not fully realized even though paper lab order slips, vital signs charts, and hospital ward records disappeared. Entering medical orders was much more difficult, involved many more clicks, and required entering redundant data. A simple request required filling in detailed forms. A physician spent an hour or more on the computer every night after her children had gone to bed. Just ordering medications and lab tests triggered dozens of mostly irrelevant alerts, all needing human reviewing and sorting.

Changes in How People Worked Together. Colleagues became more disconnected and less likely to see and help one another.

Impacts on Support Work. The new software reduced an office assistant's role and shifted more of her responsibilities to doctors. She had different screens and was not trained or authorized to use the ones doctors have. She felt disempowered. On the other hand, the use of scribes and virtual scribes became a new type of support work.

Workarounds. The use of scribes and virtual scribes was basically a workaround of shortcomings of the intended work practices. In a more modest workaround, the author reported printing out key materials before meeting with a surgery patient because it takes too long to flip between screens.

Questions About Equity and Sustainability. IKS Health in Mumbai, India provides virtual scribe service supporting thousands of patient visits in the United States. The virtual scribes are fully credentialed doctors. Many of its staffers are better paid than they would be in a local medical practice. A doctor who was quite satisfied with the virtual scribes wondered about the sustainability of having fully trained doctors in India entering data for doctors in the United States. In particular, who would take care of the patients that the scribing doctors weren't seeing?

7   Conclusion

Starting with an attempt to come to grips with the idea of RIS, this exploratory paper moved toward developing an approach for enhancing SA&D by visualizing how an IS might become more responsible. Examples in the first part of the paper and the EMR example in the second part highlight many areas in which an IS might or might not be responsible in relation to stakeholders with conflicting interests.

The themes from the EMR case study were a result of identifying issues related to IS responsibilities by using a two-dimensional checklist (available from the author in a longer version of this paper) based on facets of capabilities and stakeholders. Among many others, those issues included whether an IS has responsibility to protect its participants from burnout, whether it has responsibility to make sure that information has high quality, and whether it has a responsibility to not drain resources from other parts of the world that may need those resources. Overall, the checklist based on facets of capabilities helped in identifying many issues that might not have been anticipated by the people who designed or required the ERM software.

It is possible that a similar two-dimensional checklist could be used in SA&D both in initial deliberations and in trying to imagine otherwise unanticipated consequences of a planned system. Looking at an existing case study obviously is not equivalent to testing this paper's ideas in a research setting. While many of this paper's ideas are used to some extent in SA&D practice, the presentation of facets of capabilities in a checklist form might help designers, users, and managers visualize and deliberate upon issues that otherwise might have been overlooked.

References

1. Simon, H.A.: The Sciences of the Artificial. MIT Press, Cambridge (1996)
2. Alter, S.: The Work System Method: Connecting People, Processes, and IT for Business Results. Work System Press, Lankspur (2006)
3. Alter, S.: Work system theory: overview of core concepts, extensions, and challenges for the future. J. Assoc. Inf. Syst. 14, 72–121 (2013)
4. Authors: paper on facets of capabilities (2019, currently under review)
5. Roberts, J.J., Rapp, N.: Exclusive: Nearly 4 Million Bitcoins Lost Forever, New Study Says. Fortune, 25 November 2017
6. White, E.: Judge Orders Volkswagen to Pay $2.8B in Emission Scandal. Manufacturing Net, 21 April 2017
7. Koppel, R., et al.: Workarounds to computer access in healthcare organizations: you want my password or a dead patient? In: ITCH, pp. 215–220
8. Cowley, S., Kingson, J.A.: Wells Fargo to Claw Back $75 Million From 2 Former Executives. New York Times, 10 April 2017

9. Stechlow, S.: Why Facebook is losing the war on hate speech in Myanmar. Reuters, 15 August 2018
10. Goswani, S.: More SWIFT-Related Fraud Revealed: How Banks Must Respond. https://www.bankinfosecurity.com/more-swift-related-fraud-revealed-how-do-we-stop-it
11. Keller, L.L.: Wall Street's New Favorite Way to Swap Secrets Is Against the Rules. Bloomberg Businessweek, 30 March 2017
12. Gliklich, E., Guo, R., Bergmark, R.W.: Texting while driving: a study of 1211 US adults with the distracted driving survey. Prev. Med. Rep. **4**, 486–489 (2016)
13. Popescu, A.: Keep your head up: How smartphone addiction kills manners and moods. New York Times, 25 January 2018
14. Zuboff, S.: Big other: surveillance capitalism and the prospects of an information civilization. J. Inf. Technol. **30**(1), 75–89 (2015)
15. Chen, B.X.: In an era of 'smart' things, sometimes dumb stuff is better. New York Times, 21 February 2018
16. Alter, S.: Theory of workarounds. Commun. Assoc. Inf. Syst. **34**(55), 1041–1066 (2014)
17. Alter, S.: Beneficial Noncompliance and Detrimental Compliance, AMCIS 2015 (2015)
18. Bērziša, S., et al.: Capability Driven Development: an approach to designing digital enterprises. Bus. Inf. Syst. Eng. **57**(1), 15–25 (2015)
19. Loucopoulos, P., Kavakli, E.: Capability oriented enterprise knowledge modeling: the CODEK approach. Domain-Specific Conceptual Modeling, pp. 197–215. Springer, Cham (2016). https://doi.org/10.1007/978-3-319-39417-6_9
20. Ciborra, C.: Improvisation and information technology in organizations. In: ICIS 1996 Proceedings, 26 (1996)
21. Elbanna, A.R.: The validity of the improvisation argument in the implementation of rigid technology. J. Inf. Technol. **21**(3), 165–175 (2006)
22. Cherns, A.: Principles of sociotechnical design revisited. Hum. Relat. **40**(3), 153–162 (1987)
23. Malone, T.W., Crowston, K.: The interdisciplinary study of coordination. ACM Comput. Surv. **26**(1), 87–119 (1994)
24. Strauss, A.L.: Work and the division of labor. In: Creating Sociological Awareness, pp. 85–110. Routledge (2018)
25. Sawyer, S., Tapia, A.: Always articulating: theorizing on mobile and wireless technologies. Inf. Soc. **22**(5), 311–323 (2006)
26. Gawande, A.: Why Doctors Hate Their Computers. New Yorker, 12 November 2018

Discovering Customer Journeys from Evidence: A Genetic Approach Inspired by Process Mining

Gaël Bernard[1]([⊠]) and Periklis Andritsos[2]

[1] Faculty of Business and Economics (HEC), University of Lausanne,
Lausanne, Switzerland
gael.bernard@unil.ch
[2] Faculty of Information, University of Toronto, Toronto, Canada
periklis.andritsos@utoronto.ca

Abstract. Displaying the main behaviors of customers on a customer journey map (CJM) helps service providers to put themselves in their customers' shoes. Inspired by the process mining discipline, we address the challenging problem of automatically building CJMs from event logs. In this paper, we introduce the CJMs discovery task and propose a genetic approach to solve it. We explain how our approach differs from traditional process mining techniques and evaluate it with state-of-the-art techniques for summarizing sequences of categorical data.

Keywords: Customer journey mapping · Process mining ·
Customer journey analytics · Genetic algorithms

1 Introduction

We aim to summarize customer journeys. A customer journey is a collection of interactions (or touchpoints) between a customer and a firm. A journey can be as simple as a single activity (e.g., 'looking at a product'), but can also involve complex interactions. Concretely, a challenge faced by many practitioners is to make sense of the–potentially infinite–combination of activities that exist in order to consume a service. As a response, new methods to understand, design, and analyze customer journeys are emerging from the industry and are becoming increasingly popular among researchers. One of these methods, which is the focus of this paper, is the Customer Journey Map (CJM). A CJM is a conceptual tool used for better understanding customers' journeys when they are consuming a service. A CJM depicts typical journeys experienced by the customers across several touchpoints. To represent a CJM, we use a visual chart showing the basic components of a CJM; namely, the touchpoints, and the journeys. It possesses two axis: the y-axis lists the touchpoints in alphabetical order, while the x-axis represents the ordering of the sequence of touchpoints. Dots connected with a smooth line represent a journey.

C. Cappiello and M. Ruiz (Eds.): CAiSE Forum 2019, LNBIP 350, pp. 36–47, 2019.
https://doi.org/10.1007/978-3-030-21297-1_4

Fig. 1. ❶ A fraction of the dataset–612 sequences out of 123'706–displayed on a CJM, and ❷, a CJM that summarizes the entire dataset using three representatives.

The left part of Fig. 1 display a CJM containing all the observed journeys from customers while the right part shows how our algorithm helps in reducing a CJM's complexity by building three representative journeys that best summarize the entire dataset. Summarizing thousands of journeys using few representatives has many compelling applications. First, it allows a business analyst to discover the common customers' behaviors. Second, the representative journeys extracted from data can also serve as a basis to fuel the discussion during workshops and complement strategic CJM built by internal stakeholders. Third, by assigning each journey to its closest representative, we turn a complex type of input data into a categorical one. The latter can be used to complete the traditional types of data that are used to perform behavior segmentation (e.g., usage volume, loyalty to brand).

Our work contributes by: (1) clarifying the customer journey discovery activity which has, to the best of our knowledge, never been defined, (2) proposing ground truth datasets, which are particularly suited for evaluating this activity, and (3) introducing a genetic algorithm to discover representative journeys. Using the proposed datasets and existing cluster analysis techniques, we demonstrate that our approach outperforms state-of-the-art approaches used in social sciences to summarize categorical sequences.

The paper is organized as follows. Section 2 defines the customer journey discovery activity while Sect. 3 provides an overview of existing techniques closely related to this task. Section 4 introduces our genetic algorithm. In Sect. 5, we evaluate the results. Finally, Sect. 6 concludes the paper.

2   Customer Journey Discovery

The customer journey discovery activity can be described with the following definition: *given a set of actual journeys, find a reasonable amount of representative journeys that well summarize the data.*

Definition 1 (Touchpoint): a touchpoint is an interaction between a customer and a company's products or services [2]. 'Sharing on social network' or 'ordering a product on the website' are two typical examples of touchpoints in a retail context. Let t be a touchpoint, and let T be the finite set of all touchpoints.

Definition 2 (Journey): A journey J is a sequence of touchpoints. For instance, $J = \{\langle$'Visiting the shop', 'Testing the product', 'Sharing on social network'$\rangle\}$ is a journey with three touchpoints. For the sake of brevity, we replace the touchpoints with alphabetical characters so that J becomes $\langle ABC \rangle$.

Definition 3 (Actual Journey): An event log J_a is the set of all actual journeys observed from customers.

Definition 4 (Event Logs): Let J_A be an event log, the set of all actual journeys observed by customers.

Definition 5 (Representative Journey): A representative journey, J_r, is a journey that summarizes a subset of actual journeys $\in J_A$.

Definition 6 (Customer Journey Map): A CJM summarizes customer journeys through the use of representative journeys. Let a customer journey map J_R be the set of all the J_rs summarizing J_A. Let k_R denotes the number of journeys in a map (i.e., $|J_R|$). Typically, the part ❷ of Fig. 1 is a CJM, J_R, containing three representative journeys, J_r ($k_R = 3$), summarizing an event log J_A.

Discovering J_R from J_A is an unsupervised clustering task that entails interesting challenges. First, there is no work in the literature that deals with the optimal number of k_R. Second, the sequence that best summarizes its assigned actual journeys needs to be found.

3   Related Work

In [1], we propose a web-based tool to navigate CJMs, which is called CJM-ex (CJM-explorer). It uses a hierarchical structure so that the first layers show only the most representative journeys, abstracting from less representative ones.

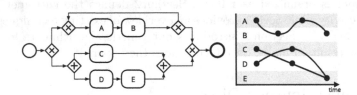

Fig. 2. Expected BPM and CJM when L = [$\langle ABAB \rangle$, $\langle DCE \rangle$, $\langle CDE \rangle$].

In [2], we show that the process mining framework as well as the input data are relevant in a customer journey analytics context. Similar to the process discovery activity in process mining, this work focuses on the *discovery* of a model from *event logs*. Our work was inspired by the approach in [3,6,14] where the authors propose discovering business process models (BPMs) using a genetic algorithm. A BPM and a CJM is not used for the same purpose. Fundamentally, the goal of a BPM is to find models that best describe how the processes are handled. In contrast, the aim of a CJM is to help internal stakeholders to put themselves in their customers' shoes. Figure 2 shows that these models convey different type of information. A CJM depicts journeys as experienced by customers while a BPM shows the available combination of activities using advanced constructs such as exclusive or parallel gateways. Overall, CJMs are used to supplement but not to replace BPMs [12].

In fact, our work is closer to the summarization of categorical sequences used in social sciences. In particular, in [8,9], Gabadinho et al. propose summarizing a list of observed sequences (i.e., actual journeys) using representative (i.e., representative journey). They define a representative set as "a set of non-redundant 'typical' sequences that largely, though not necessarily exhaustively, cover the spectrum of observed sequences" [8]. We argue that their definition matches our definition of a representative sequence summarizing a set of sequences. The authors propose five ways to select a representative. The 'frequency' (1), where the most frequent event is used as the representative. The 'neighborhood density' (2), which consists of counting the number of sequences within the neighborhood of each candidate sequence. The most representative is the one with the largest number of sequences in a defined neighborhood diameter. The 'mean state frequency' (3): the transversal frequencies of the successive states is used to find a representative using the following equation:

$$MSF(s) = \frac{1}{\ell} \sum_{i=1}^{\ell} f_{si} \tag{1}$$

where

$s = s_1 s_2 ... s_l$: Sequence of length ℓ
$(f_{s_1}, f_{s_2}, ... f_{s_l})$: Frequencies of the states at time t_ℓ

The sum of the state frequencies divided by the sequence length becomes the mean state frequency. Its value is bounded by 0 and 1 where 1 describes a situation where there is only one single distinct sequence [8]. The sequence with the highest score is the representative. The 'centrality' (4): the representative – or medoid – can be found using the centrality. Being the most central object, the representative is the sequence with the minimal sum of distances to all other sequences. Finally, the 'sequence likelihood' (5): the sequence likelihood of a sequence derived from the first-order Markov model can also be used to determine the representative. In the evaluation section, we compare our genetic approach with these five techniques using their own implementation of the package Traminer available in R [7].

4   Genetic Algorithm for CJM Discovery

As an introduction, Fig. 3 provides intuition on how the genetic algorithm builds a CJM such as the one visible in Fig. 1 (part ❷). A set of actual journeys, J_a, is

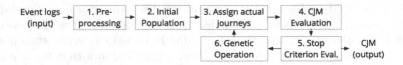

Fig. 3. Overview of the genetic algorithm to discover CJMs

provided to the algorithm. Then, during *Generation 1*, we build p number of $J_{\mathcal{R}}$, where p *is the population size*; i.e., the number of CJMs that will be evaluated after each generation. In our example $p = 3$. Each $J_{\mathcal{R}}$ is evaluated and we keep the e best $J_{\mathcal{R}}$s, called the *elite set* while we discard the other $(p - e)$ $J_{\mathcal{R}}$s. Then, we move to *Generation 2*, where we keep an untouched version of the e number of $J_{\mathcal{R}}$s in the elite set. For instance, $J_{\mathcal{R}2}$ was kept in Generation 2 because it has the best average quality in Generation 1, i.e., $J_{\mathcal{R}2}$ is intact in Generation 2. We then apply some transformation (to be discussed next) to generate $(p - e)$ new $J_{\mathcal{R}}$s that will, in turn, be evaluated. In our case, we generate $J_{\mathcal{R}4}$ and $J_{\mathcal{R}5}$. We recursively transform and evaluate the p number of $J_{\mathcal{R}}$s until a stopping criterion is met. Once a stopping criterion is met, we return the best $J_{\mathcal{R}}$. *The best $J_{\mathcal{R}}$ can be interpreted as the best set of representative journeys, J_r, representing a set of journeys from J_A that have been found given a certain evaluation criterion.* The next section describes how we generate the initial population, what various types of operations we apply on each $J_{\mathcal{R}}$ to transform them, and how we evaluate each one of them given a set of journeys in J_A.

4.1 Preprocessing

To gain in efficiency, we make the assumption that $J_{\mathcal{R}}$ will be close to the frequent patterns observed in J_a. Let Top_{ℓ_n} be the n most occurring pattern of length ℓ and $Top_n \supseteq Top_{\ell_{[2,m]}}$ be the superset of all the most occurring patterns of lengths 2 to m. Top_n is used later to form the initial population of $J_{\mathcal{R}}$ (described in Sect. 4.2), and to add a random journey to $J_{\mathcal{R}}$. Using Top_n we avoid generating journeys by picking a random number of touchpoints from T. According to our experiments, using Top_n reduces the execution time by two to get an output $J_{\mathcal{R}}$ of the same average quality.

4.2 Initial Population

The initial population is generated by adding a sequence randomly picked from Top_n (defined in Sect. 4.1).

4.3 Assign Actual Journeys

The quality of a representative journey can only be measured when knowing which actual journeys it represents. Hence, a first step toward evaluating the quality of $J_\mathcal{R}$ is to assign each journey $J_a \in J_\mathcal{A}$ to its closest journey in $J_r \in J_\mathcal{R}$. To characterize the closeness between J_a and J_r, we use the Levensthein distance borrowed from [11]. It is a metric particularly well suited to measure the distance between sequences. The Levensthein distance counts the number of edit operations that are necessary to transform one sequence into another one. There are three types of operations: deletions, insertions, and substitutions. For instance, the distance between ⟨ABC⟩ and ⟨ACCE⟩ is 2 since one substitution and one insertion are required to match them. We define the closest representative as the one having the smallest Levensthein distance with the actual journeys. Note that if a tie occurs between multiple best representatives, we assign the J_a to the J_r having the smallest amount of actual journeys already assigned to it. Once each actual journey has been assigned to its closest representative, we can evaluate $J_\mathcal{R}$ using the criteria described in the next section.

4.4 CJM Evaluation Criteria

This section introduces the evaluation criteria used to determine the quality of each $J_\mathcal{R}$, namely, (1) the fitness, (2) the number of representatives, and (3) the average quality.

Fitness. The fitness measures the distance between each sequence of activities J_a and its closest representative $J_\mathcal{R}$ using the Levenshtein distance [11].

$$Fitness(J_a, J_\mathcal{R}) = 1 - \frac{\sum_{i=1}^{|J_a|} min_{j=1}^{|J_\mathcal{R}|}(Levensthein(\sigma_{\mathcal{A}_i}; \sigma_{\mathcal{R}_j}))}{\sum_{i=1}^{|J_a|} Length(\sigma_{\mathcal{A}_i})} \tag{2}$$

where

$\sigma_{\mathcal{A}_i}$	: i^{th} actual sequence observed in event logs
$\sigma_{\mathcal{R}_j}$	: j^{th} representative contained in $J_\mathcal{R}$
$Levenshtein(x_1, x_2)$	: Levensthein distance between two sequences
$Length(x)$	: Length of the sequence of activity x

A fitness of 1 means that the representative journey perfectly catches the behavior of the actual journeys assigned to it. In contrast, a fitness close to 0 implies that many edit operations are necessary to match the sequences.

Number of Representatives. If we maximize the fitness without trying to keep a low $k_\mathcal{R}$, the CJM will become unreadable because too many representative journeys will be displayed in it. In other words, $J_\mathcal{R}$ overfits. Hence, the goal is to find a $k_\mathcal{R}$ that offers a good compromise between underfitting and overfitting. Finding the optimal number of clusters is a recurrent challenge when clustering data. We propose integrating traditional ways of determining the optimal number of clusters, such as the Bayesian information criterion [13], or the Calinski-Harabasz index [5]. The idea is to evaluate a range of solutions (e.g., from 2 to 10 journeys) and to keep the best solution. Let k_h be the optimal number of clusters returned by one of the techniques mentioned above. By integrating k_h into the evaluation, we can guide the solution toward a $k_{\mathcal{R}}$ that is statistically relevant. To evaluate the quality, we measure the distance between $k_{\mathcal{R}}$ and k_h. To do this, we propose the following distribution function:

$$NumberOfRepresentatives(k_{\mathcal{R}}, k_h, x_0) = \frac{1}{1 + (\frac{|k_{\mathcal{R}} - k_h|}{x_0})^2} \qquad (3)$$

where

$k_{\mathcal{R}}$: Number of J_r journeys on $J_{\mathcal{R}}$ (i.e., $|J_{\mathcal{R}}|$)
k_h : Optimal number of journeys (e.g., using the Calinski-Harabasz index)
x_0 : x value of the midpoint

The parameter x_0 determines where the midpoint of the curve is. Concretely, if $x_0 = 5$, $k_{\mathcal{R}} = 11$ will result in a quality of 0.5 because the absolute distance from k_h is 5. We set $x_0 = 5$ for all our experiments. Intuitively, x_0 guide the number of representatives that will be found. We set it to 5 as we believe that it is a reasonable amount of journeys to display on a single CJM. Because the number of representatives is not the only criteria to assess the quality of a CJM, the final CJM might contain more or less journeys if it increases the average quality.

Average Quality. We assign weights to the fitness and the number of representatives qualities to adjust their relative importance. According to our experiments and in line with the work from Buijs et al. [3], the results tend to be best if more weight is given to the fitness quality. Typically, weights $w_f = 3$, and $w_{k_h} = 1$ lead to the best results. Then, we get the overall quality by averaging the weighted qualities using the arithmetic mean. In the next section, we determine the stopping criterion of the algorithm.

4.5   Stopping Criterion

Before starting a new generation, we check if a stopping criterion is met. There are three ways we can use to stop the algorithm taken from [3,6]. (1) The algorithm could stop after a certain number of generations. (2) One could stop the algorithm when a certain number of generations have been created without improving the average quality. (3) We could stop the algorithm when a certain quality threshold is reached for one of the evaluation criteria. Because it is difficult to predict the quality level that can be reached, we believe that stopping the algorithm using a threshold is not advisable. For this reason, we used a combination of approaches 1 and 2 for our experiments. Once the stopping criteria have been evaluated, either the algorithm stops, or, we generate new candidates by applying genetic operators described in the next section.

4.6   Genetic Operations

Once all the CJMs have been evaluated, we rank them by their average quality and copy a fraction (i.e., e) of the best ones in *elite*. Because we keep an untouched version of the e number of $J_\mathcal{R}$s, we make sure that the overall quality will only increase or stay steady. Then, we generate $(p-e)$ new $J_\mathcal{R}$s as follows. We pick one random $J_\mathcal{R}$ from *elite*, and perform one or multiple of these four operators. *(1) Add a journey:* A sequence is randomly picked from Top_n and added to $J_\mathcal{R}$. *(2) Delete a journey:* A random journey is removed from $J_\mathcal{R}$. Nothing happens if $J_\mathcal{R}$ contains only one journey. *(3) Add a touchpoint:* A touchpoint from T is added to one of the journeys from $J_\mathcal{R}$ at a random position. *(4) Delete a touchpoint:* A touchpoint is removed from $J_\mathcal{R}$ unless removing this touchpoint would result in an empty set of touchpoints. As described in Fig. 3, once new $J_\mathcal{R}$s have been created, we go back to the evaluation phase where the new $J_\mathcal{R}$s are evaluated until one stopping criterion is met. Once such a criterion is met, we return the best $J_\mathcal{R}$s of the last generation and the algorithm stops.

5   Evaluation

5.1   Datasets

We produced several event logs that simulate journeys. Generating the event logs ourselves means that we know the ground truth represented by the generative journeys and therefore the objective is to recover these journeys from a set of actual ones we produce. *A generative journey is a known list of touchpoints from which we generate the event logs.* Let $J_\mathcal{G}$ be a set of $k_\mathcal{G}$ generative journeys used to generate a dataset composed of 1,000 actual journeys.

If we were to use only these generative journeys to generate 1,000 journeys, we would obtain only $k_\mathcal{G}$ distinct journeys. For instance, if we use $J_{g1} = \langle \text{ABC} \rangle$ and $J_{g2} = \langle \text{ABBD} \rangle$ to generate 1,000 journeys equally distributed, we obtain $J_a = \left\{ J_{g1}^{500}, J_{g2}^{500} \right\}$. A more realistic situation would depict a scenario where each group of customers can be described by a representative sequence of activities, but the actual journeys within the group can deviate from the representative one. Hence, to produce more realistic data, we inject noise for a fraction of the journeys. For instance, if the noise level is set to 50%, $J_a = J_g$ is true for half of the data. For the other half, we add noise by removing or adding touchpoints, or by swapping the ordering of activities.

We generated 8 datasets of varying characteristics. The characteristics are distinct in terms of: number of $k_\mathcal{G}$, number of touchpoints, average length of the journeys, and the standard deviation of the number of journeys assigned to each generative journey. For each dataset, we gradually apply 5 levels of noise, resulting in 40 datasets. The datasets, the detailed characteristics of them as well as the procedure followed to produce them are available at the following url: http://customer-journey.unil.ch/datasets/.

5.2   Metrics

We use both external and internal evaluation metrics. On the one hand, the external ones evaluate the results relative to the generative journeys. On the other hand, the internal evaluation uses cluster analysis techniques to assess the results. The aim is to account for the fact that the ground truth might not be the optimal solution because of the noise that was added. This section introduces these metrics. For the internal evaluation metrics, we borrowed them from [9].

External Evaluation - Jaccard Index. To evaluate the similarity between the sequences of activities from the generative journeys ($J_\mathcal{G}$) and the discovered representative journeys ($J_\mathcal{R}$), we propose to use the Jaccard index where a score of 1 indicates a perfect match.

$$JaccardIndex(J_\mathcal{R}, J_\mathcal{G}) = \frac{|J_\mathcal{R} \cap J_\mathcal{G}|}{|J_\mathcal{R} \cup J_\mathcal{G}|} \tag{4}$$

External Evaluation - Distance in Number of Journeys. This metric measures the distance between the number of generative journeys and the number of representative journeys returned by the algorithm. We propose:

$$NbJourneysDistance(k_\mathcal{G}, k_\mathcal{R}) = abs(k_\mathcal{G} - k_\mathcal{R}) \tag{5}$$

Internal Evaluation - Mean Distance [9]. The mean distance i returns the average Levensthein distance between the representative sequence i and the sequence of actual journeys that have been assigned to i, k_i being the number of actual journeys assigned to the representative journey i.

$$MeanDistanceScore_i = \frac{\sum_{j=1}^{k_i} D(J_{r_i}, J_{a_{ij}})}{k_i} \tag{6}$$

Internal Evaluation - Coverage [9]. The coverage indicates the proportion of actual journeys that are within the neighborhood n of a representative.

$$Coverage_i = \frac{\sum_{j=1}^{k_i} (D(J_{r_i}, J_{a_{ij}}) < n)}{k_i} \tag{7}$$

Internal Evaluation - Distance Gain [9]. The distance gain measures the gain in using a representative journey instead of the true center of the set, C (i.e., the medoid of the whole dataset). In other words, it measures the gain obtained in using multiple representative journeys instead of a single one.

$$DistGain_i = \frac{\sum_{j=1}^{k_i} D(C(J_a), J_{a_{ij}}) - \sum_{j=1}^{k_i} D(J_{r_i}, J_{a_{ij}})}{\sum_{j=1}^{k_i} D(C(J_a), J_{a_{ij}})} \tag{8}$$

5.3   Settings

We evaluate our genetic algorithm (approach 1) against an approach using Kmedoids clustering (approach 2) and the approaches proposed by Gabadinho et al. [7] (approach 3). Approach 1 is using our genetic algorithm with a fitness weight set to 3 and a weight for the number of representatives set to 1. Due to the non-deterministic nature of the genetic algorithm, we run it ten times. In approach 2, we build a distance matrix of the edit-distance between sequences. We then create k (found using the Calinski-Harabasz index) clusters using an implementation, [4], of the k-medoids algorithm. Finally, the medoid of each cluster becomes the representative. In approach 3 we build the same distance matrix as then one used in approach 2. Then, we used an agglomerative hierarchical clustering to define k clusters. Finally, we return the best representatives of each cluster using the frequency, the neighborhood density, the mean state frequency, the centrality, or the likelihood using the package Traminer available in R [7] (Fig. 4).

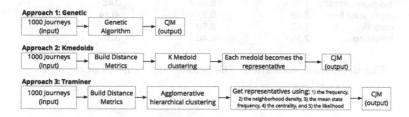

Fig. 4. Three approaches used to find the representative journeys.

5.4   Results

We present the results of the external evaluation metrics, then the internal ones and we conclude by mentioning the execution times for several datasets sizes. The external evaluation metrics are shown in Fig. 5. Here, we can see that the solution that reduces the Jaccard index the most and which is closest to the ground truth in terms of number of journeys is the genetic approach. The internal evaluation in Fig. 6 shows that the genetic algorithm outperforms the other approaches. Finally, the execution time to for 100 actual journeys is much faster using the kmedoids or using the techniques implemented in Traminer [7]. We observe that when we increase the datasets' size the performance of the genetic algorithm tend to be comparable to the kmedoids implementation and faster than the techniques implemented in Traminer (Fig. 7).

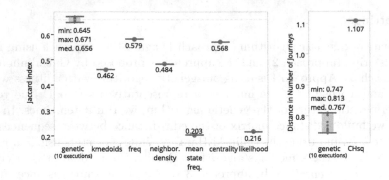

Fig. 5. External evaluation

	Avg. mean distance (the smaller, the better)	Avg. coverage (the higher, the better)	Avg. dist-gain (the higher, the better)
genetic (10 executions)	1.37 (median) min:1.37 max:1.38	0.59 (median) min:0.58 max:0.59	0.59 (median) min:0.59 max:0.60
kmedoids	1.75	0.47	0.48
freq	1.74	0.49	0.48
neighbor. density	1.72	0.46	0.48
mean state freq.	3.69	0.27	-0.14
centrality	1.62	0.50	0.51
likelihood	2.15	0.40	0.36

Fig. 6. Internal evaluation. The genetic algorithm perform best.

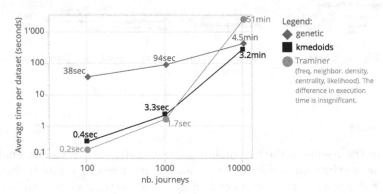

Fig. 7. Comparing the execution time per dataset for 100, 1'000, and 10'000 journeys.

6   Conclusion

In this paper, we propose two basic quality criteria to guide the evolution process of discovering the best representative journeys for a given set of actual journeys that otherwise would be unreadable. We demonstrate that they perform well on synthetic datasets. We show that techniques from social sciences are also useful for studying customer journeys. As suggested by Gabadinho et al., "The methods are by no way limited to social science data and should prove useful in many other domains" [8]. This present study supports this claim and highlights how research from social science can benefit our understanding of customers. At a time when a customer-centric culture has become a matter of survival according to [10], we anticipate that research at the crossroads between data science, marketing, and social sciences will be key to a full understanding of customer experiences.

References

1. Bernard, G., Andritsos, P.: CJM-ex: goal-oriented exploration of customer journey maps using event logs and data analytics. In: 15th International Conference on Business Process Management (BPM 2017) (2017)
2. Bernard, G., Andritsos, P.: A process mining based model for customer journey mapping. In: Proceedings of the Forum and Doctoral Consortium Papers Presented at the 29th International Conference on Advanced Information Systems Engineering (CAiSE 2017) (2017)
3. Buijs, J.C., van Dongen, B.F., van der Aalst, W.M.: A genetic algorithm for discovering process trees. In: 2012 IEEE Congress on Evolutionary Computation (CEC), pp. 1–8. IEEE (2012)
4. Bauckhage, C.: Numpy/Scipy Recipes for Data Science: k-medoids Clustering[r]. Technical report (2015). https://github.com/letiantian/kmedoids
5. Caliński, T., Harabasz, J.: A dendrite method for cluster analysis. Commun. Stat. Theory Methods 3(1), 1–27 (1974)
6. van der Aalst, W.M.P., de Medeiros, A.K.A., Weijters, A.J.M.M.: Genetic process mining. In: Ciardo, G., Darondeau, P. (eds.) ICATPN 2005. LNCS, vol. 3536, pp. 48–69. Springer, Heidelberg (2005). https://doi.org/10.1007/11494744_5
7. Gabadinho, A., Ritschard, G.: Searching for typical life trajectories applied to childbirth histories. Gendered life courses-Between individualization and standardization. In: A European Approach Applied to Switzerland, pp. 287–312 (2013)
8. Gabadinho, A., Ritschard, G., Studer, M., Mueller, N.S.: Summarizing sets of categorical sequences: selecting and visualizing representative sequences, pp. 94–106, October 2009
9. Gabadinho, A., Ritschard, G., Studer, M., Müller, N.S.: Extracting and rendering representative sequences. In: Fred, A., Dietz, J.L.G., Liu, K., Filipe, J. (eds.) IC3K 2009. CCIS, vol. 128, pp. 94–106. Springer, Heidelberg (2011). https://doi.org/10.1007/978-3-642-19032-2_7
10. Goran, J., LaBerge, L., Srinivasan, R.: Culture for a Digital Age. Technical report, McKinsey, July 2017. https://www.mckinsey.com/business-functions/digital-mckinsey/our-insights/culture-for-a-digital-age
11. Levenshtein, V.I.: Binary codes capable of correcting deletions, insertions, and reversals. Soviet physics doklady 10, 707–710 (1966)
12. Olding, E., Cantara, M., Robertson, B., Dunie, R., Huang, O., Searle, S.: Predicts 2016: business transformation and process management bridge the strategy-to-execution gap. Technical report, Gartner, November 2015. https://www.gartner.com/doc/3173020/predicts-business-transformation-process
13. Schwarz, G., et al.: Estimating the dimension of a model. Ann. Stat. 6(2), 461–464 (1978)
14. Vázquez-Barreiros, B., Mucientes, M., Lama, M.: ProDiGEN: mining complete, precise and minimal structure process models with a genetic algorithm. Inf. Sci. 294, 315–333 (2015)

Keeping Data Inter-related
in a Blockchain

Phani Chitti and Ruzanna Chitchyan$^{(\boxtimes)}$ (iD)

Department of Computer Science, University of Bristol,
MVB Building, Woodland Road, Bristol BS8 1UB, UK
{sc18092,r.chitchyan}@bristol.ac.uk

Abstract. Blockchains are gaining a substantial recognition as an alternative to the traditional data storage systems due to their tampering-resistant and decentralized storage, independence from any centralized authority, and low entry barriers for new network participants. Presently blockchains allow users to store transactions and data sets, however, they don't provide an easy way of creating and keeping relationships between data entities. In this paper we demonstrate a solution that helps software developers maintain relationships between inter-related data entities and datasets in a blockchain. Our solution runs over Ethereum's Go implementation. This is the first step towards a database management-like middleware system for blockchains.

Keywords: Blockchain · Data integrity · Referential integrity ·
Relations · Data access · Data stores

1 Introduction

Blockchains are increasingly recognised as an alternative to traditional database systems for transactional data and dataset storage. Yet, to be a feasible replacement to the currently predominating *relational databases* for the enterprise use, blockchains must also ensure that *integrity constraints*[1] hold for their stored data and for the interrelationships between such data entries. These *(data and referential) integrity constraints* ensure accuracy and consistency of data over its life-cycle and are important aspects of the design, implementation and usage of database solutions.

Data integrity refers to the overall completeness, accuracy and consistency of the stored data. *Referential integrity* ensures that data references spread across

---

[1] We note that some popular databases (e.g., NoSQL) do not address referential integrity constraints, which, we think, is one of the reasons of their slow penetration into the mainstream enterprise use.

This research is funded by the UK EPSRC Refactoring Energy Systems fellowship (EP/R007373/1).

© Springer Nature Switzerland AG 2019
C. Cappiello and M. Ruiz (Eds.): CAiSE Forum 2019, LNBIP 350, pp. 48–59, 2019.
https://doi.org/10.1007/978-3-030-21297-1_5

entities[2] are consistent. In a database, operations that modify the state of data (like inserting a new entry, updating or deleting a data record) must maintain the integrity constraints.

Presently blockchains don't provide an easy way for creating, maintaining, and using relationships between data entries, or for enforcing and utilising the integrity constraints. In this paper we demonstrate a solution that helps software developers maintain relationships between smart contracts, preserve these relations and enforce them during run-time. In short, our solution aims to provide to Ethereum blockchain users some of the functions that a traditional database management system delivers to its' users. Our solution runs over Ethereum's Go implementation.

The paper presents a motivating example for this problem in Sect. 2. The proposed architecture of the system and its components are explained in Sect. 3. Section 4 briefly discusses some related work, and Sect. 5 concludes the paper.

2   Motivating Example

To demonstrate the need for data and referential integrity, let us consider the example of a building occupancy analysis system [14]. This system collects and analyses large data sets about a building: its' sensors, equipment, energy consumption and occupancy information. Figure 1 shows a part of the conceptual schema for data representation in such a system, where inter-relations between entities are highlighted via linked boxes.

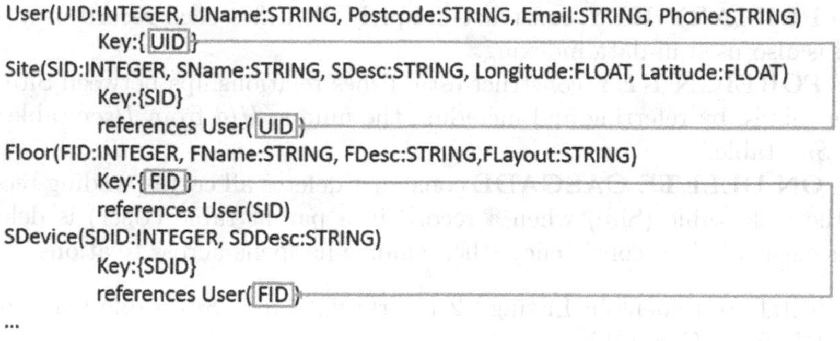

```
User(UID:INTEGER, UName:STRING, Postcode:STRING, Email:STRING, Phone:STRING)
        Key:{ UID }
Site(SID:INTEGER, SName:STRING, SDesc:STRING, Longitude:FLOAT, Latitude:FLOAT)
        Key:{SID}
        references User( UID )
Floor(FID:INTEGER, FName:STRING, FDesc:STRING,FLayout:STRING)
        Key:{ FID }
        references User(SID)
SDevice(SDID:INTEGER, SDDesc:STRING)
        Key:{SDID}
        references User( FID )
    ...
```

Fig. 1. Relational schema

Traditionally, a database management system provides means to implement such conceptual models within a database, as well as to ensure integrity when adding or maintaining their relevant data. Let us consider how relational and blockchain databases handle this.

---

[2] I.e., digital representations of the real world objects or concepts.

2.1   Integrity in a Relational Database

The *relational data model* [6,7] is built around the mathematical structure of *relation*. A *relation*, is a digital representation of an object or a concept (as defined in a schema) which is instantiated as a tabular construct (i.e., with columns for headings and rows for data entries). Constraints can be expressed over a set of columns to ensure data and referential integrity.

The Structured Query Language (SQL) CREATE TABLE command in Listing 1.1 creates a relation for the *Site* concept (shown in Fig. 1 conceptual schema).

CREATE TABLE IF NOT EXISTS Site (
SID INT **NOT NULL** , SName VARCHAR(255) **NOT NULL** ,
SDesc VARCHAR(255) **NOTNULL** ,
...
UId INT NOT NULL,
PRIMARY KEY (SID) ,
FOREIGN KEY ('UId')   **REFERENCES**   'User' ('UId')
                ON DELETE CASCADE)

Listing 1.1. Create SQL Statement

the text that is highlighted in bold in Listing 1.1 indicates the data and referential integrity constrains over corresponding columns as explained below:

- **NOT NULL** construct prevents the corresponding column from accepting NULL values, thereby ensuring that a valid data entry always has a non-null value in this column.
- The **PRIMARY KEY** construct uniquely identifies each record in a table and is also used in data indexing.
- The **FOREIGN KEY** construct establishes relationships between Site and User tables, by referring and including the unique *UId* from *User* table into the *Site* table.
- The **ON DELETE CASCADE** construct deletes all corresponding records in the child table (Site) when a record in a parent table (User) is deleted, thus ensuring data consistency when change happens across relations.

The INSERT Statement in Listing 1.2 inserts data into *Site* table while referencing *UId* from *User* table.

INSERT INTO Site VALUES(1 , ' ' Site − 1 '' , ' ' First Site '' ,
                − 2.774757 , 50.628323 , 1)

Listing 1.2. Insert SQL Statement

Since the database management system ensures the data and referential integrity constraints when updating data entries, the erroneous data entry is prevented. For instance, it is not possible to enter a NULL or a STRING value for *SID* attribute of *Site* table, as the respective constrains (as per Listing 1.1) reject such data entries. Similarly it is not possible to enter *Site* details for a User who is not present in *User* table, as the FOREIGN KEY('UId') constraint in Listing 1.1 ensures that the UId must be an existing unique ID in *User* table. The database management system performs corresponding actions for aforementioned integrity related constructs during insert, update and delete operations to ensure the data and referential integrity.

2.2   Integrity in a Blockchain

Ethereum blockchain is an immutable chain of interlinked blocks maintained in a network of untrusted peers. Ethereum blockchain can be used as a data store by modelling entities as smart contracts and deploying them to blockchain. Given the conceptual schema in Fig. 1, a sample outline for the contract representing the *User* entity (written in Solidity [9] language) is shown in Listing 1.3.

```
contract User {
    //Specify data Layout representing the
    //attributes of the entity
    struct UserDetail{
                uint16 UId;
                string UName;
                string Postcode;
                string email;
                string phone;
    }
    //mapping data structure used to store the Rows
    mapping(int => UserDetail) uDetails;
    //counter for key in mapping
    uint32 counter = 0;
    constructor() public { }
    //The Set methods inserts data row
    function SetData(address hash, uint16 uid, ...)
            public returns(string) {
        //Get the next key value by increasing the counter
        counter++;
        //Create a row using UserDetail Struct
        //Append the row to uDetails mapping using the counter as key
    }
    //The Get method return required data from
    //the mapping data store.
    function GetData(address hash) public view
                    returns (uint16 uid, ...) {
    ...
    }
}
```

Listing 1.3. User Smart Contract

The text that is highlighted in bold in Listing 1.3 shows the constructs that set out the data layout, and functions for data insertion and access.

– **struct:** Solidity's *struct* construct specifies the data column layout for attributes along with their data types. The UserDetail struct defines the data layout for *User* as per the conceptual schema defined in Fig. 1.

- **mapping:** The *mapping* data structure specifies the data row layout for *User* entity; it stores data in key-value pairs. Alternatively the *event* construct can be used to store data. However, the drawback of using events is that the data cannot be easily accessed and marked when it is updated or deleted.
- **SetData:** the SetData function receives data from an application and inserts data into blockchain by appending a row in the *uDetail* mapping.
- **GetData:** many variants of the GetData function (as needed for the data requested by the caller) retrieve data from the *mapping* structure and return to the caller.

This approach has the following drawbacks:

- Uniqueness of a column: There is no straightforward way to ensure the uniqueness of an entity's "key" column. As a result, it is possible to insert two rows that have the same UId. The *mapping* uDetails then stores both records, as shown in Table 1, where user ID is duplicated.

Table 1. Mapping structure containing the inserted values for User contract

Key	Value
1	1, "ABC", "BS8 1PT", "xyz@bristol.ac.uk", "745967262"
2	1, "DEC", "BS9 3PT", "abc@bristol.ac.uk", "749857262"

- Referential integrity: To enforce referential integrity constraints (e.g., checking that a valid user with an ID '2' exists in the User contract, before inserting a data for ID '2' into Site contract), Ethereum requires use of a structured process [18]. So, for the above example, the Site contract will have to call the getData function of the User contract to check the legitimacy of ID '2'. The steps involved in this process are that:
  - The callee contract (User) must be deployed into blockchain beforehand (i.e., prior to Site calling it), to get its address.
  - The Application Binary Interface (ABI) of the deployed contract (User) must be specified in the caller contract along with the address of the deployed smart contract.
  - Public functions of the callee can be used via the ABI code and address. This is a rigid process and makes the modelling cumbersome (when compared to the simple SQL statement definition).

As a result, when the entities are modelled as individual contracts, without efficiently implementing data and referential integrity features, it is possible to have redundant, inconsistent and erroneous data.

Thus, below we present a solution that delivers (some of the) same features for the Ethereum users, that the database management systems deliver to the relational database system users. Our management system allows users to define relationships between smart contracts, preserves these relationships and ensures the referential integrity is maintained while performing operations on data. The relationships between smart contracts are represented as a Directed Acyclic Graph (DAG) and are stored in an underlying blockchain along with metadata.

3 Proposed Solution

The proposed system's architecture is presented in Fig. 2. Here the entities and their attributes (that were identified in the conceptual schema in Fig. 1) are modelled as smart contracts and deployed into the blockchain (Fig. 2, box a). The relationships between entities are captured in a directed acyclic graph (Fig. 2, box b) and will be handled by the Management System (Fig. 2, box c). Accordingly, the system has two main components: the data model, and the management system.

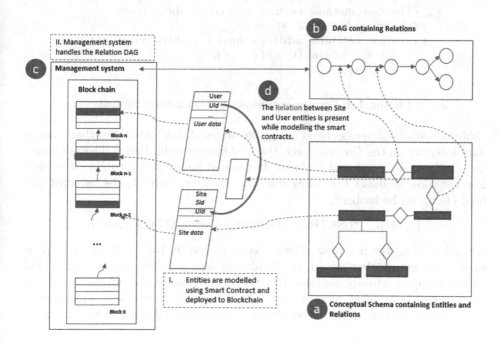

Fig. 2. Architecture overview

3.1 Ethereum-Based Data Model

This data model uses the Ethereum smart contract as the data structure to model entities, and their attributes in a conceptual schema. The smart contract for management system's user entity defined in a conceptual schema is displayed in Listing 1.4, titled msUser.

The Listing 1.3 *User* smart contract is similar to the *msUser* in Listing 1.4 except for the *Detail* mapping definition. To achieve data integrity, the proposed system is using *Address* as a key in the mapping data structure.

```
contract msUser {
    //Specify data Layout representing the
    //attributes of the entity
    struct UserDetail{
        uint16 UId;
            ...
    }
    //mapping data structure used to store the Rows
    mapping(address => UserDetail) uDetails;
        constructor() public { }
    //The Set methods inserts data row
        function setData(address hash, uint16 uid, ...)
                        public returns(string)
        { ... }
    //The Get method return required data from
    //the mapping data store.
    function getData(address hash) public view returns
            (uint16 uid, ...)
        { ... }
}
```

Listing 1.4. User smart contract in Management System

Address is hash value calculated using the values of 'key' attributes that ensures data integrity. In the *User* contract, the *UId* is a key field. Hence the hash would be calculate on the value of *UId* and then would be inserted into *User* contract. For instance, to insert the below row into *msUser* contract, the value of *UId* field (1) would be hashed[3].

{1, "ABC", "BS8 1PT", "xyz@bristol.ac.uk", "745967262"}.

After insertion, the mapping uDetails is as shown in Table 2. If an attempt is made to insert another row in which value of *UId* is 1, the insertion would fail as the mapping already contains this key. This ensures the uniqueness of the column and hence data integrity. In case of a multi-column key, a cumulative hash will be generated. Where an entity in a conceptual schema does not have

Table 2. Mapping structure containing the inserted values with Hash

Key	Value
0xabXn3f6d....2Ccd1P6LG	1 "ABC", "BS8 1PT", "xyz@bristol.ac.uk", "745967262"

---

[3] Hashing is used for creating a single-string key for establishing uniqueness, given that both single and multi-column references would need to be handled, as discussed below.

a key column (i.e., single column data set), the hash will be calculated from the value of the column and used as a key.

3.2 Management System

The Management system achieves the referential integrity and has two responsibilities: representing the relationships and ensuring the referential integrity among data entities. The following sections explain each of them in detail.

Representing Relationships

The Directed Acyclic Graph (DAG) data structure is used to represent the relationships among the entities. The DAG is defined as

$$Relations(DB) = <N, E>$$

Where N is a set of nodes relating to all entities in the DB (database) schema and E is a set of edges indicating relationships among entities. For the conceptual schema defined in building occupancy analysis example, N and E are defined as:

- $N = \{$User, Site, Floor, SDevice, MultiSensor, SmartEquipment$\}$
- $E = \{$User–Site, Site–Floor, Floor–SDevice, SDevice–Multisensor, SDevice–SmartEquipment$\}$

The graph is represented as an adjacency matrix. The elements of the matrix indicate the relationships between entities. The in-degree of an entity (number of incoming relationships) can be computed by summing the entries of the corresponding column, and the out-degree (number of outgoing relationships) can be computed by summing the entries of the corresponding row. The adjacency matrix in Table 3 indicates the relationships among entities in the aforementioned conceptual schema of Fig. 1. In the Boolean representation of adjacency (shown in Table 3), 1 represents a relationship between entities and 0 indicates absence of a relationship. The entities *User* and *Site* are related hence the corresponding element is represented with 1 in the Matrix. It can be seen from the matrix that the entity *Site* has an incoming relationships from User and an outgoing relationship to *Floor*.

Table 3. Adjacency Matrix representing the relations among entities

	User	Site	Floor	SDevice	MultiSensor	SmartEquipment
User	0	1	0	0	0	0
Site	0	0	1	0	0	0
Floor	0	0	0	1	0	0
SDevice	0	0	0	0	1	1
MultiSensor	0	0	0	0	0	0
SmartEquipment	0	0	0	0	0	0

Referential Integrity

The Management System ensures the validity of data references among different entities using the metadata about deployed contracts and relationships among them. The metadata stores information about entities and their attributes in predefined smart contracts. These predefined smart contracts are as follows:

- *SCRepository* contract stores the addresses of deployed smart contracts that represent the entities. This smart contract also provides functionality to obtain the address of the corresponding smart contract given an entity name and vice-versa.
- *SCEntityMetada* contact stores metadata about an entity, the data layout and other integrity related information. The data layout contains a list of columns and their data types in the order they are entered. This smart contract also provides functionality to obtain an entity's metadata given an entity name and vice-versa.
- *SCRelationDetails:* as discussed before, the management system stores the adjacency matrix representing the relationships among entities. The set of entities N will be stored as per the order they are arranged in the adjacency matrix. Keeping the node order is important as the relationships are defined based on this order. The set of relationships E is converted to a sequence of 1s and 0s, as shown below:

$$\{E = 0,1,0,0,0,0,1,0,1,0,0,0,0,1,0,1,0,0,0,0,1,0,1,1,0,0,0,1,0,0,0,0,0,1,0,0\}.$$

The SCRelationDetails smart contact stores relationship information among different entities and also provides functionality to obtain relationship data from an entity metadata given the address of an entity.

Figure 3 shows the sequence of actions taken by the Management System to ensure the referential integrity during a data insertion operation. The below row would be inserted into *Site* contract as the value for *UId* is present in *User* contract.

$$\{2, \text{"Site2"}, \text{"Second Floor"}, -2.773238, 50.844838, 1\}.$$

Table 4 shows the data in the *Site* contract, after successfully inserting the row.

Table 4. Mapping structure containing the inserted values for Site contract

Key	Value
0xbdhe3a0d819....j2Lsd3D3AF	1,"Site2","Second Floor",-2.773238,50.844838,1

The below rows can not be added to *Site* contract, as the value provided for *UId* is not present in *User* contract, ensuring the referential integrity.

$$\{1, \text{"Site1"}, \text{"First Floor"}, -2.773838, 50.883838, 2\}.$$

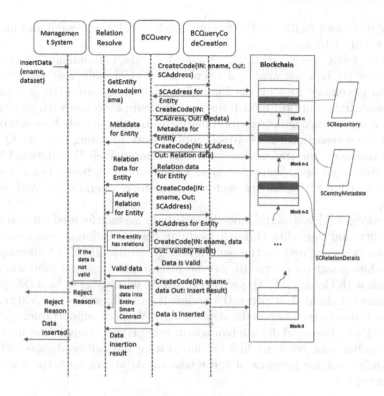

Fig. 3. Sequence diagram

4 Related Work

Since emergence of Bitcoin [17] a wide range of research and development activities is under way on using blockchain as a data storage mechanism. A small selection of such related work is presented below.

One area of research is in transferring properties of blockchain to centralised databases and/or database properties to blockchains. For instance, BigchainDB [4] integrates properties of a blockchain into a database, while using an Asset as a key-concept. Asset represents a physical or digital entity which starts its' life in BigchainDB with CREATE Transaction and lives further using TRANSFER Transaction. Each Asset contains Metadata to specify details about the Asset. The life-cycle of a BigchainDB Transaction is described in [5]. Each node in BigchainDB will have a MongoDB [15] instance and will maintain the same set of data. The Tendermint [19] is used as consensus protocol, which ensures the data safety even if 1/3 of nodes are down in the network. Traditional database features, like indexing and query support are carried out through the underlying MongoDB.

Mystiko [3] is another attempt in the same direction where Cassandra [2] is used in every node in the network as a database. Cassandra is a No-SQL column store database and facilitates the features such as full text search and indexing options for Mystiko users.

Another focus area is creating customised private/permissioned blockchains. Hyperledger [1] is a permissioned open source blockchain and related tools, started in December 2015 by the Linux Foundation. Quorum [16] is a permissioned blockchain platform built from the Ethereum codebase with adaptations to make it a permissioned consortium platform. Ethereum code base is modified with private transactions, consensus (Proof-of-work to voting system). Quorum creators increased the transaction rate. The Energy Web Foundation(EWF)'s Energy Web is an open-source, scalable Ethereum blockchain platform specifically designed for the energy sector's regulatory, operational, and market needs [8].

Hyperledger [1] is a permissioned blockchain system focused on scalability, extensibility and flexibility through modular design. Different consensus algorithm can be configured to this solution (e.g., Kafka, RBFT, Sumeragi, and PoET) while smart contracts [10] can be programmed using a platform called Chaincode with Golang [11]. Hyperledger uses Apache Kafka to facilitate private communication channels between the nodes. It can achieve up to 3,500 transactions per second in certain popular deployments. Work to support query [12] and indexing [13] on temporal data in blockchain using Hyperledger is also underway.

In a similar vein, our work looks at integrating the well established relationship management mechanisms of the relational databases with the blockchain infrastructure.

5   Conclusions and Discussion

In this paper we have presented an initial implementation of a middleware that preserves relationships among entities while storing data in a blockchain. This middleware has two components, the Ethereum-based data model that supports users in modelling entities as smart contracts and a management system that maintains relationships between entities.

However, as this is an initial proof-of-concept implementation, it has a number of limitations, such as:

- Dependency on *solc* tool, which is used to compile smart contracts to create ABI, BIN and .GO files. The *solc* changes whenever the solidity specification changes. Currently, our middleware will have to change to adapt to such tool changes.
- Time delay in blockchain response, caused by the need to carry out additional validation activities while carrying out the usual insert/update operations. This could be unacceptable, particularly when working on processing high frequency data.
- Storing temporary files: while compiling a smart contract, a set of files (.abi .bin and *.go) are generated which must be available to create GO programs that interact with the blockchain. Over the lifetime of the system these files would grow in number and size, which could cause storage considerations.

Our immediate future research will focus on addressing the above pointed limitations, always working towards making blockchains a more widely usable database solution.

References

1. Androulaki, E., et al.: Hyperledger fabric: a distributed operating system for permissioned blockchains. In: EuroSys, NY, USA, pp. 30:1–30:15. ACM (2018)
2. Apache: Apache Cassandra. http://cassandra.apache.org/. Accessed 14 Feb 2019
3. Bandara, E., et al.: Mystiko-blockchain meets big data. In: IEEE Big Data, pp. 3024–3032, December 2018
4. BigchainDB: Bigchaindb..the Blockchain Database. https://www.bigchaindb.com/. Accessed 14 Feb 2019
5. B. Blog: Lifecycle of a BigchainDB Transaction - The BigchainDB Blog. https://blog.bigchaindb.com/lifecycle-of-a-bigchaindb-transaction-c1e34331cbaa. Accessed 14 Feb 2019
6. Chen, P.P.-S.: The entity-relationship model-toward a unified view of data. ACM Trans. Database Syst. **1**(1), 9–36 (1976)
7. Codd, E.F.: A relational model of data for large shared data banks. Commun. ACM **13**(6), 377–387 (1970)
8. EWF: The Energy Web Blockchain-Energy Web Foundation. Accessed 20 Feb 2019
9. E. Foundation: Solidity - Solidity 0.4.24 Documentation. https://solidity.readthedocs.io/en/v0.4.24/. Accessed 14 Feb 2019
10. E. Foundation: White paper.ethereum/wiki wiki github. https://github.com/ethereum/wiki/wiki/White-Paper. Accessed 14 Feb 2019
11. Google: The Go Programming Language (2019). https://golang.org/. Accessed 13 Feb 2019
12. Gupta, H., Hans, S., Aggarwal, K., Mehta, S., Chatterjee, B., Jayachandran, P.: Efficiently processing temporal queries on hyperledger fabric. In: 2018 IEEE 34th International Conference on Data Engineering (ICDE), pp. 1489–1494, April 2018
13. Gupta, H., Hans, S., Mehta, S., Jayachandran, P.: On building efficient temporal indexes on hyperledger fabric. In: 2018 IEEE 11th International Conference on Cloud Computing (CLOUD), pp. 294–301, July 2018
14. Ioannidis, D., Tropios, P., Krinidis, S., Stavropoulos, G., Tzovaras, D., Likothanasis, S.: Occupancy driven building performance assessment. J. Innov. Digit. Ecosyst. **3**(2), 57–69 (2016)
15. MongoDB: Open Source Document Database — MongoDB. https://www.mongodb.com/. Accessed 14 Feb 2019
16. Morgan, J.: Quorum — JP Morgan. Accessed 20 Feb 2019
17. Nakamoto, S.: Bitcoin: A Peer-to-Peer Electronic Cash System (2008)
18. Peh, B.: Calling a Function Another Contract in Solidity. https://medium.com/@blockchain101/calling-the-function-of-another-contract-in-solidity-f9edfa921f4c. Accessed 06 Mar 2019
19. Tendermint: Blockchain Consensus - Tendermint (2019). https://tendermint.com/. Accessed 14 Feb 2019

Finding Non-compliances with Declarative Process Constraints Through Semantic Technologies

Claudio Di Ciccio[2(✉)], Fajar J. Ekaputra[1], Alessio Cecconi[2],
Andreas Ekelhart[1], and Elmar Kiesling[1]

[1] TU Wien, Favoritenstrasse 9-11, 1040 Vienna, Austria
{fajar.ekaputra,andreas.ekelhart,elmar.kiesling}@tuwien.ac.at
[2] WU Vienna, Welthandelsplatz 1, 1020 Vienna, Austria
{claudio.di.ciccio,alessio.cecconi}@wu.ac.at

Abstract. Business process compliance checking enables organisations to assess whether their processes fulfil a given set of constraints, such as regulations, laws, or guidelines. Whilst many process analysts still rely on ad-hoc, often handcrafted per-case checks, a variety of constraint languages and approaches have been developed in recent years to provide automated compliance checking. A salient example is DECLARE, a well-established declarative process specification language based on temporal logics. DECLARE specifies the behaviour of processes through temporal rules that constrain the execution of tasks. So far, however, automated compliance checking approaches typically report compliance only at the aggregate level, using binary evaluations of constraints on execution traces. Consequently, their results lack granular information on violations and their context, which hampers auditability of process data for analytic and forensic purposes. To address this challenge, we propose a novel approach that leverages semantic technologies for compliance checking. Our approach proceeds in two stages. First, we translate DECLARE templates into statements in SHACL, a graph-based constraint language. Then, we evaluate the resulting constraints on the graph-based, semantic representation of process execution logs. We demonstrate the feasibility of our approach by testing its implementation on real-world event logs. Finally, we discuss its implications and future research directions.

Keywords: Process mining · Compliance checking · SHACL · RDF · SPARQL

1 Introduction

Declarative business process specification approaches rely on a normative description of processes' behaviour by means of inviolable rules. Those rules, named *constraints*, exert restrictions on the process behaviour. DECLARE [1],

© Springer Nature Switzerland AG 2019
C. Cappiello and M. Ruiz (Eds.): CAiSE Forum 2019, LNBIP 350, pp. 60–74, 2019.
https://doi.org/10.1007/978-3-030-21297-1_6

Dynamic Condition Response Graphs (DCR Graphs) [24], and the Case Management Model and Notation (CMMN)[1] are examples of such declarative process specification languages. Declarative process discovery is the branch of the process mining discipline [2] aimed at extracting the constraints that specify a process by their verification over execution data, namely event logs. To date, research in the area has mainly focused on devising of efficient algorithms for mining constraints verified in the event log [9,11,14,32]. All of these approaches return constraints that are never (or rarely) violated in the event log, thus implicitly assuming that rarity corresponds to noise. Similarly, approaches have been proposed to verify the compliance and conformance of event logs with declarative process specifications [28–30,39], indicating whether and to what extent constraint sets are satisfied by process executions.

However, it is often not sufficient to solely assess whether constraints are satisfied or not. Especially in cases with rare exceptions, knowing when and why certain constraints are violated is key. Those circumstances apply in many scenarios: To mention but a few, inspecting the root cause of enactment errors [15], deriving digital evidence of malicious behaviour [25], identifying the origin of drifts in the process [31], or identifying illicit inflows into digital currency services [26].

Against this background, we leverage semantic technologies for the verification and querying of event logs, in an approach that *(i)* checks whether they comply with provided declarative process specifications, and *(ii)* if not, reports on the cause of violations at a fine-grained level. We evaluate our technique by applying our prototype to real-world event logs. We empirically show the insights into detected violations provided by detailed reports. The opportunities brought about by the use of semantic technologies go well beyond the promising results presented in this vision paper. We thus endow the discussion on the evaluation of our approach with considerations on potential improvements over the current achievements, especially in regard to further semantic analyses of the current results.

The remainder of the paper is structured as follows. Section 2 provides an overview of the literature on declarative process mining and semantic technologies. Section 3 describes our approach, i.e., its workflow and components, from the bare event log to its semantic representation and reasoning. Section 4 evaluates and discusses the feasibility of the approach against real-life logs. Section 5 concludes the paper and highlights future research directions.

2   Background and State of the Art

Our approach draws on two main strands of research: on the one hand, it is grounded in state-of-the-art process mining techniques for declarative specifications; on the other hand, it adopts validation concepts developed in the semantic web research community and applies them to fine-grained compliance checking.

---

[1] https://www.omg.org/spec/CMMN/1.1.

Declarative Process Mining. A *declarative process specification* defines a process behaviour through a set of temporal rules (constraints) that collectively determine the allowed and forbidden traces. Specifically, constraints exert conditions that allow or forbid *target* tasks to be executed, depending on the occurrence of so-called *activation* tasks. A declarative specification allows for any process executions that do not violate those constraints. Each constraint is defined using a template that captures the semantics of the constraint, parametric to the constrained tasks. The number of parameters denote its cardinality. DECLARE [1] is a well-established declarative process specification language. Its semantics are expressed in Linear Temporal Logic on Finite Traces (LTL_f) [10]. It offers a repertoire of templates extending that of the seminal paper of Dwyer et al. [16]. Table 1 shows some of those. RESPONSE, for example, is a binary template stating that the occurrence of the first task imposes the second one to occur eventually afterwards. RESPONSE(a, b) applies the RESPONSE template to task a and b, meaning that each time that a occurs in a trace, b is expected to occur afterwards. ALTERNATERESPONSE(a, b) is subsumed by RESPONSE(a, b) as it restricts the statement by adding that a cannot recur before b. PRECEDENCE(a, b) switches activation and target as well as the temporal dependency: b can occur only if a occurred before. NOTSUCCESSION(a, b) establishes that after a, b cannot occur any more. Finally, PARTICIPATION(a) is a constraint stating that in every process execution, a must occur. It applies the PARTICIPATION unary template.

The fundamental input for process mining is the event log, i.e., a collection of recorded process executions (traces) expressed as sequences of events. For the sake of simplicity, we assume events to relate to single tasks of a process. The eXtensible Event Stream (XES) format is an IEEE standard[2] for the storage and exchange of event logs and event streams, based on XML. In *declarative process mining*, constraints are verified over event logs to measure their *support* (i.e., how often they are satisfied in the traces), and optionally their *confidence* (i.e., how often they are satisfied in traces in which their activation occurs), and *interest factor* (i.e., how often they are satisfied in traces in which both activation and target occur) [14,32]. Table 1 reports traces that satisfy or violate the aforementioned constraints. For instance, a trace like caacb satisfies RESPONSE(a, b) (increasing its mining measures) but violates ALTERNATERESPONSE(a, b) (decreasing it). Although a trace like bcc satisfies RESPONSE(a, b), it does not contribute to its confidence or interest factor, since the activation (a) does not occur. Support is thus an aggregate measure for compliance as those traces that do not comply with a constraint, decrease its value.

Semantic Web Technologies provide a comprehensive set of standards for the representation, decentralised linking, querying, reasoning about, and processing of semantically explicit information. We mainly base our approach on two elements of the semantic web technology stack: *(i)* the Resource Description Framework (RDF), which we use as a uniform model to express process information, declarative constraints, and validation reports, and *(ii)* the SHACL

---

[2] https://doi.org/10.1109/IEEESTD.2016.7740858.

Table 1. A collection of DECLARE constraints with their respective natural language explanation, and examples of accepted (✓) or violating (×) traces.

Constraint	Explanation	Examples			
PARTICIPATION(a)	a occurs at least *once*	✓ bcac	✓ bcaac	× bcc	× c
RESPONSE(a, b)	If a occurs, then b occurs eventually after a	✓ caacb	✓ bcc	× caac	× bacc
ALTERNATERESPONSE(a, b)	Each time a occurs, then b occurs eventually afterwards, and no other a recurs in between	✓ cacb	✓ abcacb	× caacb	× bacacb
PRECEDENCE(a, b)	b occurs only if preceded by a	✓ cacbb	✓ acc	× ccbb	× bacc
ALTERNATEPRECEDENCE(a, b)	Each time b occurs, it is preceded by a and no other b can recur in between	✓ cacba	✓ abcaacb	× cacbba	× abbabcb
NOTSUCCESSION(a, b)	a can never occur before b	✓ bbcaa	✓ cbbca	× aacbb	× abb

Shapes Constraint Language (SHACL), which provides a constraint specification and validation framework on top of RDF. In the following, we provide a brief overview of both these standards.

RDF is a data representation model published by the World Wide Web Consortium (W3C) as a set of recommendations and working group notes.[3] It provides a standard model for expressing information about *resources*, which in the context of the present paper represent traces, tasks, events, actors, etc. An RDF dataset consists of a set of statements about these resources, expressed in the form of triples $\langle s, p, o \rangle$ where s is a *subject*, p is a *predicate*, and o is an *object*; s and o represent the two resources being related whereas p represents the nature of their relationship. Formally, we define an RDF graph G as a set of RDF triples $(v_1, v_2, v_3) \in (U \cup B \cup L) \times U \times (U \cup B \cup L)$ where: U is an infinite set of constant values (called RDF *Uniform Resource Identifier (URI) references*); B is an infinite set of local identifiers without defined semantics (called *blank nodes*); and L is a set of values (called *literals*). For instance, a trace expressed in RDF may contain a statement such as eventA xes:nextEvent eventB to describe the temporal relationship between two particular events. A key advantage of RDF as a data model is its extensible nature, i.e., additional statements about eventA and eventB can be added at any time, adding concepts and predicates from various additional, potentially domain-specific vocabularies.

Furthermore, ontology specification languages such as the Web Ontology Language (OWL)[4] can be used to more closely describe the semantic characteristics of terms. Although beyond the scope of the present paper, this extensible semantic web technology stack opens up opportunities for the use of reasoners in

---

[3] http://www.w3.org/TR/rdf11-primer/.
[4] http://www.w3.org/TR/owl2-primer/.

compliance checking and in the interpretation of violations (e.g., generalisations, root cause analyses, etc.) [4,17]. Other benefits of RDF include interoperability, i.e., information expressed in RDF using shared vocabularies can be exchanged between applications without loss of meaning. Furthermore, it makes it possible to apply a wide range of general purpose RDF parsing, mapping, transformation, and query processing tools.

Finally, once transformed into RDF, information (such as process information and compliance checking rules) can be easily published online, interlinked, and shared between applications and organisations, which is particularly interesting in the context of collaborative processes.

SHACL is a W3C Recommendation and language for validating RDF graphs against a set of conditions.[5] These conditions are specified in the form of RDF *shape graphs* which can be applied to validate *data graphs*. SHACL thereby provides a flexible declarative mechanism to define arbitrary validity constraints on RDF graphs. Specifically, these constraints can be formulated using a range of constraint components defined in the standard, or as arbitrary constraints implemented in SPARQL Protocol and RDF Query Language (SPARQL).[6] Validation of a data graph against a shapes graph produces a validation report expressed in RDF as the union of results against all shapes in the shapes graph. Importantly, compliance checking in SHACL is performed gradually by validating each individual so-called *focus node* against the set of constraints that apply to it. Compliance checks therefore produce detailed validation reports that not only conclude whether a data graph conforms globally, but also reports on the specific violations encountered. In the context of process compliance checking, this provides a foundation to not only determine whether a process trace conforms, but to also report on the specific declarative rules that are violated.

Semantic Approaches to Compliance Checking. Several approaches have been developed to support organisations in their compliance efforts, each offering their own functional and operational capabilities [5,22]. The underlying frameworks, such as Process Compliance Language (PCL) [20], DECLARE [1], and BPMN-Q [3], offer different levels of expressiveness, and consequently, varying reasoning and modelling support for normative requirements [23]. Three main strategies for business process compliance checking have been proposed in the literature to date [22]: *(i) runtime monitoring* of process instances to detect or predict compliance violations (runtime compliance checking, online monitoring, compliance monitoring); *(ii) design-time* checks for compliant or non-compliant behaviour during the design of process models; *(iii) auditing* of log files in an offline manner, i.e., after the process instance execution has finished. Based on DECLARE, techniques such as the one described in [34] can discover declarative models, use them to check process compliance, and apply the model constraints in online monitoring. Presently, however, all reported result are at the granularity of a trace, without pointing at the cause. Remarkably, Maggi et al. [33] apply

---

[5] https://www.w3.org/TR/shacl/.

[6] http://www.w3.org/TR/sparql11-query/.

the outcome of that technique to repair BPMN [15] process models according to the constraints to which an event log is not compliant.

In our approach, we implement DECLARE constraints with semantic technologies. Related work on semantic approaches in process mining include Thao Ly et al. [38], which presents a vision towards life-time compliance. The authors motivate the creation of global repositories to store reusable semantic constraints (e.g., for medical treatment). and advocate the importance of intelligible feedback on constraint violations. This includes the reasons for the violations, to help the user to devise strategies for conflict avoidance and compensation. Furthermore, the results of semantic process checks must be documented. In our paper, we address these requirements. To reason about the data surrounding a task, semantic annotations of tasks are introduced in [19,21] as logical statements of the PCL language over process variables, to support business process design. Governatori et al. [18] show how semantic web technologies and languages like LegalRuleML (based on RuleML)[7] can be applied to model and link legal rules from industry to support humans in analysing process tasks over legal texts. They apply semantic annotations in the context of a regularity compliance system. To that end, they extend their compliance checker Regorous [21] with semantics of LegalRuleML. An approach to include additional domain knowledge to the process perspective is introduced in [39]. The authors extract additional information from domain models and integrate this knowledge in the process compliance check. Pham et al. [36] introduce an ontology-based approach for business process compliance checking. They use a Business Process Ontology (BPO) and a Business Rules Ontology (BRO) including OWL axioms and SWRL[8] rules to model compliance constraints. They do not, however, systematically translate compliance rules as in our approach, and mention

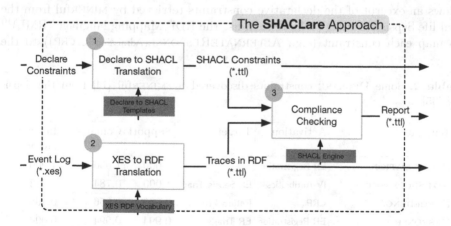

Fig. 1. SHACLARE components architecture

---

[7] http://wiki.ruleml.org/index.php/RuleML_Home.
[8] https://www.w3.org/Submission/SWRL.

that performance is a key problem with standard reasoners. Our focus is different from the work presented in that our main aim is not to validate process models against rules, but to verify declarative specifications on existing process executions.

A Folder-Path enabled extension of SPARQL called FPSPARQL for process discovery is proposed in [6]. Similarly, Leida et al. [27] focus on the advantages of process representation in RDF and show the potential of SPARQL queries for process discovery. Our approach also builds on semantic representations of process data but explores how compliance checking can be conducted with semantic technologies.

3 Approach

Our approach applies a set of semantic technologies, including SHACL on event logs to check their compliance with DECLARE constraints.[9] As depicted in Fig. 1, the SHACLARE compliance checking workflow is composed as follows. ① We generate SHACL compliance constraints for a target process from a set of DECLARE constraints. To this end, we translate the DECLARE constraints through respective SHACL templates. ② Because SHACL constraints can only be validated against RDF graphs, we next transform the event log into RDF. This step takes an event log in XES format as input and produces a traces file in RDF. ③ At this point, we have all necessary inputs to perform the SHACL compliance check, which results in a detailed report on each constraint violation.

① **DECLARE to SHACL.** In this first step, we generate SHACL compliance constraints for a target process. As input, we take a set of DECLARE constraints, which can be automatically discovered with tools such as MINERful [12]. Table 2 shows an excerpt of the declarative constraints retrieved by MINERful from the real-life Sepsis event log [35]. We then use the RDF Mapping language (RML)[10] to map each constraint (e.g., ALTERNATERESPONSE(Admission IC, CRP)) to the

Table 2. Some DECLARE constraints discovered by MINERful [14] from the Sepsis log [35]

Template	Activation	Target	Support	Confidence	Interest factor
PARTICIPATION	ER Registration		1.000	1.000	1.000
NOTSUCCESSION	IV Antibiotics	ER Sepsis Triage	1.000	0.784	0.783
PRECEDENCE	CRP	Return ER	0.996	0.956	0.268
RESPONSE	ER Registration	ER Triage	0.994	0.994	0.994
ALTERNATERESPONSE	Admission IC	CRP	0.974	0.102	0.098

---

[9] Hence, we call it SHACLARE.
[10] http://rml.io/RMLmappingLanguage.

```
 1  @prefix xes: <http://semantics.id/ns/xes#> .
 2  @prefix dec: <http://semantics.id/ns/declare#> .
 3  @prefix decs: <http://semantics.id/ns/declare-shacl#> .
 4  % ... deliberately left out rdf,rdfs,sh,owl, and xsd
 5  <decs:param_URI>
 6      a sh:NodeShape ;
 7      sh:targetClass xes:Trace ;
 8      decs:baseConstraint <decs:param_declare> ;
 9      decs:baseConstraintClass dec:AlternateResponse ;
10      sh:sparql [
11          a sh:SPARQLConstraint ;
12          sh:message "Each time 'decs:param_value1' occurs, then 'decs:param_value2' occurs afterwards,
            before 'decs:param_value1' recurs. Cause event: {?object}" ;
13          sh:prefixes decs:namespace ;
14          sh:select """
15              SELECT $this ?object
16              WHERE {
17                  $this xes:hasEventList/rdf:rest*/rdf:first ?object .
18                  {
19                      # check if there is no "decs:param_value2" after "decs:param_value1"
20                      ?object rdfs:label "decs:param_value1" .
21                      FILTER NOT EXISTS {
22                          ?object ^rdf:first/rdf:rest+/rdf:first ?object2 .
23                          ?object2 rdfs:label "decs:param_value2" .            }            }
24                  UNION         {
25                      # check if there is no "decs:param_value2" between two "decs:param_value1"s
26                      ?object rdfs:label "decs:param_value1" .
27                      ?object ^rdf:first/rdf:rest+/rdf:first ?object2 .
28                      ?object2 rdfs:label "decs:param_value1" .
29                      FILTER NOT EXISTS {
30                          ?object ^rdf:first/rdf:rest+/rdf:first ?item .
31                          ?object2 ^rdf:first/^rdf:rest+/rdf:first ?item .
32                          ?item rdfs:label "decs:param_value2" .
33                  }}}"""  ;
34      ] ;.
```

Listing 1. SHACL template excerpt for ALTERNATERESPONSE

respective DECLARE RDF data model elements (available at http://semantics.id/ns/declare).

To enable SHACL validation on DECLARE constraints, we developed a complete set of SHACL templates to represent the DECLARE ones. Specifically, we analysed the DECLARE constraint semantics and derived a set of equivalent SHACL constraint templates, similarly to what Schönig et al. [37] did with SQL. These SHACL templates are publicly available at http://semantics.id/resource/shaclare as documents written using the RDF Turtle notation.[11] Listing 1 shows an excerpt of SHACL template that represents ALTERNATERESPONSE in RDF Turtle notation. Lines 1–4 list the namespaces used in the templates. In addition to the standard rdf, rdfs, and shacl vocabularies defined by the W3C, we introduce the following vocabularies: (i) desc: provides a set of properties and parameters used in the template, which are specific to the SHACLARE approach, (ii) dec: defines the RDF classes and properties to describe the DECLARE language, and (iii) xes: provides the terms used to represents XES data in RDF. Line 5 contains a placeholder that will be replaced by the name of the particular DECLARE constraint instance during the compliance checking runtime. Lines 6–7 signify that the constraint will be validated against instances of class xes:Trace. Lines 8–9 specify that the SHACL constraint will evaluate ALTERNATERESPONSE, while line 12 provides a template for the violation constraint message. Lines 14–34 are the main part, representing the ALTERNATERESPONSE DECLARE constraint template in its SHACL-SPARQL representation.

---

[11] https://www.w3.org/TR/turtle/.

Subsequently, we translate the DECLARE constraints into SHACL constraints by injecting the constraint parameters `Activation` and `Target` in the SHACL template. All generated SHACL constraints are stored in memory for later execution, but also get persisted as a SHACL shape graph in the RDF Turtle `.ttl` format as a reference.

② **From XES to RDF.** The transformation takes as input an event log in XES format and translates it in RDF. To that end, we developed an XES RDF vocabulary (available at http://semantics.id/ns/xes), which provides the terms and concepts to represent XES data in RDF. We transform into main classes the basic XES objects: *(i)* `xes:Log` for the complete event log, *(ii)* `xes:Trace` to refer to individual traces, and *(iii)* `xes:Event` for single events. In addition to those classes, we define a set of data properties for the optional event attributes, such as `xes:timestamp` and `xes:transition`. Object properties (relation) bind together the elements, e.g., `xes:hasTrace` to relate `xes:Log` and `xes:Trace`, and `xes:hasEventList` to relate an `xes:Trace` and an `rdf:List` that contains event sequences.

③ **SHACL Compliance Checking.** Given the SHACL DECLARE constraints (①) and the RDF event log (②), we have all the required input to run the SHACL *Compliance Checking* component. All generated SHACL constraints are grouped according to their template (e.g., ALTERNATERESPONSE) and subsequently checked one by one by a SHACL validation engine. The result of a SHACL validation is an RDF graph with one `ValidationReport` instance. In case the `conforms` attribute of a `ValidationReport` is false, a `result` instance provides further details for every violation, including: *(i)* `focusNode`, which points to the trace in which the violation occurred; *(ii)* `sourceShape`, linking the SHACL constraint instance which triggered the result; *(iii)* `resultMessage`, explaining the reason for the constraint violation with a natural-language sentence.

4   Evaluation

To demonstrate the efficiency and effectiveness of our compliance checking approach, we developed a proof-of-concept software tool, available for download at gitlab.isis.tuwien.ac.at/shaclare/shaclare. In this section, we report on its application on publicly available real-world event logs. In particular, we focus on the report produced on a specific event log to demonstrate the capability of SHACLARE to provide detailed insights into compliance violations. The experiment environment, as well as the full set of input and output files are available on the aforementioned SHACLARE GitLab project page.

The Prototype. The prototype is implemented in Java, using a number of open source libraries,[12] including *(i)* Apache Jena, for RDF Graph manipulation and processing, *(ii)* OpenXES, for accessing and acquiring XES data into

---

[12] Apache Jena: http://jena.apache.org/; OpenXES: http://code.deckfour.org/xes/; caRML: https://github.com/carml/carml/; TopBraid: https://github.com/topquadrant/shacl.

RDF Graph, *(iii)* caRML, for acquiring RDF representation of DECLARE constraints, and *(iv)* the TopBraid SHACL engine, for compliance checking. Based on the SHACLARE approach description in Sect. 3, the following functions are available: ① translation of DECLARE to SHACL constraints, ② translation of XES event logs to its RDF Graph representations, and ③ compliance checking of event logs against defined constraints.

Table 3. An excerpt of the SHACLARE validation report

Constraint	Trace	Message
dec:AlternateResponse_Admission+IC_CRP	xesi:trace/c677627d-079b-4585-87e4-8ea4ff11ff2a	Each time 'Admission IC' occurs, then 'CRP' occurs afterwards, before 'Admission IC' recurs. Cause event: xesi:event/A657AD0E-AD65-4E6F-B141-871A8C340B37
dec:Precedence_CRP_Return+ER	xesi:trace/4f1aff3f-b078-48e8-8e94-72c38c0ce6b7	If 'Return ER' occurs, 'CRP' must occur beforehand. Cause event: xesi:event/2BEFECDC-88C0-40E1-83D1-B41089C6A7C1

Insights into Violations. The steps are illustrated on the example of the Sepsis treatment process event log [35]. That event log reports the trajectories of patients showing symptoms of sepsis in a Dutch hospital, from their registration in the emergency room to their discharge. Because of the reported flexibility of the healthcare process [35] and its knowledge-intensive nature, it is a suitable case for declarative process specification [13].

After running our prototype with the mined DECLARE constraints and the Sepsis event log as inputs, we receive as output the compliance report, the traces in RDF, and the set of checked constraints in SHACL (cf. Fig. 1). Those files form the basis of our analysis. We thus import the report and trace triples in GraphDB[13] to query and visualise the result data structures. An excerpt of non-compliant validation results is shown in Table 3.

Next, we explore why particular constraints are violated. For instance, the constraint ALTERNATERESPONSE(Admission IC, CRP) dictates that after every admission at the Intensive Care unit (Admission IC), a C-Reactive Protein test (CRP) must be performed later on, and the patient should not be admitted again at the IC before the CRP. As it can be noticed in Table 2, the support of the constraint is high (0.974), therefore we are interested in understanding what event(s) determined its violation. We thus extract the event xesi:event/A657AD0E-AD65-4E6F-B141-871A8C340B37 signalled by the report and visualise it from the XES RDF representation. Figure 2(a) depicts a graph with the violating event and the connected events from its trace. We observe that

---

[13] http://graphdb.ontotext.com/.

the violation is due to the fact that the two events are swapped in the trace (CRP occurs before Admission IC). The right-hand side in the screenshot features a sample of metadata on the selected event (the violating activation, namely Admission IC). The tool allows us to scroll through all available properties and navigate through the trace, thus providing the user a powerful tool to inspect the violations in detail. Similarly, Fig. 2(b) shows that despite the high support of PRECEDENCE(CRP, Return ER) in the event log (0.996 as per Table 2), in one trace it was recorded that the patient was discharged and sent to the emergency room (Return ER), although no CRP took place before.

(a) ALT.RESPONSE(**Admission IC,CRP**)   (b) PRECEDENCE(**CRP,Return ER**)

Fig. 2. Graphs illustrating the violations of constraints in the traces.

The analysis can be further extended through the integration of additional context information on the traces, which may be specified in domain-specific vocabularies. Furthermore, the by-products and results of our approach can be utilised for further analyses via semantic technologies. This can provide a rich interpretation context for the qualitative analysis of constraint violations. An important aspect is that it is possible to use all the metadata information directly in the SHACL constraints or later on in a SPARQL query. Therefore, the analysis is readily extensible beyond the control flow perspective. The investigation of those extensions draws future plans for our research, outlined in the next section.

5   Conclusion and Future Work

In this vision paper, we proposed a novel approach for compliance checking leveraging semantic technologies, named SHACLARE. In particular, we provide a set of templates to translate DECLARE constraints into SHACL constraints, and subsequently validate them against a graph representation of XES process execution data. Thereby, we overcome a typical limitation of existing compliance checking approaches, which lack granular information on violations and their context. The compliance reports SHACLAREprovides contain links to the respective traces, as well as to the events triggering constraint violations. Due to the semantically explicit representation, we can easily query and visualise connected events and inspect all metadata provided in the original log files. The preliminary results attained illustrate how our approach could be used and extended further for auditability of event logs.

This new approach opens opportunities for future work in various directions. We aim at leveraging Linked Data frameworks so as to conduct compliance checking over multiple process data sources beyond single event logs, inspired by the seminal work of Calvanese et al. [8]. In that regard, the checking of richer constraints encompassing perspectives other than the usual control flow (i.e., data, time, resources, etc.) [7], draws our future research endeavours, driven by the capabilities readily made available to that extent by SHACL and SPARQL. This paper analysed the compliance checking setting, thus the analysis of constraints violations. If the goal is also to analyse the relevance of satisfaction, verification of a formula is not sufficient and the vacuity problem must be taken into account [12]. We will investigate how our approach can be extended to tackle this problem. Online compliance checking is another topic of interest. It would be worth exploring how SHACL constraints can be checked in a streaming fashion, potentially based on stream reasoning engines. In addition, we aim to further (automatically) enrich the metadata extracted from the log data, using Natural Language Processing (NLP) and ontologies. From a formal analysis viewpoint, we will investigate the semantic equivalence of the SHACL constraints with respect to DECLARE LTL$_f$ formulas, and more generally the expressive power of those languages. Finally, additional compliance checking tools could be developed to provide users with easy-to-use and feature-rich options to adopt this approach in their process management strategies.

Acknowledgements. This work was partially funded by the Austrian FFG grant 861213 (CitySPIN), the Austrian FWF/netidee SCIENCE grant P30437-N31 (SEPSES), the EU H2020 programme under MSCA-RISE agreement 645751 (RISE_BPM), the Christian Doppler Research Association, the Austrian Federal Ministry for Digital and Economic Affairs and the National Foundation for Research, Technology and Development.

References

1. van der Aalst, W.M.P., Pesic, M., Schonenberg, H.: Declarative workflows: balancing between flexibility and support. Comput. Sci. Res. Dev. **23**(2), 99–113 (2009)
2. van der Aalst, W.M.P.: Process Mining - Data Science in Action, 2nd edn. Springer, Heidelberg (2016). https://doi.org/10.1007/978-3-662-49851-4
3. Awad, A., Decker, G., Weske, M.: Efficient compliance checking using BPMN-Q and temporal logic. In: Dumas, M., Reichert, M., Shan, M.-C. (eds.) BPM 2008. LNCS, vol. 5240, pp. 326–341. Springer, Heidelberg (2008). https://doi.org/10.1007/978-3-540-85758-7_24
4. Balduini, M., et al.: Reality mining on micropost streams. Semant. Web **5**(5), 341–356 (2014)
5. Becker, J., Delfmann, P., Eggert, M., Schwittay, S.: Generalizability and applicability of model-based business process compliance-checking approaches – a state-of-the-art analysis and research roadmap. Bus. Res. **5**(2), 221–247 (2012)

6. Beheshti, S.-M.-R., Benatallah, B., Motahari-Nezhad, H.R., Sakr, S.: A query language for analyzing business processes execution. In: Rinderle-Ma, S., Toumani, F., Wolf, K. (eds.) BPM 2011. LNCS, vol. 6896, pp. 281–297. Springer, Heidelberg (2011). https://doi.org/10.1007/978-3-642-23059-2_22

7. Burattin, A., Maggi, F.M., Sperduti, A.: Conformance checking based on multi-perspective declarative process models. Expert Syst. Appl. **65**, 194–211 (2016)

8. Calvanese, D., Kalayci, T.E., Montali, M., Santoso, A., van der Aalst, W.: Conceptual schema transformation in ontology-based data access. In: Faron Zucker, C., Ghidini, C., Napoli, A., Toussaint, Y. (eds.) EKAW 2018. LNCS (LNAI), vol. 11313, pp. 50–67. Springer, Cham (2018). https://doi.org/10.1007/978-3-030-03667-6_4

9. Chesani, F., Lamma, E., Mello, P., Montali, M., Riguzzi, F., Storari, S.: Exploiting inductive logic programming techniques for declarative process mining. In: Jensen, K., van der Aalst, W.M.P. (eds.) Transactions on Petri Nets and Other Models of Concurrency II. LNCS, vol. 5460, pp. 278–295. Springer, Heidelberg (2009). https://doi.org/10.1007/978-3-642-00899-3_16

10. De Giacomo, G., Vardi, M.Y.: Linear temporal logic and linear dynamic logic on finite traces. In: IJCAI, pp. 854–860 (2013)

11. Debois, S., Hildebrandt, T.T., Laursen, P.H., Ulrik, K.R.: Declarative process mining for DCR graphs. In: SAC, pp. 759–764. ACM (2017)

12. Di Ciccio, C., Maggi, F.M., Montali, M., Mendling, J.: On the relevance of a business constraint to an event log. Inf. Syst. **78**, 144–161 (2018)

13. Di Ciccio, C., Marrella, A., Russo, A.: Knowledge-intensive Processes: characteristics, requirements and analysis of contemporary approaches. J. Data Semantics **4**(1), 29–57 (2015)

14. Di Ciccio, C., Mecella, M.: On the discovery of declarative control flows for artful processes. ACM Trans. Manage. Inf. Syst. **5**(4), 24:1–24:37 (2015)

15. Dumas, M., La Rosa, M., Mendling, J., Reijers, H.A.: Fundamentals of Business Process Management, 2nd edn. Springer, Heidelberg (2018). https://doi.org/10.1007/978-3-662-56509-4

16. Dwyer, M.B., Avrunin, G.S., Corbett, J.C.: Patterns in property specifications for finite-state verification. In: ICSE, pp. 411–420 (1999)

17. Francesconi, E.: Semantic model for legal resources: annotation and reasoning over normative provisions. Semant. Web **7**(3), 255–265 (2016)

18. Governatori, G., Hashmi, M., Lam, H.-P., Villata, S., Palmirani, M.: Semantic business process regulatory compliance checking using LegalRuleML. In: Blomqvist, E., Ciancarini, P., Poggi, F., Vitali, F. (eds.) EKAW 2016. LNCS (LNAI), vol. 10024, pp. 746–761. Springer, Cham (2016). https://doi.org/10.1007/978-3-319-49004-5_48

19. Governatori, G., Hoffmann, J., Sadiq, S., Weber, I.: Detecting regulatory compliance for business process models through semantic annotations. In: Ardagna, D., Mecella, M., Yang, J. (eds.) BPM 2008. LNBIP, vol. 17, pp. 5–17. Springer, Heidelberg (2009). https://doi.org/10.1007/978-3-642-00328-8_2

20. Governatori, G., Rotolo, A.: A conceptually rich model of business process compliance. In: APCCM, pp. 3–12. Australian Computer Society, Inc. (2010)

21. Governatori, G., Shek, S.: Regorous: a business process compliance checker. In: ICAIL, pp. 245–246. ACM (2013)

22. Hashmi, M., Governatori, G.: Norms modeling constructs of business process compliance management frameworks: a conceptual evaluation. Artif. Intell. Law **26**(3), 251–305 (2018)

23. Hashmi, M., Governatori, G., Wynn, M.T.: Normative requirements for business process compliance. In: Davis, J.G., Demirkan, H., Motahari-Nezhad, H.R. (eds.) ASSRI 2013. LNBIP, vol. 177, pp. 100–116. Springer, Cham (2014). https://doi.org/10.1007/978-3-319-07950-9_8

24. Hildebrandt, T., Mukkamala, R.R., Slaats, T.: Nested dynamic condition response graphs. In: Arbab, F., Sirjani, M. (eds.) FSEN 2011. LNCS, vol. 7141, pp. 343–350. Springer, Heidelberg (2012). https://doi.org/10.1007/978-3-642-29320-7_23

25. Kävrestad, J.: Fundamentals of Digital Forensics - Theory, Methods, and Real-Life Applications. Springer, Cham (2018). https://doi.org/10.1007/978-3-319-96319-8

26. Kuzuno, H., Karam, C.: Blockchain explorer: an analytical process and investigation environment for bitcoin. In: eCrime, pp. 9–16. IEEE (2017)

27. Leida, M., Majeed, B., Colombo, M., Chu, A.: A lightweight RDF data model for business process analysis. In: Cudre-Mauroux, P., Ceravolo, P., Gašević, D. (eds.) SIMPDA 2012. LNBIP, vol. 162, pp. 1–23. Springer, Heidelberg (2013). https://doi.org/10.1007/978-3-642-40919-6_1

28. de Leoni, M., Maggi, F.M., van der Aalst, W.M.: An alignment-based framework to check the conformance of declarative process models and to preprocess event-log data. Inf. Syst. **47**, 258–277 (2015)

29. Letia, I.A., Goron, A.: Model checking as support for inspecting compliance to rules in flexible processes. J. Vis. Lang. Comput. **28**, 100–121 (2015)

30. Gómez-López, M.T., Parody, L., Gasca, R.M., Rinderle-Ma, S.: Prognosing the compliance of declarative business processes using event trace robustness. In: Meersman, R., et al. (eds.) OTM 2014. LNCS, vol. 8841, pp. 327–344. Springer, Heidelberg (2014). https://doi.org/10.1007/978-3-662-45563-0_19

31. Maaradji, A., Dumas, M., Rosa, M.L., Ostovar, A.: Detecting sudden and gradual drifts in business processes from execution traces. IEEE Trans. Knowl. Data Eng. **29**(10), 2140–2154 (2017)

32. Maggi, F.M., Bose, R.P.J.C., van der Aalst, W.M.P.: Efficient discovery of understandable declarative process models from event logs. In: Ralyté, J., Franch, X., Brinkkemper, S., Wrycza, S. (eds.) CAiSE 2012. LNCS, vol. 7328, pp. 270–285. Springer, Heidelberg (2012). https://doi.org/10.1007/978-3-642-31095-9_18

33. Maggi, F.M., Marrella, A., Capezzuto, G., Cervantes, A.A.: Explaining noncompliance of business process models through automated planning. In: Pahl, C., Vukovic, M., Yin, J., Yu, Q. (eds.) ICSOC 2018. LNCS, vol. 11236, pp. 181–197. Springer, Cham (2018). https://doi.org/10.1007/978-3-030-03596-9_12

34. Maggi, F.M., Montali, M., Westergaard, M., van der Aalst, W.M.P.: Monitoring business constraints with linear temporal logic: an approach based on colored automata. In: Rinderle-Ma, S., Toumani, F., Wolf, K. (eds.) BPM 2011. LNCS, vol. 6896, pp. 132–147. Springer, Heidelberg (2011). https://doi.org/10.1007/978-3-642-23059-2_13

35. Mannhardt, F., Blinde, D.: Analyzing the trajectories of patients with sepsis using process mining. In: RADAR+EMISA, pp. 72–80. CEUR-ws.org (2017)

36. Pham, T.A., Le Thanh, N.: An ontology-based approach for business process compliance checking. In: IMCOM, pp. 1–6. ACM SIGAPP (2016)

37. Schönig, S., Rogge-Solti, A., Cabanillas, C., Jablonski, S., Mendling, J.: Efficient and customisable declarative process mining with SQL. In: Nurcan, S., Soffer, P., Bajec, M., Eder, J. (eds.) CAiSE 2016. LNCS, vol. 9694, pp. 290–305. Springer, Cham (2016). https://doi.org/10.1007/978-3-319-39696-5_18

38. Thao Ly, L., Göser, K., Rinderle-Ma, S., Dadam, P.: Compliance of semantic constraints - a requirements analysis for process management systems. In: GRCIS (2008)
39. Ly, L.T., Rinderle-Ma, S., Dadam, P.: Design and verification of instantiable compliance rule graphs in process-aware information systems. In: Pernici, B. (ed.) CAiSE 2010. LNCS, vol. 6051, pp. 9–23. Springer, Heidelberg (2010). https://doi.org/10.1007/978-3-642-13094-6_3

The SenSoMod-Modeler – A Model-Driven Architecture Approach for Mobile Context-Aware Business Applications

Julian Dörndorfer[1(✉)], Florian Hopfensperger[2], and Christian Seel[1]

[1] University of Applied Science Landshut,
Am Lurzenhof 1, 84036 Landshut, Germany
{julian.doerndorfer,christian.seel}@haw-landshut.de
[2] IBM Deutschland GmbH,
Mies-van-der-Rohe-Straße 6, 80807 Munich, Germany
florian.hopfensperger@de.ibm.com

Abstract. The ubiquity and the low prices of mobile devices like smartphones and tablets as well as the availability of radio networks hold the opportunity for companies to reorganize and optimize their business processes. These mobile devices can help users to execute their process steps by showing instructions or by augmenting reality. Moreover, they can improve the efficiency and effectiveness of business processes by adapting the business process execution. This can be achieved by evaluating the user's context via the many sensor-data from a smart device and adapting the business process to the current context. The data, not only collected from internal sensors but also via networks from other sources, can be aggregated and interpreted to evaluate the context. To use the advantages of context recognition for business processes an simple way to model this data collection and aggregation is needed. This would enable a more structured way to implement supportive mobile (context-aware) applications. Today, there is no modeling language that supports the modeling of data collection and aggregation to context and offers code generation for mobile applications via a suitable tool. Therefore, this paper presents a domain specific modeling language for context and a model-driven architecture (MDA) based approach for mobile context-aware apps. The modeling language and the MDA-approach have been implemented in an Eclipse-based tool.

Keywords: Domain specific modeling · Context-aware modeling · Mobile business processes

1 Development of Mobile Business Applications

The availability of broadband radio networks, like 3G, 4G and soon 5G, and the decreasing prices for mobile devices, like smartphones, smartwatches and tablets, hold the opportunity for companies to optimize their business processes via these mobile devices. The design, execution, controlling and evaluation of business processes are a standard procedure in theory and practice [1–4]. However, business processes must

© Springer Nature Switzerland AG 2019
C. Cappiello and M. Ruiz (Eds.): CAiSE Forum 2019, LNBIP 350, pp. 75–86, 2019.
https://doi.org/10.1007/978-3-030-21297-1_7

become more flexible due to the continuously changing business environment. These changes are necessary to react on new legislation or rising competitors [5]. Business processes should therefore be able to react to such alterations or disturbances in the sense that they have to be flexible enough to consider environmental changes [6]. Mobile devices are able to improve the flexibility and quality of business processes [7] and to transform them into a mobile business process [8].

However, mobile devices are not only capable of improving the execution of a business process. Moreover, they have, depending on the concrete devices, many sensors which enable context recognition in the execution phase of a business process [9]. This context recognition makes a mobile business process context-aware. The aim of such mobile context-aware business processes is to support the process execution to improve the efficiency and effectiveness. This can be done by a mobile application on mobile devices, which for example changes the appearance of the application or autofills forms. However, to recognize the context is sometimes not a trivial task for the software architect or the developer. For example, when should the appearance of an app be adjusted, from which sensors can the context be measured? In addition, sometimes only end users, which will use the mobile application in the end, can describe why a certain behavior of the application is necessary and how it can be measured. Therefore, we decided to create a Domain Specific Modeling Language (DSML) [10] and develop a modeling tool which will also be able to generate code from the model. This model-driven architecture (MDA) approach allows to model a context model platform and technology independent. This enables to model where the data for a context will be collected and how the data can be aggregated. The development of the modeling tool was conducted by following the design science approach by HEVNER et al. [11]. To communicate and show the usefulness of the modeling tool, the development of the tool will be described, and a proof of concept will be conducted. Therefore, we formulate the following research questions (RQ):

RQ. 1: How can a modeling tool for the DSML be developed?
RQ. 2: How can the context model be transferred into application code?

The remaining paper is structured as follows: In Sect. 2 the related work for this topic will be presented and discussed. The tool development is described in Sect. 3 (RQ. 1) which comprises in Sect. 3.1 a framework selection for the modeling tool. Section 3.2 describes the code generation from the context model (RQ 2). An evaluation which is in this case a proof of concept will be shown in Sect. 4. The paper ends with a conclusion and outlook to further research about this topic.

2   Related Work

Context is "any information that can be used to characterize the situation of an entity. An entity can be a person, place or object which is considered relevant to the interaction between a person and an application" [12]. DEY gives a very precise definition of context because he distinguishes between data and context. Moreover, he and ABOWD [13] also define a context-aware application "if it uses context to provide relevant information and/or services to the user, where relevancy depends on the user's task".

This means, if a mobile application, which supports the fulfillment of a business process, has to be context-aware, it must use context to provide relevant information and/or services. In consequence, a mobile context-aware application has to be conscious of the user's and business process' context, like the weather, machines nearby or process steps to fulfill. The data to evaluate a context, can be derived and aggregated from sensors. This potentially very complex task can be facilitated with a modeling language and tool. ROSEMANN et al. [14] postulated that modeling languages have to be more flexible to cope with contextual influences and therefore decrease the time-to-market for products [5]. This leads to a higher demand for process flexibility [6]. In consequence, ROSEMANN and VAN DER AALST developed an extension for the event-driven process chain (EPC) to address the flexibility problems of the EPC. However, this approach does not address context evaluation in particular, it only made EPC more flexible. Efforts to consider context in business processes at design- [15–19] and runtime [20, 21] have also been made. While they focus on extending business process languages and made it possible to consider contextual influences, they do not offer a way to model where the data for the context evaluation can be collected and how the data can be aggregated to context information. A more detailed summary of the consideration of context in business processes with an in-depth literature review can be found in [22]. Domain Specific Languages (DSL) for context aggregation on mobile devices [23] and context-aware systems [24] have also been found. However, they both focus on the transformation of applications across different platforms and not on data aggregation for context evaluation.

The approach of generating source code from models is already pursued in Model-Driven Software Development (MDSD). According to STAHL and BETTIN [25], MDSD is a generic term for techniques that automatically generate *executable* software from models. On the contrary, the Object Management Group (OMG) coined the term Model-Driven Architecture (MDA) [26] as an approach to develop *parts* of software from models. MDA can improve the productivity, quality and longevity outlook [27]. There are three different abstraction levels for model languages according to the OMG [28]. The Computation Independent Model (CIM) describes a software system at the domain level, while the Platform Independent Model (PIM) describes the functionality of a software component independently of the given platform. A platform could be the Java Enterprise Edition. The last abstraction level is the Platform Specific Model (PSM), which knows the platform and implements a PIM. The modeling language SenSoMod introduced in this paper can be classified according to the OMG as a PIM, because it is necessary to create a model in the language SenSoMod, which then describes a context-aware application independent of the target platform.

3 A Modeling Tool for SenSoMod – The SenSoMod-Modeler

SenSoMod is a DSML for modeling the data collection and aggregation for context. The reason to develop a new DSML instead of extending an existing modeling language (e.g. BPMN) was that this would be an extensive enlargement which would lead to large and overloaded models. SenSoMod was developed after the visualization principles by DEELMAN and LOOS [29] and is introduced in [10].

The functional and non-functional requirements are typically derived from the system context and the use case. In addition, to being able to create a model, add elements or attributes to it and connect the elements, it should also be possible to validate the created model and generate Java source code from it. In contrast, the non-functional requirements are usually measurable and allow a better understanding for the application to be created. The operating system independence, robustness and usability are important non-functional requirements. Furthermore, the modeling tool to be developed should not be created from scratch, instead a development framework should be used to assist the software architect or business process modeler in formulating requirements for a context-aware system as quickly as possible.

3.1   The Selection of a Development Framework

This section selects the appropriate tool to create a modeling tool for the DSML SenSoMod, according to the requirements (RQ. 1). There are different approaches to create a model which varies in its complexity. For example, models can be created using paper and pencil without any restrictions. However, as soon as this has to be digitized in order to prevent media breaks, a supportive program is required. The easiest way are simple drawing programs (such as Microsoft Paint). However, they do not offer a way to define available elements and their possible relationships to each other. These restrictions are defined by means of a metamodel. A good example for modeling languages is the unified modeling language (UML). In practice, the UML class diagram is considered as the de facto standard to model a software architecture. Modeling tools can be divided into several groups. The following list shows the individual groups with known representatives:

- Visualization tool (Microsoft Visio)
- Analysis and Modeling tool (ARIS Platform)
- Computer Aided Software Engineering tool (IBM Rational Rose)
- Integrated Development Environment (Microsoft Studio)

None of the mentioned tool groups are on their own sufficient for the implementation of the SenSoMod-Modeler. Rather, one or more groups would have to be combined. FOWLER [30] coined the term 'Language Workbench' in 2005. It describes a development environment (IDE) in which a DSL and its tool support can be developed. The definition of a new DSL using the Language Workbench is usually done in three steps which are referred to below:

1. Schema Definition of the semantic model (metamodel) of a language
2. Definition of an editor to be able to display the language textually or graphically
3. Definition of a generator which describes how a concrete model is transformed into an executable representation.

Over the years, many applications have been created that can be assigned to the Language Workbench field [30]. The various representatives differ in several points, such as the type definition of the metamodel (graphical or textual). A representative of a Language Workbench is the Obeo Designer [31]. This tool is an installable and customized Eclipse environment, developed by the French company Obeo and has fully integrated the Sirius framework. They also have an active forum, which can be used for any kind of question about Sirius. Furthermore, it provides tools which have the purpose to create a simple graphical representation, such as diagrams or tables. Creating a modeling tool in Obeo Designer for a DSML is usually done in three steps:

1. Creating a metamodel in Ecore, the meta model language of the Eclipse Modeling Framework, that contains the concepts of the domain (elements), the relationships between the elements, and the properties of the elements.
2. Once the metamodel has been created, Ecore generates the metamodel implementation. When the metamodel has been defined, this step creates the semantic model and the graphical representation like a diagram, table, or tree. The Obeo Designer uses viewpoints to achieve this. A viewpoint is a graphical representation (specification) to characterize or solve a specific problem. This means that several viewpoints can be created for one modeling language.
3. The final step is done with a tree-based editor by defining the appearance (e.g. icon, color, size) of all elements of the modeling language. Furthermore, the elements of the metamodel are bound to the elements of the viewpoint. The available Elements of the drawing palette of the modeling tool are also described therein.

3.2 The Implementation of the SenSoMod-Modeler

Based on the steps described in Sect. 3.1, the implementation of the SenSoMod-Modeler starts with the creation of the metamodel in Ecore. The metamodel is constructed by modeling the language elements of SenSoMod and their relationships to each other by creating new classes, attributes, and relations. Figure 1 shows the metamodel in Ecore. The model elements Sensor, Context and ContextDescription are created and derived from the abstract class Node. This inheritance enables the above-mentioned elements to have the attributes name and description as properties. Furthermore, it is necessary that all elements are bound to the class 'Model' by means of composition relation. This condition can be attributed to the fact that a model must consist of none or several nodes (cardinality 0…*). Ecore and the viewport approach of Sirius have another special feature: relations between two model elements have to be represented by a simple reference relation. The relationship between two model elements (e.g. ContextDescription to Context) is created with the help of a reference relation. Parallel to the definition of the metamodel, the Ecore engine creates a so-called genemodel in the background. This model is a readable text file in XML Metadata Interchange (XMI) format. XMI is an independent, open exchange format for metadata in distributed software structures based on the Extensible Markup Language (XML). The XMI from a concrete model can later be used to derive the Java classes. Before a viewpoint can be created, the created files have to be executed in a new Obeo instance. The executed instance must be used to create viewpoints. To enable modeling with the SenSoMod elements viewpoints have to be defined. Therefore, a new representation (Diagram Description) with the name SenSoMod is created.

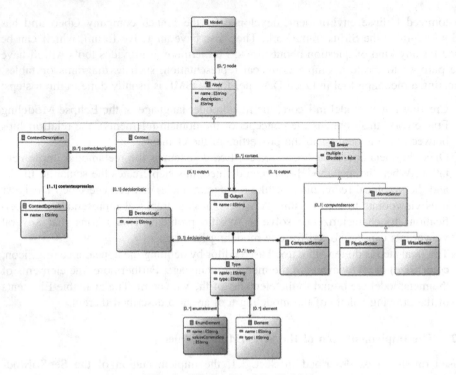

Fig. 1. Metamodel of SenSoMod

This viewpoint requires the reference to the metamodel which is needed to access the individual elements of the modeling language. With the use of a tree-based editor it is possible to define the individual nodes (Context, ContextDescription and Sensors), relations, tools and their appearance. After the node design has been created, it is possible to realize the assignments of a concrete SenSoMod model in the form of node connections. For example, it should be possible to connect a physical sensor to a context or computed sensor, but not to a context description. To achieve this the 'Atomic Sensor to Computed Sensor', 'Atomic or Computed Sensor to Context' and the 'Context to Context Description' flows were established. The cardinalities of the edges (e.g. how often a certain sensor can be connected to different contexts) have already been defined in the metamodel and therefore have not to be specified again.

After the creation of the SenSoMod-Editor has been realized in the Obeo-Designer by means of a suitable modeling tool, the source code generator will be explained (RQ. 2). The goal of the source code generator is to derive source code from a SenSoMod model. This source code should not be executable as independent software, but the modeled logic and structure should be mapped in to Java classes and methods. These classes and methods can then be used in a concrete information system (e.g. context-aware application) by adapting them to the specific requirements. Furthermore, the software developer has still the choice of the application architecture (e.g. Model-View-Controller Pattern). The concrete PIM can be used to create a context-aware application in the Java programming language. One reason why Java was chosen is that

Java is still one of the most widely used programming languages according to ratings like the TIOBE [32] or the IEEE spectrum [33]. Furthermore, Java is platform-independent and can be used in the mobile, desktop and web development. Moreover, the focus is to speed up the development of a mobile context-aware application for which Android, a java-based programming language, is the most widely used programming language. The generation of Java code from a SenSoMod-model will be conducted in several steps. Basically, Java code is generated by parsing the xml document. Each SenSoMod project has an automatically generated xml file in which the created model is described. First, the super classes for each used element type will be created. In a second step, the classes for each element will be created. For example, for the Location element a superclass Context (which is the type of the element) will be created as well as a Location.java class. The Location.java class will also include a method with the decision logic and the variables from the output field. In order to make this possible a new Obeo Designer plug-in must be created. Therefore, a SenSo-Mod2Java script was programmed. The library JavaParser [34] will be used to transform the xml to java code. First the node Id is extracted from the sensor and context elements, which represent the relation between the language elements. To assign the relations the XML document is processed twice. In the first cycle, all node names (e.g. WIFI) are stored in an ArrayList. The second cycle is used to read the relation ID from a node, which is stored with the node name in a MultiMap. In contrast to a map, a MultiMap allows to assign several values to one key. After both passes are completed, MutltiMap stores the relations of the nodes to each other. Hereafter, the XML document is parsed one last time. In this run, the names of the nodes and their attributes are finally written to Java files. The complete SenSoMod-Modeler can be found on GitHub[1] including installation and demo videos, the source code of the modeler and generator.

4 Evaluation

The evaluation is performed as a proof of concept by creating an example application which is simplified in its scope but contains a typical characteristic of a context-aware application. Based on the requirements of the context-aware application, a SenSoMod-model with the previously created tool will be modeled. Hereafter, the Java code will be generated and refined until the application functionality can be provided. In comparison, the equivalent application will be programmed without prior modeling and thus without source code generation. The application to be developed is intended to support IT staff in the maintenance of printers. Printer data such as paper quantity or fill level of the cartridges should be managed with the help of a context-aware application. The context awareness is characterized by the requirement that only printers that are in the geographical vicinity of an IT staff member can be displayed and managed. The current position of the employee can be determined using the GPS or WIFI sensor of his/her smartphone. The first approach will be the implementation of the described

---

[1] https://github.com/HAWMobileSystems/sensomod-modeler.

context-aware application using the SenSoMod-Modeler. It starts by modeling the elements which can be derived from the description above:

- **Physical Sensor WIFI:** The current location of an employee is to be determined using WIFI.
- **Physical Sensor PrinterStatus:** The various printer states are represented by using this sensor.
- **Computed Sensor UserLocation:** The data from the WIFI sensor will be used to determine the current user location. For example: If the WIFI sensor has determined the SSID_1, the user can be located near room 1, since the WIFI access point is installed in this room. This logic is descripted in the DL-Area of the sensor notation.
- **Context PrinterManagement:** Depending on the identified user location and the printer status, the different contexts and therefore the various tasks for the user depending on the context can be determined. For example, if an employee is near printer 1 and the printer has no paper available, the task is to refill the paper.
- **Context Descriptions** RefillPaper, OrderCartridge, NothingToDo: Depending on the determined context, these language elements represent the tasks to be fulfilled.

The corresponding elements are dragged step by step from the toolbar onto the drawing sheet and the properties are adapted. Figure 2 shows the final model of the printer management example. The advantage of this approach is that the created model can now be used in order to present it to the management as well as to the IT staff for a discussion. If any changes must be made because of the discussion it is no problem to alter the model. Furthermore, Java source code can be generated by means of the developed plug-in and is available to the application developers. After the generation, they can implement the user interface as well as the rest of the context-aware application. Another advantage of this approach is that no other diagram (e.g. UML class diagram or activity diagram) must be created beforehand, since the program structure and logic is already present in the model as well as in the generated Java files and can therefore be directly used. The last step is to develop the rest of the context-aware application, like the user interface. The various Java Swing elements (e.g. buttons and labels) were developed, then an object of the PrinterManagement class was created which contains the entire logic of the context-aware application, and a 'click' action was defined for each button. The complete source code can also be found on GitHub. In contrast to implementing the context-aware application by using the SenSoMod-Modeler, the 'traditional' development after SOMMERVILLE [35] was conducted. Based on the requirements, a UML class diagram was defined that visualizes the program structure. Compared to the SenSoMod-model, all elements must be captured in the form of classes with associated attributes. However, the decision logic and output elements of the concrete context- or computed sensor classes cannot be provided with associated logic. Furthermore, special attention must be paid to inheritance, otherwise it is no longer possible to determine the type (sensor or context) of a class. If this information were not captured the structure and organization of the context-aware application would be lost. For example, it is necessary to create a PhysicalSensor superclass from which the classes WIFI and PrinterStatus are derived. This will automatically be generated in the SenSoMod-Modeler. Moreover, the UML does not provide a way to generate a method to specify that the specific sensor or context has a decision logic and output attributes.

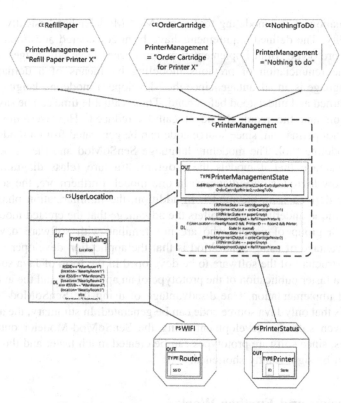

Fig. 2. SenSoMod model: printer management

This circumstance is particularly important because all conditions have to be recorded and documented in a different form. Furthermore, the created class diagram only describes the program structure, but not the context-aware application flow. A flow means in this context that one or more conditions must be fulfilled before the next event is triggered. In the described example, two elementary context conditions must be fulfilled. For example, as soon as an employee is near a printer and at the same time the printer has the status 'paper is empty', the paper for this printer must be refilled. The UML family offers the so-called activity diagram for this purpose, but a separate diagram must be created for each use case (respectively for each context description). After the diagrams necessary for the implementation have been modeled, the program code must now be developed. There are two possible alternatives. On the one hand, the source code could be generated from the class diagram similar to the SenSoMod Model and refined step by step. Alternatively, classes, methods and attributes could be taken from the created class diagram without prior generation by programming them from scratch. Both alternatives lead to the same result, but the second variant will take more time. Furthermore, the basic context-aware application logic described by activity diagrams must be implemented for both alternatives. After the application logic has been programmed, the GUI must be implemented like in the SenSoMod-Modeler approach.

The evaluation of the modeling tool SenSoMod-Modeler has basically confirmed its functionality. The defined requirements have been considered and implemented in the software prototype. Both implementation approaches have advantages and disadvantages. The renunciation of previous modeling by means of a domain-specific modeling language is an advantage, since the (developed) modeling languages do not have to be learned and understood beforehand. Thus, valuable time can be saved during implementation and the required budget can be reduced. However, this temporal advantage is not permanent, since source code can be generated from a model with the help of a modeling tool. The modeling language SenSoMod and the associated tool have the advantage that it models the program structure (class diagram) and the application flow logic (activity diagram) in one model. Furthermore, the source code can be partly derived from the model. In addition, the familiarization phase in Sen-SoMod is a unique undertaking and offers the advantage that the created models can be presented to a group of people who are not familiar with software development. A further advantage of using SenSoMod is that the application developer is provided with a basic structure of the software to be developed in the form of Java source code. This enables a faster publication of the prototype of an application and the avoidance of errors during implementation. One disadvantage of using the SenSoMod-Modeler at the moment is that only Java source code can be generated. In summary, the advantages of model-driven software development using the SenSoMod-Modeler outweigh the disadvantages, since software prototypes can be created much faster and thus the time-to-market can be significantly shortened.

5   Conclusion and Further Work

In this paper a modeling tool for SenSoMod was introduced and its development has been shown. For this purpose, the selection of a development framework was introduced which eases the implementation for a DSML modeling tool. An evaluation was conducted which showed a realization of a mobile context-aware application with the SenSoMod-modeler and without it. This comparison showed that the modeler has advantages in time saving since the source code can be generated directly from the model. Furthermore, the model and with it the application logic and data aggregation can be discussed with non-IT specialists. However, SenSoMod has to be understood and learned before it can be applied in practice. To confirm these results the evaluation will have to be conducted in a more comprehensive way. Possible scenarios would be field experiments or case studies for the practical impact and a laboratory experiment. The latter could mean that two groups have to implement a context-aware application: One group models and implements it with the SenSoMod-modeler, the second group without it. This would bring solid information about the time saving assumption.

References

1. Becker, J., Kugeler, M., Rosemann, M. (eds.): Process Management. A Guide for the Design of Business Processes. Springer, Berlin (2011)
2. Vom Brocke, J., Rosemann, M. (eds.): Handbook on Business Process Management 2. Strategic Alignment, Governance, People and Culture. Springer, Heidelberg (2010). https://doi.org/10.1007/978-3-642-01982-1
3. Scheer, A.-W.: ARIS–Business Process Modeling. Springer, New York (2000). https://doi.org/10.1007/978-3-642-57108-4
4. Bichler, M., et al.: Erratum to: theories in business and information systems engineering. Bus. Inf. Syst. Eng. **58**(5), 327–328 (2016)
5. Rosemann, M., Recker, J., Flender, C.: Designing context-aware business processes. In: Siau, K., Chiang, R., Hardgrave, B.C. (eds.) Systems Analysis and Design, People, Processes and Projects, pp. 51–73. M.E. Sharpe, Armonk (2011)
6. Soffer, P.: On the notion of flexibility in business processes. In: Proceedings of the CAiSE 2005 Workshops, pp. 35–42 (2005)
7. Falk, T., Leist, S.: Effects of mobile solutions for improving business processes. In: Avital, M., Leimeister, J.M., Schultze, U. (eds.) ECIS 2014 Proceedings, 22th European Conference on Information Systems; Tel Aviv, Israel, June 9–11, 2014. AIS Electronic Library (2014)
8. Gruhn, V., Köhler, A., Klawes, R.: Modeling and analysis of mobile business processes. J. Enterp. Inf. Manag. **20**, 657–676 (2007)
9. Dörndorfer, J., Seel, C.: The impact of mobile devices and applications on business process management. In: Barton, T., Herrmann, F., Meister, V., Müller, C., Seel, C. (eds.) Prozesse, Technologie, Anwendungen, Systeme und Management 2016. Angewandte Forschung in der Wirtschaftsinformatik, pp. 10–19 (2016)
10. Dörndorfer, J., Seel, C., Hilpoltsteiner, D.: SenSoMod – a modeling language for context-aware mobile applications. In: Paul, D., Burkhardt, F., Peter, N., Lin, X. (eds.) Multikonferenz Wirtschaftsinformatik (MKWI), pp. 1435–1446 (2018)
11. Hevner, A.R., Chatterjee, S.: Design Research in Information Systems Theory and Practice. Integrated Series in Information Systems, vol. 22. Springer, Heidelberg (2010). https://doi.org/10.1007/978-1-4419-5653-8
12. Dey, A., Abowd, G., Salber, D.: A conceptual framework and a toolkit for supporting the rapid prototyping of context-aware applications. Hum.-Comput. Interact. **16**, 97–166 (2001)
13. Dey, A.K., Abowd, G.D.: Towards a better understanding of context and context-awareness. In: Tremaine, M. (ed.) CHI 2000 extended abstracts (2000)
14. Rosemann, M., Recker, J.C., Flender, C.: Contextualisation of business processes. Int. J. Bus. Process Integr. Manag. **3**(1), 47–60 (2008)
15. de la Vara, J.L., Ali, R., Dalpiaz, F., Sánchez, J., Giorgini, P.: Business processes contextualisation via context analysis. In: Parsons, J., Saeki, M., Shoval, P., Woo, C., Wand, Y. (eds.) ER 2010. LNCS, vol. 6412, pp. 471–476. Springer, Heidelberg (2010). https://doi.org/10.1007/978-3-642-16373-9_37
16. Saidani, O., Nurcan, S.: Towards context aware business process modelling. In: Workshop on Business Process Modelling, Development, and Support, p. 1. Norway (2007)
17. Al-alshuhai, A., Siewe, F.: An extension of class diagram to model the structure of context-aware systems. In: The Sixth International Joint Conference on Advances in Engineering and Technology (AET) (2015)

18. Al-alshuhai, A., Siewe, F.: An extension of UML activity diagram to model the behaviour of context-aware systems. In: Computer and Information Technology; Ubiquitous Computing and Communications; Dependable, Autonomic and Secure Computing; Pervasive Intelligence and Computing (CIT/IUCC/DASC/PICOM), pp. 431–437 (2015)
19. Dörndorfer, J., Seel, C.: A meta model based extension of BPMN 2.0 for mobile context sensitive business processes and applications. In: Leimeister, J.M., Brenner, W. (eds.) Proceedings der 13. Internationalen Tagung Wirtschaftsinformatik (WI), pp. 301–315. St. Gallen (2017)
20. Heinrich, B., Schön, D.: Automated Planning of Context-Aware Process Models. University of Münster, Münster (2015)
21. Conforti, R., La Rosa, M., Fortino, G., ter Hofstede, A.H.M., Recker, J., Adams, M.: Real-time risk monitoring in business processes. A sensor-based approach. J. Syst. Softw. **86**, 2939–2965 (2013)
22. Dörndorfer, J., Seel, C.: Research agenda for mobile context sensitive business processes. AKWI, 28–37 (2017)
23. Kramer, D., Clark, T., Oussena, S.: MobDSL. a domain specific language for multiple mobile platform deployment. In: 2010 IEEE International Conference on Networked Embedded Systems for Enterprise Applications, pp. 1–7. IEEE (2010)
24. Hoyos, J.R., García-Molina, J., Botía, J.A.: A domain-specific language for context modeling in context-aware systems. J. Syst. Software **86**, 2890–2905 (2013)
25. Stahl, T., Bettin, J.: Modellgetriebene Softwareentwicklung. Techniken, Engineering, Management. Dpunkt-Verl., Heidelberg (2007)
26. Object Management Group (OMG): Model Driven Architecture (MDA). How Systems Will Be Built. https://www.omg.org/mda/
27. Frankel, D.: Model Driven Architecture. Applying MDA to Enterprise Computing. Wiley, New York (2003)
28. Truyen, F.: The Fast Guide to Model Driven Architecture. The Basics of Model Driven Architecture (2006)
29. Deelmann, T., Loos, P.: Grundsätze ordnungsmäßiger Modellvisualisierung. In: Rumpe, B. (ed.) Modellierung 2004. Proceedings, pp. 289–290. Ges. für Informatik, Bonn (2004)
30. Fowler, M.: Language Workbenches: The Killer-App for Domain Specific Languages? https://www.martinfowler.com/articles/languageWorkbench.html
31. Obeo: The Professional Solution to Deploy Sirius - Obeo Designer. https://www.obeodesigner.com/en/
32. TIOBE software BV: TIOBE Index | TIOBE - The Software Quality Company. https://www.tiobe.com/tiobe-index/
33. Cass, S.: The 2018 Top Programming Languages. https://spectrum.ieee.org/at-work/innovation/the-2018-top-programming-languages
34. van Bruggen, D.: JavaParser. http://javaparser.org/about/
35. Sommerville, I.: Software Engineering. Pearson Higher Education, München u.a (2012)

Blurring Boundaries

Towards the Collective Team Grokking of Product Requirements

Rob Fuller[✉]

Electrical and Computer Engineering,
The University of British Columbia, Vancouver, B.C., Canada
rfuller@ece.ubc.ca

Abstract. Software development has become increasingly software 'product' development, without an authoritative 'customer' stakeholder that many requirements engineering processes assume exists in some form. Many progressive software product companies today are empowering cross-functional product teams to 'own' their product – to collectively understand the product context, the true product needs, and manage its on-going evolution – rather than develop to a provided specification.

Some teams do this better than others and neither established requirements elicitation and validation processes nor conventional team leadership practices explain the reasons for these observable differences. This research examines cross-functional product teams and identifies factors that support or inhibit the team's ability to collectively create and nurture a shared mental model that accurately represents the external product domain and its realities. The research also examines how teams use that collective understanding to shape development plans, internal and external communications, new team member onboarding, etc.

We are engaged with several software product companies using a constructivist Grounded Theory method towards the research question.

Early results are emerging as organisational factors, within and surrounding the teams. One emerging observation relates to the degree to which functional distinctions are treated as demarcations or blurred boundaries. The other observation is the impact an expectation of mobility has on an individual's sense of feeling part of the collective team versus solely being a functional expert. This also becomes a factor in the first observation.

The research is in-progress but early observations are consistent with a basic element of empathy that a certain blurring of the boundaries is necessary for a period of time in order to better understand the other context. Future research will examine whether the observed organisational factors are pre-conditions for the team being able to collectively understand the context of the product requirements, collectively and deeply.

Keywords: Empathy-driven development · Collective sensemaking ·
Design science · Requirements validation · Team learning ·
Knowledge management · Complex adaptive systems ·
Tacit knowledge · Product team organisation

© Springer Nature Switzerland AG 2019
C. Cappiello and M. Ruiz (Eds.): CAiSE Forum 2019, LNBIP 350, pp. 87–98, 2019.
https://doi.org/10.1007/978-3-030-21297-1_8

1 Introduction

For those unfamiliar with its popular culture roots, the Oxford English Dictionary [1] defines the verb 'grok' as "understand (something) intuitively or by empathy." Increasingly, the success of cross-functional software product development teams depends on the degree to which the team collectively groks, more than simply the product requirements, but the context for those requirements, the world for which their products are intended.

2 Historical Context

During the 1990s, three factors collectively contributed to a massive shift in the software landscape. The first was the continuing improvement in the price/performance ratio of computing which had brought PCs to every desktop in the workplace and to a great number of homes, creating a much more broad and diverse demand for software and carrying with it a broader range of needs and desires. The second contributing factor was the widespread introduction of graphical user interfaces on personal computers which caused the industry to examine human-computer interaction (HCI) in entirely new and vastly more complex ways. The third factor was the arrival of the Internet which affected everything from how we thought of using technology to business models themselves. These factors combined dramatically changed the 'art of the possible' in software.

By the late 1990s, a "model revolution" [2] began to emerge that took a different view on change, risk, and uncertainty. These 'agile' models typically embraced the possibility that requirements could change throughout the development effort in contrast to many earlier Software Development LifeCycles (SDLCs) that strived to lock down requirements in the specification and planning stages. They took the form of iterative and incremental approaches to solution development using cross-functional teams that attempt to 'discover' the needs throughout the development effort. This model viewed emergence as a fact of life rather than a failure of the requirements elicitation and analysis activities.

These process models had a greater focus on the software development 'team', usually cross-functional, as a critical success factor in delivering software. These teams often have the necessary collection of functional expertise and capacity in each functional area to be essentially self-sufficient. Many software development companies have gone even further, empowering their cross-functional teams to 'own' the product. This approach is now quite common, no longer adopted only by industry thought-leaders. It is these organisations and teams that are the main focus of this research.

3   The Problem

While agile models improve many of the issues that were breaking down during the crisis period of the 1990s, they still generally cling to the notion that there is a 'customer', an authoritative voice that the development team can interact with iteratively to clarify requirements and validate results. However, as software development has become less bespoke development and more 'product' development intended for a market, a new and critical challenge exists for software teams, especially those now empowered to own the product, and that is how to gain a deep understanding of the world for which their product is intended. Certainly, techniques to 'hear' from the market are helpful but, as Polyani [3] noted, this is tacit knowledge that these market participants have and people can know more than they can tell and they also know more than can be easily observed. A form of this problem commonly occurs with the popular 'user story' technique of communicating end-user requirements when it's later discovered that the story doesn't reflect an actual need but rather simply an articulation of what someone wants, resulting in, "I know that's what I said I wanted but that doesn't seem to be what I need." … they know more than they can tell or IKIWISI (I'll Know It When I See It).

It is also important that the entire team gain this deep understanding. Team members (individually and in sub-teams), in all functional roles, make decisions almost continually based on their understanding of the requirements and within their understanding of the context of those requirements. Much of this understanding is also tacit.

The problem exists in the midst of a current controversy. Some agile development thought-leaders such as Cohn are blunt: "The idea of eliciting and capturing requirements is wrong." [4, p. 52]. While many hold to prevailing views, believing that we just need better techniques to improve effectiveness, others are taking Cohn's critique even further and fundamentally suggesting that the notion of requirements itself may be counterproductive (e.g. Ralph [5], Mohanani et al. [6], Guinan et al. [7]) or even illusory (Ralph [8].)

This controversy aside, it still behooves teams to strive for a deep, collective understanding of the context of their product, that other world for which their product is intended, a shared mental model of the supra-domain since many large and small, conscious and unconscious design and implementation decisions are made within the team's understanding of the domain context. The success of the team, of their product, and often of the software company itself rests upon how well they do this. Teams do this with varying degrees of success. Some achieve reasonable success seemingly instinctively, while many struggle ineffectively. Software development leaders are often able to observe this phenomenon but have no theories that help explain why.

While some labels are being used to describe what they think development teams have to do to achieve a profound understanding (grokking) of that external world (e.g. "empathy-driven development"), there does not appear to be any clear definition of what that is, but rather simply a label of what some think may be happening but there lacks a true understanding of how this may be occurring.

4   Research Question and Importance

The purpose of this qualitative research study is to develop a substantive theory that answers the following general research question:

"what factors influence the degree to which cross-functional software product teams, empowered to own their product, collectively achieve a deep understanding of the environment for which their product is intended?"

This theory will help industry practitioners explain why certain prevailing techniques and empirical approaches for understanding software solution needs are often inadequate, why some succeed while others do not. It is also likely to offer interpretive insights into how creativity and innovation occurs within software product teams and offer guidance for more effective software development approaches.

In addition to assisting practitioners in industry, this interpretive theory aspires to illuminate areas of potential further research. For example, how are technically-oriented people (primarily millennials) working in teams (typically cross-functional) and following a rational process to create software solutions able to develop, nurture, and incorporate 'squishier' skills into a process that strives to be as rational and deterministic as possible? What does this suggest regarding teaching of problem-solving skills for software engineers in the future? Or, how does that which cannot be easily observed nor expressed be equally understood and preserved within a team? Or, how does empathic appreciation of the context of a software solution translate across individuals, organisations, business domains, cultures?

5   Focus of the Research and Challenges

As the saying goes, "a fish doesn't know it's in water", thus the intended users of software solutions often cannot envisage an ideal (or, sometimes, even a conceptually different) solution nor clearly communicate the context in which they operate because they are trapped in that context. Thus, for software development teams to understand and define that which they cannot easily see, to understand 'why' more than 'what', to understand the functionality needs and the supra-functionality requirements and context, it is necessary to somehow become one of the people targetted to use a software solution, and to truly learn from that immersion. This is difficult because it involves somehow blurring the perceptual boundaries between the team members and the target environment. To be an outsider and obtain an insider's perspective and knowledge is not only difficult, it is messy logistically. This does not easily fit into established software engineering practices nor is it well-supported by software engineers' training. Considering that software solutions are a result of a collaborative cross-functional team effort, the messiness is even more acute.

Thus, the focus of this research is practicing software product teams in action, specifically teams empowered to own their product. It examines the empirical adaptations these teams make to established software engineering practices and to methods of user interaction design to support empathic-based development towards an ever-growing and increasingly accurate understanding of the context in which their users operate, the supra-domain - the business needs, technology, culture, and politics. The research also examines how software development individuals and teams, who are trained and encouraged to apply their best judgement, suspend those judgements and opinions in order to connect with and exercise empathy for the domain for which their solution is intended. Finally, it examines important organizational factors that either allow or inhibit a team's ability to collectively grok the domain.

One challenge identified early in the study was how to detect or measure a team's grokking ability. A team's ability to execute is not a suitable indicator since it is culturally and contextually dependent and that those factors may not be the same as the ones that influence the ability of a team to grok. Individual and collective engagement, however, is a necessary condition and the existence, or lack of, has been very easily detected in the field experience to-date, so I am using this as a first-level differentiator.

A second challenge has been the impact an organizational structure has on a team's collective understanding. To-date, my approach is to identify these as critical factors (intended or otherwise) and the insights as guidance for technical leaders.

6 Literature Review

A modest review of the literature was done determine if this topic was previously explored in a different context, perhaps with a different vocabulary. Nothing was found that referred to this research topic. Much was found that looked at intra-team dynamics within software development teams, but this does not get to the focus of my inquiry.

Literature was also reviewed in 3 main areas (requirements engineering (specifically elicitation), design science, and collective sensemaking) as well as certain tangential areas (management decision-making, information system success models, and cognitive and organisational models).

My research may be viewed as falling fully within the topic of software requirements engineering, specifically requirements elicitation (attempting to obtain and understand the true needs). I looked at all the accepted papers for the IEEE International Requirements Engineering Conference over the past 10 years, plus many related papers published in other publications. There are increasingly more views being expressed - consistent with the problem and views I reference in Sect. 3 - that acknowledge the shortcomings of prevailing approaches to requirements elicitation which have tended to focus on techniques and methods rather than deep practitioner understanding. This is evidence that some software product development efforts still operate in the 'process-driven' paradigm and are experiencing what Kuhn [2] described as the incommensurability across paradigms. While acknowledging that the 'techniques and methods' approach is entirely appropriate in certain domains, my focus is on problem domains that don't lend themselves well to clear specifications and, thus, I find myself firmly planted philosophically in the new paradigm and sharing the incommensurate view of 'requirements'. Setting labels and practices aside, I acknowledge that the intent of requirements elicitation has always been to understand the true software needs and, therefore, this research will contribute to the requirements engineering discipline, relabelled or not.

To establish a broader positioning of this research in the literature, I reviewed a significant amount of relevant literature in the design science field since design would appear to have some relationship to my research which is looking at teams trying to grok someone else's world (empathic ability). I also reviewed relevant literature of sensemaking as my research will examine the collective team effort to under-stand (collective sensemaking).

In the design science space, I found a considerable scholarship regarding empathy-driven design, e.g. (Koppen and Meinel [9], van Rijn et al. [10], Postma et al. [11], Wood-cock et al. [12], Dong et al. [13], Kourprie and Visser [14], Kolko [15]). However, this research falls short of addressing my inquiry questions in three critical respects: (1) the focus is solely on the design activity as part of an essentially sequential product development process rather than design as part of an on-going continuous product development effort, (2) it tends not to consider the whole development team, rather tends to focus on the design individual or design team, and, (3) when it does consider the design team, it is not viewed as a unit to consider regarding its empathic ability. There are design science models described by Wieringa [16] that acknowledge the challenge that empathy-driven requirements understanding attempts to address (using very different vocabulary) but he stops short of suggesting how those challenges are, or could be, addressed. I believe the results of my research could enrich those models and generally contribute to the design science field.

In the organisational sensemaking field, the focus of many researchers is mainly on the social process of individual identity in successive spheres of membership through interactions with others. The collective (team) is usually considered only insofar as its relationship to the organisation, not to its understanding of a specific domain outside of the organisation. Some researchers, notably Russell [17] from a Human-Computer Interaction (HCI) perspective, look at sensemaking for a broader purpose - to collect and organise information in order to gain insight, to analyse, to transfer. However, although his view establishes sensemaking in a collective location (an information world), he describes a style of engagement of sensemaking that is essentially personal, not collective. The Cynefin framework (Kurtz & Snowden [18]) is a sensemaking framework that is particularly useful for collective sensemaking in that it is designed to allow shared understandings to emerge which could be insightful with respect to how teams ingest, socialise, and collectively store insights. As with other collective sensemaking models, it has resonance in early problem-solving stages and for formal and finite periods of time. Other researchers (Klein et al. [19], Naumer et al. [20], Kolko [21]) elaborate further by bringing data-framing into the picture and defining design synthesis as a process of sense-making, trying to make sense of chaos. The data-framing activity of sensemaking lends itself to being part of a long-term collective effort to understand and therefore may have some relevance to this research.

In the more tangential areas, there is scholarship in the management decision-making field that have parallels to this inquiry, e.g. Isabella [22] work on how man-agement team interpretations evolve should be compared and contrasted with how software development teams evolve their understanding of needs, and Weick and Roberts [23] work on the collective mind could help frame how software teams socialise learning and maintain a relevant team memory. My research is about obtaining understanding upon which decision-making would be based and not about decision-making per se, so I have not surveyed this space thoroughly although I intend to do so once core categories have emerged in my study.

Finally, once the core categories do emerge, I intend to compare my findings to information systems success models such as: Technology Acceptance Model (Davis [24]) based on the Theory of Reasoned Action, DeLone and McLean Information Systems Success Model (DeLone and McLean [25]), and the IS-Impact Model (Gable et al. [26]). Also models from other disciplines are likely to have comparative value such as the Expectation Confirmation Theory (Oliver [27, 28], Bhattacherjee, [29] and theories from Organisational Learning – mental models, shared vision, team learning, and systems thinking.

7   Method of the Research

As the primary interest is on substantive theory generation, rather than extending or verifying existing theories, I am taking an interpretive epistemological stance, employing a Grounded Theory approach, as developed by Glaser and Strauss [30], and using the Constructivist Grounded Theory methodology described by Charmaz [31]. Grounded Theory is highly applicable in research such as this because it is explicitly emergent. I am interested in generating theory relating to a specific research situation and this research calls for a qualitative approach. This is an area that is a relatively new, where there has been limited research, and where field data will come from observations and interviews, conditions for which Grounded Theory is particularly well suited.

More specifically, Grounded Theory is applicable for this research because the current Agile paradigm for software development focusses on people and interactions and Grounded Theory, as a qualitative research method, allows for the study of complex, multi-faceted social interactions and behaviour. Grounded Theory has been used success-fully as a research method to study Agile software development teams: Adolph et al. [32], Dagenais et al. [33], Coleman and O'Connor [34], Martin [35], Hoda [36].

The research uses theoretical sampling (Charmaz [32]) where the analysis of the data collected prior informs the selection of and inquiry with the next participants. Individual participants and corporate sites selected are ones involved with software product development (teams developing software for market) and that claim to have cross-functional product development teams. The primary data collection method is semi-structured interviews with open-ended questions that will allow real issues to emerge. I con-duct observations of team meetings and team interactions to enrich interview data.

I carefully recruit participants through my professional networks, from product study groups, and via direct outreach to select software product organisations. Where per-mitted, I hold interviews in the participant's workplace to allow for record review to enrich the interview data. Also, where I have approval from the organisations involved, I locate myself as unobtrusively as possible in the workplace to allow for direct observation as an additional data source and for those observations to direct further data collection and analysis. The interviews conducted are primarily with individuals and recorded whenever permitted. Group interviews may be held if data analysis suggests, although, to date, this need has not surfaced. My many years of leader-ship with the types of people that are participants affords me considerable comfort, understanding, and rapid rapport with them.

Iterative data collection and analysis (formulation, testing, and redevelopment of propositions) allows the sample of participants and questions to purposefully evolve as patterns emerge in the data until I reach a theory. I use the NVivo software tool to analyse the unstructured qualitative data collected. The current expectation is to interview 25–30 team members representing 5–8 different teams, more if the analysis suggests. Data collection will stop once the analysis indicates the achievement of theoretical saturation, the point at which gathering more data reveals no new properties nor yields any further theoretical insights about the emerging grounded theory (Charmaz [31]). This ensures a certain degree of consistency in the analysis.

I recognise that my professional experience allows for a certain considered positionality and that this shapes my objectivity and subjectivity of many aspects of perspective in this study. While acknowledging the challenges, I consider this experience, and the bias it creates, to be an asset to this research. As Eisner [37] suggests, the expert ability to "see what counts" – the sensitivity to tacit elements of the data, meanings and connotations – will guide the research, supported fully by the collected data, towards questions that matter.

Quality in research of this nature is generally assessed in terms of validity and generalizability, which, together, determine some measure of usefulness. During the research, I employ various strategies (Maxwell [38]) to mitigate threats to validity (credibility, dependability, reliability). Intensive, on-going involvement (extended participation, the ability to 'live' in the participants' workplace) provides richer types of data, more direct and less dependent on inference, opportunity for repeated observations and interviews, all which will help rule out spurious associations and premature theories. The collection and use of rich data (transcribed inter-views, thick descriptive note-taking of observations) help provide a more complete and revealing picture of what is going on. Participant checks (obtaining participant and peer feedback on the data collected and conclusions drawn) help rule out possibilities of misinterpretation. Triangulation (collection from a range of participants and settings) reduces the risk of chance associations and systematic biases. Finally, I will be transparent with any discrepant evidence or negative cases. In short, applying disciplined rigor to the grounded theory methodology. I intend to assess transferability of the results within the context of software product development primarily via peer reviews of the resulting theory with software product development leaders and, further, to draw comparisons with non-product software development teams to further refine the specificity of transferability claims.

8 Status of the Research

Fieldwork began in 2017 and, to-date, I have been working with 4 software companies, all of which produce commercial software products, are leaders in their product markets, and range in size and maturity from early-stage to well-established (>12 years). With 8 participating teams across these companies, I have conducted 15 individual, semi-structured interviews and 17 team planning observation sessions. More interviews and observation sessions are scheduled and more organizations and teams are being actively recruited.

9 Emerging Observations

The first emerging observation is that whether or not there is a functional organisation model surrounding the cross-functional team, the team dynamics, individual participation and sense of primary allegiance are significantly impacted. Where there is, e.g., a software engineering department, a design department, and a product management department, all contributing resources into cross-functional product teams, the inter-team dynamics are often strikingly different than when there is no functional organisation surrounding the teams. In the former case, team members are more likely to temper their contributions, identifying more with their functional affiliation than with the product mandate. The analogy I use here is that they're wearing a functional tee-shirt (e.g. I'm wearing the software engineering department t-shirt with a small insignia that says I happen to be assigned to this particular product at the moment). In addition to observing this in team interactions, this also appears in the language, "*I just do my job and they do theirs*", "*I trust them*", "*I think someone else is looking after that*", "*I just do what Product Management (or Product Design) says*", "*I'm on this team for now*". A software engineer in this environment is much more likely to care about the 'how' and defer to others on 'what' and 'why'. In contrast, organisations that do not have a functional structure surrounding the cross-functional product teams tend to see the teams have a more complete sense of ownership for their product and richer inter-team interactions. The tee-shirt analogy is that they're all wearing the same product tee-shirt with perhaps an insignia that identifies their functional competency. On these teams, sense of team is much stronger, thus the language does not refer to 'them'. All team members are more likely to care about 'what', 'why', and 'how' because they feel a stronger sense of ownership for the product overall, not just their particular contribution to it. I plan to probe this phenomenon further and look at definitions of success and how they may be defined similarly or not across these two models.

The second emerging observation relates to expectation of mobility. I've observed two pressures that inhibit an individual's inclination to be 'all-in'. One pressure is where there is a high degree of staff churn that impacts product development team resourcing. After a certain length of time, people in these environments come to expect they will be reassigned soon and thus have a certain tentativeness to their commitment to the product and the product team and tend to apply their focus to functional excellence only. The other pressure is similar, however, intended, and this is where an HR policy exists that encourages a high degree of mobility with respect to team assignment, e.g. 20% of technical staff should change teams every year. This seems to stem from a belief that this is healthy for the individual and/or adds to corporate robustness. A telling quote from an engineering manager, "I don't know how a true 'team' can emerge this way."

10 Discussion

Product development is a social process, thus the organizational dimension is the 'elephant in the room', a critical factor for success or failure of software product teams. The two observable phenomena surfacing strongly in the analysis thus far both fall into a category of what an organisation may do, consciously or otherwise, to support or inhibit a cross-functional team to be all it can be.

In the context of requirements engineering, I use the definition of empathy as *the ability to imaginatively step into another domain, understand the perspectives of those in that domain, and use that understanding to guide decisions* [39]. Stepping into that other domain involves a certain temporarily *'blurring of the boundaries'* in order to truly understand perspectives in that domain.

Although these observations point to internal conditions that impact a team's ability to perform, it appears that both these observations point to a certain *blurring of the boundaries* that may be a pre-condition for a cross-functional team to collectively grok (have deep, empathic understanding for) the world for which their product is intended.

This is consistent with a basic notion of empathy, namely that, in order to truly understand another world, one has to blur the boundaries somewhat for a period of time in order to better understand. Further work is needed to explore this, particularly as it applies to the collective cross-functional product development team.

References

1. Grok: Oxford English Dictionary. Oxford University Press, Oxford (1989)
2. Kuhn, T.S.: The Structure of Scientific Revolutions, 4th edn. University of Chicago Press, London (2012)
3. Polanyi, M.: The tacit dimension. In: Knowledge in Organisations (1997)
4. Cohn, M.: User Stories Applied: For Agile Software Development. Addison-Wesley Professional, Boston (2004)
5. Ralph, P.: The illusion of requirements in software development. Requirements Eng. 18(3), 293–296 (2013)
6. Mohanani, R., Ralph, P., Shreeve, B.: Requirements fixation. In: Proceedings of the 36th International Conference on Software Engineering, pp. 895–906 (2014)
7. Guinan, P.J., Cooprider, J.G., Faraj, S.: Enabling software development team performance during requirements definition: a behavioral versus technical approach. Inf. Syst. Res. 9(2), 101–125 (1998)
8. Ralph, P., Mohanani, R.: Is requirements engineering inherently counterproductive?. In: Proceedings - 5th International Workshop on the Twin Peaks of Requirements and Architecture, TwinPeaks 2015 (2015)
9. Koppen, E., Meinel, C.: Knowing people: the empathetic designer. Des. Philos. Pap. 10(1), 35–51 (2012)
10. Van Rijn, H., Sleeswijk Visser, F., Stappers, P.J., Özakar, A.D.: Achieving empathy with users: the effects of different sources of information. CoDesign 7(2), 65–77 (2011)
11. Postma, C., Zwartkruis-Pelgrim, E., Daemen, E., Du, J.: Challenges of doing empathic design: experiences from industry. Int. J. Des. 6(1) (2012)

12. Woodcock, A., McDonagh, D., Osmond, J., Scott, W.: Empathy, design and human factors. In: Advances in Usability and User Experience, pp. 569–579 (2018)
13. Dong, Y., Dong, H., Yuan, S.: Empathy in design: a historical and cross-disciplinary perspective. In: Baldwin, C. (ed.) AHFE 2017. AISC, vol. 586, pp. 295–304. Springer, Cham (2018). https://doi.org/10.1007/978-3-319-60642-2_28
14. Kouprie, M., Sleeswijk-Visser, F.: A framework for empathy in design: stepping into and out of the user's life. J. Eng. Des. **20**(5), 437–448 (2009)
15. Kolko, J.: Well-Designed: How to Create Empathy to Create Products People Love. Harvard Business Review Press, Boston (2014)
16. Wieringa, R.: Design Science Methodology for Information Systems and Software Engineering. Springer, Berlin (2014). https://doi.org/10.1007/978-3-662-43839-8
17. Russell, D., Pirolli, P.: An Overview of Sensemaking: A View from the Workshop CHI 2009. Sensemaking Work. CHI, pp. 1–2 (2009)
18. Kurtz, C.F., Snowden, D.: The new dynamics of strategy: sense-making in a complex-complicated world. IBM Syst. J. **42**(3), 462–483 (2003)
19. Klein, G., Moon, B., Hoffman, R., Associates, K.: Making Sense of Sensemaking 2: a macrocognitive model. IEEE Intell. Syst. **21**(5), 88–92 (2006)
20. Naumer, C., Fisher, K., Dervin, B.: Sense-Making: a methodological perspective. In: CHI 2008 Work. Sense-Making Florence (2008)
21. Kolko, J.: Sensemaking and framing: a theoretical reflection on perspective in design synthesis. In: 2010 Design Research Society Conference, pp. 1–9 (2010)
22. Isabella, L.A.: Evolving interpretations as a change unfolds: how managers construe key organisational events. Acad. Manag. J. **33**(1), 7–41 (1990)
23. Weick, K.E., Roberts, K.H.: Collective mind in organizations: heedful interrelating on flight decks. Adm. Sci. Q. 357–381 (1993)
24. Davis, F.D.: Perceived usefulness, perceived ease of use, and user acceptance of information technology. MIS Q. **13**(3), 319–340 (1989)
25. DeLone, W.H., McLean, E.R.: The DeLone and McLean model of information systems success: a ten-year update. J. Manag. Inf. Syst. **19**(4), 9–30 (2003)
26. Gable, G., Sedera, D., Taizan, C.: Re-conceptualizing information system success: the IS-Impact measurement model. J. Assoc. Inf. Syst. **9**(7), 1–32 (2008)
27. Oliver, R.L.: Effect of expectation and disconfirmation on post exposure product evaluations - an alternative interpretation. J. Appl. Psychol. **62**(4), 480 (1977)
28. Oliver, R.L.: A cognitive model of the antecedents and consequences of satisfaction decisions. J. Mark. Res. **17**, 460–469 (1980)
29. Bhattacherjee, A.: Understanding information systems continuance: an expectation - confirmation model. MIS Q. **25**(3), 351–370 (2001)
30. Glaser, B.G., Strauss, A.L.: The Discovery of Grounded Theory: Strategies for Qualitative Research. Aldine Transaction, Piscataway (1967)
31. Charmaz, K.: Constructing Grounded Theory: A Practical Guide Through Qualitative Analysis. Sage, London (2006)
32. Adolph, S., Hall, W., Kruchten, P.: Using grounded theory to study the experience of software development. Empirical Softw. Eng. **16**(4), 487–513 (2011)
33. Dagenais, B., Ossher, H., Bellamy, R.K.E., Robillard, M.P., De Vries, J.P.: Moving into a new software project landscape. In: ICSE 2010 Proceedings of the 32nd ACM/IEEE International Conference on Software Engineering, pp. 275–284 (2010)
34. Coleman, G., O'Connor, R.: Using grounded theory to understand software process improvement: a study of Irish software product companies. Inf. Softw. Technol. **49**(6), 654–667 (2007)

35. Martin, A.M.: The role of customers in extreme programming projects. Ph.D. thesis. Victoria University of Wellington, New Zealand (2009)
36. Hoda, R.: Self-organizing agile teams : a grounded theory. Ph.D thesis. Victoria University of Wellington, New Zealand (2011)
37. Eisner, E.W.: The Enlightened Eye: Qualitative Inquiry and The Enhancement of Educational Practice. Prentice-Hall, Upper Saddle River (1998)
38. Maxwell, J.A.: Qualitative Research Design: An Interactive Approach. SAGE Publications, Thousand Oaks (2012)
39. Krznaric, R.: Empathy: Why It Matters, And How to Get It. Penguin Random House, New York (2014)

Towards an Effective and Efficient Management of Genome Data: An Information Systems Engineering Perspective

Alberto García S.[✉][iD], José Fabián Reyes Román[iD], Juan Carlos Casamayor, and Oscar Pastor[iD]

PROS Research Center, Universitat Politècnica de València, Valencia, Spain
{algarsi3,jreyes,jcarlos,opastor}@pros.upv.es

Abstract. The Genome Data Management domain is particularly complex in terms of volume, heterogeneity and dispersion, therefore *Information System Engineering* (ISE) techniques are strictly required. We work with the *Valencian Institute of Agrarian Research* (IVIA) to improve its genomic analysis processes. To address this challenge we present in this paper our *Model-driven Development* (MDD), conceptual modeling-based, experience. The selection of the most appropriate technology is an additional relevant aspect. NoSQL-based solutions where the technology that better fit the needs of the studied domain – the IVIA Research Centre using its Information System in a real-world industrial environment– and therefore used. The contributions of the paper are twofold: to show how ISE in practice provides a better solution using conceptual models as the basic software artefacts, and to reinforce the idea that the adequate technology selection must be the result of a practical ISE-based exercise.

Keywords: Conceptual modeling · Genomics · Neo4J · Data management

1 Introduction

Understanding the internals of the genome is one of the greatest challenges of our time. The complexity of the domain is tremendous and we have just begun to glimpse the vast knowledge we can extract it. Technology has improved over the years, allowing to sequencing in mass not only the genome of humans but of any organism at an increasingly lower cost. Not only the fast growing of the domain information, but the complexity, variety, variability or velocity makes it a Big Data domain. Special attention has been paid to the understanding of the human genome projected on the potential benefits on our health in the field of *Precision Medicine* (PM) [6]. But not only the study of the human genome can report us a benefit. Keeping the interest in the relationship between genotype and

© Springer Nature Switzerland AG 2019
C. Cappiello and M. Ruiz (Eds.): CAiSE Forum 2019, LNBIP 350, pp. 99–110, 2019.
https://doi.org/10.1007/978-3-030-21297-1_9

phenotype, the focus can be put on other species in order to achieve also relevant results. For instance, the improvement in food characteristics has a positive effect on our health. Increasing the concentration of vitamins or improving resistance to weather anomalies are just some examples of possible benefits [13]. Through the years, the costs of DNA sequencing have dropped severally. In 2017 the cost of sequencing a genome has reduced from 100 million dollars in 2007 to 1.000 dollars in 2018. This decreasing in cost has come with increasing speed of sequencing thanks to new techniques [11]. Because of these two factors, the amount of generated data is massive. As an example, the US healthcare system reached 150 exabytes in 2013 [18]. This high volume has followed *Conceptual Modelling* (CM) principles in a very limited way. The result is the existence of a very heterogeneous and disperse data from thousands of data sources. Each one of these data sources stores the information following its own defined structure. Great challenges arise and make necessary the execution of data science-oriented projects to integrate this heterogeneous data. Even though some standards are defined [7], most of the genomics data is mainly unstructured. Dealing with a variety of structured and non-structured data greatly increases complexity. These characteristics hinder the value of the data and make mandatory to accomplish complex data analysis tasks with the goal of extract the hidden value.

The IVIA Research Centre is a recognized centre of reference in the domain of Citrus genome data management [22]. Based on our previous experience on structuring the process of discovering relevant genomic information in the PM domain [14], in this paper we report our work on how their genomic studies methods and the corresponding data management strategies have been improved. This is what we mean by improving efficacy and efficiency from an *Information Systems Engineering* (ISE) perspective: firstly, to apply a rigorous CM process in order to identify and delimit the domain core concepts. This task is essential in such a complex and disperse domain. Secondly, to design and implement the corresponding *Information System* (IS) emphasizing the need to select the most appropriate data management technology.

To accomplish this goal, after this introduction the paper discusses in Sect. 2 the state of the art by studying how CM is applied to the genomic domain and how graph-oriented databases, our selected technology, are used in this domain. Section 3 describes the characteristics of the data that the IVIA manages, and how they are currently working with it, emphasizing the complexity of the working domain. Section 4 introduces the proposed solution, namely, a *Citrus Conceptual Schema* (CiCoS). This CiCoS is the key artefact used to design and develop the associated IS. Up to three types of representative complex queries are used to guide their genomic processes and the selection of the most appropriate data management technology. We present a brief real-world use case in which the schema is successfully used through the implementation of a prototype to obtain value from the data. Section 5 exposes the conclusions and future work.

2   State of the Art

We study the state of the art in two different fields. Firstly, we describe how CM is applied in the genomics domain in order to provide deep knowledge to generate value. Secondly, we study the use of Neo4J in the Genomic Data Management domain.

2.1   Conceptual Modeling in the Genomic Domain

The CM defines the activities of obtaining and describing the general knowledge needed for a particular IS [12]. The main goal of CM is to obtain that description, called *"conceptual schema"*. The conceptual schemas (CS) are written under so-called *"Conceptual Modelling Languages"* (CML). CM is an important part of requirement engineering, the first and most important phase in the development of an IS [1,12]. The use of this approach in previous work showed how CM grant a clear definition of the domain, allowing a deeper understanding of the involved activities and their relations. For this reason, it is widely accepted that using CM eases the comprehension of complex domains, namely, genomic domain. One of the first presented papers regarding the application of CM to the genome was written by Paton [17]. His work focused on describing the genome from different perspectives. These perspectives were the description of the genome of a eukaryote cell, the interaction between proteins, the transcriptome and other genomic components, though this work was discontinued.

CM has been also used to model proteins [19], which included a great amount of data with a deeply complex structure. This study was based on search and comparison through the 3D structure of a protein and this goal was easier to achieve thanks to the use of CM. Other approaches arose with the objective of representing genome concepts, i.e., the representation offered by GeneOntology[1]. It aims the unification of terms used on the genomic domain and obtains a thesaurus of terms (see more in [2]). Despite the huge amount of genomic data sources publicly available, it is not usual to find underlying stable CS. This is mainly caused because the accessible data is focused on the solution space and do not tackle the process of conceptualizing the analyzed domain. CM is not only used as an approach to describe and represent a specific domain but also helps on software production. Particularly, MDD has already been used on bioinformatic domain [16,20]. Gardwood et al. (2006) created user interfaces to examine biological data sources using MDD [9]. Note that CS are rare to find on the genomics domain. On the citrus domain, no other intent of defining a conceptual schema has been found.

The relational databases are a mature, stable and well-documented technology. It has been around several decades and can face and solve almost every use case. Nevertheless, relational databases struggle with highly interconnected data. Relational databases deal poorly with relationships. Relationships are generated at modelling time as a result of the execution of multiple joins over the tables.

---

[1] http://www.geneontology.org/.

As the model complexity and stored data size increases, so does the impact on performance. The more complex and interconnected is a domain, the more the efficiency will drop when interrogating that domain. This is caused, in part, by how relational databases physically store the relationships between entities, namely, by using *foreign keys*. The relational model makes some kind of queries very easy, and others more complex. Join tables add extra complexity since it mixes business data with foreign key metadata. Foreign key constraints add additional development and maintenance overhead. With exploratory queries, relations are translated into expensive join operations. This is even worse with recursive questions, where the complexity increases as the degree of recursion increases.

2.2   Graphs as Genomic Modelling Entities

Graph structure fits particularly well the genomic domain. Life can be modelled as a dense graph of several biological interactions that semantically represents the core concepts.

Pareja-Tobes et al. created Bio4J (2015) [15]. Bio4J is a bioinformatic graph platform that provides a framework for protein related information querying and management. It integrates most data available in Uniprot, Gene Ontology, UniRef, NCBI Taxonomy and Expasy Enzyme DB webs. Storing information on a graph-oriented solution allowed them to store and query in a way that semantically represents its own structure. McPhee et al. (2016) [10] used graph DB to record and analyse the entire genealogical history of a set of genetic programming runs and demonstrated the potential of Neo4J as a tool for exploring and analyzing a rich matrix of low-level events. Balaur et al. (2017) [3] used Neo4J to implement a graph database for colorectal cancer. This database is used to query for relationships between molecular −*genetic* and *epigenetic*− events observe at different stages of colorectal oncogenesis. They probed that graph DB facilitate the integration of heterogeneous and highly connected data over relational databases. Besides, it offers a natural representation of relationships among various concepts and helped to generate a new hypothesis based on graph-based algorithms. The same author created Recon2Neo4J, that offers a computational framework for exploring data from the Recon2 human metabolic reconstruction model (2017) [21]. Using graph-oriented DB facilitated the exploration of highly connected and comprehensive human metabolic data and eased the identification of metabolic subnetworks of interest.

As we can observe, bioinformatic and genomic domains rely heavily on graph database technology and in Neo4J in particular in a significant way. Neo4J is widely used in the genomic domain for the benefits it brings when modeling the information and eases working with complex and highly interconnected data. These examples show the usage of Neo4J as the technology to implement in the genomics context.

3   Data Characteristics and IVIA Context

The IVIA research centre has as main goals the development of plant improvement programs in order to obtain agricultural products with greater resilience and adaptation to increase their diversification and competitiveness. It has several lines of investigation and we collaborated with the one dedicated to obtaining, improvement and conservation of citrus varieties. They get new citrus varieties by irradiation and selection directed by genomic methods and establish phenotype-genotype *relations* through genomic analysis. They work with hundreds of citrus varieties and with a very heterogeneous and diverse set of external data sources. The studies they perform can be of two types. Firstly, to compare citrus groups to determine their differences at a DNA level and then try to establish a correlation with their phenotype: from genotype to phenotype. Secondly, starting from a protein, enzyme or pathway −*functional annotations*− of interest identify the variations that directly intervene with them: from phenotype to genotype. Based on these studies, three types of queries have been defined. The first one obtains differences on the genome of groups of citrus that have different characteristics −*phenotype*− from a global perspective to determine which variations cause these differences. The second one starts from a particular functional annotation and identifies only the variations that directly affect it. The third, unlike the first type of query, focuses the search not on the global genome but in very specific regions of interest. Two challenges arise. The first challenge is how to store and retrieve the data in a quick and, especially, cost-effective way; here lays the importance of selecting the right technology. The second challenge is to integrate all the heterogeneous data they work with in order to be able to extract and analyse it together. This heterogeneity leads to three different problems: technological heterogeneity, schema technology and instance heterogeneity. Based on these conflicts, three strategies can be used: (i) conflict ignoring, (ii) conflict-avoiding and (iii) conflict resolution [4].

The technological heterogeneity is resolved by integrating the data. The schema heterogeneity is resolved by defining a conceptual schema. This schema defines the final data structure and guides the data transformations. It acts as a global source of knowledge and helps on the process of resolving technological heterogeneity by easing the data science project. This conceptual schema is explained in more detail in Sect. 4.1. Regarding the instance heterogeneity, until now the strategy used to deal with was conflict ignoring. This changed to conflict resolution by the application of filters to allow scientists to dynamically remove not sufficiently truthful data from their analysis by defining parametrizable quality filters.

The objective is to extract knowledge by building genotype-phenotype relations in order to establish clear and direct relations between a desired or undesired effect and its genetic source. Let the following idea be a simple example to recognise the potential value of the data that is been working on: determine what variations cause acidness in a specific citrus variety and be able to revert that condition obtaining a sweeter version of that variety.

4   Proposed Solution

This section illustrates the generated conceptual schema (CiCoS), the result of an iterative process of discussions with the experts of PROS and IVIA Research centres, and the implemented IS, that is being used in a real industrial environment.

4.1   Citrus Conceptual Schema

CM has a vital role in the development of conforming applications. In a such a complex domain, the importance of accurately identifying and define concepts is essential. CM arises as the solution to properly generate the knowledge domain that is needed. The generated schema serves us as an ontological basis and provides all the necessary information. Several sessions were needed to implement the schema. On one hand, the IVIA experts provided their vast biological knowledge to correctly understand and interpret the available data. This knowledge allowed to successfully transform an immense amount of data into a well defined conceptual schema in order to extract value using data analysis. On the other hand, the PROS researchers provided their proved years of experience in CM to properly design and implement the conceptual model. In the course of these sessions, all data was carefully analyzed in order to identify the elements of higher importance. Through an iterative process multiple models where created and expanded until accomplishing a stable version. The resulting schema is a precise representation of the genomic domain tailored to the specific needs of the IVIA. This schema can be grouped into three main views: (i) *the functional annotation view*, (ii) *the structural view* and (iii) *the variations view*.

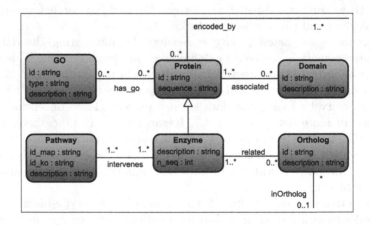

Fig. 1. Functional annotations view

On Fig. 1 the functional annotations view can be found. These view groups information related to functional annotations. Functional annotations are defined as every element that is related to a gene and has a specific function inside the biological domain (*main elements*). On this view auxiliary elements that add additional information (*secondary elements*) are also included. The objective of this view is to get effective information about how a gene interacts with the organism. Three main elements can be found, namely, the *proteins* −and the *enzymes*, by extension, since an enzyme is a type of protein− and the *pathways*. A protein can be understood as a molecule made of a set of amino acids that are physically arranged in a particular way. A pathway can be understood as chains of biological reactions that happen inside a cell and modifies it in some way. Secondary elements are *domains*, to characterize proteins, *GO* to specify protein functionality and *orthologs* that relates genes with a common ancestor with the enzyme that encode them.

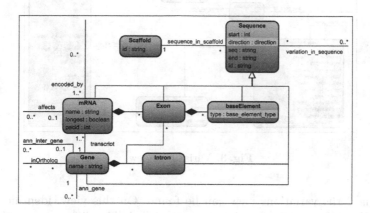

Fig. 2. Structural view

On Fig. 2 the structural view can be found. This view establishes a hierarchical structure of the identified genomic elements. This view is not intended to be a comprehensive organizational model but rather tries to ease the analysis process that will be carried on. The most important elements are the *gene* and the *messenger RNA (mRNA)* that is transcripted from the genes. These two elements act as hooks between the other two views. These elements are affected by the elements of the variations view and modify the behaviour of the elements of the functional annotations view. The elements move from general to specific, that is, from larger sequences to smaller ones. All these elements are a kind of sequence. A *sequence* is the parent of all the elements and allows us to abstract the structural hierarchy details from the variations view. Since a variation can be located in multiple sequences we can range between the level of specificity. These sequences are grouped into *scaffolds*. We can understand the concept of the scaffold as an equivalent of a chromosome although a scaffold does not contain the full chromosome sequence. Instead, it contains some gaps of known distance where the sequence content is unknown. On top of this organization, the gene and the mRNA can be found, a gene can be transcripted to multiple mRNAs and each mRNA translated into a protein. The second stage is formed by the *exon* and *intron* elements, the exon is the part of the gene that is transcripted while the intron is the part that is not transcripted. Finally, the third stage contains the so-called base elements. These elements are the parts that are part of an exon, namely the *coding sequence − CDS−*, the *5 prime untranslated region* and the *3 prime untranslated regions*.

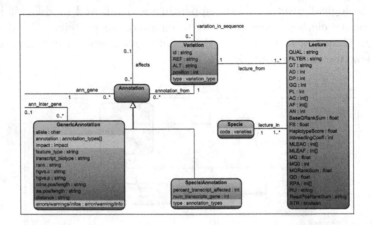

Fig. 3. Variations view

On Fig. 3 the variations view can be found. On this view, identified *variations* on the different citrus varieties are modelled. The different variations can be found in one or more citrus varieties and each occurrence has some values related to how the variation was identified and isolated. These values depend, among others, on the technology used to perform the sequencing, the curation filters and specific varieties characteristics such as the allele frequency or the allele depth. The variations are annotated using SnpEff software [5]. This software predicts the effect an *annotation* will produce on an organism. These annotations are incorporated into the model differentiating the different types of annotations the software can produce: the generic, most common, annotation, and *loss of functionality* −the variation produces a change that provokes a loss of functionality of the protein translated, also known as LOF− and *Nonsense mediate decay* −when the variation degrades the mRNA causing not to be translated into a protein, also known as NMD− annotations, represented as special annotations since they are rather rare. Generic annotations has an attribute called "*annotation_impact*" that determines the degree of impact of the variation.

4.2   Use Case: IVIA Research Centre Genomic Analysis

After developing the CiCoS, a prototype has been implemented. This prototype is being currently used by the IVIA Research Centre to perform genomic analysis in a real industrial environment. This helps us get feedback to improve and fine-tune the prototype to finally release a stable version. The prototype helps this analysis process by defining a set of queries that generate value from the stored data. The prototype can be defined as a web application that interacts with an API to execute the defined queries. For this example, we will focus on one of the three types of queries defined.

The data analysis process carried out on our genomic data has proven to be useful to properly identify core concepts of the domain and help in the process of generating effective knowledge, namely, genomic data value. We proceed to evince a use case where the implemented conceptual schema has helped to obtain valuable knowledge through the execution of the first query defined previously.

To detail more in-depth the chosen query, we start by defining two arbitrary groups of citruses. Typically, these groups will share some common characteristic, namely *sweetness* versus *acidness*. The goal is to determine how different the groups are from a genomic perspective. This objective is accomplished by finding which variations are present on one of the groups −the first− and not on the other one −the second−. The aim is to find variations present in all the varieties of the first group and not present in any of the varieties of the second group.

In order to fine-tune the query, we need to be able to apply restrictions regarding multiple parameters. Throughout the sequencing process, each variety comes characterized by a set of quality attributes that defines the degree of truthfulness of it. These attributes can be used to filter additional variations in order to be included or not on the sets depending on the degree of strictness we want to use. Three attributes are used for this purpose, namely, Approximate read depth, Conditional genotype quality and Allele Depth. More information about these attributes can be found at [7].

Additionally, there are three more criteria to filter variations. We refer to the concept of positional depth as the first criterion. It is used to filter variations based on their physical position. As seen on the structural view, multiple types of sequences are defined based on a hierarchical organization. It is of interest to filter variations based on any of the elements of the defined hierarchical organization. This additional filter allows the researchers to focus on more limited regions of the genome. There is another interesting point regarding data quality and the second criterion addresses it. Due to sequencing failures, false positives or false negatives may arise. To deal with these undesirable events, it is imperative to provide flexibility to the group selection: suppose two groups of varieties. We may want to indicate that the variations of interest must be present not in 100% varieties, but in 90% of them. Another possibility is that the variations may be present in at most one of the varieties where they should not appear. The third and last criterion deals with the degree of impact of a variation predicted by an annotation, making it possible to discard variations based on the impact they have on the varieties and allowing us to focus on critical, undefined or neutral variations.

The result is displayed on a table showing information about the selected variations, including the gene or genes they affect and the functional annotations related to that genes. A more detailed approach on how the data is displayed can be found in [8].

5   Conclusions and Future Work

The complexity of the problem that we have solved cannot be faced without using sound ISE techniques. We want to emphasize with our work that using an ISE perspective is essential to provide valid and efficient solutions to complex problems. We have done it working in two main directions. Firstly, the use of CM and MDD has facilitated the understanding of a given domain. Secondly, having a precise, well-defined and standardized conceptual base on which to discuss has eased the knowledge transference that the project required. These techniques also improve data and processes management and allow a more efficient exploitation.

After a study of the genomic domain, analyzing its characteristics and the available technologies, it has been determined that graph-oriented databases are the technological environment that better fits this domain. CM allowed us to define the key artefact to develop the associated IS. Using a technology that makes easier to manage the conceptual model of the relevant domain data allowed us to rapidly adapt and evolve the schema as the understanding of the domain increases. The Graph-oriented databases allow to *capture* and *model* the genomic domain in a more natural way since the domain is composed of highly interconnected interdependent data.

The generated IS is currently being used by the IVIA Research Centre to obtain valuable feedback to implement improvements that allow to speed up more their genomic analysis process. The objective is to extend the CiCoS with the IVIA researchers feedback. Likewise, we want to compare this schema with the PROS Research Centre *Conceptual Schema of the Human Genome* (CSHG) [20]. This will allows us to point out similarities and differences and start the process of unifying models in order to generate a conceptual schema of the genome (CSG) independent of the species.

Acknowledgments. This work was supported by the Spanish Ministry of Science and Innovation through Project DataME (ref: TIN2016-80811-P) and the Generalitat Valenciana through project GISPRO (PROMETEO/2018/176). The authors would like to thank members of the PROS Research Centre Genome group, the IVIA Research group, especially Manuel Talón and Javier Terol for the fruitful discussions and their valuable assistance regarding the application of CM in the genomics domain and José Marín Navarro for his advice and help.

References

1. Aguilera, D., Gómez, C., Olivé, A.: Enforcement of conceptual schema quality issues in current integrated development environments. In: Salinesi, C., Norrie, M.C., Pastor, Ó. (eds.) CAiSE 2013. LNCS, vol. 7908, pp. 626–640. Springer, Heidelberg (2013). https://doi.org/10.1007/978-3-642-38709-8_40

2. Ashburner, M., et al.: Gene ontology: tool for the unification of biology, May 2000. https://doi.org/10.1038/75556
3. Balaur, I., et al.: EpiGeNet: a graph database of interdependencies between genetic and epigenetic events in colorectal cancer. J. Comput. Biol. **24**(10), 969–980 (2017). https://doi.org/10.1089/cmb.2016.0095
4. Batini, C., Scannapieco, M.: Data and Information Quality. DSA. Springer, Cham (2016). https://doi.org/10.1007/978-3-319-24106-7
5. Cingolani, P., et al.: A program for annotating and predicting the effects of single nucleotide polymorphisms, SnpEff: SNPs in the genome of Drosophila melanogaster strain w1118; iso-2; iso-3. Fly **6**(2), 80–92 (2012)
6. Collins, F.S., Varmus, H.: A new initiative on precision medicine. N. Engl. J. Med. **372**(9), 793–795 (2015). https://doi.org/10.1056/NEJMp1500523
7. Danecek, P., et al.: The variant call format and VCFtools. Bioinformatics **27**(15), 2156–2158 (2011). https://doi.org/10.1093/bioinformatics/btr330
8. García Simón, A.: Gestión de datos genómicos basada en Modelos Conceptuales (2018). https://hdl.handle.net/10251/111666
9. Garwood, K., et al.: Model-driven user interfaces for bioinformatics data resources: regenerating the wheel as an alternative to reinventing it. BMC Bioinf. **7**(1), 532 (2006). https://doi.org/10.1186/1471-2105-7-532
10. Mcphee, N.F., Donatucci, D., Helmuth, T.: Using Graph Databases to Explore the Dynamics of Genetic Programming Runs, pp. 185–201 (2016). https://doi.org/10.1007/978-3-319-34223-8_11
11. NHGRI: DNA Sequencing Costs: Data - National Human Genome Research Institute (NHGRI) (2015). https://www.genome.gov/sequencingcostsdata/
12. Olive, A.: Conceptual Modeling of Information Systems, 1st edn. Springer, Heidelberg (2007)
13. Paine, J.A., et al.: Improving the nutritional value of Golden Rice through increased pro-vitamin a content. Nat. Biotechnol. **23**(4), 482–487 (2005). https://doi.org/10.1038/nbt1082
14. Palacio, A.L., López, Ó.P., Ródenas, J.C.C.: A method to identify relevant genome data: conceptual modeling for the medicine of precision. In: Trujillo, J.C., et al. (eds.) ER 2018. LNCS, vol. 11157, pp. 597–609. Springer, Cham (2018). https://doi.org/10.1007/978-3-030-00847-5_44
15. Pareja-Tobes, P., Pareja-Tobes, E., Manrique, M., Pareja, E., Tobes, R.: Bio4j: an open source biological data integration platform. In: Rojas, I., Guzman, F.M.O. (eds.) IWBBIO. p. 281. Copicentro Editorial (2013). http://iwbbio.ugr.es/papers/iwbbio_051.pdf
16. Pastor, O.: Conceptual modeling of life: beyond the homo sapiens. In: Comyn-Wattiau, I., Tanaka, K., Song, I.-Y., Yamamoto, S., Saeki, M. (eds.) ER 2016. LNCS, vol. 9974, pp. 18–31. Springer, Cham (2016). https://doi.org/10.1007/978-3-319-46397-1_2
17. Paton, N.W., et al.: Conceptual modelling of genomic information. Bioinformatics **16**(6), 548–557 (2000). https://doi.org/10.1093/bioinformatics/16.6.548
18. Pérez, J.A., Poon, C.C.Y., Merrifield, R.D., Wong, S.T.C., Yang, G.: Big data for health. IEEE J. Biomed. Health Inform. **19**(4), 1193–1208 (2015). https://doi.org/10.1109/JBHI.2015.2450362
19. Ram, S., Wei, W.: Modeling the semantics of 3D protein structures. In: Atzeni, P., Chu, W., Lu, H., Zhou, S., Ling, T.-W. (eds.) ER 2004. LNCS, vol. 3288, pp. 696–708. Springer, Heidelberg (2004). https://doi.org/10.1007/978-3-540-30464-7_52

20. Reyes Román, J.F.: Diseño y Desarrollo de un Sistema de Información Genómica Basado en un Modelo Conceptual Holístico del Genoma Humano. Ph.D. thesis, Universitat Politècnica de València (2018). https://riunet.upv.es/handle/10251/99565

21. Swainston, N., et al.: Recon 2.2: from reconstruction to modelof human metabolism. Metabolomics **12**(7), 109 (2016). https://doi.org/10.1007/s11306-016-1051-4

22. Wu, G.A., et al.: Genomics of the origin and evolution of Citrus. Nature **554**(7692), 311–316 (2018). https://doi.org/10.1038/nature25447

A Data Streams Processing Platform for Matching Information Demand and Data Supply

Jānis Grabis(✉), Jānis Kampars, Krišjānis Pinka, and Jānis Pekša

Institute of Information Technology, Riga Technical University,
Kalku 1, Riga 1658, Latvia
{grabis,janis.kampars,krisjanis.pinka,
janis.peksa}@rtu.lv

Abstract. Data-driven applications are adapted according to their execution context, and a variety of live data is available to evaluate this contextual information. The BaSeCaaS platform described in this demo paper provides data streaming and adaptation services to the data driven applications. The main features of the platform are separation of information requirements from data supply, model-driven configuration of data streaming services and horizontal scalable infrastructure. The paper describes conceptual foundations of the platform as well as design of data stream processing solutions where matching between information demand and data supply takes please. Light-weight open-source technologies are used to implement the platform. Application of the platform is demonstrated using a winter road maintenance case. The case is characterized by variety of data sources and the need for quick reaction to changes in context.

Keywords: Data stream · Adaptation · Context · Model-driven

1 Introduction

Data-driven applications (DDA) rely on data availability and intelligent processing to guide their execution. These applications have certain information demands, which can be formally described as their execution context. On the other hand modern information and communication technologies provide ample opportunities for data capture though organizations often struggle with applying these data [1], especially if different types of external data are used. The external data are often characterized by high level of volatility and lack of meta-information about their content and usefulness. The organizations might know their information needs while it is difficult to identify appropriate data sources and to transform data in a suitable form [2].

The Capability Driven Development methodology [3] addresses the aforementioned challenges of developing DDA. It provides methods and guidance to develop context-aware and adaptive applications. Computational tools have been developed to support the methodology. The BaSeCaaS platform described in this demo paper furthers development of tools specifically dealing with processing of data streams for

© Springer Nature Switzerland AG 2019
C. Cappiello and M. Ruiz (Eds.): CAiSE Forum 2019, LNBIP 350, pp. 111–119, 2019.
https://doi.org/10.1007/978-3-030-21297-1_10

needs of DDA. It is intended for application cases characterized by: (1) variety of stakeholders (i.e., data suppliers and information consumers); (2) distributed, volatile and heterogeneous data sources; (3) high volume data streams; (4) computationally demanding application adaptation algorithms; and (5) near real-time response. The main features of the BaSeCaaS are: (1) model-based specification of data streams processing requirements; (2) automated deployment of horizontally scalable data streams processing environment; (3) separation of information requirements and data sources; and (4) decoupling of computationally intensive DDAs adaptation logics from the core business logics.

The survey [4] of more than 30 data stream processing tools reveals that the field is mature though there is strong emphasis on using push based processing, processing languages have variable expressiveness and topology of systems is a concern of further research. Another survey [5] identifies requirements towards streaming tools and points out that processing language and historical/current data integration are two major limitations. These tools mainly address technical concerns while BaSeCaaS focuses on making data stream processing accessible to consumers. Similar concerns are addressed in [6] proposing a knowledge based approach to deal with data heterogeneity. Data markets and platforms [7] dealing with matching data consumers and providers are relatively early stages of development for data streaming applications.

The objective of these demo paper is to describe the overall design of BaSeCaaS and to demonstrate its application case. The platform supports model-driven development and it consists of three main layers, namely, modeling, service and infrastructure layers. The modeling layer is responsible for representing the data processing problem, the service layer implements data processing services and the infrastructure layer provides scalable computational resources of execution of the services. The platform is implemented using a set of open-source lightweight technologies. The application case considered deals with the winter road maintenance problem.

The rest of the paper is structured as follows. Section 2 describes conceptual foundations of the BaSeCaaS. The platform's application scenario is discussed in Sect. 3. Technological solutions are presented in Sect. 4 and a brief demonstration is provides in Sect. 5. Section 6 concludes.

2 Foundations

The platform is developed on the basis of the Capability Driven Development metamodel [3] and focuses on parts dealing with context processing. Figure 1 shows its key concepts. The information demand is defined using context elements (CE), where context characterizes DDA execution circumstance. The context elements are thought to have a clear business interpretation (i.e., they drive execution of the DDA). Adjustments define actions to be performed as a result of changes in the context what can be perceived as context dependent adaptation of the application. Raw observations of DDA execution circumstances are referred as to measurable properties (MP). They specify available data and often there is no clear idea about their usage. Context providers for MP are physical endpoints of the context acquisition channel in BaSeCaaS. They are used by providers to post context observations.

Relations among CE and MP are established using Context Calculation element, which specifies transformation of raw data streams into useful information. This way raw observations are decoupled from information consumption and the context calculations can be modified depending on data availability and other considerations. In the boundary case without available data providers, the DDA becomes a static application. Similarly, the Adjustment trigger binds adjustments with context. The adjustment is enacted if context elements assume specific values. The adjustments also use the context elements to determine an appropriate action.

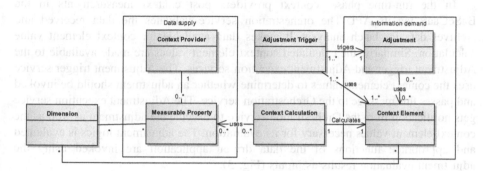

Fig. 1. Key concepts used in the BaSeCaaS platform

The data stream processing problem is tackled in two phases: (1) design time; and (2) run time. The design time phase (Fig. 2) deals with definition of the data processing problem following a model-driven approach. On the demand side, information requirements are represented as context elements and context-aware adaptation of DDA

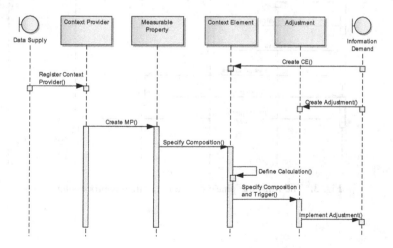

Fig. 2. The design phase of data streams processing

is specified using adjustments. On the supply side, context data providers are registered with the platform and appropriate MP are specified. As indicated above, the demand and supply sides are linked via context calculations and MP used to calculate CE are specified and joint together by creating context element composition (i.e., rules for joining multiple streams). In the context calculation, the MP are filtered by using sliding window and aggregation functions. The context calculations can be specified in a form of rules or arbitrary calculations. The adjustments implement the adaptation logics of data driven applications and passes decisions made onto these applications via their interfaces. That allows of target application independent modification and execution of computationally demanding and volatile adaptive functions.

In the run-time phase, context providers post context measurements in the BaSeCaaS via its API. The orchestration service validates the data received and archives data for batch analysis. It makes data available for context element value calculation. Similarly, the calculated context element values are made available to the Adjustment trigger and Adjustment execution services. The Adjustment trigger service uses the context element values to determine whether an adjustment should be invoked and passes this message to the Orchestration service. The Adjustment execution service gets notification from the Orchestration service to execute the adjustment as well as the context element values necessary for its evaluation. The adjustment logics is evaluated and appropriate functions of the data driven application are invoked using the adjustment evaluation results as inputs (Fig. 3).

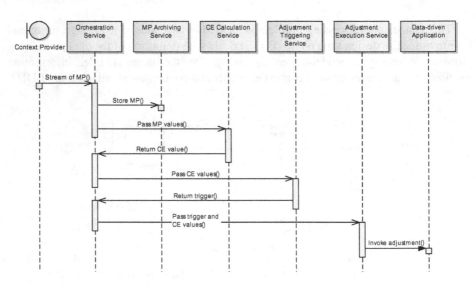

Fig. 3. The run-time phase of the data streams processing

3 Scenario

The application case considered is winter road maintenance (WRM) [8]. The case is characterized by the need for timely reaction to changes in road conditions due to snow and icing. The delayed action might cause traffic accidents with severe consequences. Additionally, there are many information consumers ranging from road maintenance and emergency services to drivers. From the data supply perspective, there is a diversity of data sources. The bulk of data are provided by field surveying, which has relatively low frequency and varying coverage. There are road monitoring weather-stations and cameras operated by different entities. Their data are comprehensive though limited to major sections of the road network. In the case of insufficient coverage, non-conventional data sources such as mobile fleet and crowd-sourced data.

As an example the following information needs are considered:

- Road conditions – road conditions characterize visual appearance of the road with possible values Bare, Partly Covered and Covered;
- Driving conditions – forecasting driving conditions with values Good, Fair, Caution and Poor;
- Recommended speed – depending on road conditions speed limit is changed;
- Snow removal needs – the level of urgency of the snow removal.

The adjustments defined are:

- Snow removal prompt – depending on snow removal needs a road maintenance company receives a notification;
- Change recommended speed – depending on recommended speed information is changed in smart road signs;
- Road conditions warning – depending on road conditions, on-line road maps are updated;
- Driving conditions warning – depending on driving conditions notification to drivers and other stakeholders are provided.

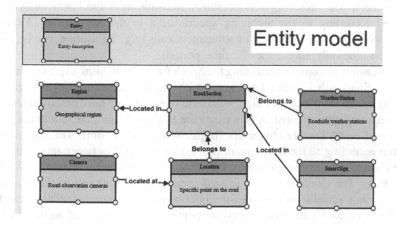

Fig. 4. The entity model as specified in the BaSeCaaS platform

The entities defining the WRM problem are specified in the Entity model (Fig. 4). The road maintenance is performed for specific Road Sections belonging to a Region. There are smart road signs (SmartSigns) providing information for the whole road section as well as weather-stations. The road cameras are installed at specific locations. There is a number of MP. For instance, driving conditions are evaluated according to temperature and precipitation MP provided by road side weather-stations as well as weather service. However, the weather service provides data only at the regional level. Aggregation of measurements is performed according to the relations specified in the entity model.

The BaSeCaaS platform is domain-independent and can be used various use cases. Management of distributed data centers and identification of security threats also has been analyzed.

4   Technical Solution

The technical solution underlying BaSeCaaS consists of three layers (Fig. 5). The platform is model-driven and both information demand and data supply are specified in a form of data models. MP and CE characterize certain entities in the problem domain. These entities and their relationships are defined in the entity model (Fig. 4). MP and CE are also specified and there is a number of predefined filtering, sliding and aggregation functions. Every entity has several instances and entities are used to define dimensions of MP and CE while instances are used as dimensions' indices. For example, entity is a weather-station and MP is temperature, then a single data stream contains temperature values from multiple weather-stations (i.e., instances of the entity). If several data streams are used to compute values of CE or Adjustment trigger then composition models are used to specify the way data streams are joined together. The joint is made along the matching dimensions.

The models are used to configure services. The Orchestration service controls stream processing workflow and ensures delivery of data streams from publishers to subscribers. Messaging topics are created according to the model as well as subscribers and publishers. MP archiving service stores measurements for batch analysis. It is configured according to the archiving specification in the MP model. Adjustment locking service controls frequency of adjustment calls (e.g., adjustment can be invoked for the next time only after a specific time period).

The streaming is implemented using the Spark framework (https://spark.apache.org). A separate Spark job is created for every MP and CE according to the data stream processing model. In the case of high, workload these jobs are horizontally scaled in the cloud computing environment. Adjustments are evaluated using the Computing cluster implemented using Docker containers (https://www.docker.com). The containers are also setup according to the data stream processing model. Containerization allows for flexible choice of adjustment implementation technologies and scalability of intensive computations. The Queuing service is implemented using Kafka (https://kafka.apache.org) supporting scalable processing of high volume data streams. Casandra (http://cassandra.apache.org/) database is used for persistent data storage of archived MP.

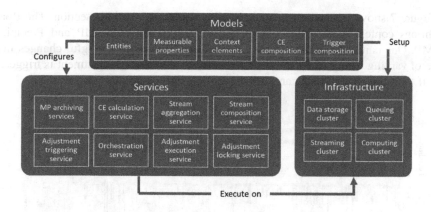

Fig. 5. Layers of the BaSeCaaS platform

5 Demonstration

The WRM case is implemented as demonstration following the design process as showed in Fig. 2. Figure 6a shows the winter road maintenance CE created in the system as well as dialogs for specifying context element composition and calculation. A Spark job is created for every context element. For instance, the context element DrivingConditionsCE is created to characterize current perception of driving condition ranging from normal to poor. This context element is mainly used to provide warnings to various stakeholders. These warnings are implemented as adjustments (Fig. 6b). RoadConditionsWarrningAdj sends a message to the data driven application that context has changed. The triggering rule depends on value of the context elements as specified in the trigger composition. The adjustments can be frozen for a specific period to avoid excessive messaging. The adjustment can be implemented using various technologies and JavaScript is used in this case. The event log keeps trace of adjustments invoked. It is important to note that different data driven applications might need different responses to changes in the context and the platform is able to provide specific adjustments. The adjustments are not limited notifications and complex adaptive logics can be specified within their containers. In the road maintenance case, one of the adjustments evaluates a need to deice the roads.

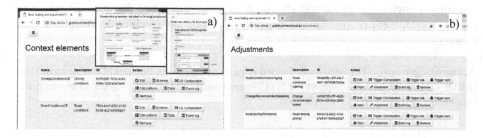

Fig. 6. Definition of (a) context elements and (b) adjustments in the BaSeCaaS platform

Figure 7 shows context element evaluation results for one road section. The Road conditions context element is computed using MP TemperatureMP and PrecipitationMP. One can observe continuous changes of MP while meaningful changes in a sense of varying values of CE occur more rarely. The warning adjustment is triggered only if the locking conditions are met preventing unnecessary nervousness.

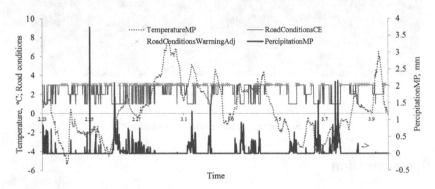

Fig. 7. Sample MP measurements and CE evaluation results for a selected road section

6   Conclusion

BaSeCaaS simplifies development of data streams processing solutions. It supports model driven specification of key data streams processing functions, configuration of streaming services and automated setup of infrastructure. These are important preconditions for making data streams processing as widely used as classical data processing. CE represent information needs in DDA while MP represent data supply. Various combinations of MP can be used to evaluate CE depending on data availability, privacy, business and other considerations. The adjustments are decoupled from DDA to separate intensive computations and frequently changing adaptation logics from the core application. The platform is also horizontally scalable. Application of the proposed platform has been preliminary also for security monitoring in federated computer networks and providing real-time support to users of enterprise applications. The model driven configuration is restricted to the implemented set of stream processing functions. It is not intended to support all types of stream processing functions out-of-the-box rather branching of the platform for specific application cases or domains is envisioned to support custom requirements. One of the main directions of future development of pre-defined adjustments based on machine learning and data mining.

Acknowledgements. This study was funded in parts by European Regional Development Fund (ERDF), Measure 1.1.1.5 "Support for RTU international cooperation projects in research and innovation". Project No. 1.1.1.5/18/I/008.

References

1. Philip Chen, C.L., Zhang, C.: Data-intensive applications, challenges, techniques and technologies: a survey on Big Data. Inf. Sci. **275**, 314–347 (2014)
2. L'Heureux, A., Grolinger, K., Elyamany, H.F., Capretz, M.A.M.: Machine learning with big data: challenges and approaches. IEEE Access **5**, 7776–7797 (2017)
3. Sandkuhl, K., Stirna, J.: Capability Management in Digital Enterprises. Springer, Cham (2018). https://doi.org/10.1007/978-3-319-90424-5
4. Cugola, G., Margara, A.: Processing flows of information: from data stream to complex event processing. ACM Comput. Surv. **44**, 3 (2012)
5. Gorawski, M., Gorawska, A., Pasterak, K.: A survey of data stream processing tools. In: Czachórski, T., Gelenbe, E., Lent, R. (eds.) Information Sciences and Systems 2014, pp. 295–303. Springer, Cham (2014). https://doi.org/10.1007/978-3-319-09465-6_31
6. Esposito, C., Ficco, M., Palmieri, F., Castiglione, A.: A knowledge-based platform for big data analytics based on publish/subscribe services and stream processing. Knowl.-Based Syst. **79**, 3–17 (2015)
7. Auer, S., et al.: The BigDataEurope platform – supporting the variety dimension of big data. In: Cabot, J., De Virgilio, R., Torlone, R. (eds.) ICWE 2017. LNCS, vol. 10360, pp. 41–59. Springer, Cham (2017). https://doi.org/10.1007/978-3-319-60131-1_3
8. Dey, K.C., Mishra, A., Chowdhury, M.: Potential of intelligent transportation systems in mitigating adverse weather impacts on road mobility: a review. IEEE Trans. Intell. Transp. Syst. **16**, 1107–1119 (2015)

Co-location Specification for IoT-Aware Collaborative Business Processes

Paul Grefen[1]([⊠]), Nadja Brouns[1], Heiko Ludwig[2],
and Estefania Serral[3]

[1] Eindhoven University of Technology, Eindhoven, Netherlands
p.w.p.j.grefen@tue.nl
[2] IBM Almaden Research, San José, CA, USA
[3] KU Leuven, Louvain, Belgium

Abstract. Technologies from the Internet of Things (IoT) create new possibilities to directly connect physical processes in the 'real' world to digital business processes in the administrative world. Objects manipulated in the real world (the 'things' of IoT) can directly provide data to digital processes, and these processes can directly influence the behavior of the objects. An increasing body of work exists on specifying and executing the interface between the physical and the digital worlds for *individual* objects. But many real-life business scenarios require that the handling of *multiple* physical objects is synchronized by digital processes. An example is the cross-docking of sea containers at ports: here we have containers, ships, cranes and trucks that are all 'things' in the IoT sense. Cross-docking processes only work when these 'things' are properly co-located in time and space. Therefore, we propose an approach to specify this co-location in multi-actor, IoT-aware business process models, based on the concept of spheres. We discuss consistency checking between co-location spheres and illustrate our approach with container cross-docking processes.

Keywords: Internet of Things · Business process · Location specification · Time specification · Co-location

1 Introduction

The concept of the Internet of Things (IoT) aims at the integration of physical 'things' (physical objects with sensors and/or actuators) with digital information processing in the Internet, thereby arriving at a highly distributed, cyber-physical information system. IoT technologies bring new possibilities to directly connect physical processes in the 'real' world to digital business processes in the administrative world. Objects manipulated in the real world (the 'things' of IoT) can directly provide data to the digital processes using various kinds of sensors. Activities in digital business processes can directly influence the behavior of physical objects through various kinds of actuators. For the handling of individual physical objects in digital processes, an increasing body of work exists that shows how to specify and execute the interface between the physical and the digital worlds. But many real-life business scenarios require that the handling

© Springer Nature Switzerland AG 2019
C. Cappiello and M. Ruiz (Eds.): CAiSE Forum 2019, LNBIP 350, pp. 120–132, 2019.
https://doi.org/10.1007/978-3-030-21297-1_11

of multiple physical objects is synchronized by digital processes. We see this for example in real-time manufacturing [Gre17] and in intelligent transport systems for urban mobility [Lu18]. Another domain is logistics. We elaborate an example from this domain in this paper: cross-docking of sea containers at ports. In the example process, we have containers, ships, cranes and trucks that are all 'things' in the IoT sense – and cross-docking processes only work when these 'things' are properly coordinated in space and time. This coordination should take place in a hard real-time fashion and with a high level of automation. Hard real-time processing is important to not have process management slow down physical processes – in physical processes, 'time is money'. A high level of automation is required because many of these scenarios process large amounts of physical objects and hence require large numbers of instances of IoT-aware business processes. To illustrate this with numbers from sea container example: in 2016, the Port of Rotterdam handled approximately 7.4 million sea containers [PoR17] and a single large container ship can transport over 10,000 large (40 foot) sea containers.

In this paper, we propose a novel approach to specify physical co-location in models of inter-organizational, collaborative business processes. In these processes, multiple actors (business organizations or parts thereof) physically and digitally collaborate to achieve a common goal. We re-use the concept of 'sphere' that was developed to group activities in process specifications that are related through transactional characteristics. We re-apply the concept in a novel way to group steps in multi-actor process models that are related through IoT characteristics. We apply our conceptual approach in process specification languages like BPMN. We illustrate our approach with the mentioned application of cross-docking containers.

2   Related Work

We discuss related work from three perspectives. The first perspective is the confluence of the domains of business process management (BPM) and the internet of things (IoT), which is the context of this paper. Secondly, we discuss the perspective of specifying time and location attributes in information system models, which is the aspect of the confluence we address. The third perspective is the use of the concept of sphere, as this is the basis for the approach that we propose in this paper.

Confluence of BPM and IoT. As discussed, there is a confluence of digital and physical business processes in many application domains. But the worlds of BPM (traditionally concerned with highly digital processes) and IoT (traditionally concerned with rather isolated activities involving physical entities) are still weakly connected. Consequently, the need for research on the combination of BPM and IoT has been explicitly confirmed [Jan17]. There is some work already available though. Work has been performed on specification of IoT-aware business processes, typically concentrating on extending existing business process specification languages with elements that can cater for physical objects, e.g. [Ser15]. Another example project is the European IoT-A project. An overview of the current state of the art in this field is given in a recent research report [Bro18]. Other work deals with business processes that handle physical objects without a very explicit reference to IoT, for example projects that address the digital support for complex transport and logistics processes. An effort in this class is the GET Service European project, which addresses the near-real time planning of processes for synchro-modal container logistics [Bau15]. The IoT character of the processes is however not explicitly reflected in the business process models, but in the complex event processing mechanism that provides business process management with decision information.

Specifying Time and Location. In the field of information systems, there have been various proposals for the specification of time and location attributes of activities. To the best of our knowledge, the most elaborate approaches have their origins in the world of ontologies. To specify temporal attributes of activities, the OWL Time Ontology [W317] provides an elaborate framework. The standard provides elements for the specification of temporal attributes of individual activities, but also elements for the specification of relations between temporal elements, such as 'interval overlaps'. To specify location attributes of activities, the W3C Geospatial Ontologies [W307] provide an elaborate framework. As with the Time Ontology, many primitives in this standard address individual location. The standard briefly discusses coordinate reference systems or spatial reference grids to denote individual geographic relations. But the W3C standard also covers (geo-)spatial or 2D topological relationships, which are related to the geographic co-locations we discuss in this paper. Neither of the two discussed ontological standards are applied in the context of automated support for multi-actor business processes.

Using Spheres to Group Activities. The concept of sphere has been proposed to specify semantic coherence of activities in business processes. It has mainly been applied in complex transaction management in database applications. One of the early concepts is that of *saga* [Gar87] to denote a set of transactions that together form a higher-level transaction with relaxed transactional. In this work, sagas can be seen as transactional spheres. This concept is extended in the two-layer approach to transaction management developed in the WIDE project [Gre97]. In this approach, business process models are annotated with two levels of spheres, where the higher level denotes global transactions with loose properties (based on the saga concept) and the lower level (which is nested in the higher level) denotes local transactions with strict properties. This transactional approach was later extended to be applied in dynamic service outsourcing [Von03]. In our current work, we use the concept of spheres in business processes for a different purpose: not for transactional characteristics, but for physical co-location properties of activities in collaborative business processes.

3   A Motivating Case

As announced in the introduction of this paper, we take our motivating case from container logistics. This is a business domain with complex business processes that have both a digital (administrative) and a physical (container handling) aspect. For the sake of brevity, we limit the scope of our case in this paper to the unloading process of a container in an international sea port like Rotterdam. A simplified overview of this process is shown in Fig. 1. Note that the model is simplified as process starts, ends and alternative paths have been omitted – but these are not essential to the line of reasoning in this paper. In this figure, we see a process with five pools, where each pool represents an actor in the process: an intelligent sea container (with an on-board IoT computing unit), a crane that unloads containers from docked ships (*Crane1*), an automated guided vehicle that transports containers from the quay to a holding location (*AGV*), a crane that unloads containers from AGVs (*Crane2*) and the customs office that inspects the contents of containers (for the sake of simplicity, we assume that every container is inspected).

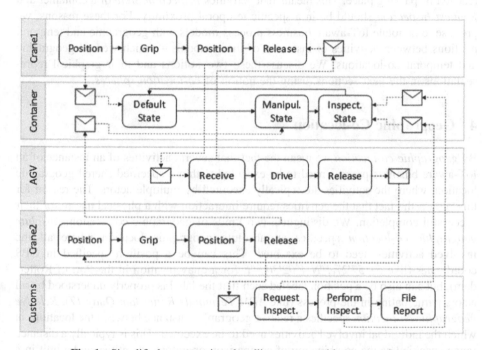

Fig. 1. Simplified sea container handling process with message flows

The container can be in a *Default State* (e.g. during sea transport), in which it reports its status on a periodic basis or an exceptional basis (for example when it is moved unexpectedly), but it also has active states: the *Manipulated State* in which it expects to be moved (and will not raise an exception because of this) and the *Inspected State* in which it will unlock its doors and deactivate its tampering detectors for a specific period of time. The figure also shows message flows between activities. All messages in this case are IoT messages: they are automatically generated machine-to-machine messages. For example, activity *Position* of *Crane1* sends a message to the *Container* to request a transfer from *Default State* to *Manipulated State*. Activity *Release* of *Crane2* sends a message to the *Container* to notify that it can leave *Manipulated State*. The *Container* now knows it can go into *Inspected State*, which is actually activated by a message from the activity *Request Inspection* of *Customs*.

Apart from the fact that most activities and all messages in Fig. 1 have an IoT connotation, the process model looks like a 'traditional' business process. The IoT connotation has important implications, though, because physical activities are being executed. For example, a container cannot be gripped by a crane when it is out of physical reach of that crane – a problem that does not occur in traditional business processes where objects are digital. In the example, the execution of activities *Grip* of the crane and *Manipulated State* of the container must be executed in a specific geographic proximity. Also, timing is an important issue when dealing with physical objects. For example, we want a container inspected by customs soon after it has reached its parking place. This means that activities *Inspection State* of a container and *Request Inspection* should be in a specific temporal proximity. For these reasons, we propose to annotate IoT-aware business process models with geographic and temporal relations between activities of instances of these models – which we call geographic and temporal co-locations. We discuss these two notions and their graphical representations in the next sections, using the notion of *co-location spheres*.

4 Geographic Co-location

By *geographic co-location* we mean the fact that several activities of an instance of an IoT-aware business process need to be executed within a specified shared geographic location, where the activities are typically executed by multiple actors. The reason for this need is the fact that the activities require interaction with a physical nature for their successful completion. We distinguish two kinds of geographic co-location. *Absolute geographic co-location* specifies an absolute geographic location where all the involved activities need to be executed. This can be a position specified in GPS coordinates (like *51°57'27.1"N 4°02'30.5"E* for a quay position in the Port of Rotterdam), but can also be a position labeled such that the label is properly understood by all actors participating in the process (like *APM Terminals Rotterdam Quay 17*). *Relative geographic co-location* specifies a relative geographic distance between the locations at which the individual involved activities need to be executed. This is typically a distance range specified as the combination of comparison operators, quantities and a unit in a metric length system (like *between* 2 *and* 12 m). Both types of geographic co-location can be combined with an exception handler: a specification of the action that must take place if the co-location constraint is violated.

We graphically represent geographic co-location in a process model using *spheres* that are drawn as regions around the involved process activities. As co-location often involves multiple actors in a process, these spheres are often drawn across two or more process pools. Geographic co-location spheres are indicated with a single location pin symbol for absolute co-location and a double location pin symbol for relative co-location. The symbols are parameterized with a location indication for absolute co-location or a distance indication for relative co-location, and optionally an exception handler label. Examples of geographic co-location in our example case are shown in Fig. 2. In this figure, we have omitted the message flows of Fig. 1 to avoid clutter. The figure contains two relative geographic co-location spheres and one absolute sphere. The first relative sphere specifies that the activities for moving a container from a ship must take place between 5 and 25 m from each other, as this is the operating reach of the specific crane type. The absolute location is not relevant here, as there are many quays and cranes in the port that can be used. The second relative sphere specifies that for moving a container from an AGV, the distance must be between 2 and 10 m, as a smaller crane is used here. We use the symbol γ to indicate geographic distance. Both relative spheres specify *restart* as the exception handler (indicated by the exclamation mark symbol): the activities in the sphere must be restarted if the co-location constraint is violated. The absolute sphere specifies that the container should be released and inspected at the custom grounds (*CustGrnd*). Here, the symbol γ is used to indicate geographic location and the @-symbol is followed by a specification of that location. The exception handler here is *alarm*, indicating that process monitoring must be escalated to a human decision maker.

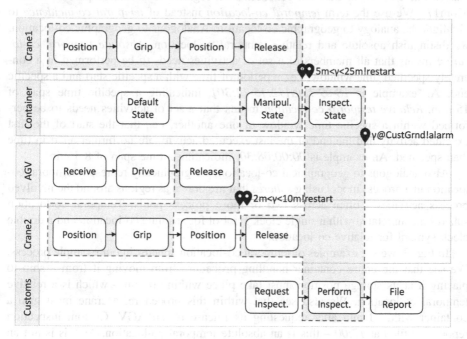

Fig. 2. Geographic co-location specification in case process

For the specification of a geographic co-location, we use the simple syntax shown below, formulated in production rules (following BNF convention [Wik19]): pointy brackets denote non-terminals, symbols in quotes denote terminals, square brackets denote optional elements and a vertical line denotes choice.

```
<GeoCoLoc>      ::= (<AbsGeoCoLoc> | <RelGeoCoLoc>) ["!" <ExceptionHandlerID>]
<AbsGeoCoLoc>   ::= "γ" "@" <AbsLoc>
<AbsLoc>        ::= <AbsLocID> | <AbsLocGPS>
<RelGeoCoLoc>   ::= [<Distance> "<"] "γ" ["<" <Distance>]
<Distance>      ::= <Number> <DistanceUnit>
```

The syntax can be extended to grow towards a more complete framework, like the W3C Geospatial Ontologies [W307] (see Sect. 2). It can be converted to XML for easy integration with business process specification languages like BPMN or BPEL.

5 Temporal Co-location

We use the concept of *temporal co-location* to specify that activities of an IoT-aware business process instance should be performed in a shared time window, where the activities are typically executed by multiple actors, i.e., are in different process model pools. Note that this is a more general concept than the notion of temporal constraints on consecutive tasks in process models, which is already supported by existing languages like BPMN, or duration constraints on regions of structured process models [Com17]. We use the term *temporal co-location* instead of *temporal co-incidence* to highlight the analogy to geographic co-location. Analogous to geographic co-location, we distinguish absolute and relative temporal co-location. *Absolute temporal co-location* means that all members of a set of activities needs to be performed in a concretely specified time window, i.e., a period of time with a specific start and a specific end. An example is *18-09-18@[12:15-12:30]*, indicating a specific time span of 15 min. *Relative temporal co-location* means that a set of activities needs to be performed within a specific time window of one another, i.e., that the start of the first executed activity and the end of the last executed activity are no further apart in time than specified. An example is *00:00:08:30*, indicating a time span of 8.5 min.

Also analogous to geographical co-location, we graphically represent temporal co-location in a process model using *spheres* that are drawn as regions around the involved process activities - often across two or more process pools. Temporal co-location spheres are annotated with a single clock symbol for absolute co-location and a double clock symbol for relative co-location.

In Fig. 3, we see examples of temporal co-location spheres in our example process. We see that the entire container handling procedure from moving it from a ship to placing it at its storage position must take place within 60 min – which is a relative temporal co-location. We also see that within this procedure, a crane must grip a container within 1 min after requesting its release by an AGV. Custom inspection reports are filed at *17:00* – this is an absolute temporal co-location. As this is not an action the failure of which will leave physical objects in an undesirable state, there is no exception handling here.

From Fig. 3, we can observe that absolute spheres can contain only a single activity (for relative spheres this obviously doesn't make sense). Although strictly speaking, this is not co-location, we do not exclude this to provide more modeling freedom. We can also observe that spheres can overlap – we address this topic in the next section.

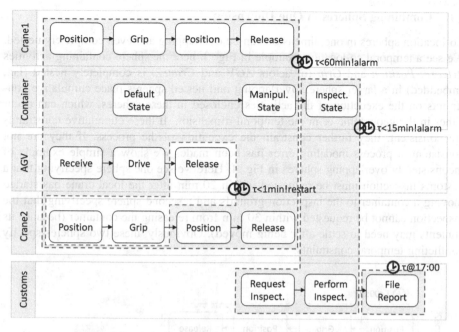

Fig. 3. Temporal co-location specification in case process

Similar to geographic co-location, we can use a simple syntax to specify temporal co-location expressions:

```
<TempCoLoc>        ::= (<AbsTempCoLoc> | <RelTempCoLoc>) ["!" <ExceptionHandlerID>]
<AbsTemoCoLoc>     ::= "τ" "@" <AbsTemp>
<AbsTemp>          ::= <AbsTempID> | <AbsTempSpec>
<AbsTempSpec]      ::= [<date>] "," [<time]
<RelTempCoLoc>     ::= [<TimePeriod> "<"] "τ" ["<" <TimePeriod>]
<TimePeriod>       ::= <Number> <TimeUnit>
```

The syntax can be extended to grow towards a more complete framework, like the OWL Time Ontology [W317], and can be converted to XML for easy integration with business process specification languages.

6   Combining Spheres

So far, we have mainly looked at individual co-location spheres: we have seen multiple spheres in one IoT-aware business process model, but these spheres are (mostly) semantically (and pragmatically) independent. When spheres overlap though, they become semantically (and possibly pragmatically) related. This can occur both within one co-location dimension and in the combination of the two dimensions of space and time. We discuss both cases in this section.

6.1   Combining Spheres in One Dimension

Co-location spheres in one dimension can be overlapping and even completely nested. We see a temporal co-location example in Fig. 3: here the sphere containing activities *Release*, *Position* and *Grip* (of actors *AGV* and *Crane2*) is completely nested (i.e., embedded) in a larger sphere. Overlapping and nested spheres place cumulative constraints on the execution of the activities enclosed in these spheres, which can occur either in the geographic or in the temporal dimension. If these cumulative constraints are consistent, they further constrain the execution of the process. If they are not consistent, a process modeling error has been made. We show a simple example of inconsistently overlapping spheres in Fig. 4. Here we see one sphere specifying that a customs inspection must be requested within 20 min after the local crane has started moving a container to the inspection grounds and a second sphere specifying that the inspection cannot be requested within 30 min from releasing the container (because its contents may need to settle after being moved). Obviously, these two spheres specify conflicting temporal constraints.

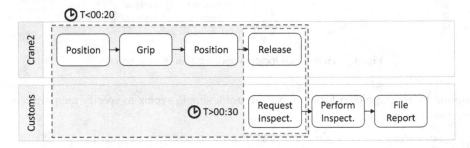

Fig. 4. Inconsistent temporal co-location spheres

6.2   Combining Spheres in Multiple Dimensions

We have respectively discussed the notions of geographical and temporal co-location spheres, representing physical activity co-location in two dimensions: place and time. For complete specification of IoT-aware business processes, we need to combine these two notions. Put simply, it implies the superposition of two sets of spheres from different dimensions. Although two dimensions are in principle orthogonal, the superposition may introduce semantic or pragmatic inconsistencies if spheres overlap. A typical example is the case where relative temporal co-location specifies that a pair of activities should be executed within a time window t, whereas geographical co-location specifies that the pair activities should be executed with a minimum distance d, in a situation where it is impossible to bridge d within t.

We show a stylized example of this situation in Fig. 5. Here we see that a container must be picked up by an AGV at *Dock12*, handled after delivery by the AGV at *Customs*, and that the inspection request by customs must be performed within 10 min after loading the container onto the AGV. Although this model is syntactically and semantically correct, it is pragmatically inconsistent if the distance between *Dock12*

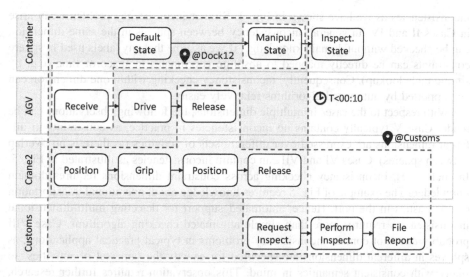

Fig. 5. Co-location spheres with inter-dimensional pragmatic inconsistency

and Customs *cannot* be driven by the AGV within 10 min (note that port grounds in locations like Rotterdam are fairly large).

6.3   Checking Consistency Between Spheres

In checking consistency between spheres, several cases arise depending on the number of dimensions involved and the way the spheres overlap. We give an overview of the possibilities for two spheres *s1* and *s2* in Table 1 – we limit the discussion here to two spheres for reasons of simplicity. The rows of the table indicate the cases in which the spheres are both defined in a single co-location dimension, or each is defined in a different dimension (we have discussed only two dimensions so far, but more are possible, as we discuss in the conclusions). The columns indicate the way the spheres overlap in terms of the activities they contain: not at all, partial overlap without embedding, embedding (subset relation), equality (contain exactly the same activities). In total, we have eight cases.

Table 1. Possible combinations of two spheres $s1$ and $s2$

Dimension(s)	$s1 \cap s2 = \emptyset$	$s1 \cap s2 \neq \emptyset$	$s1 \subset s2$	$s1 = s2$
Single	I	II	III	IV
Multiple	V	VI	VII	VIII

With respect to the cases involving a single dimension, we can make the following observations. Case I is in general 'harmless' with respect to inconsistencies, but may contain inconsistencies if absolute time constraints are used in temporal co-location spheres in which activities are linked by process control flow. Case III can contain inconsistencies as we have shown in Fig. 4. Similar inconsistency problems can arise in Cases II and IV. In general, inconsistency between spheres in the same dimension can be checked without domain knowledge, if we assume that any labels used in sphere constraints can be directly mapped to absolute coordinates in space or time (e.g. by simple table lookup). Consequently, inconsistency checking within one dimension can be supported by automated algorithms relatively easily.

With respect to the cases in multiple dimensions, the following observations can be made. Case V typically contains no inconsistencies in practice, as constraints in different dimensions are expressed over different sets of activities (as there is no overlap between spheres). Cases VI and VII can contain inconsistencies as illustrated in Fig. 5. In such cases, inconsistency checking across constraint dimensions requires domain knowledge. The example of Fig. 5 requires knowledge about operational transportation characteristics in the port. Hence, automated support for detecting multi-dimensional inconsistencies requires more than simple automated checking algorithms. Case VIII probably does not contain inconsistency problems in typical practical applications, as spheres in different dimensions are specified for exactly the same set of activities, so likely with consistent semantics in mind. This observation requires further research, however – certainly for complex cases where the equality of spheres in terms of activities they contain can be a mere coincidence. Consistency checking for Case VIII will be simpler than for Cases VI and VII as the conjunction of sphere conditions is the same for all activities in both spheres.

7 Conclusion and Future Work

In this paper, we introduce the concept of geographic and temporal *co-location* of activities in an IoT-aware business process. The concept of co-location is required to specify that 'things' participating in business processes need to 'meet each other' in space and time to produce specific effects. The 'meeting point' can be specified in an absolute or relative way. We are aware that introducing these concepts into IoT-aware business processes adds to their complexity. In our container handling example, the full process specification emerges when we 'super-impose' Figs. 1, 2 and 3 (and this is a simplified process to start with). But cyber-physical business processes in practice are complex – and executing them in an automated way requires dealing with this complexity. Consequently, the adoption of our approach in real practice will require adequate support for design, specification and validation of processes.

In future work, the approach presented in this paper will be extended. A first extension will be the inclusion of *state co-location*. This form of co-location is used to specify requirements that the actors are in compatible states when executing specific activities. We see simple examples of in current pairing protocols (as in the Bluetooth standard) where compatible states are required to achieve common results. This form of co-location can also be expressed using co-location spheres. We also consider extending our framework with more physical dimensions. An example is the temperature dimension, where *temperature co-location* spheres indicate that activities must be executed within a certain common temperature range. An application domain is advanced fine mechanics in Industry 4.0 settings, where small tolerances in processes require very strict temperature control between multiple activities.

The semantics of spheres needs attention in further research. Where semantics are often obvious in spheres with two process activities, they can be ambiguous in cases of multi-activity spheres, as they represent n-ary relations. Our work on inconsistency checking requires further analysis too – this exploratory paper only presents initial thoughts with rather intuition-based underpinning. To make multi-dimensional co-location specification practical in complex real-world applications (such as logistics), automated support for consistency checking will be indispensable.

Related work that is currently in execution is in the direction of extending the BPM + IoT coupling to distributed analytics, as we advocate in recent work [Gre18]. The fact that activities in a process are linked in a co-location sphere implies that these activities have a pragmatic link – or more concretely, have a common business goal. To plan the execution of these sets of activities in an evidence-based way, analytics needs to become part of the game. In complex, distributed IoT environments (like logistics), the analytics may be of a distributed nature as well. The link of co-location spheres to analytics, for example by specifying the nature of data to be generated, may become part of the specification of the spheres.

References

[Bau15]   Baumgraß, A., Dijkman, R., Grefen, P., Pourmirza, S., Völzer, H., Weske, M.: A software architecture for transportation planning and monitoring in a collaborative network. In: Camarinha-Matos, L.M., Bénaben, F., Picard, W. (eds.) PRO-VE 2015. IAICT, vol. 463, pp. 277–284. Springer, Cham (2015). https://doi.org/10.1007/978-3-319-24141-8_25

[Bro18]   Brouns, N., Tata, S., Ludwig, H., Serral Asensio, E., Grefen, P.: Modeling IoT-Aware Business Processes. IBM Research Reports (2018)

[Com17]   Combi, C., Oliboni, B., Zerbato, F.: Modeling and handling duration constraints in BPMN 2.0. In: Proceedings of the ACM Symposium on Applied Computing, pp. 727–734 (2017)

[Gar87]   Garcia-Molina, H., Salem, K.: Sagas. In: Proceedings of the SIGMOD Conference, pp. 249–259. ACM (1987)

[Gre97]   Grefen, P.W.P.J., Vonk, J., Boertjes, E., Apers, P.M.G.: Two-layer transaction management for workflow management applications. In: Proceedings of the Database and Expert Systems Applications Conference, pp. 430–439 (1997)

[Gre17]   Grefen, P., Vanderfeesten, I., Boultadakis, G.: Supporting hybrid manufacturing: bringing process and human/robot control to the cloud. In: Proceedings of the 5th International Conference on Cloud Networking, pp. 200–203. IEEE (2016)

[Gre18]   Grefen, P., et al.: Complex collaborative physical process management: a position on the trinity of BPM, IoT and DA. In: Camarinha-Matos, L.M., Afsarmanesh, H., Rezgui, Y. (eds.) PRO-VE 2018. IAICT, vol. 534, pp. 244–253. Springer, Cham (2018). https://doi.org/10.1007/978-3-319-99127-6_21

[Jan17]   Janiesch, C., et al.: The internet-of-things meets business process management: mutual benefits and challenges. arXiv:1709.03628 (2017)

[Lu18]   Lu, M., et al.: Cooperative and connected intelligent transport systems for sustainable european road transport. In: Proceedings of the 7th Transport Research Arena (2018)

[Ser15]   Serral, E., De Smedt, J., Snoeck, M., Vanthienen, J.: Context-adaptive petri nets: supporting adaptation for the execution context. Expert Syst. Appl. **42**(23), 9307–9317 (2015)

[Von03]   Vonk, J., Grefen, P.: Cross-organizational transaction support for e-services in virtual enterprises. Distrib. Parallel Databases **14**(2), 137–172 (2003)

[W307]   Lieberman, J., Singh, R., Goad, C.: W3C Geospatial Ontologies. W3C Incubator Group Report 23 (2007) http://www.w3.org/2005/Incubator/geo/XGR-geo-ont-20071023/. Accessed Aug 2018

[W317]   Cox, S., Little, C., Hobbs, J., Pan, F.: Time Ontology in OWL. W3C Recommendation 19 October 2017. https://www.w3.org/TR/2017/REC-owl-time-20171019/. Accessed Aug 2018

[Wik19]   Wikipedia. Backus–Naur Form. https://en.wikipedia.org/wiki/Backus-Naur_form. Accessed Aug 2018

[PoR17]   Facts & Figures, A Wealth of Information, Make it Happen. Port of Rotterdam, Information Report (2017)

Towards Risk-Driven Security Requirements Management in Agile Software Development

Dan Ionita[1]([✉]), Coco van der Velden[2], Henk-Jan Klein Ikkink[2], Eelko Neven[2], Maya Daneva[1], and Michael Kuipers[2]

[1] Department Cybersecurity and Safety, University of Twente,
Enschede, The Netherlands
{d.ionita,m.daneva}@utwente.nl
[2] Centric B.V., Gouda, The Netherlands
{coco.van.der.velden,henk-jan.klein.ikkink,eelko.neven,
michael.kuipers}@centric.eu
https://scs.ewi.utwente.nl/

Abstract. The focus on user stories in agile means non-functional requirements, such as security, are not always explicit. This makes it hard for the development team to implement the required functionality in a reliable, secure way. Security checklists can help but they do not consider the application's context and are not part of the product backlog.

In this paper we explore whether these issues can be addressed by a framework which uses a risk assessment process, a mapping of threats to security features, and a repository of operationalized security features to populate the product backlog with prioritized security requirements. The approach highlights the relevance of each security feature to product owners while ensuring the knowledge and time required to implement security requirements is made available to developers. We applied and evaluated the framework at a Dutch medium-sized software development company with promising results.

Keywords: Secure software development · Security requirements ·
Risk assessment · Empirical research method

1 Introduction

Agile software development relies on the team's ability to decompose, refine, and operationalize high-level user requirements such as user stories. The majority of users and customers lack awareness of the security risks in the implementation and usage of the software and settle for compliance. Furthermore, most agile

Supported by The Netherlands Organisation for Scientific Research (NWO) in the context of cyber-security research (grant number 628.001.011).

© Springer Nature Switzerland AG 2019
C. Cappiello and M. Ruiz (Eds.): CAiSE Forum 2019, LNBIP 350, pp. 133–144, 2019.
https://doi.org/10.1007/978-3-030-21297-1_12

teams do not have a security expert on board. Therefore, product owners (POs) have a hard time identifying and prioritizing security requirements and developers often rely on security checklists which are not integrated with agile project management processes and tools. This results in software which fails to properly mitigate many risks relevant to its users or its application domain.

To address this, we propose a secure software development framework consisting of (1) a high-level risk assessment process to be undertaken with the application's stakeholders, (2) a mapping of threats to security requirements and (3) a searchable repository of security requirements integrated with agile project management tools. The goal of the risk assessment is to identify and prioritize risks, the mapping is used to derive high level security requirements (i.e. features) based on these risks, and the repository makes it easy to inject these features together with their operationalizations into the agile development workflow. The three components work together to support risk-driven selection, prioritization and implementation of security requirements in a way that requires minimal security knowledge and effort from users, customers, and POs. As a whole, the approach is designed to provide traceability of security requirements and forces the development team to consider the effort required to implement security features in their planning.

The framework aims to align with the agile manifesto [3]. First, it provides a means to discuss security with the customer of an agile project. Second, it produces a list of prioritized requirements in a format that can be directly imported into product backlogs. Third, it leaves it up to the teams to break down the requirements into tasks and add these to sprints. Fourth, it includes control points for testing the implementation. Fifth, it is able to respond to changes in the risk landscape. Furthermore, the framework was applied in a real-life organization and its evaluation shows promising results.

In what follows, Sect. 2 summarizes our research methodology. Sections 3 and 4 position our work in relation to the real-world problems that we want to address as well as related publications. Section 5 introduces our framework based on a practical example of how this was implemented at Centric, a medium-sized software development company. Section 6 discusses our preliminary evaluation and Sect. 7 draws wraps up with conclusions and future work.

2   Research Methodology

This paper is the result of an extensive collaboration between the University of Twente and Centric B.V., a medium-sized Dutch application provider. Therefore, the underlying methodology applied throughout the research is Technical Action Research (TAR): a technique is designed and applied to a real-life problem in order to draw conclusions about both the technique and the problem. TAR helps both the company, in that it is provided with a working solution, and the researcher, in that he/she has the opportunity to perform real-life validation [20].

Problem Investigation. To better understand the problem context, we did a literature survey on security requirements management in agile software development. In parallel, we interviewed security coordinators, penetration testers, developers, POs, as well as the management and governance team working on various projects within Centric. The findings are summarized in the Sect. 3.

Treatment Design. To define our solution direction, we explored literature on strategies for incorporating security in agile workflows. The findings are summarized in Sect. 4. We designed a framework which aligns with some of these strategies while addressing the issues highlighted by the problem investigation. Each component of the framework was developed iteratively in consultation with relevant stakeholders from Centric. The framework is described in Sect. 5.

Treatment Validation. To validate the proposed treatment we ran five focus groups within Centric where we applied the risk assessment methodology described in Sect. 5.1. We systematically compared the results of applying the mapping described in Sect. 5.2 to the judgment of security experts. Finally, we created a template project according to the repository structure proposed in Sect. 5.3 in a major issue tracking software and ran a survey to assess its usability and utility.

3   Motivation and Background

Established approaches to security engineering as part of software development fail to address the particular needs of agile [2]. As a result, security considerations in agile software development are often based on security baselines, despite the fact that best practice insists security should be risk-driven [1,4,8]. "Discrete techniques" such as security checklists integrate very poorly into agile approaches [18]. The requirements listed in baselines and checklists don't always have an owner and are often considered towards the end of development [19].

Daneva and Wang [5] indicate that security requirements engineering in agile boils down to documenting risks and mitigations. But POs, as well as developers, often lack security knowledge [19]. Our framework provides assistance in formulating risk scenarios and centralizes security knowledge, making it easily reusable across teams and even across projects.

Daneva and Wang also point out that the gate-keeping role of the PO often hampers the elicitation and implementation of security requirements. This is mainly because agile is business-value-driven [3] and security is hard to "sell" [6]. We propose mitigating this by highlighting the business value – in terms of risk reduction – that each security requirements provides.

Furthermore, our informal interviews and conversations with domain experts and stakeholders revealed that:

- Security requirements are not risk-based. We mitigate this by maintaining a mapping base of risks and requirements.

- Security requirements are not user-driven. We mitigate this by prescribing a non-technical risk assessment methodology.
- Security requirements are not application-specific. We mitigate this by linking requirements to the result of the risk assessment.
- Penetration tests are standardized. We mitigate this by generating a list of the most important security requirements to be tested.
- Security requirement documents are missing implementation-specifics. We mitigate this by maintaining a central repository of operationalized security features.
- It's hard to keep track of the implementation status of security requirements. We mitigate this by making security requirements available on issue trackers.

4   Related Work

Siponen et al. [18] conclude that an agile security requirements management technique must include a quantified risk assessment in the requirements analysis phase. Security requirements should be explicitly included in the design phase, their implementation must be monitored throughout the implementation phase and they should be tested in the testing phase. Our proposal mandates starting with a risk assessment, including the resulting requirements in the planning and effort estimations, and making sure acceptance criteria are known and tested.

A notable approach for eliciting security requirements in agile are *abuser stories*. Similar to abuse cases, they document threat scenarios [14, 15]. However, this approach has some caveats. E.g. several threat scenarios can be mitigated by the same security feature, sometimes with different efficiency. And since most issue trackers do not allow a backlog item to have multiple parents, defining these as backlog items results in many security requirements being duplicated. This would also fail to reflect the relative importance of security features with regard to their efficacy and the number of threat scenarios they mitigate. In order to avoid these issues, our approach maintains a separate overview of threat scenarios as part of the risk assessment document described in Sect. 5.1.

Terpstra et al. [19] performed a practitioner survey of problems and coping strategies for handling security requirements in agile project management and agile software development projects. The methodology proposed in this paper aligns well with many of these strategies. For example, by adding security features – including acceptance criteria - to the backlog we are making sure they are considered during effort estimations, and that these features are part of the definition of "done".

5   The Proposed Framework

The aim of the framework is to support the identification, prioritization and implementation of security requirements in an agile workflow. Its application consists of three phases:

1. **Risk assessment:** Each risk is quantified and mapped to one or more of threats in consultation with relevant stakeholders (the left side of Fig. 1). This performed according to a pre-defined *risk assessment methodology* described in Sect. 5.1 below.
2. **Prioritization of security requirements:** Based on the ranked list of threats resulting from the risk assessment, a prioritized list of security requirements is automatically derived (the middle part of Fig. 1). This is achieved by means of an intermediary *threat-requirement map* described in Sect. 5.2 below.
3. **Populate product backlog:** The PO imports the relevant security requirements with associated priorities to the product backlog of his agile issue tracking tool of choice (the right side of the Fig. 1). This is facilitated by means of a *security requirements repository* described in Sect. 5.3 below.

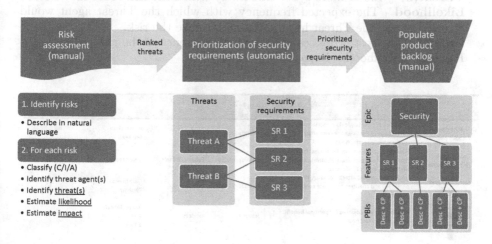

Fig. 1. Overview of the proposed framework

5.1   The Risk Assessment Methodology

Most secure software development guidelines such as the CIP Overheid [12] or the ISO 27000x series [9–11] recommend performing a risk or threat assessment as early in the software lifecycle as possible. This helps avoid architectural risks and reduces the amount of work needed to fix security issues late in the project. But more importantly, it provides a good understanding of the most significant threats and risks.

In our framework, risk assessment serves as a starting point. Its results are to be correlated with the mapping described in the following section in order to produce a ranked list of security requirements. To this end, the risk assessment must be correct and complete, and should therefore be performed in close consultation with the PO and customer in order to make sure the most relevant risks are identified, that the impact estimations are accurate, and that the resulting mitigations are taken into consideration during agile planning. In addition, the assessment must produce output which can be consumed by the threat-requirement map, namely a quantitative ranked list of pre-defined threats.

Structure. We use a spreadsheet as the basis for our assessment, see Fig. 2. It consists of the following columns:

Risk label - a brief description of the risk.
Explanation - an description of the process by which the risk could materialize.
Type - Confidentiality, Integrity, or Availability.
Threat agent(s) - An individual or group which are likely to try to materialize the risk.
Threat(s) - One or more cyber-threats by which the risk could materialize.
Likelihood - The expected frequency with which the Threat agent would attempt to use the Threat in order to materialize the risk.
Impact - The cost or loss caused by the occurrence of the risk.
Rating - Likelihood x Impact.

Risk label	Explanation	Type C/I/A	Threat agent(s)	Threat(s)	Likelihood (0-100)	Impact (0-100)
Expose data of famous people	Employee accidentaly leaks personal (sensitive) information of Politicians or celeberties. E.g.HR reviews, medical info, leave.	Confidentiality	Insiders	Information leakage	50	50
Data breach - famous people	Hacker beach the system. Politicians, Royal and celeberties have personal (sensitive) exposed. E.g. HR reviews, medical info, leave.	Confidentiality	Cyber-criminals	Data breach	20	55
Hacktivist leak sensitive info	Hacktivist - targeted attack e.g. salary data of politicians and charities, to expose controversial information.	Confidentiality	Hacktivists	Data breach, Phishing	5	65
Fraudulent contract adjustments	HR contracts are adjusted for personal benefit. E.g. salary, or contract hours.	Integrity	Insiders	Insider threat, Web-based attack	10	15

Fig. 2. Fragment of a risk assessment

Process. The table (Fig. 2) is filled in from left to right, however, we found that first selecting a likely threat agent stimulates creativity. This is in line with the philosophy of the Intel's Threat Agent Risk Assessment [17] which starts by agreeing on a list of relevant threat agents. Each risk is given a label, described in free text, and classified in terms as confidentiality, integrity, or availability. In order to further scope down the risk and ensure consensus among participants, a relevant threat agent(s) is chosen if one was not chosen already. It is possible that the same risk produces a different impact, or manifests with a different likelihood depending on the threat agent and their purpose. Therefore, the same risk may appear on multiple rows, but mapped to a different threat agent. Then, each risk is mapped to one or more of the pre-defined threats. Finally, each risk is quantified in terms of likelihood and impact which are multiplied in order to obtain a risk rating.

5.2   The Threat-Feature Map

To arrive at the ranked list of security requirements needed to populate the product backlog, a mapping between the threat taxonomy used in the risk assessment and a set of security features is necessary. To strengthen the usability and justifiability of the mapping, the list of threats should be based on an established threat taxonomy such as ENISA's [7] or Intel's [17], and the list of requirements should be based on established secure software development guidelines such as OAWSP [16] or Grip on SSD [13]. Note that there is a many-to-many relationship between threats and requirements. Furthermore, this relationship is not binary; some security requirements are better at mitigating a threat than others. This *relevance factor* should also be reflected in the mapping.

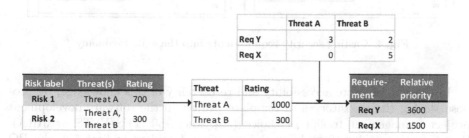

Fig. 3. A simple example of using the threat-requirements map for prioritization

Figure 3 shows a simple example of using the mapping to automatically derive a list of prioritized requirements:

1. Sum up the rating of each risk where a particular threat is mentioned, we obtain a ranked list of threats with relative ratings.
2. Then, for each security requirement, sum up the relative rating of each threat it mitigates multiplied by the threats' relevance factor.

What we end up with is a ranked list of security requirements with relative ratings. These rating is finally normalized to a scale which matches the one used in sprint planning, usually 1 to 4.

5.3   The Security Requirements Repository

An important aspect of the proposed methodology is that it helps the development team account for security requirements during sprint planning by making prioritized security requirements available on the product backlog. Therefore, the ranked list of requirements produced by applying the threat-requirement mapping to the results of the risk assessment needs to find their way into the product backlog. Furthermore, these requirements need to be operationalized. To facilitate this, we propose creating a repository of security requirements in the agile issue tracking software being used by the development team. To be able to do so, we overload established agile terminology to accommodate security requirements, as shown in Fig. 4 below. The security features stored in the mapping of Sect. 5.2 are defined as Features and their respective requirements are stored as User Stories.

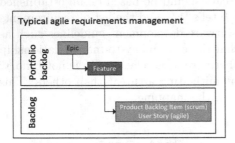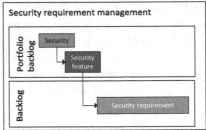

Fig. 4. Casting security requirements into the agile taxonomy

In order to promote accessibility and re-usability of this knowledge, we propose storing the repository as a template project in the software development project management toolkit of choice (e.g. Microsoft TFS/VSTS or JIRA). Based on the results of applying the mapping described in Sect. 5.2, the PO can import the relevant security features from the repository and assign priorities to them. This can be done manually or by means of an extension such as "Issue templates for JIRA"[1]. As long as the selected features are imported together with their children (i.e. the associated backlog items), then all relevant information will be visible on the developer's backlog.

Implementation of the requirements can then take place as per the agile philosophy: the requirements are broken down into tasks, effort estimations are performed, and the tasks assigned to sprints, based on the priorities of their parent features.

6   First Evaluation

In order to evaluate the proposed framework, we tested each of its three components individually in practical settings. Specifically, we investigated whether:

1. the *risk assessment methodology* is usable;
2. the *threat-requirement map* produces a correct ranking of security features;
3. and the *security requirements repository* is able to store a security requirements knowledge base.

We used ENISA's Threat Landscape [7] as a source for threats and CIP Overheid's Grip on Secure Software Development [13] as a source of security features

---

[1] https://marketplace.atlassian.com/apps/1211044/issue-templates-for-jira.

and requirements. Both knowledge bases are well established in academia as well as practice and are actively maintained. The threats were added as a drop-down to the risk assessment spreadsheet, the requirements were added to the security requirements repository, and they were both mapped to each other in the threat-feature map.

The Risk Assessment Methodology. We performed a total of five assessments together with the PO and one other stakeholder of five different applications from a variety of domains: finance, HR, retail, social, and privacy. The risk assessment sessions lasted between two and three hours and resulted in the identification of an average of 18 risk scenarios per assessment. All assessments were facilitated by at least one of the authors.

We observed the participants found the exercise engaging and simply going through each threat helped them identify risks they had not considered. We also administered a questionnaire after each session, the results of which are shown in Table 1.

Table 1. Practitioner feedback on the risk assessment methodology

Question	Average rating (1–5)
Has the assessment helped you identify risks?	3.2
Has the assessment helped you understand risks?	3
Has the assessment helped you select security requirements?	3
Would you execute the assessment with clients?	3.2
How easy was performing the assessment?	3.4
Would you recommend the assessment to others?	4.4
Is the assessment suitable for agile processes?	1.8

After the assessment, participants felt they have a better awareness and understanding of the risks their application is exposed to. Even though the questionnaire was administered before the participants were shown the resulting feature prioritization, many stated the assessment helped them think of important security requirements. On average, the participants felt the assessment was not difficult, despite lacking security expertise and having no security experts in the session. Participants also indicated they would perform the assessment with a client and that they highly recommend other teams perform one. The assessment was not deemed suitable for agile processes. However, the assessment is meant as an entry point in order to obtain a list of requirements and priorities without security knowledge; once the requirements are copied to the project backlog, their implementation can take place in an agile way. Furthermore, changes to the application's risk profile can be reflected in the assessment in order to re-calibrate the priorities at any time.

The Threat-Feature Map. In order to assess the feasibility of defining a mapping of threats to security features, the authors manually mapped the 15 threats maintained by ENISA [7] to the 27 security features part of the CIP Overheid's Grip on SSD [13]. For each threat, we evaluated the likelihood (high-medium-low) it would exploit common one of the web-application vulnerabilities used internally for penetration testing. Then, for each vulnerability, we specified which security feature is able to mitigate it. The result was a matrix of relevance factors for each threat-feature tuple.

We asked three security experts in our partner organization to manually assign priorities of 0 (do not implement) to 4 (critical) to each of the security features in our mapping given the results of one of the risk assessment. Each expert was given the assessment of a different application but none of the experts were familiar with the application itself nor were they involved in creating the mapping. The threat-feature map only uses the threat and risk rating columns, however, the human assessors could base their judgment on the entire table.

Table 2 compares the automated prioritization to the manual one for each application. In two of the three assessments the automatically generated results differed significantly from the expert judgment. However, the automatically assigned priorities were similar to the manual ones for the HR system. Across the three assessments 1-in-4 of security features were assigned the same priority by the mapping and the expert. Of the features which were assigned different priorities, 57% deviated by one.

Table 2. Statistical comparison of the automated prioritisation vs. expert judgment

Application	Privacy	HR	Taxes
Correct guesses	3	8	9
Off by 1	14	14	7
Correlation	−0.18	0.28	0.12
p-value	0.82	0.07	0.26

Despite promising results with the HR application, the mapping has overall failed to deliver a prioritization significantly better than random when compared to expert judgment. Either (1) the mapping is incorrect or incomplete, or (2) judging the priorities is difficult and error-prone. Both explanations could be investigated given higher availability of experts by (1) using the expert judgments to infer a mapping or (2) measuring inter-expert agreement.

The Security Requirements Repository. To validate our claim that the structure proposed in Fig. 4 is able to encode any security requirement we defined a template project in Microsoft Team Foundation Server (TFS) and used it to store the entire set of high-level security requirements, operationalized requirements, and control points mandated by the CIP Overheid's Grip on Secure

Software Development. We also wrote a script which is able to import these requirements into any other TFS project. We are currently working on a graphical TFS extension to make this process easier and allow users to also assign priorities during the import (more on this in Sect. 7).

7 Conclusions

Simply performing a risk assessment as described in Sect. 5.1 raises awareness of security issues. Experts did not always agree with the priorities assigned by the threat-requirement mapping, but found manual prioritization difficult. Finally, we showed how the availability, usability, and maintainability of a security baseline can be improved by storing it as a linked collection of backlog items. We believe our framework can help agile development teams take security into account during by providing a first indication of the most important security features, their priority, and the tasks required. Security experts should still be involved during implementation and testing; they can use the assessment and initial prioritization as a starting point or reference.

The proposed framework was developed and tested at a single Dutch software developer, and only applied to mobile and web applications. However, the developer makes use of standard stacks, development practices, and supporting tools. Therefore, following Wieringa [20], we think that the framework could potentially be applicable to other organizations that have similar organizational and software development context to the one of our partnering Dutch company.

Nevertheless, we are looking for industry partners to refine the threat-feature map and strengthen our evaluation. We also want to extend the security requirements repository with technology-specific and domain-specific requirements to enable selection as well as prioritization. Finally, we are exploring using Artificial Intelligence to prioritize requirements based on prioritizations of experts.

References

1. Hammoudeh, A.: A risk-driven approach to security, from check boxes to risk management frameworks (2016). https://securityintelligence.com/a-risk-driven-approach-to-security-from-check-boxes-to-risk-management-frameworks/
2. Baskerville, R.: Agile security for information warfare: a call for research. In: ECIS 2004 Proceedings p. 13 (2004)
3. Beck, K., et al.: Manifesto for Agile Software Development (2001)
4. Boehm, B.W.: A spiral model of software development and enhancement. Computer **21**(5), 61–72 (1988)
5. Daneva, M., Wang, C.: Security requirements engineering in the agile era: How does it work in practice? In: 2018 IEEE 1st International Workshop on Quality Requirements in Agile Projects (QuaRAP), pp. 10–13, August 2018. https://doi.org/10.1109/QuaRAP.2018.00008
6. Davis, A.: Return on security investment-proving it's worth it. Netw. Secur. **2005**(11), 8–10 (2005)

7. ENISA Threat Landscape 2017: 15 Top Cyber-Threats and Trends. Technical report, European Union Agency for Network and Information Security (2017). https://doi.org/10.2824/967192
8. Goldfarb, J.: Risk-driven security: The approach to keep pace with advanced threats (2015). https://www.securityweek.com/risk-driven-security-approach-keep-pace-advanced-threats
9. Information technology - Security techniques - Information security management systems - Requirements. Standard ISO 27001:2005, International Organization for Standardization (ISO) (2005)
10. Information technology - Security techniques - Code of practice for information security management. Standard ISO 27002:2005, International Organization for Standardization (ISO) (2005)
11. Information technology - Security techniques - Information security risk management. Standard ISO 27005:2011, International Organization for Standardization (ISO) (2011)
12. Koers, M., Paans, R., van der Veer, R., Kok, C., Breeman, J.: Grip on secure software development (SSD): 'the client at the helm', version 2.0. Technical report, Centrum voor Informatiebeveiliging en Privacybescherming (CIP), March 2015. https://www.cip-overheid.nl/wp-content/uploads/2018/01/20160622_Grip_on_SSD_The_method_v2_0_EN.pdf
13. Koers, M., Tewarie, W.: Grip on secure software development (SSD): security requirements for (web) applications, version 2.0. Technical report, Centrum voor Informatiebeveiliging en Privacybescherming (CIP), October 2014. https://www.cip-overheid.nl/wp-content/uploads/2018/08/20180821-Grip-on-SSD-Security-requirements-v2.0-2.pdf
14. McDermott, J.: Abuse-case-based assurance arguments. In: Proceedings 17th Annual Computer Security Applications Conference, ACSAC 2001, pp. 366–374. IEEE (2001)
15. McDermott, J., Fox, C.: Using abuse case models for security requirements analysis. In: Proceedings of the 15th Annual Computer Security Applications Conference. (ACSAC 1999), pp. 55–64. IEEE (1999)
16. OWASP: Top 10–2013: The ten most critical web application security risks. The Open Web Application Security Project (2013)
17. Rosenquist, M.: Prioritizing information security risks with threat agent risk assessment. Intel Corporation White Paper (2009)
18. Siponen, M., Baskerville, R., Kuivalainen, T.: Integrating security into agile development methods. In: Proceedings of the 38th Annual Hawaii International Conference on System Sciences. HICSS 2005, pp. 185a–185a. IEEE (2005)
19. Terpstra, E., Daneva, M., Wang, C.: Agile practitioners' understanding of security requirements: insights from a grounded theory analysis. In: 2017 IEEE 25th International Requirements Engineering Conference Workshops (REW), pp. 439–442. IEEE (2017)
20. Wieringa, R.J.: Design Science Methodology for Information Systems and Software Engineering. Springer, Heidelberg (2014). https://doi.org/10.1007/978-3-662-43839-8

Detection and Resolution of Data-Flow Differences in Business Process Models

Ivan Jovanovikj[1]($\boxtimes$), Enes Yigitbas[1], Christian Gerth[2], Stefan Sauer[1], and Gregor Engels[1]

[1] SI-Lab - Software Innovation Lab, Paderborn University, Paderborn, Germany
{ivan.jovanovikj,enes.yigitbas,sauer,engels}@upb.de
[2] Hochschule Osnabrück, Osnabrück, Germany
c.gerth@hs-osnabrueck.de

Abstract. Business process models have an important role in enterprises and organizations as they are used for insight, specification or configuration of business processes. After its initial creation, a process model is very often refined, by different business modelers and software architects in distributed environments, in order to reflect changed requirements or changed business rules. At some point, the different resulting process model versions need to be merged in an integrated version. In order to enable comparison and merging, an approach which comprises difference representation as well as a discovery method for differences is needed. Regarding control-flow, such approaches already exist. As the specification of data-flow is also important, an approach for dealing with data-flow differences is also needed. In this paper, we propose a model for representation of data-flow differences as well as a method able to discover, visualize, and resolve data-flow differences.

Keywords: Business process models · Data-flow ·
Change management

1 Introduction

Every enterprise or organization has organizational and business goals. In order to achieve these goals, a simple activity or set of related activities comprising a business process are conducted [16]. A business process model is a model which describes the workflow of a business process an it plays an important role as is it is used for gaining insight, documentation, performance analysis, specification, implementation or configuration [1]. The Business Process Model and Notation (BPMN) [12] provides a graphical notation for specifying business process models. A process model may comprise different perspectives of a process. The order of execution of activities in a process is represented by the control-flow. The data-flow is another perspective which represents what kind of information is the input and output of a process and the activities inside a process. Further, data-flow specifies where data comes from and goes to, and where data is stored.

C. Cappiello and M. Ruiz (Eds.): CAiSE Forum 2019, LNBIP 350, pp. 145–157, 2019.
https://doi.org/10.1007/978-3-030-21297-1_13

After its initial creation, a process model underlines a constant change, in order to reflect changed requirements or changed rules of business processes. Therefore, an additional activity may be added, or an existing activity is deleted or modified. Very often, this is done by different business modelers and software architects in distributed environments. As a consequence, we come to a point where two or more different versions exist. At some point in time, all different versions have to be compared and merged [9] in an integrated business process model. Therefore, an effective change management approach [5] that results in a consistent integrated model is needed. Considering the field of business process model analysis, in recent years, several techniques [4–6,10] have been developed for analyzing different aspects of business process models. In these approaches, the most attention has been devoted to the control-flow perspective. To the best of our knowledge, the data-flow perspective has not considered too much attention. Maybe one of the reasons is the lack of a good support by modeling tools. Nevertheless, this does not indicate that the role of the data in process models is unimportant. For example, the routing in process models is based on data which means that the control-flow often depends on data.

In this paper, we present an approach that builds upon an existing work that considers the control-flow perspective [5,8]. We extend the existing approach by consideration of a data-flow in process models. The main concern of this work is the representation of data-flow differences in process models in terms of change operations, as well as their detection and resolution, by providing a discovery and a resolution method, respectively.

This paper is organized as follows: Sect. 2 presents a difference model for representation of data-flow differences. The discovery method is presented in Sect. 3. Then, in Sect. 4, the dependencies between data-flow differences are discussed and in Sect. 5 we address the resolution of the differences. At the end, Sect. 6 gives an overview of the work and sketches possible directions for future work.

2   Difference Model for Data-Flow Differences

We represent differences in terms of change operations. All differences that can be detected in a data-flow, comprise the difference model for data-flow differences. Similarly to [5], our difference model consists of the *Primitive Difference Model* (Fig. 1) and the *Compound Difference Model* (Fig. 3). The change operations from the *Primitive Difference Model* are related directly to data-flow elements such as *Data Objects*, *Data Stores*, and *Data Associations*. The *Compound Difference Model* contains compound change operations, where each compound change operation consists of one or more primitive change operations. The compound change operations are on a higher level of abstraction and are much more understandable to a business user. We evaluate our difference representation against the requirements defined in [5] as follows:

R1-Completeness: The difference representation must contain all data-flow differences that can occur between two process models.

R2-Understandability: The difference representation of data-flow differences must be compact and easy understandable for business users.

R3-Directly Resolvable: Data-flow differences between process models shall be directly resolvable using their operational representation.

R4-Connected Process Model: The difference representation shall support the creation of connected merged data-flow of process models.

2.1 Primitive Change Operations

Primitive change operations modify a single data-flow element in a process model. For each data-flow element class, there is a meta class for the insertion and deletion in the primitive difference meta-model which is visualized in Fig. 1. An *InsertDataArtifact*(BPMN Process Model, Data Artifact), for example, inserts a single Data Artifact, e.g. a Data Object or a Data Store into an BPMN Process Model. The inverse operation of *InsertDataArtifact* is *DeleteDataArtifact*. Figure 2 shows the application of the *InsertDataArtifact(V, 'Order')* operation which inserts the Data Object *'Order'* and its inverse operation, the *DeleteDataArtifact*. Summarized, both **R1** and **R3** are successfully addressed, as all differences between different model versions

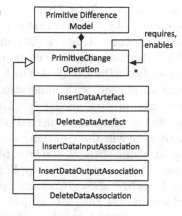

Fig. 1. Meta-model for primitive change operations

are represented and directly resolvable by applying them. However, it is very difficult to identify and understand the actual high level change (**R2**). Moreover, the business user should know which operation can be applied independently in order to obtain a correct process model (**R4**). To overcome these drawbacks, in the next section, we introduce compound change operations.

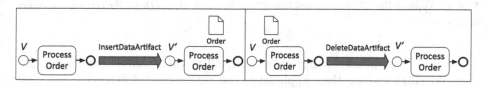

Fig. 2. Application of *InsertDataArtifact* and *DeleteDataArtifact* operations

2.2 Compound Change Operations

Compound change operations are conceptually much closer to the actual change as they represent how the accesses to data artifacts have changed. Technically, a compound change operation comprises one or more primitive change operations.

Compound change operations are split into two groups: data object related and data store related change operations. Regarding data objects, as depicted in Fig. 3, four different types are considered (creation, read, update, and deletion). Regarding data store related change operation, read and update are considered.

An *InsertDataObjectCreation* operation, for example, has as input a BPMN Process Model, a Data Object and an Activity. For example, *InsertDataObjectCreation(V, do, c)* represents an insertion of a Data Object *do* which is created by the Activity *c* in the BPMN Process Model *V*. It consists of the following primitive change operations: *InsertDataArtifact* which inserts data object *do* with annotation *[new]* into the process model *V*. The data object *do* is then connected with the activity *c* via data output association by applying *InsertDataOutputAssociation*. Figure 4 shows the application of an *InsertDataObjectCreation* operation which inserts the data object *'Order'*

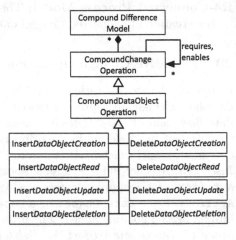

Fig. 3. An excerpt of the meta-model for compound change operations

which is created by the activity *'Create Order'*, and the opposite compound operation *DeleteDataObjectCreation(V, c, do)*.

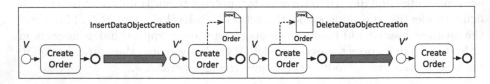

Fig. 4. Application of *InsertDataObjectCreation* and *DeleteDataObjectCreation* operations

By using compound change operations, all possible differences can be represented (**R1**) and by their application the represented difference is resolved (**R3**). The compound change operations successfully address **R2** as they are closer to the actual high level change. Also, the application of each compound change operation leads to a correct and connected process model (**R4**). Hence, the compound change operations address successfully all four requirements.

3   Method to Discover Data-Flow Differences

Based on the difference model introduced in the previous section, we present our approach for discovering data-flow differences. The main goal of the discovery method is to detect data-flow differences in terms of how accesses to data artifacts have changed between different process model versions of a process model. The input of the discovery method are two versions of a single process model. The discovery method comprises four steps (Fig. 5). Before explaining the steps in detail, in the next section, we firstly introduce the access triples, the base for the difference detection.

3.1   Access Triples

Access triples represent a specific data access, i.e., a particular way in which an activity accesses a data artifact, either a data object or a data store. Basically, the goal is to identify differences between two versions of a process model, i.e., how data accesses in a data-flow have changed. More formally, an access triple is defined as follows:

Definition 1 (Access Triple). *An Access triple is a substructure consisting of an activity, a data association, and a data artifact (a data object or a data store). It represents a specific access of an activity to a data artifact.*

Four different types of interaction between activity and data object exist: create, read, update, and delete access. As there is no way in BPMN to implicitly denote a creation of a data object or a deletion of a data object, we use the extension proposed in [11]. There, two annotations are defined: *[new]* for data object creation and *[delete]* for data object deletion. We formalize data access types in the following definition:

Definition 2 (Data Access Type). *A Data access type specifies the actual interaction between an activity and a data artifact. Four different data access types exist: create (C), read (R), update (U), and delete (D) access type. In a concrete data-flow, data access types can be determined according the following four rules:*

1. *A Data Output Association with a target reference a Data Object annotated with [new] represents a create access type*
2. *A Data Input Association always represents a read access type*
3. *A Data Output Association with a target reference a Data Object without annotation or a Data Store represents an update (write) access type*
4. *A Data Output Association with a target reference a Data Object annotated with [delete] represents a delete access type.*

According to the contained data artifact, the following two types of triples are defined: *Data Object-Access Triple* and *Data Store-Access Triple*. Regarding the access type, the following four types of triples are specified: *Create-Access Triple, Read-Access Triple, Update-Access Triple,* and *Delete-Access Triple*.

3.2 Detection of Access Triples

The access triple detection process consists of the following steps: (1) We iterate over all data associations; (2) For each data association, the source and the target reference are checked and corresponding access triple are created; (3) Each formed access triple is then extended by a corresponding activity and a data artifact; (4) Applying Definition 2, the type of the access triple is determined. The detection process continues until all data associations are analyzed. The process results in a complete set of access triples.

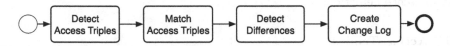

Fig. 5. Steps of difference detection process

3.3 Correspondences of Data-Flow Elements and Access Triples

A correspondence is used to establish relations between model elements from one process model to another [5,13]. They express that a specific element has or does not have a counterpart in the other version of a process model. Firstly, correspondences between data-flow elements, *Data Artifacts* and *Data Associations*, are established. Based on these correspondences correspondences between access triple are established. A correspondence between data-flow elements is defined as follow:

Definition 3 (Correspondences of Data-Flow Elements). *Let V_1 and V_2 be two process models. Let x and y be two data-flow elements (Data Artifacts or Data Association). The following types of correspondences can be defined between x and y:*

- *A 1-1 correspondence connects two data-flow elements x and y in V_1 and V_2 if x is represented by y and vice versa. x is represented by y if they are of the same type and the activity and the data artifact are equal ($C_{1-1}^{DO}(V_1, V_2)$ correspondence set).*
- *A 1-0 correspondence is attached to a data-flow element x in V_1 if x is not represented by a data-flow y in V_2 ($C_{1-0}^{DO}(V_1, V_2)$ correspondence set).*
- *A 0-1 correspondence is attached to a data-flow element y in V_2 if y is not represented by a data-flow x in V_1 ($C_{0-1}^{DO}(V_1, V_2)$ correspondence set).*

Based on this, we define correspondences between access triples as follows:

Definition 4 (Correspondences of Access Triples). *Let V_1 and V_2 be two process models. Let x and y be two access triples. The following types of correspondences can be defined between x and y:*

- *A 1-1 correspondence connects two access triples x and y in V_1 and V_2 if x is represented by y. We say that a x is represented by y if the activities are in 1-1 correspondence and also the data-flow elements are in 1-1 correspondence.*

- *A 1-0 correspondence is attached to an access triple x in V_1 if x is not represented by an access triple y in V_2.*
- *A 0-1 correspondence is attached to an access triple y in V_2 if y is not represented by an access triple x in V_1.*

3.4   Matching of Data-Flow Elements and Access Triples

In this step, we firstly, match data-flow elements. The input of this step are the initial and the update versions od the process model. At the end of the matching process, we have 1-1, 1-0, and 0-1 correspondence sets for both Data Artifacts and Data Associations.

Let suppose that we are comparing the process model versions V_1 and V_2 and let the $M(V_1, V_2)$ be the resulting mapping. We iterate through data-flow elements of a source version V_1 and we try to find matching data-flow elements in the target version V_2. Firstly, we iterate over all Data Artifacts and if two compared Data Artifacts have same name, then we establish 1-1 correspondence. If an element from V_1 does not have counterpart in V_2, it is assigned with 1-0 correspondence. At the end, all the elements from V_2 without counterpart in V_1 are assigned with 0-1 correspondence. In the case of Data Associations, two Data Associations match if they are of the same type (Data Input Association or Data Output Association) and have the same source and the target reference.

Based on the correspondences between data-flow elements, we match access triples. We iterate over the activities in V_1 and for each activity all related access triples are checked. As we assume that correspondences between activities are already established, we use them in our matching process directly. When an activity has a 1-0 correspondence, the access triple is also assigned with 1-0 correspondence. When an activity has a 1-1 correspondence, the data association is also checked and if it is assigned with 1-0 correspondence, the access triple is assigned 1-0 correspondence as well. If the data association has 1-1 correspondence, then the access triple is assigned with 1-1 correspondence. Once all the access triples in the source version are checked, we check the access triples in the target version. Similarly, we iterate over all activities and all access triples which are not assigned with 1-1 or 1-0 correspondence, are assigned with a 0-1 correspondence.

3.5   Difference Detection

A particular data access may be added, deleted or updated. Hence, we define three main type of differences: insert, delete, and update differences as follows:

Definition 5 (InsertDifference).   *Given two business process models V_1 and V_2, an access triple x and 0-1 correspondence sets. We define the **InsertDifference** as an access triple x that is in the 0-1 correspondence set.*

Analogously, *DeleteDifference* is defined, with a minor difference that the 1-0 correspondence set is used.

Definition 6 (UpdateDifference). *Given two business process models V_1 and V_2, access triples x and y and 1-0 and 0-1 correspondence sets. The access triple x is in the 1-0 correspondence set (**DeleteDifference**) and the access triple y that is in the 0-1 correspondence set (**InsertDifference**). First, x and y are of same type and are either a Create-Access Triple or a Delete-Access Triple. Second, accessed data objects in both access triples are same. If the previously mentioned conditions hold, then such combination of an **InsertDifference** and a **DeleteDifference** is defined as an **UpdateDifference**.*

According to the definitions, out of the access triple correspondence set differences are derived. For example, considering Definition 5, *InsertDifferences* are identified. Then, for each *InsertDifference* an appropriate INSERT compound change operation is defined.

4   Dependencies Between Differences

Identifying dependencies between change operations is very important because an execution of dependent operation may lead to incorrect data-flow in a process model. Therefore, for example, a data object shall not be updated until it is created in the process. We analyzed the dependencies between data-flow change operations as well as the dependencies between data-flow and control-flow change operations. Due to the space constraint, in the following, we only discuss the dependencies between data-flow change operations. We base our dependency analysis on the data-flow anti-pattern "Missing Data" defined in [15]. This anti-pattern describes the case when a data object is accessed (read or deleted), but it has not been previously created. Based on this anti-pattern, we define the invariant as follows: *Every data object in the process model must be created and that can be done only by one particular activity.* Consequently, dependant operations are formalized as follow:

Definition 7. *[Dependent Compound Change Operations ([7])] Let op1 and op2 are two change operations and op1 transforms the process model V to V_1 and op2 transforms process model V_1 to V_2. If the change operation op2 is not applicable on the process model V, but it is applicable on V_1, then op2 is dependent on op1.*

	InsertDataObjectOCreation (pm, do1, b)
InsertDataObjectCreation (pm, do, a)	
InsertDataObjectRead (pm, do, a)	do=do1
InsertDataObjectUpdate (pm, do, a)	do=do1
InsertDataObjectDeletion (pm, do, a)	do=do1

Fig. 6. Dependencies between INSERT data-flow change operations

According to the invariant and Definition 7, two main consequences are defined: *(i) No change operations can be applied to a data object until the operation that creates that data object is applied; (ii) If a creation of data object is removed, all other accesses to that data object must be removed.* Having the invariant and the consequences defined, we systematically compare every change operation with every other change operation in order to detect all the dependencies between them. The result of that comparison are pairs of dependent change operations, i.e., pairs of operations where one operation creates a model structure that is needed by the other one.

Dependencies are identified in the following cases: between insert operations, between delete operations, and between update and delete operations. Due to space constraint, in the following, we just discuss the dependency between insert operations namely, between the *InsertDataObjectCreation* and *InsertDataObjectUpdate* operation. Let us assume that *InsertDataObjectCreation(pm, x, a)* is detected, i.e., the activity a creates the data object x. Also, *InsertDataObjectUpdate(pm, x, b)* is detected, i.e., the activity b updates the data object x. The connection between these two operations is clear, as they specify the insertion of a write access to the same data object. The pre-condition of the *InsertDataObjectUpdate* is that the data object x must be created. On the other hand, this is the post-condition of the *InsertDataObjectCreation* operation, created data object x. Therefore, the *InsertDataObjectUpdate* operation requires the application of an *InsertDataObjectCreation* operation, i.e., it is dependent on this operation. We visualize dependencies between change operations by using a dependency matrix as shown in Fig. 6. To explain how the dependency matrix represents the dependencies, we consider the *InsertDataObjectRead* operation. According to the dependency matrix, this operation is dependent on the *InsertDataObjectCreation* if the data object *do* from the *InsertDataObjectRead* operation is equal to the data object *do1* used in the *InsertDataObjectCreation* operation.

5   Resolution of Differences

In order to merge the different versions, the differences should be resolved, which is done by applying the change operations. The user selects change operations, according to her needs, in an iterative and manual way. We support the two-way merging strategy, which means that two process models are merged, a source version and an updated version of a given process model. Due to two-way merging, conflicts between operations do not exist. At the moment when the desired integrated model is obtained, the iterative process ends. When a change operation is selected, a dependency check is performed. If the selected operation is dependent on another operation which is not applied yet, the dependent change operation cannot be resolved. It becomes applicable when all of the operations that it is dependent on are applied (Fig. 7).

The change operations that are in bold style are directly applicable (Fig. 8). All other change operations are disabled, i.e., not applicable. Initially, the control-flow change operation *7. InsertActivity* is applied. As a consequence, the change operations *8. InsertDataObjectRead* and *9. InsertDataObjectCreation* become enabled, as both of them were dependent on the *InsertActivity* operation. The updated log and the updated process modelV_1 are shown in Figs. 9 and 10 respectively. The operations 11 and 12 are dependent on two operations, 9 and 10. Hence, they can only be applied when both operations 9 and 10 are applied. For example, the operation *11. InsertDataObjectRead* can be applied

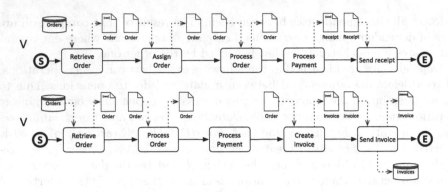

Fig. 7. Process models V_1 and V_2

```
Δ(V₁, V₂)
 1. DeleteActivity(V₁,"Assign Order","Retrieve Order","Process Order")
   2. DeleteDataObjectRead(V₁, "Order", "Assign Order") [ || 1.]
   3. DeleteDataObjectUpdate(V₁, "Order", "Assign Order") [ || 1.]
 Activity Process Payment
   4. DeleteDataObjectCreation(V₁, "Receipt", "Process Payment")
 5. DeleteActivity(V₁, "Send Receipt","Process Payment","Close Order")
   6. DeleteDataObjectRead(V₁, "Receipt", "Send Receipt") [ || 4.] [ || 5.]
 7. InsertActivity(V₁, "Create Invoice","Process Payment", "Close Order")
   8. InsertDataObjectRead(V₁, "Order", "Create Invoice") [→ 7.]
   9. InsertDataObjectCreation(V₁, "Invoice", "Create Invoice") [→ 7.]
 10. InsertActivity(V₁, "Send Invoice","Process Payment","Close Order")
   11. InsertDataObjectRead(V₁, "Invoice", "Send Invoice") [→ 9.] [→ 10.]
   12. InsertDataObjectDeletion(V₁, "Invoice", "Send Invoice") [→ 9.] [→ 10.]
   13. InsertDataStoreWrite(V₁, "Invoices", "Send Invoice") [→ 10.]
```

Fig. 8. The extended hierarchical change log with dependencies between differences for the process model versions V_1 and V_2

only when the change operations *9. InsertDataObjectCreation* and *10. InsertActivity* are applied. Delete data-flow change operations can be applied without any restriction. However, some of them may be denoted by || (e.g., *2. DeleteDataObjectRead [|| 1.]*). This suggests that the *DeleteDataObjectRead* operation is automatically applied when the corresponding operation *1. DeleteActivity* is also applied. This comes from the fact that the *DeleteDataObjectRead* operation is a prerequisite for the application of the *DeleteActivity* operation, i.e., the

```
Δ(V₁, V₂)
 ...
 Activity Create Invoice
   8. InsertDataObjectRead(V₁, "Order", "Create Invoice")
   9. InsertDataObjectCreation(V₁, "Invoice", "Create Invoice")
 10. InsertActivity(V₁, "Send Invoice","Create Invoice","Close Order")
   11. InsertDataObjectRead(V₁, "Invoice", "Send Invoice") [→ 9.] [→ 10.]
   12. InsertDataObjectDeletion(V₁, "Invoice", "Send Invoice") [→ 9.] [→ 10.]
   13. InsertDataStoreWrite(V₁, "Invoices", "Send Invoice") [→ 10.]
```

Fig. 9. The updated change log after resolution step 1

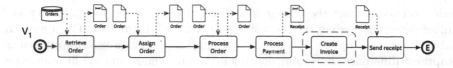

Fig. 10. The updated process model V_1 after the resolution step 1

DeleteActivity operation is dependent on the *DeleteDataObjectRead* operation. In the next resolution step we apply the *9. InsertDataObjectCreation* operation. The application of this operation enables the data-flow change operations under number 11 and 12 (Fig. 11). Now, they are dependent only on the control-flow change operation *10. InsertActivity*. Figure 12 represents the updated process model V_1.

```
Δ(V₁, V₂)
...
Activity Create Invoice
  8. InsertDataObjectRead(V₁, "Order", "Create Invoice")
  Creates: Invoice
  10. InsertActivity(V₁, "Send Invoice","Create Invoice","Close Order")
    11. InsertDataObjectRead(V₁, "Invoice", "Send Invoice") [→ 10.]
    12. InsertDataObjectDeletion(V₁, "Invoice", "Send Invoice") [→ 10.]
    13. InsertDataStoreWrite(V₁, "Invoices", "Send Invoice") [→ 10.]
```

Fig. 11. The updated change log after resolution step 2

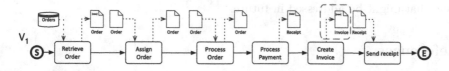

Fig. 12. The updated process model V_1 after the resolution step 2

6 Related Work

In general, two different groups of approaches regarding change management of business process models can be observed: change-based and state-based. In the change-based approaches [6,10,14], mostly, changes are represented in terms of operations which transform a process model from a particular state to the next one. In [10] for instance, the operations are recorded during the development phase of a process model. The *CoObRA* framework presented in [14] is a lightweight framework which provides recovery, versioning and multi-user functionality. As differences are detected on an elementary level, there is a possibility for the user to group them. Beside these approaches, there are also state-based approaches [2–5]. The basic idea is to compare different versions of a process model and reconstruct the change log. Most of them support dependency and conflict detection mechanisms as well as resolution of differences. The approach, we build our work upon [5], is a language-specific and state-based approach. It comprises: difference detection, dependency, equivalence and conflict analysis, and resolution of differences. Similarly to the previously mentioned approaches, it is focused on control flow-differences.

7   Conclusion and Future Work

In this paper, we presented an approach for detection and resolution of data-flow differences. Firstly, we presented the difference model which contains all possible differences that can occur between different versions of a process model. Then, we presented our detection method which is capable of detecting data-flow differences. As dependencies are possible between differences, we also provided a dependency analysis. At the end, we presented an iterative method for resolution of differences. However, there are some open questions that might be addressed in future. An ongoing work is to provide a tool support that serves as a proof of concept. Then, our dependency analysis for data-flow change operations was based on one invariant which must hold in a process model and it specifies that a data object must be created in order to be accessed. Including additional data-flow anti patterns from [15] in our dependency analysis step, should guarantee an error-free data-flow. Our approach support only two-way merging, i.e., merging of one source version and one updated version. However, in most of the cases we have at least two updated versions which should be compared and merged with the source version. Supporting a three-way merging definitely is an important issue that might be addressed in future.

References

1. van der Aalst, W.M.P.: Process Mining - Discovery, Conformance and Enhancement of Business Processes. Springer, Heidelberg (2011). https://doi.org/10.1007/978-3-642-19345-3
2. Alanen, M., Porres, I.: Difference and union of models. In: Stevens, P., Whittle, J., Booch, G. (eds.) UML 2003. LNCS, vol. 2863, pp. 2–17. Springer, Heidelberg (2003). https://doi.org/10.1007/978-3-540-45221-8_2
3. Altmanninger, K., et al.: AMOR - towards adaptable model versioning. In: 1st International Workshop on Model Co-Evolution and Consistency Management (MCCM 2008), Workshop at MODELS 2008, Toulouse, France (2008)
4. Brun, C., Pierantonio, A.: Model differences in the eclipse modeling framework. Eur. J. Inform. Prof. **9**, 29–34 (2008)
5. Gerth, C.: Business Process Models - Change Management. LNCS, vol. 7849. Springer, Heidelberg (2013). https://doi.org/10.1007/978-3-642-38604-6. Ph.D. thesis, University of Paderborn
6. Koegel, M., Herrmannsdoerfer, M., Li, Y., Helming, J., David, J.: Comparing state- and operation-based change tracking on models. In: EDOC, pp. 163–172. IEEE Computer Society (2010)

7. Küster, J.M., Gerth, C., Engels, G.: Dynamic computation of change operations in version management of business process models. In: Kühne, T., Selic, B., Gervais, M.-P., Terrier, F. (eds.) ECMFA 2010. LNCS, vol. 6138, pp. 201–216. Springer, Heidelberg (2010). https://doi.org/10.1007/978-3-642-13595-8_17
8. Küster, J.M., Gerth, C., Förster, A., Engels, G.: Detecting and resolving process model differences in the absence of a change log. In: Dumas, M., Reichert, M., Shan, M.-C. (eds.) BPM 2008. LNCS, vol. 5240, pp. 244–260. Springer, Heidelberg (2008). https://doi.org/10.1007/978-3-540-85758-7_19
9. Küster, J.M., Koehler, J., Ryndina, K.: Improving business process models with reference models in business-driven development. In: Eder, J., Dustdar, S. (eds.) BPM 2006. LNCS, vol. 4103, pp. 35–44. Springer, Heidelberg (2006). https://doi.org/10.1007/11837862_5
10. Lippe, E., van Oosterom, N.: Operation-based merging. In: Proceedings of the Fifth ACM SIGSOFT Symposium on Software Development Environments, pp. 78–87. SDE 5. ACM (1992)
11. Meyer, A., Pufahl, L., Fahland, D., Weske, M.: Modeling and enacting complex data dependencies in business processes. In: Daniel, F., Wang, J., Weber, B. (eds.) BPM 2013. LNCS, vol. 8094, pp. 171–186. Springer, Heidelberg (2013). https://doi.org/10.1007/978-3-642-40176-3_14
12. Object Management Group (OMG): Business Process Model and Notation (BPMN) Version 2.0 (2011). http://www.omg.org/spec/BPMN/2.0
13. Pottinger, R.A., et al.: Merging models based on given correspondences. In: VLDB, pp. 826–873 (2003)
14. Schneider, C., Zündorf, A., Niere, J.: CoObRA - a small step for development tools to collaborative environments. In: Workshop on Directions in Software Engineering Environments; 26th International Conference on software Engineering (2004)
15. Trčka, N., van der Aalst, W.M.P., Sidorova, N.: Data-flow anti-patterns: discovering data-flow errors in workflows. In: van Eck, P., Gordijn, J., Wieringa, R. (eds.) CAiSE 2009. LNCS, vol. 5565, pp. 425–439. Springer, Heidelberg (2009). https://doi.org/10.1007/978-3-642-02144-2_34
16. Weske, M.: Business Process Management: Concepts, Languages, Architectures. Springer, Secaucus (2007). https://doi.org/10.1007/978-3-642-28616-2

Modeling Reverse Logistics Networks: A Case Study for E-Waste Management Policy

Paola Lara(✉) Ⓘ, Mario Sánchez Ⓘ, Andrea Herrera Ⓘ,
Karol Valdivieso, and Jorge Villalobos Ⓘ

Bogotá, Colombia
{p.lara1081,mar-san1,a-herrer,km.valdivieso,
jvillalo}@uniandes.edu.co

Abstract. Reverse Logistics (RL) groups the activities involved in the return flows of products at the end of their economic life cycle. Enterprises and policy makers all over the world are currently researching, designing and putting in place strategies to recover and recycle products and raw materials, both for the benefit of the environment and to increase profits. However, the management of return flows is complex and unpredictable because consumer behavior introduces uncertainties in timing, quantity, and quality of the end-of-life products. To proactively cope with these concerns, we propose a metamodel that serves as a foundation for a domain specific modeling language (DSML) to understand RL processes and apply analysis techniques. This DSML can also be used to examine aspects such as RL strategies, capacity of the facilities, and incentives (e.g., sanctions and tax reliefs introduced by regulators). The core element of this approach is an extensible metamodel which can be used for analyzing specific applications of RL such as E-waste management.

Keywords: Reverse Logistics · Metamodel · DSML · E-waste management

1 Introduction

In a supply chain (SC), reverse flows consist of products at the end of their life cycle (EOL), or products that have been returned at other stages in the forward SC. The logistics of these flows, known as Reverse Logistics (RL), is formally defined as "the process of planning, implementing and controlling flows of raw materials, in-process inventory, and finished goods, from a manufacturing, distribution, or use point to a point of recovery or point of proper disposal" [15]. Growing concerns derived from global competitiveness, higher customer expectations, and superior SC performance have made RL all the more relevant. Lambert et al. [10] found that RL issues have been divided into three main concerns: recovery/distribution, production and inventory, and SC management. In all of these, quantitative and qualitative analysis techniques are used, together with approaches such as case studies, literature reviews, and conceptual descriptions. More recently, Suyabatmaz et al. [18] conclude that due to the high complexity and heterogeneity of reverse flows, problem-specific methodologies as well as generalized models are required and call for research efforts to study RL issues by

C. Cappiello and M. Ruiz (Eds.): CAiSE Forum 2019, LNBIP 350, pp. 158–169, 2019.
https://doi.org/10.1007/978-3-030-21297-1_14

incorporating analytical and simulation models. In particular, methods are noticeably needed to improve RL capabilities and to fulfill needs over short- or long-time periods.

Thus, a need has been identified for systematic approaches to understand, design and deal with the uncertainty of reverse flows along a SC and to reduce their increasing environmental impact. Along these lines, research has been conducted in specific industries such as in bottled products [9] and mobile phones [14]. Nowadays, RL scenarios involving E-waste management-i.e., electronic components that are considered obsolete or no longer functioning - are of particular interest: it contains valuable materials that should be recovered, as well as hazardous substances that require special handling to minimize pollution concerns. In addition, the increasing number of products containing electronic components have made this the fastest growing global waste stream. The Global E-waste Monitor 2017 has estimated that worldwide a staggering 44.7 million metric tons (Mt) of E-waste was generated in 2016, equal to 6.1 kilograms per inhabitant (kg/inh) annually. It has also predicted an alarming increase to 52.2 Mt alike to 6.8 kg/inh, by 2021 [3]. All of this has made imperative to design, implement, measure and improve strategies and public policies involving RL activities for E-waste management.

In order to proactively cope with these growing concerns on RL, we built a proposal to allow researchers, practitioners and decision makers to analyze, understand, and perform experiments with short- or long-term scenarios. In particular, we enable the exploration of "what-if" scenarios in RL networks with respect to costs, quality and sustainability outcomes. The core of this work is an extensible Domain Specific Modeling Language (DSML) [7] to create RL scenarios for analysis purposes. The language is built on top of a RL metamodel, product of a thorough literature review, capturing the fundamental RL concepts and relations that enable modeling the entire process.

This paper focuses on the modeling aspects of the metamodel for the RL process. The remaining sections are organized as follows: Sect. 2 presents a brief overview of RL providing a context for the rest of the work. Sections 3, 4 and 5 present our overall approach and details the construction and structure of the RL metamodel. Particularly, Sect. 5 illustrates its usage, by creating a scenario based on the recently promulgated laws for E-waste management in Colombia. Section 6 discusses how the metamodel can be extended to support dynamic analysis methods such as system dynamics (SD); and in Sect. 7, we draw initial conclusions, and future research avenues.

2   A Brief Reverse Logistics Background

This section focuses on presenting an overview of RL: its definition, main differences with forward logistics, and current streams of research. While forward logistics refers to the flow of a product from the manufacturer to the end consumer, Reverse Logistics is the process in which goods are recovered from an end point in order to either recapture value or to properly dispose them. Compared to forward logistics, the management of these flows is highly complex and less predictable because consumer behavior introduces uncertainties in timing, quantity, and quality of the EOL products [6]. As stated by Suyabatmaz et al. [18], reverse flows are complex and heterogeneous, and its study requires problem-specific methodologies as well as generalized models.

There are three main forces driving current work on RL: regulations, economic factors, and consumer awareness [4]. There is also an emerging trend which includes sustainability, and has adopted analysis techniques such as SD [8]. Current industry efforts to tackle reverse logistics issues include, for example, the Supply Chain Operations Reference (SCOR) [17], which provides a detailed description of the activities and the possible indicators that can be measured. However, the SCOR scope regarding RL is very limited and cannot model the behavior of the full reverse chain. While these initiatives have recognized the importance of putting in place a proactive strategy for RL, the management of return flows is easier said than done. The design and analysis of RL networks is a topic that is far from settled and offers a great number of opportunities. Likewise, the conceptual structure of the field is not yet fully established: there are some key concepts that are shared by most approaches and have well accepted definitions, yet there are also concepts that are included in only a small number of works and have definitions that are vague or even contradictory. Therefore, there is a need to further standardize the elements, definitions and relationships in the domain.

3   A Model-Based Approach to Understand Reverse Logistics

The proposal to support the understanding and analysis of RL networks is based on three main ideas that can be illustrated through phases (see Fig. 1). The first one is creating a metamodel for the RL domain. The second phase is to extend and refine said metamodel in order to adapt it to the needs of specific scenarios. This is because distinct scenarios can have particular requirements depending on the product entailed in the RL process and the specific country of analysis (e.g., E-waste management in Colombia). The third phase further extends the metamodel with new concepts, attributes and relations that depend on the type of analysis that is intended to be applied to modeled scenarios (e.g., SD, discrete event simulation). This metamodel is crucial in the construction of a subsequent RL DSL.

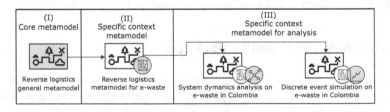

Fig. 1. General approach for RL modeling

Section 4 describes the first phase, that is the construction of the RL metamodel that formalizes the DSML's abstract syntax and is used to define its elements, relationships and modeling rules [5]. This metamodel is the result of a systematic review of the RL literature identifying the domain's core concepts along with its key attributes and relationships. The RL metamodel is the foundation of our approach for modeling and analyzing RL scenarios, using a domain-specific formalism [4]; and it aims to fulfill the needs of industries no matter their RL process. However, as products and legislation change among industries and countries, decision makers (e.g., government entities) will have the need to create specific models to analyze a given RL network. Hence, the need for a second phase where metamodel extensions are created, as illustrated in Sect. 5. This section first describes the mechanisms to extend the RL metamodel and then illustrates them in the context of current E-waste management regulations for Colombia.

The third phase entails the creation of further extensions to the metamodel that focus on the analysis methods that decision makers require to analyze their scenarios. For example, with the phase II metamodels it is impossible to apply techniques such as discrete event simulation, agent simulation, or SD because these metamodels focus mainly on static, structural aspects. However, by introducing additional concepts, attributes and relations targeted toward a specific analysis technique, it becomes possible to apply said technique on models created with the extended RL metamodel. This strategy of metamodel extension guided by the analysis technique has been applied in past works. For example, Manzur et al. [11] enriched ArchiMate [19] by adding elements to make possible the creation of architectural models for discrete event simulation.

4 The Reverse Logistics Metamodel

Next, we present the process to build a RL metamodel based on existing literature and expressive enough to address all of our concerns. To identify the core elements for the metamodel, we performed a systematic review of the RL literature. We limited the scope of our search to studies published in ranked peer-reviewed academic journals. A previous literature review by Agrawal et al. [1] on RL issues was found, which covers publications from 1986 to 2015. We updated this review by following the same selection and classification process for the missing period 2015 to 2018. Accordingly, six databases were considered: Elsevier, Emerald, Springer, Taylor and Francis, Wiley, and Informs. Given the main objective of our research, another exclusion criterion was defined: articles studying specific RL networks (e.g., closed-loop supply chains) or specific industrial applications were not considered. This resulted in a final set of 42 papers to complement those found in Agrawal et al.'s work [1].

As part of our analysis, we found that in the selected articles there is no agreement on the vocabulary to describe RL processes. To deal with this, we identified five clusters of terms used to describe closely related concepts: (i) Activity; (ii) Actor; (iii) Facility; (iv) Product; (v) and Regulator. Each cluster contains secondary clusters with finer grained terms also found in the literature review. Table 1 illustrates this by showing the Activity cluster which has 11 secondary clusters and the 66 terms.

Table 1. Cluster characterization for activities in RL

Main cluster	Secondary cluster	Related terms
Activity	Storing	Storing (A), warehousing (A), inventory (A), inspection (H)
	Sell	Sell to secondary market (H), sales (A), marketed (A), resell (A)
	Disposal	Disposition (A), disposition cycle time (A), disposal (A), incineration (H), secure disposal (A), littering (H), land filling (A), destruction (H)
	Pollute	Pollute (A), leachate (H)
	Manufacture	Production, manufacturing, product assembly (H), parts fabrication (H), modules subassembly (H), re-manufacture (H), reprocessing (H), re-produce (H)
	Recycle	Asset recovery (H), material recovery (H), cannibalization of parts (H), reuse (H), informal recycle (H), upcycled (H)
	Recover	Recover (A), asset recovery (A), reutilization (H), refurbish (A), product recovery (A), repair (A), reconditioning (A), disassembly (H), product upgrade (A), renovation (A)
	Transportation	Reverse distribution (H), reverse transportation (H), distribution (A), delivering goods (A), redistributed (A)
	Collection	Retrieval (A), collecting used products (A), gate keeping (H)
	Purchase	Sale (A), consumption (H), purchase (A)
	Return	Return (A), return to supplier (H), commercial return (H), end of use return (H), EOL return (H), non-defective return (H), customer return (H), warranty return (H), service return (H)

Following recommendations of the work by Babur et al. [2], which considers the definition and similarity of terms to discover clusters of elements, we established two types of relationships between terms in the literature: (i) analogous relations (A), when the terms are synonyms (e.g., manufacturing and production); (ii) and hyponym relations (H), which refers to subordinate connections in between concepts (e.g., manufacturing and product assembly). The complete literature review and the classification by clusters can be found on our website.

4.1   The Proposed Reverse Logistics Metamodel

The RL core metamodel defines and structures the key RL concepts identified after the literature review. Moreover, it allows the modeling of the network's controllable, static aspects, including a minimal subset of forward logistics concepts. Figure 2 depicts the core elements of each concept, the root of the metamodel (Return Flow) and their primary associations. It is possible that the attributes included in the metamodel may not be sufficient to model every specific RL scenario. Thus, this set of attributes is not set in stone and we have included the mechanisms to make it extensible: modelers might add more attributes and even new concepts in order to satisfy particular needs of analysis, as we explain in the following sections. The RL metamodel is organized around five clusters (see Fig. 2): (i) Activities, which refer to processes occurring in the RL scenarios; (ii) Actors, who guide and participate in those activities; (iii) Facilities, where the activities are performed or where production outputs are stored; (iv) Product related components, which represent the products themselves and their parts, their raw materials, their packaging, and the waste and pollution left after their usage and consumption; and (v) components related to Regulator entities that can create or terminate incentives for performing RL activities such as recycling.

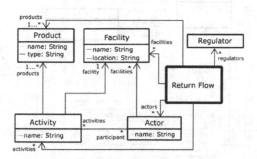

Fig. 2. The RL metamodel main concepts

Figure 3 shows the complete metamodel with the five key concepts and the root of the metamodel in bold lines, and with the elements that belong to each cluster as close as possible to them. Next, we present a brief overview of the metamodel, by following the typical sequence of a RL flow. The first activities serve to represent manufacturing or production, storage, transportation, and purchasing processes. Although these activities are widely regarded as belonging to the forward logistics domain, these activities are more likely to be controlled, thus enduring less uncertainty when starting from this point in the application of dynamic analysis to the RL models. To complement these activities, the metamodel includes related actors (e.g., manufacturer, and customer), facilities (e.g., factory, and warehouse), and sales channels which are all connected through associations. These elements were deliberately designed in a high-level manner to prevent the metamodel from becoming too large to be practical.

The second part of the metamodel refers to activities that pertain to the RL domain: disposal, pollute, recovery, recycling, collection, and returns. Disposal refers to activities that involve throwing away wastes in a facility such as a landfill. Likewise, to pollute refers to disposing pollutants into the natural environment (e.g., toxic wastes in a river). Recovery encompasses activities that return products to a state where they can be sold again for their original purpose (e.g., refurbishing, and reconditioning), as previously shown in Table 1. Similarly, recycling activities reduce products to their basic elements which can then be reused [15]. Recycling may refer to packaging, raw material, or any product part. Unfortunately, recycling and recovering can create their own waste and pollution. Collection is the selected term for activities such as gathering, filtering, and transporting previously sold products [15]. Return activities involve an actor who sends back a product to its manufacturer because the product either fails to meet his needs or fails to perform [15]. The final part of the metamodel includes regulators, which are in charge of the decision-making processes and influence RL chains by means of policies and controls. Regulators are not actors because they are not in direct contact with flows of products. However, they perform a critical role and have to be included in order to study how their actions influence the models' behavior.

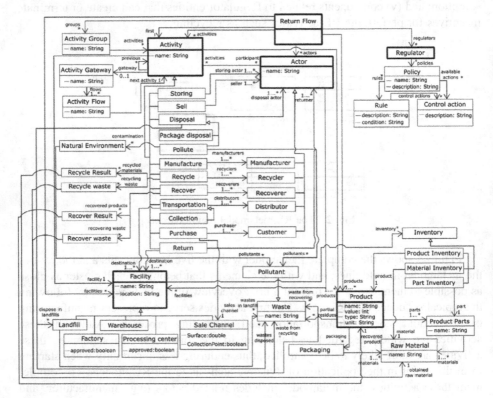

Fig. 3. The RL metamodel

5   Reverse Logistics in a Specific Context: E-Waste Case Study

While the RL metamodel groups the core concepts of any RL scenario, it is often necessary to have more specialized concepts to support the creation of more expressive models. In this section, we show how this can be achieved by extending and specializing the metamodel and illustrate this with a preparatory case study based on the E-waste management in Colombia. This case study is of interest because it targets a specific kind of waste with particular necessities regarding RL, and because the geographical localization provides a specific framework with respect to regulations. Over the last two decades, the amount of Electrical and Electronic Equipment (EEE) has continuously increased because of the rapid changes in information technologies, its increased accessibility, a downward trend in EEE prices, and a reduced lifetime for most products. As a result, a fast-growing number of EEE goods are reaching their EOL, generating vast amounts of E-waste [13]. An EEE is considered E-waste when it reaches its EOL and loses its original functionality, for instance, non-functioning or obsolete TVs, computers and mobile phones.

Given the importance of properly caring for E-waste streams, many countries have taken measures and have introduced policies to regulate its management. Based on a systematic review of the guiding legislations, we have identified one main principle and one derivative principle, described in Table 2 [14]. Today, most countries have EPR programs and policies in place. Nonetheless, their specific features and outcomes vary significantly across countries and industries. These variations cause a shift in the different RL processes and scenarios; this is where the need for extensions emerges, as the models shift from one country to another. For example, in South Korea the collection, treatment and costs are fully covered by producers through a collective scheme. To study how the metamodel adapts to the implementation of the EPR principle, we next analyze the case for E-waste management in Colombia.

Table 2. Principles for E-waste management

Principle	Description
Extended Producer Responsibility (EPR)	Forces the producers or importers of EEE to be financially responsible for the entire life cycle of their products, especially when they become obsolete; and assumes that the producer will minimize the costs of E-waste management from the design phase of the product
Shared Responsibility (SR)	All actors (producer, retailer, government, final consumer) participate in the waste management and are responsible for its success

5.1   Modeling E-Waste in Colombia

Colombia is one of the Latin American countries with the largest generation of E-waste. Estimations in 2010 shows that for a Colombian population of 46.3 million inhabitants, the E-waste generation is nearly 110.000 tons per year [12]. To deal with this situation the Colombian government has begun to regulate the EEE industry with the Law 1672 of 2013 and the Decree 284 of 2018, from the Ministry of Environment and Sustainable Development. This scheme follows the EPR principle and stimulates the adoption of RL practices since the producers are responsible for the recovery of E-waste. The Decree identifies all the actors involved in the E-waste management: producers, retailers, consumers, E-waste managers, environmental authorities, and territorial entities; and lists their obligations according to their role. In Colombia, customers can use the channels provided by both producers and retailers to deliver obsolete EEE devices to E-waste managers, who are responsible for either taking it back to producers (in its original form or as raw material), or to dispose them in a proper way. In this scenario, the government monitors and supervises parts of the RL network (actors, facilities, activities, inventories) and through incentives and penalties promotes a proper E-waste management aiming to reduce the use of informal alternatives.

To analyze the behavior of the presented case for E-waste management, it is necessary to extend the basic metamodel and adapt it to the specific context. Figure 4 presents the extensions added with newly added attributes and are shown in a grey shade. The elements added to the original metamodel arise from the study of the rules in the Colombian Decree that the core metamodel is not capable of supporting. The main extensions are: (i) definition of two additional attributes in the "Actor" entity allowing us to assess the responsibility of producers with the return of products: "Collection System" validates that the producers have an active collection scheme, and "Registry" validates that producers, distributors and E-waste managers are registered with the regulatory entities. Likewise, we added an attribute called "Fines" that sums up the value of all penalties imposed to an actor for breaking the law. (ii) definition of two attributes to "Sale Channel" that model the surface area of these points and the existence of collection points in them, as well as an attribute that guarantees that the "Processing Center" and "Factory" facilities are approved by relevant regulatory entities. (iii) addition of two "Action" specializations that specify the measures taken to enforce compliance with the law. These new actions are: "Penalty", applied to monitored actors for any breach of the law, or "Facility Closure", for lack of licenses and permits to operate. These extensions guarantee the expressiveness of the metamodel to describe the behavior of E-waste management in Colombia.

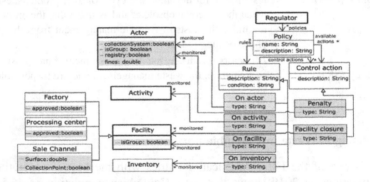

Fig. 4. Changes in the RL extended metamodel for the E-waste scenario in Colombia

6   Metamodel Extensions for Dynamic Analysis

In RL, it is often useful to explore "what-if" scenarios. These allow researchers, practitioners and decision makers to understand, analyze, and prepare for different outcomes regarding costs, quality and sustainability, whether they consider short- or long-term decisions. Thus, it is suitable to perform dynamic analyses, using techniques such as simulation, to comprehend the effects of the uncertainty in RL networks. However, for this to be possible, the metamodel must include elements, attributes, and relations representing dynamic aspects, and supporting specific analysis techniques, which can be achieved through an extension of a specific context metamodel for RL.

Using the same scenario, we exemplify the creation of an extension of the metamodel that can be used for dynamic analysis. The technique that is being applied to extend the metamodel is SD [16]. SD is a simulation technique to study nonlinear behaviors, centered around the concepts of flows and stocks: flows represent the movement of an element and stocks refer to the quantity of an element at a given time. In the metamodel, flows can be represented through RL activities and stocks can be stored in facilities. In order to support SD analysis of RL scenarios, the metamodel was first enriched with attributes to describe the outputs of activities (cost, value and quantity), and the stocks stored in facilities (initial and maximum capacities). It also requires a system to handle multiple units of measurement to perform unit conversions. Additionally, we can describe equations to specify changes in outputs or stocks of the model. The resulting metamodel is shown in Fig. 5 with the new extensions highlighted in grey. This metamodel extends the one proposed for E-waste management in Colombia in Fig. 4.

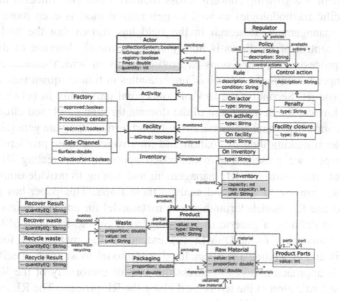

Fig. 5. Specific context metamodel extension: E-waste Colombian scenario for SD analysis

With this metamodel it is possible to establish a transformation schema from RL models to SD models that can be run with specific tools such as Stella's iThink. In this way, a modeler only has to construct RL models because their equivalent SD models can be automatically generated. The transformation schema, while not overly complicated, is more than an equivalence table: for each element in the RL model many elements may appear in the SD model. For example, for each kind of product and each facility where a product may be handled in the RL model, a stock has to be created in the SD model.

SD is not the only type of dynamic analyses that can be applied to the proposed metamodel. Any dynamic analyses can be used by including new elements and modifying current attributes and relationships with the dynamic components. For example, the E-waste metamodel for Colombia can also be adapted to support discrete event simulations (DES). These simulations differ from SD as they consider a discrete event in a given time, and each time an event occurs there is a change in the system's state. Thus, a model that supports DES has to consider components such as a system state, a time or clock, the events, and conditions in the system. DES has many suitable uses in the RL context, for example, process diagnosis, testing policies and prediction models.

7   Conclusions

RL management is a growing concern across industries and governments that requires problem-specific methodologies as well as generalized models even more so than in forward SC management. Research in the field has shown that the understanding, analysis and control of RL flows is highly complex mainly because of three issues. Firstly, RL processes face decisions in environments in which consumer behavior introduces unpredictability as a result of uncertainties in timing, quantities, and quality of an EOL product. Secondly, the lack of conceptual uniformity in between actors in the RL field hinders the development of the domain through combined efforts. Finally, the decisions and changes on a process are not short termed, they are generally reflected over a long term making their evaluation and improvement more problematic.

In this paper, we presented a model-based approach for creating RL scenarios considering the main issues of RL management and aiming to provide domain experts with tools they can use to study and analyze these flows. This paper has presented a proposal to create RL models through a core metamodel for analysis purposes and has focused on: (i) defining a generic metamodel, based on the RL state-of-the-art, that serves as a foundation for a DSML; (ii) extending the metamodel for particular domains; (iii) and extending the specialized metamodel to support specific analysis methods. This approach allows to address the lack of uniformity of the RL concepts through a standardization of the terms used along the RL process. The RL metamodel's concepts groups terms which describe the same or closely related concepts through the definition of clusters. Likewise, the metamodel allows domain experts to study and analyze using static and dynamic methods through the metamodel's extension mechanism. Particularly, this approach should be useful for regulators, which define RL policies and need to study "what-if" scenarios to improve RL capabilities, propose viable changes, or compare models' sustainability under different scenarios/policies. These extensions enable applying different analysis techniques to manage the RL flows in spite of the high uncertainty in the environment. For example, by giving information about the behavior of a network under an actual policy in the short, and long term, allowing to identify possible problems in the long term that are not visible at the beginning.

Based on the span of the literature review, the methodology used to identify the core concepts and the results with the preparatory case study on the E-waste Colombian scenario, we strongly believe that our proposal contributes to the main open issues in the field. Further research will provide domain experts with additional experimentation tools based on other simulation approaches (e.g., discrete events and agents).

References

1. Agrawal, S., et al.: A literature review and perspectives in reverse logistics. Resour. Conserv. Recycl. **97**, 76–92 (2015)
2. Babur, Ö., et al.: Hierarchical Clustering of Metamodels for Comparative Analysis and Visualization. Presented at the (2016)
3. Baldé, C.P., et al.: Quantities, Flows, and Resources. The Global E-waste. Global E-waste Monitor (2017)
4. Barker, T.J., Zabinsky, Z.B.: Reverse logistics network design: a conceptual framework for decision making. Int. J. Sustain. Eng. **1**(4), 250–260 (2008)
5. Cengarle, M.V., Grönniger, H., Rumpe, B.: Variability within modeling language definitions. In: Schürr, A., Selic, B. (eds.) MODELS 2009. LNCS, vol. 5795, pp. 670–684. Springer, Heidelberg (2009). https://doi.org/10.1007/978-3-642-04425-0_54
6. Fleischmann, M., et al.: Quantitative models for reverse logistics: a review. Eur. J. Oper. Res. **103**(1), 1–17 (1997)
7. Frank, U.: Domain-specific modeling languages: requirements analysis and design guidelines. In: Reinhartz-Berger, I., et al. (eds.) Domain Engineering, pp. 133–157. Springer, Berlin (2013). https://doi.org/10.1007/978-3-642-36654-3_6
8. Ghisolfi, V., et al.: System dynamics applied to closed loop supply chains of desktops and laptops in Brazil: a perspective for social inclusion of waste pickers. Waste Manag. **60**, 14–31 (2017)
9. González-Torre, P.L., et al.: Environmental and reverse logistics policies in European bottling and packaging firms. Int. J. Prod. Econ. **88**(1), 95–104 (2004)
10. Lambert, S., et al.: A reverse logistics decisions conceptual framework. Comput. Ind. Eng. **61**(3), 561–581 (2011)
11. Manzur, L., et al.: xArchiMate: Enterprise Architecture simulation, experimentation and analysis. Simulation **91**(3), 276–301 (2015)
12. Ministerio de Ambiente y Desarrollo Sostenible: Política Nacional: Gestión Integral de Residuos de Aparatos Eléctricos y Electrónicos, p. 104 (2017)
13. de Oliveira, C.R., et al.: Collection and recycling of electronic scrap: a worldwide overview and comparison with the Brazilian situation. Waste Manag. **32**(8), 1592–1610 (2012)
14. Rathore, P., et al.: Sustainability through remanufacturing in India: a case study on mobile handsets. J. Clean. Prod. **19**(15), 1709–1722 (2011)
15. Rogers, D.S., et al.: Going Backwards: Reverse Logistics Trends and Practices. Reverse Logistics Executive Council (1999)
16. Sterman, J.: Business Dynamics: Systems Thinking and Modeling for a Complex World. McGraw-Hill, Irwin (2000)
17. Supply Chain Council: SCOR® supply chain operations reference model. The Supply Chain Council, Inc. (2008)
18. Suyabatmaz, A.Ç., et al.: Hybrid simulation-analytical modeling approaches for the reverse logistics network design of a third-party logistics provider. Comput. Ind. Eng. **70**, 74–89 (2014)
19. The Open Group: ArchiMate® 3.0 specification (2016)

Using Conceptual Modeling to Support Machine Learning

Roman Lukyanenko[1](✉), Arturo Castellanos[2], Jeffrey Parsons[3],
Monica Chiarini Tremblay[4], and Veda C. Storey[5]

[1] HEC Montreal, Montreal, QC, Canada
roman.lukyanenko@hec.ca
[2] Baruch College, CUNY, New York, NY, USA
arturo.castellanos@baruch.cuny.edu
[3] Memorial University of Newfoundland, St. John's, NL, Canada
jeffreyp@mun.ca
[4] William and Mary, Williamsburg, VA, USA
monica.tremblay@mason.wm.edu
[5] Georgia State University, Altanta, GA, USA
vstorey@gsu.edu

Abstract. With the transformation of our society into a "digital world," machine learning has emerged as an essential approach to extracting useful information from large collections of data. However, challenges remain for using machine learning effectively. We propose that some of these can be overcome using conceptual modeling. We examine a popular cross-industry standard process for data mining, commonly known as CRISP-DM Directions, and show the potential usefulness of conceptual modeling at each stage of this process. The results are illustrated through an application to a management system for drug monitoring. Doing so demonstrates that conceptual modeling can advance machine learning by: (1) supporting the application of machine learning within organizations; (2) improving the usability of machine learning as decision tools; and (3) optimizing the performance of machine learning algorithms. Based on the CRISP-DM framework, we propose six research directions that should be explored to understand how conceptual modeling can support and extend machine learning.

Keywords: Machine learning · Conceptual modeling · Applications ·
Data mining · CRISP-DM

1 Introduction

Machine learning within business contexts (advanced business analytics [1, 2]) is a key driver of organizational competitive advantage [3, 4]. Despite the organizational and societal impact of machine learning [5], many challenges remain to both the effectiveness of machine learning and its widespread adoption. These include: interpreting the models used; executing machine learning algorithms effectively; and integrating machine learning into organizational processes. As a result of these challenges, organizations continue to struggle to implement successful machine learning solutions [6]. The objective of this research is to analyze how challenges specific to machine learning

C. Cappiello and M. Ruiz (Eds.): CAiSE Forum 2019, LNBIP 350, pp. 170–181, 2019.
https://doi.org/10.1007/978-3-030-21297-1_15

can be addressed by incorporating conceptual modeling principles in the machine-learning toolbox. Specifically, we show how many challenges related to machine learning could be potentially addressed with the help of conceptual modeling techniques that have been used for decades to support information systems development and database design.

Conceptual models formally describe "some aspects of the physical and social world around us for the purposes of understanding and communication" [7]. Here, we expand the usefulness of conceptual modeling from the domain of information systems development to the task of improving machine learning processes and outcomes. The contribution of this research is to show that conceptual modeling can improve in the application of machine learning algorithms. We illustrate our results by applying conceptual modeling to a management system for psychotropic drug monitoring. Section 2 reviews relevant machine learning and conceptual modeling research. Section 3 shows how characteristics of conceptual modeling can be applied to a machine learning process. Section 4 summarizes the paper and proposes future research directions.

2 Background: Machine Learning and Conceptual Modeling

2.1 Machine Learning

Machine learning (ML) is considered to have the potential to transform organizations and society [8, 9]. According to Gartner's 2016 Hype Cycle for Emerging Technologies, machine learning is one of "three key trends that organizations must track to gain competitive advantage" [3]. It has passed the early proof-of-concept phase and is now at the "Peak of Inflated Expectations." That is, it is now a popular mature technology, complete with major successes and failures [3].

Traditionally, machine learning proceeds without support from external knowledge sources (e.g., domain models) and relies heavily on the training data and learning algorithms. Recent research is exploring ways to encode additional semantics so that (some) rules do not have to be learned from training example [8, 10, 11]. For example, a model may reference a domain ontology and incorporate rules such as "all birds are animals." Then, a model does not need to learn the concept of "animal." Instead, through the domain ontology, it can automatically infer that a new instance labeled as a bird is also an animal. This work is narrowly focused on infusing the learning algorithms with additional knowledge, without requiring assistance from users.

Given the focus of machine learning on data and algorithms, several issues are evident. First, the quality of data inputs is critical to the performance of machine learning techniques [12]. Second, given the complexity of models such as neural networks and deep learning, the ability to explain the decisions or predictions made by ML techniques needs to be improved for such models to be adopted in many settings [13]. Finally, machine learning models should also provide guidelines for developers regarding appropriate deployment (e.g., the populations, cases, or processes to which the results of the model generalize).

2.2   Conceptual Models

Traditionally, conceptual modeling is a major phase of information systems development that formally captures user requirements to support the development of information systems. Research has led to the development of different kinds of conceptual models, including data models, process models, models of business activity and goals, and models of enterprise and systems architecture [14, 16–27].

Conceptual models are typically diagrams that contain graphics and text and are widely used in IS development to facilitate communication, improve domain understanding among stakeholders, and guide IS development activities such as database design, user interface design, and programming [22–28]. Conceptual models have played an especially important role in database design, where grammars such as the Entity-Relationship model have become a de facto standard way of formally representing the structure of data to be stored and are widely used to derive database tables, fields and relationships.

Researchers have investigated the benefits of conceptual models for information systems development. These can be summarized through the three basic needs that conceptual models address [29]:

1. *Need to cope with complexity.* Conceptual models reduce complexity of information systems development by focusing on the relevant aspects, structuring and organizing the requirements.
2. *Need for shared understanding.* Information systems development typically involves many people with different backgrounds, beliefs, expertise and training. Such diversity creates potential for conflicts, and if left unresolved, may lead to project failures. Conceptual models are designed with the general objective of being boundary objects [30].
3. *Need to solve problems.* Information technologies are typically created to address some organizational or societal need, although it is often unclear how to best design a system with the many options that typically exists. Conceptual modeling supports analysis of a domain and supports specific design solutions.

These three needs, although studied in the context of information systems development, are also present in the context of machine learning. Therefore, the conceptual modeling techniques used in systems development might also be useful in resolving challenges related to the development, adoption, and effectiveness of ML techniques by organizations.

However, research at the intersection of conceptual modeling and ML remains rare and lacks an overarching agenda. Machine learning is absent from the authoritative conceptual modeling agenda set by Wand and Weber [28] and has not been part of active discourse in conceptual modeling [31, 32].

In addition to the paucity of efforts to apply conceptual modeling to machine learning, existing efforts appear narrowly focused on some specific issue (e.g., modeling sentiment or supporting business simulations). A general assessment of the potential of conceptual modeling to support machine learning is missing, as is an agenda that can support future research. We propose an approach intended to stimulate broad efforts in the research community to find synergies between the two fields.

3   Using Conceptual Modeling to Support Machine Learning

Conceptual modeling can be used as an effective and standard activity in machine learning to support activities in various phases of the machine learning process. Specifically, conceptual modeling can be useful to identify and specify problems, improve understanding of the data that is used for training, increase the predictive accuracy and performance of machine learning algorithms, and model the process change needed to introduce machine learning into organizational processes.

We demonstrate the application of conceptual modeling and ML in a real case, which uses ML within the context of a US foster care system tasked with placing and monitoring children in foster families. The evidence is based on our direct observations and experience with developing ML solutions for several agencies that are part of the foster care system. A major challenge for the foster care system is the ever-increasing number of children entering foster care. For processes such as monitoring medication intake or criminal activities by foster children, the load increase can be detrimental, which may put a child's mental and physical health at serious risk. The promise of ML algorithms is to enable automated and rapid detection of potential issues with a child in a foster family (e.g., medication overdose, other physical and mental problems), based on past records written by case workers.

We illustrate the potential of conceptual modeling to benefit each stage of the Cross-Industry Standard Process for Data Mining (CRISP-DM) (i.e., Business Understanding, Data Understanding, Data Preparation, Modeling, Evaluation, and Deployment) [33]. CRISP-DM was originally developed for data mining, but became widely adopted for ML as well [34, 35].

Business Understanding. The first phase of the CRISP-DM process seeks to understand the project objectives and requirements from a business perspective [33]. Business understanding is also a phase of information systems development. Traditionally, conceptual models have been used to support this phase. Effective ML is impossible without first carefully examining and understanding the business objectives for a particular ML project, and the specific goals the project seeks to achieve. Acquiring this information is akin to eliciting information systems requirements, a phase of systems development that has benefited historically from the use of conceptual models. Common notations to support this phase could be process and goal-oriented conceptual modeling grammars and methods, such as i*, BPMN, UML, or BIM (Business intelligence model).

Conceptual models can represent specific objectives and goals for an ML project. Monu and Woo [36] demonstrate the value of goal-oriented actor-based modeling to model goals, objectives and resources of intelligent systems. Finally, conceptual models can assist managers and other parties in comprehending the scope of ML interventions (i.e., identify the organizational processes affected by ML).

Returning to the case management in foster care example, new mandates required monitoring children who were taking, and may potentially be overprescribed, psychotropic medication (drugs used to treat psychiatric conditions). This adds a new task to the workload of caseworkers, namely, analyzing random samples of existing home-visit notes (notes that document the interaction between the caseworker and the child at

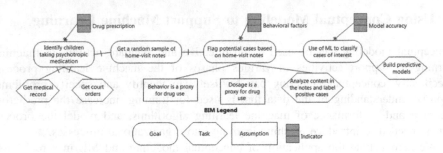

Fig. 1. BIM diagram fragment showing case management goals

their home) to identity cases of children who might be taking these medications. There can be hundreds of notes written for each child, making it difficult to identify the cases of interest. We turn to modeling (using BIM) to document the new objectives set for case workers (see Fig. 1). Based on this example and emerging research [e.g., 37], we propose the following for conceptual modeling research:

Direction 1: *Investigate the application of conceptual modeling techniques to increase business understanding in the context of machine learning projects.*

Data Understanding. The data understanding phase of CRISP-DM starts with the acquisition of data suitable for the business problem identified in Phase 1. Modelers then review the data, consider any data quality issues, and prepare it to be imported into the ML software. Conceptual modeling is especially well suited for modeling and understanding data. Common notations to support this phase include popular conceptual modeling grammars (e.g., ER, UML).

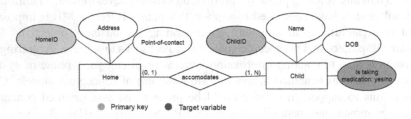

Fig. 2. Fragment of a (color-coded) conceptual model showing home-child relationship (Color figure online)

Modeling can also be used to document data provenance [38] and to help ascertain data quality. Conceptual models can suggest whether there is enough data for learning (i.e., show the scope of the domain and the attributes available for ML), identify where to obtain additional data (e.g., by showing connections between entities), and show how to best use the data in ML (e.g., what attributes to impute). For case management, without a conceptual model we may assume that home-visit notes are written in such a manner that they represent each of the children in a home. However, from the conceptual model in Fig. 2, one home can have multiple children and there might be cases where, under the same household, one child is taking psychotropic medication and another is not. If we assign labels to every given note (for the training set), how do we handle these cases? This may suggest the need to obtain data at the child level, rather than the home level, in order to acquire a more complete data set that can produce reliable models.

Consider another scenario, in which a particular data source could have missing values for an attribute 'dosage' of medication. Many ML approaches suggest imputing values for missing data before building a model [39]. However, a conceptual model of the data might indicate that 'dosage' is an optional property of medication, as shown in Fig. 3. In this case, some (or all) missing values in the data might not be applicable to the instances for which it is missing, instead of missing from the data source. This can indicate the need for subclasses of the phenomena of interest –in this case, medication. Moreover, it might be necessary to build different models for medications that have strict *physician-prescribed dosage* (e.g., prescription drugs) and medications that do not (e.g., nutrition supplements, where dosage is recommended, but not physician-prescribed), rather than impute missing values for some cases where the attribute does not apply.

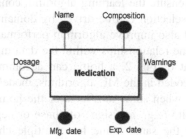

Fig. 3. Sample conceptual model with optional property shown as unfilled circle

Following our case management case, if we find references to dosage information within the home-visit notes, this can be an indication that the child is taking a pre-scribed medication (potentially a psychotropic medication). We propose:

Direction 2: *Investigate the application of conceptual modeling techniques to increase understanding of available training data for machine learning tasks and support data preparation activities for machine learning tasks.*

Data Preparation. The data preparation phase of CRISP-DM involves all activities (e.g., data transformations) required to construct the final dataset to be used for the learning algorithm. This phase involves multiple transformations of the original data source by performing extract-transform-load (ETL) procedures. Prior research in conceptual modeling has demonstrated the use of process models (e.g., BPMN, EPCs) to document the ETL process [40, 41]. The transformation process within ML software is analogous to the ETL processes used in the context of data warehousing.

Furthermore, conceptual data modeling grammars can be extended to better reflect the needs of ML. For example, grammars could allow color-coding of attributes included in the ML process as inputs, using one color to indicate a target attribute (e.g., in Fig. 2 the target variable is green) and a different color for attributes that cannot be used in a predictive model due to compliance to regulations (e.g., gender or race). In this way, conceptual modeling can graphically communicate the aspects of the business on which the ML process is based. This, in turn, may contribute to better understanding of the results and compliance with data protection regulations. We propose the following direction for conceptual modeling research:

Direction 3: *Investigate the application of conceptual modeling techniques to support attribute selection, transformation, cleaning and other activities involved in preparing training and validation data for machine learning algorithms.*

Modeling. The dataset that emerges from the transformation procedures of the previous stage is supplied to ML algorithms for training, learning, and validation.

Conceptual models can be used to support the selection of learning algorithms and the modeling process. For example, if knowledge from a certain part of the domain is important, a modeler may choose to select inputs manually based on known domain semantics (as opposed to automatically, using dimension reduction or attribute selection algorithms). This will ensure the learning algorithm considers these inputs.

The decision on input selection can be driven by domain knowledge. The use of conceptual modeling could also improve algorithm performance. This can be accomplished by hard-coding some relationships within the data inputs. To illustrate, in the conceptual model fragment of Fig. 2, a home can accommodate multiple children. Unless this is explicitly encoded in the ML algorithms, models might potentially differ in performance, especially when some attributes of the home-visit notes are used to predict attributes of the child (e.g., has signs of abuse or neglect, lack of focus). For example, for cases where the same home has multiple children there could be a conflicting signal from the home's attributes mapped to the children, whereas these conflicts would not exist in one-to-one cases. Understanding the conceptual model may help address these conflicts. When analyzing the home-visit notes, if there is a home with two children (one child requires psychotropic medication and the other does not), the home-visit may: (a) focus on aspects common to both children; (b) focus on the child taking psychotropic medication and reporting this in the home-visit note; or (c) focus on the child not taking psychotropic medication and not having anything in the case notes that reflects medication intake. In each of these cases, there would be the same entry associated to two instances with two different outcomes, degrading the performance of ML classifiers. Accordingly, we propose the following research direction:

Direction 4: *Investigate the application of conceptual modeling techniques to enhance effectiveness of machine learning algorithms.*

Evaluation. This step of the CRISP-DM method assesses the degree to which the model learned from Phase 4 meets the original business objectives. This phase also involves interpreting the results of the model by converting the structures generated by the learning algorithms into language accessible to business users.

Here, conceptual models can help by highlighting which inputs were used to train the model, relative to all the attributes that exist in the domain. An especially valuable addition that conceptual models can bring to the evaluation phase of ML is to improve the understandability of complex ML models. One prominent concern regarding the use of ML is the lack of transparency of complex models (e.g., neural networks, random forests, support vector machines). This "black box" property of many models constitutes a major barrier for wider adoption of ML, especially in critical or sensitive applications [42].

There is a growing interest in increasing the transparency and interpretability of complex models. Much of this research, however, is effective only with the variables used by a given algorithm. For example, perhaps the most common approach to increasing the interpretability of ML is by showing the relative importance of a feature with respect to the target variable [42]. Another approach to obtaining the same result is to build a tool that allows users to interact with individual components within a model (e.g., individual neurons within a neural network), and then measure how highlighting a particular component affects the target variable [42]. However, existing approaches, only consider variables that are already part of the model. Another limitation is that these approaches do not typically present the variables as belonging to a particular conceptual structure (e.g., influence is typically shown as ordered lists of variables).

As mentioned above, a principal role of conceptual models is to simplify, abstract and conceptualize a domain. Furthermore, conceptual modeling practice and research have long dealt with the issue of transparency. For example, research on conceptual modeling has been developing and evaluating methods and design approaches to improve the comprehensibility and understandability of models [32, 42–44]. Research on conceptual modeling has investigated these issues within the context of both dynamic models (e.g., process models) and static models (e.g., data models) [15].

Applying conceptual models to the problem of interpreting results may offer additional benefits because conceptual models can depict both variables included in the model, as well as those discarded due to lack of predictive power or those manually excluded for ethical or other reasons [42], providing a more comprehensive view of which aspects of the domain the model affects. Another possibility is to combine existing techniques to show the weights of variables with conceptual models. Then, the variables can be grouped into entity types, as opposed to presenting them as a list sorted by their contribution size. The advantage is in their ability to show relationships among the variables, and their groupings.

Some research has used conceptual models (e.g., actor-based, goal-oriented, BIM) to improve the transparency of intelligent agents and text-mining processes, with calls for more research in this area [36, 45]. However, no theory, framework or set of principles has been proposed. Further research is needed to apply conceptual modeling to the problem of ML transparency. This could include studies that investigate specific applications, as well as research that develops general principles and approaches for using conceptual modeling to improve the transparency and interpretability of ML results. We propose the following research direction:

Direction 5: *Investigate the application of conceptual modeling techniques to increase transparency, comprehensibility and understandability of the outputs of machine learning algorithms.*

Deployment. Creation of the model is generally not the end of an ML project. If the model addresses business objectives, its performance is sufficient. If the inner workings of the model are sufficiently understood, the model is introduced as an intervention into a real-world process. For example, a neural network can serve as a decision support tool to prioritize cases of interest.

Analogous to Phase 1, conceptual models may be used to document the objectives and goals behind an ML intervention. Once ML deployment occurs, business users can refer back to the original goals and objectives captured in the conceptual models from Phase 1 to assess the compliance of this intervention with the original requirements and goals. Furthermore, because deployment of ML in an organization typically results in changing an existing business process, process models and enterprise models can be used to document this change and communicate to stakeholders which part(s) of the enterprise the process affects (see Fig. 4).

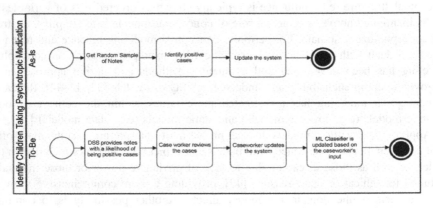

Fig. 4. As-Is and To-Be BPMN Model for psychotropic drug monitoring

The ML classifier serves as a decision support tool for the caseworker. As the BPMN diagram in Fig. 4 shows, the ML process is relatively similar to the traditional way of doing things. Models such as the one in Fig. 4 allow case managers to draw conclusions about the impact of the new process on human and material resources in the US foster care system and may suggest strategies for the deployment of ML within the US foster care system.

Direction 6: *Investigate application of conceptual modeling techniques to support deployment of machine learning in organizations, and to document and support process changes result of the introduction of machine learning in organizational processes.*

4   Conclusion

We propose that conceptual modeling can be used as a standard activity in machine learning applications. After identifying machine learning challenges, we employed a popular cross-industry standard process, CRISP-DM, to highlight the potential ways in which conceptual modeling can make this process more effective by proposing specific research directions for future conceptual modeling research. To illustrate, the results were applied to a real case of psychotropic drug monitoring within the US federal foster care system. Machine learning promises to help cope with a severe shortage of case-workers and might even save lives. The results of using conceptual modeling demonstrate the broad potential of conceptual modeling to advance ML by: (1) supporting the process change associated with introducing ML within organizations, (2) improving the usability of ML as a decision tool (e.g., by making the models and results more transparent); and (3) improving the performance of ML algorithms (e.g., by imbuing them with domain knowledge).

Future research is needed to demonstrate empirically the benefits of combining conceptual modeling and machine learning. Understanding the intersection between conceptual modeling and ML may help extend the development of ML algorithms and best practices for using ML. For example, it might be possible to directly encode the cardinalities of relationships between entities into ML algorithms. In this manner, the learner becomes aware of the entities to which the inputs belong, as well as how the entities (and therefore the inputs) are related to one another. Future research should use conceptual modeling to achieve transparency of ML models. Furthermore, although this research has proposed and illustrated the potential of conceptual modeling for each of the processes of CRISP-DM, each of these processes needs to be examined in detail and empirically assessed.

Finally, ML can add a new impetus to a recent push by conceptual modeling researchers to expand the scope of conceptual modeling (or, issues related to domain representations) beyond the traditional IS development context [e.g., 29, 31, 46, 47]. The application of conceptual modeling within the ML context can further expand the scope of conceptual modeling research and practice, foster new interdisciplinary connections and demonstrate the continued importance and value of conceptual modeling research.

References

1. Davenport, T., Harris, J.: Competing on Analytics: Updated, with a New Introduction: The New Science of Winning. Harvard Business Press, Cambridge (2017)
2. Khatri, V., Samuel, B.: Analytics for managerial work. Commun. ACM **62**, 100–108 (2019)
3. Forni, A., Meulen, R.: Gartner's 2016 Hype Cycle for Emerging Technologies Identifies Three Key Trends That Organizations Must Track to Gain Competitive Advantage (2016)
4. Ransbotham, S., Kiron, D.: Analytics as a source of business innovation. MIT Sloan Manag. Rev. **58**, 3–16 (2017)
5. McAfee, A., Brynjolfsson, E.: Machine, platform, crowd: Harnessing our digital future. WW Norton & Company, New York (2017)

6. Ransbotham, S., Kiron, D., Prentice, P.K.: Beyond the hype: the hard work behind analytics success. MIT Sloan Manag. Rev. **57**, 3–15 (2016)
7. Mylopoulos, J.: Conceptual modelling and Telos. Conceptual Modeling Databases CASE Integrated View of Information Systems Development, pp. 49–68. Wiley, New York (1992)
8. Jones, N.: The learning machines. Nature **505**, 146 (2014)
9. Waldrop, M.M.: No drivers required. Nature **518**, 20 (2015)
10. Tsymbal, A., Zillner, S., Huber, M.: Ontology – supported machine learning and decision support in biomedicine. In: Cohen-Boulakia, S., Tannen, V. (eds.) DILS 2007. LNCS, vol. 4544, pp. 156–171. Springer, Heidelberg (2007). https://doi.org/10.1007/978-3-540-73255-6_14
11. Zhou, L., Chaovalit, P.: Ontology-supported polarity mining. J. Assoc. Inf. Sci. Technol. **59**, 98–110 (2008)
12. Alonso, O.: Challenges with label quality for supervised learning. J. Data Inf. Qual. JDIQ **6**, 2 (2015)
13. Castelvecchi, D.: Can we open the black box of AI? Nat. News **538**, 20 (2016)
14. Azevedo, C.L., Iacob, M.-E., Almeida, J.P.A., van Sinderen, M., Pires, L.F., Guizzardi, G.: Modeling resources and capabilities in enterprise architecture: a well-founded ontology-based proposal for ArchiMate. Inf. Syst. **54**, 235–262 (2015)
15. Burton-Jones, A., Weber, R.: Building conceptual modeling on the foundation of ontology. In: Computing Handbook: Information Systems and Information Technology, Boca Raton, FL, United States, pp. 15.1–15.24 (2014)
16. Davies, I., Green, P., Rosemann, M., Indulska, M., Gallo, S.: How do practitioners use conceptual modeling in practice? Data Knowl. Eng. **58**, 358–380 (2006)
17. Mylopoulos, J., Chung, L., Yu, E.: From object-oriented to goal-oriented requirements analysis. Commun. ACM **42**, 31–37 (1999)
18. Pentland, B., Recker, J., Kim, I.: Capturing reality in flight? Empirical tools for strong process theory. In: ICIS 2017, Seoul, South Korea, pp. 1–12 (2017)
19. Recker, J., Rosemann, M., Green, P., Indulska, M.: Do ontological deficiencies in modeling grammars matter? MIS Q. **35**, 57–79 (2011)
20. Soffer, P., Kaner, M., Wand, Y.: Assigning ontology-based semantics to process models: the case of petri nets. In: Bellahsène, Z., Léonard, M. (eds.) CAiSE 2008. LNCS, vol. 5074, pp. 16–31. Springer, Heidelberg (2008). https://doi.org/10.1007/978-3-540-69534-9_2
21. Taghavi, A., Woo, C.: The role clarity framework to improve requirements gathering. ACM Trans. Manag. Inf. Syst. TMIS **8**, 9 (2017)
22. Aguirre-Urreta, M.I., Marakas, G.M.: Comparing conceptual modeling techniques: a critical review of the EER vs OO empirical literature. ACM SIGMIS Database **39**, 9–32 (2008)
23. Batra, D.: Conceptual data modeling patterns: representation and validation. J. Database Manag. **16**, 23 (2008)
24. Kung, C.H., Solvberg, A.: Activity modeling and behavior modeling. In: Proceedings of the IFIP WG 8.1 Working Conference on Information Systems Design Methodologies: Improving the Practice, pp. 145–171. North-Holland Publishing Co. (1986)
25. Mylopoulos, J.: Information modeling in the time of the revolution. Inf. Syst. **23**, 127–155 (1998)
26. Rizzi, S.: Conceptual modeling solutions for the data warehouse. Data Wareh. OLAP Concepts Archit. Solut. 1–26 (2007)
27. Rossi, M., Siau, K.: Information Modeling in the new Millennium. IGI Global, Hershey (2000)
28. Wand, Y., Weber, R.: Research commentary: Information systems and conceptual modeling - a research agenda. Inf. Syst. Res. **13**, 363–376 (2002)

29. Lukyanenko, R.: Rethinking the role of conceptual modeling in the introductory IS curriculum. In: Thirty Ninth International Conference (ICIS 2018) on Information Systems, San Francisco, CA, USA, pp. 1–9 (2018)
30. Mark, G., Lyytinen, K., Bergman, M.: Boundary objects in design: an ecological view of design artifacts. J. Assoc. Inf. Syst. **8**, 34 (2007)
31. Jabbari, M., Lukyanenko, R., Recker, J., Samuel, B., Castellanos, A.: Conceptual modeling research: revisiting and updating Wand and Weber's 2002 research agenda. In: AIS SIGSAND, pp. 1–12 (2018)
32. Recker, J.C., Indulska, M., Rosemann, M., Green, P.: Do process modelling techniques get better? A comparative ontological analysis of BPMN (2005)
33. Jackson, J.: Data mining; a conceptual overview. Commun. Assoc. Inf. Syst. **8**, 19 (2002)
34. Turban, E., Sharda, R., Delen, D.: Decision Support and Business Intelligence Systems (required). Google Sch. (2010)
35. Buczak, A.L., Guven, E.: A survey of data mining and machine learning methods for cyber security intrusion detection. IEEE Commun. Surv. Tutor. **18**, 1153–1176 (2016)
36. Monu, K., Woo, C.: Intelligent agents as a modeling paradigm. In: ICIS 2005 Proceedings, p. 15 (2005)
37. Nalchigar, S., Yu, E.: Conceptual modeling for business analytics: a framework and potential benefits. Presented at the 2017 IEEE 19th Conference on Business Informatics (CBI) (2017)
38. Ram, S., Liu, J.: A new perspective on semantics of data provenance. Presented at the Proceedings of the First International Conference on Semantic Web in Provenance Management, vol. 526 (2009)
39. Nelwamondo, F.V., Mohamed, S., Marwala, T.: Missing data: a comparison of neural network and expectation maximization techniques. Curr. Sci. **93**, 1514–1521 (2007)
40. Trujillo, J., Luján-Mora, S.: A UML based approach for modeling ETL processes in data warehouses. Presented at the International Conference on Conceptual Modeling (2003)
41. Simitsis, A., Vassiliadis, P.: A method for the mapping of conceptual designs to logical blueprints for ETL processes. Decis. Support Syst. **45**, 22–40 (2008)
42. Hall, P., Gill, N.: An Introduction to Machine Learning Interpretability (2018)
43. Samuel, B.M., Khatri, V., Ramesh, V.: Exploring the effects of extensional versus intentional representations on domain understanding. MIS Q. **42**(4), 1187–1209 (2018)
44. Storey, V.C., Trujillo, J.C., Liddle, S.W.: Research on conceptual modeling: themes, topics, and introduction to the special issue (2015)
45. Gu, N., Singh, V., London, K.: BIM ecosystem: the coevolution of products, processes, and people. In: Building Information Modeling: BIM in Current and Future Practice, pp. 197–210 (2015)
46. Parsons, J., Lukyanenko, R., Wiersma, Y.: Easier citizen science is better. Nature **471**, 37 (2011)
47. Lukyanenko, R., Parsons, J., Wiersma, Y., Maddah, M.: Expecting the unexpected: effects of data collection design choices on the quality of crowdsourced user-generated content. MIS Q. **43**(2), 634–647 (2019)

Analyzing User Behavior in Search Process Models

Marian Lux[1,3](✉) and Stefanie Rinderle-Ma[1,2]

[1] Faculty of Computer Science, University of Vienna, Vienna, Austria
{marian.lux,stefanie.rinderle-ma}@univie.ac.at
[2] ds@univie, Vienna, Austria
[3] LuxActive KG, Vienna, Austria

Abstract. Search processes constitute one type of Customer Journey Processes (CJP) as they reflect search (interaction) of customers with an information system or web platform. Understanding the search behavior of customers can yield invaluable insights for, e.g., providing a better search service offer. This work takes a first step towards the analysis of search behavior along paths in the search process models. The paths are identified based on an existing structural process model metric. A novel data-oriented metric based on the number of retrieved search results per search activity is proposed. This metric enables the identification of search patterns along the paths. The metric-based search behavior analysis is prototypically implemented and evaluated based on a real-world data set from the tourism domain.

1 Introduction

Mapping and understanding Customer Journey Processes (CJP) has become a new trend recently. Signavio, for example, names customer journeys a *"strategic imperative"*[1]. This is underpinned by case studies in several domains including tourism [6] and entertainment [8]. In a nutshell, customer journey describes the customer touchpoints/interactions with a company's information system [9]. Search processes constitute one type of CJP as they reflect search (interaction) of customers with an information system or web platform. According to literature, *"a better understanding of user search behavior"* [2] is essential, however, has been restricted to the analysis of single events and sequences so far. We aim to bring together process-oriented analysis with the full range of patterns in a process model (cf. http://www.workflowpatterns.com/) and search behavior analysis.

Search process models can become complex as typically customer behavior tends to be diverse [7]. Hence, we proposed a structural metric for assessing the complexity of search process models in [7]. It was shown that together with semantic pre- and post-processing it is possible to derive search paths in the models at a structural level.

---

[1] https://www.signavio.com/post/customer-journeys-as-a-strategic-imperative/.

© Springer Nature Switzerland AG 2019
C. Cappiello and M. Ruiz (Eds.): CAiSE Forum 2019, LNBIP 350, pp. 182–193, 2019.
https://doi.org/10.1007/978-3-030-21297-1_16

In order to tackle the challenge of complexity, in this work, we focus on search paths in search process models and try to find out what the customer was searching for when following a certain path in the model. This is reflected by the key research question of this work:

RQ : How to assess search behavior along search paths?

Being able to answer this question yields a competitive edge for companies, for example, by providing specific offers along the search paths. Also the customers are empowered to inspect and improve their search experience.

In this work, we tackle **RQ** in a quantitative way, i.e., based on a search behavior metric. This metric requires an extension of the search process model definition provided in [7], i.e., considering the total number of search results of a search activity as data element. Search path patterns are suggested based on literature and the search behavior metric. With these patterns, search paths can be assessed with respect to the search behavior along these paths. One example, is a decreasing of search results in the search behavior which might hint at using more and more specialized search terms in this path. Also "jumping" as search behavior can yield interesting insights for the analysts.

The search path metric is prototypically implemented and the approach is applied to a real-world data set from the tourism domain. Several search paths can be identified and suggestions for the search offering of the company can be derived.

The paper is structured as follows: Sect. 2 repeats the structural metric and introduces the new search metric for search process models. Section 3 introduces and discusses search path patterns. Section 4 describes the evaluation and the application to a real-world data set. Section 5 discusses related work and Sect. 6 the presented approach.

2   Search Path Metrics

The goal of this work is to analyze (structural paths) in search process models with respect to the search behavior of the users along these paths. One parameter reflecting and influencing the search behavior is the number of search results [12]. If a user, for example, receives a too large number of results for a certain query she/her might decide to narrow down the search in order to obtain a lower number and hence a more targeted search result. Definition 1, hence, extends the definition of search process models from [7] by adding the number of search results obtained per search activity:

Definition 1 (Search Process Model with Search Results). *Let S be the set of all search terms. A search process model with search results is defined as directed graph $SP := (N, E, l, nsr)$ where*

- *N is a set of nodes*
- *$E \subseteq N \times N$ denotes the set of control edges*

- $l : N \mapsto S$ denotes a function that maps each node to its label, i.e., $\forall n \in N$ n is a search term.
- $nsr : N \mapsto \mathbb{N}_0$ maps each node to the total number of results achieved by the search.

Note that nsr refers to the total number of search results and not to the number of results that are possibly shown to the user (cf. paging). Figure 1 shows an example search process model consisting of four search activities (plus explicit start and end node). The number on the edges reflect the number of instances for which a the path containing the edge has been executed. Also shown is the corresponding process execution log L that contains the execution events for five instances $I1$ to $I5$. Each log entry reflects the execution of one activity together with the number of retrieved search results, e.g., the execution of fitness with 50 results for instances $I1$, $I2$, $I3$, and $I4$.

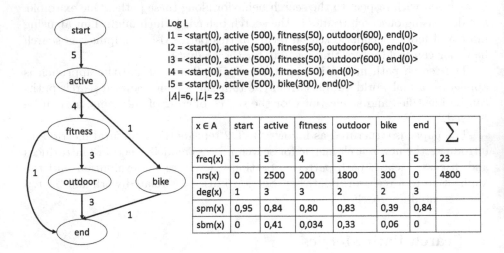

Log L
I1 = <start(0), active (500), fitness(50), outdoor(600), end(0)>
I2 = <start(0), active (500), fitness(50), outdoor(600), end(0)>
I3 = <start(0), active (500), fitness(50), outdoor(600), end(0)>
I4 = <start(0), active (500), fitness(50), end(0)>
I5 = <start(0), active (500), bike(300), end(0)>
|A|=6, |L|= 23

$x \in A$	start	active	fitness	outdoor	bike	end	Σ
freq(x)	5	5	4	3	1	5	23
nrs(x)	0	2500	200	1800	300	0	4800
deg(x)	1	3	3	2	2	3	
spm(x)	0,95	0,84	0,80	0,83	0,39	0,84	
sbm(x)	0	0,41	0,034	0,33	0,06	0	

Fig. 1. Example search process with sbm and spb metrics

In our previous work [7], the search process quality metrics (spm metric) was found useful to assess the complexity of search process models and to find relevant search paths. The spm metric relates the degree and frequency of a node to the overall number of activities and number of entries in the underlying log (the one the search process model was mined from). The table in Fig. 1 contains the spm metric for each of the activities. For activity fitness, for example, spm turns out as $1 - \frac{3*6}{4*23} = 0.8$. One path of interest can be detected based on spm as active $\rightarrow$ fitness $\rightarrow$ outdoor.

To assess the user behavior along a search path in the search process model we introduce the *search behavior metric sbm* that is based on the number of search results. According to [12] search includes an iterative execution of "query formulation + reformulation" and "evaluation of the results", following certain strategies that depend on the satisfaction with the number of retrieved search results [11]. The number of search results is also considered in web search analysis [10]. The sbm metrics hence takes the number of search results into consideration and for an activity of interest puts it into relation with the overall success of the search in the search process model. Moreover, it weighs the search results by the relative number of executions of the activity that has produced the search results. Doing so enables to differentiate whether, for example, a high number of search results has been produced by a single activity execution or by several activity executions. The latter shall result in a higher value of sbm as more users have conducted the same search.

Definition 2 (Search Behavior Metric). *Search process model, L the corresponding log, and A the corresponding set of distinct activities. Let further freq: $A \mapsto \mathbb{N}_0$ count the occurrence of an activity $x \in A$ in L. Then the search behavior metric for x sbm(x) is defined as*

$$sbm(x) := (1 - \frac{freq(x)}{\sum_{n \in N} freq(n)}) * \frac{nsr(x)}{\sum_{n \in N} nsr(n)}$$

with $\sum_{n \in N} freq(n) > 0 \wedge \sum_{n \in N} nsr(n) > 0$.

If activity x does not produce any search results (i.e., $nsr(x) = 0$), the metric yields a value of 0. As $|L| > 0$ and $|A| \leq |L|$, $|A| > 0$, $sbm(x) \in [0; 1)$ holds.

Consider again Fig. 1 where the sbm metrics is shown for all activities. Along the search path `active` → `fitness` → `outdoor` first sbm(`active`) = 0, 41 is achieved, followed by an obvious narrowing down of the search to sbm(`fitness`) = 0, 034. Then interestingly, the search is again widened to sbm(`outdoor`) = 0, 33. Such "jumps" in the search behavior in one path might indicate a shift in the search strategy. How this search behavior can be analyzed and interpreted will be discussed in the Sect. 3.

3   Revealing Search Behavior on Paths in Search Process Models

In the following, we suggest search path patterns suggested in literature and investigate whether and how these patterns can be applied to analyzing search behavior along paths in search process models. The authors in [12] identify two iteratively executed search steps "query formulation + reformulation" and "evaluation of the results" in user search. They further name two basic search strategies applied during these phases, i.e., narrowing and broadening. Narrowing is applied if the number of search results is perceived as too high. It uses more keywords, conjunction (AND), or negation (NOT). Broadening is employed if the number of search results is perceived too low; it uses less keywords, disjunctions, or text processing techniques such as stemming. Also the use of ontologies, resolving synonyms/homonyms, and adding/removing constraints can support both of the strategies.

We "unroll" the steps "query formulation + reformulation" and "evaluation of the results" and their strategies according to [12] into search paths in the search process model reflecting one line of search that was possibly shared by multiple users. The following patterns are based on a full combination of the strategies "narrowing/no narrowing" and "broadening/no broadening"[2]. Aside the description of the pattern it is discussed how the strategy can be revealed based on the development of the sbm metric of the nodes in the path. The interrelation between the number of search results and the frequency of a node is further elaborated after the pattern descriptions.

Search Path Pattern 1 – Decreasing corresponds to the strategy of narrowing and no broadening, i.e., applying different strategies on the search terms in order to decrease the number of search results along the activities in a path. The manifestation of this pattern in a search process model is a path for which the contained activities unfold a decreasing sbm metric (cf. Fig. 2a).

Search Path Pattern 2 – Increasing corresponds to the strategy of broadening and no narrowing, i.e., increasing the number of search results along the path of interest. This pattern can be deduced from the search process model based on decreasing sbm metric values along a path (cf. Fig. 2b).

Search Path Pattern 3 – Jumping reflects search behavior that jumps between narrowing and broadening along a path, i.e., search results increase and decrease reflected by an increasing and decreasing sbm along a path. This can be caused by using different search terms within one path. We denote the points in the path where the sbm changes from decreasing to increasing and vice versa as jumping points (cf. Fig. 2c).

Search Path Pattern 4 – Constant Search reflects search behavior that produces a similar number of search results along a path, i.e., the variability in the sbm metric is low (cf. Fig. 2d). This pattern can result from using different search terms resulting in a similar amount of search results: *(a)* By accident or if narrowing / broadening strategies are not effective, e.g., a specification of the search term does not result in any narrowing. *(b)* If entered terms hardly limit search results because the provided search functionality follows the strategy not to limit search results but sorting them by relevance, e.g., during the search, ontology support helps to broaden and sort the results by considering the original entered search terms first, followed by its synonyms, specializations and finally its generalizations. *(c)* The underlying overall quantity of possible search results in an information system is small, e.g., an information systems contains merely 10 substantially different documents to search for and most search terms return generally 1 search result. Therefore, most frequent search results contain 1 or 0 search results.

Let us dig a bit deeper into the behavior of the sbm metric for nodes in a path. Let $x_1, x_2 \in N$ be two nodes in a path of a search process model $SP = (N, D, l, nsr)$ where x_2 is a direct successor of x_1 (see Fig. 2). Then:

$$sbm(x_2) > sbm(x_1) \text{ if } nsr(x_2) > \frac{\sum_{n \in N} freq(n) - freq(x_1)}{\sum_{n \in N} freq(n) - freq(x_2)} * nsr(x_1) \quad (1)$$

---

[2] Note that we only use conjunction in this work.

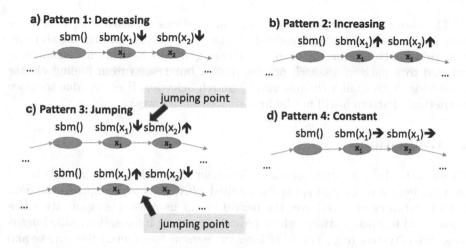

Fig. 2. Overview search patterns and search metric sbm

Equation 1 holds accordingly for sbm decrease by replacing $>$ by $<$. We fathom Eq. 1 by analyzing corner cases.

$$sbm(x_2) > sbm(x_1) \text{ if } \begin{cases} nsr(x_2) > nsr(x_1) & freq(x_1) \approx freq(x_2) \\ nsr(x_2) > \frac{nsr(x_1)}{\sum_{n \in N} freq(n) - 1} & freq(x_1) \gg freq(x_2) \\ nsr(x_2) > nsr(x_1) * (\sum_{n \in N} freq(n) - 1) & freq(x_1) \ll freq(x_2) \end{cases}$$

In the first case, if the frequencies of x_1 and x_2 are roughly the same, the development of sbm follows the development of the search results, i.e., we can directly interpret the results on the strategies narrowing and broadening as described for the search patterns. The second case illustrates the case where $freq(x_1) \gg freq(x_2)$. Hence we put $freq(x_1) = \sum_{n \in N} freq(n) - 1 \wedge$ $freq(x_2) = 1$ as extreme values. Then the number of search results for x_2 has to exceed the number of search results for x_1 divided by the overall number of node frequencies. For high overall frequency, this can mean a drop in search results for x_2 when compared to x_1, i.e., x_2 has to produce less results than x_1. If in the third case $freq(x_1) \ll freq(x_2)$, i.e., we set extreme values $freq(x_1) = 1 \wedge freq(x_2) = \sum_{n \in N} freq(n) - 1$, the number of search results for x_2 has to be higher than the number of search results for x_1 multiplied by the overall frequency. For corner cases two and three this can mean quite a difference in how the number of search results evolves for x_2, however, typically it can be assumed that the number of search results will exceed the number of node frequencies which will cushion the effect. Altogether the sbm metric provides a balanced tool of evaluating the effects of higher or lower search results, but considering the node frequencies that contributed to the search results.

Note that for the abstract example in Sect. 2 the evaluation of the sbm metric does not allow any conclusion as the search results have been synthesized in an arbitrary manner. The conclusiveness of the proposed search behavior path patterns will be evaluated on a real-world data set in Sect. 4.

The above set of patterns covers all combinations of "narrowing", "no narrowing", "broadening", "no broadening". However, further patterns are conceivable. **Search Behavior Pattern 5 – Homogeneous Search**, for example, is not tied to a path in a search process model, but results from finding cluster of activities with similar (homogeneous) search behavior. However, due to space restrictions, Pattern 5 will not be investigated in this work.

4 Evaluation

We evaluate the assessment of search behavior in search process models based on a log from a real-world application called *oHA*. This log comprises the data of four instances executed over the period of *1.5* months. The application is a commercial tourism platform which provides touristic information, called *activities*, from Austria (e.g., points of interest, events, tours, etc.) to tourists and as well locals[3]. The platform is accessible for users as progressive web app[4] and contains about *294,000* activities. The keyword based search functionality for activities has a location based filter method with the option to define an individual search radius around a current or a selected position. An online ontology support guides users through the search functionality by showing suggestions for search terms based on their previous entered search terms and the same ontology is used to broaden, and as well to sort, the results by taking into account, synonyms, generalizations, and specializations.

The search logs are accessible through a *PostgreSQL* database and used as input to calculate sbm results on a mined search process model from these logs. One log record contains the following fields: The field *case device* contains a unique id which is automatically generated per user device. It is used to trace a users' search path. *action time* contains the time stamp when a particular log entry was generated for representing the order of occurred activities inside a search path and is therefore used to calculate the edges in a process model. The *search string* represents the activity which results as node in a process model. Finally, the *search result count* shows the number of returned results and is used to calculate the number of search results *nsr*.

The search functionality has some characteristics, which may influence the resulting process model and are described in the following: There exists a special activity * which signals that the user just hit the search button without considering a search term as query input. The activity * is also automatically executed by the system, if a user enters the search functionality the first time, after manually selecting a new the search position or after deleting the whole search query by pressing a clean button. This results in many *-activities in the logs which are naturally reflected in the mined process models. As mentioned before, the system also shows recommendations for search terms which can be selected by users. After such a term is selected, a new search will be automatically performed by the system with the added search term (e.g., the first

---

[3] https://austria.myoha.at.

[4] https://developers.google.com/web/progressive-web-apps/.

query had *tours* and a user selects *mountain* as recommendation, an automatic search query *tours mountain* will be performed). Therefore the search results will be predominantly refined through the before described behaviour. In addition to the search query, the number of returned results is influenced by the user-selected position and distance radius. Therefore, the same search query – and thus activity – can return a different number of results.

Figure 3 depicts the process model mined in Disco (https://fluxicon.com/disco/).

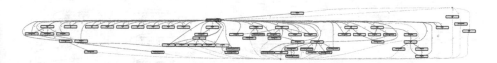

Fig. 3. *oHA* search process model with 10% of the most frequent activities

With a prototypical implementation in Java the spm and sbm metrics were calculated and annotated to the nodes in the search process model. Nodes with high spm results (which are closer to 1) indicate a clear path. Hence, we filter the model depicted in Fig. 3 for nodes with a spm metric, for example, of at least 0.96 (result see Fig. 4).

Then we visually inspect the search behavior based on sbm results of the contained nodes. Since the activity * appears predominantly in every search path, at least at the beginning as described before, we ignore this activity for the pattern recognition and treat it as "outlier". We can identify all four search behavior path patterns introduced in Sect. 3. Note that the logs are produced by the platform with a German and an English user interface. Most users used the German user interface. Therefore, the vast majority of the search paths contain German search terms, which are translated into English in the following for a better comprehensibility: *"familie"* = *"family"*, *"Spielplatz"* = *"playing area"*, *"touren"* = *"tours"*, *"wandertouren"* = *"hiking tours"*, *"tipp"* = *"advice"*, *"sehenswuerdigkeiten"* = *"sights"*, *"kulinarik"* = *"cuisine"*, *"kinder"* = *"children"*. The following paths are selected for further discussion regarding the identified pattern for the path, e.g., set P1 contains selected paths for which Search Behavior Path Pattern 1 – Decreasing can be revealed:

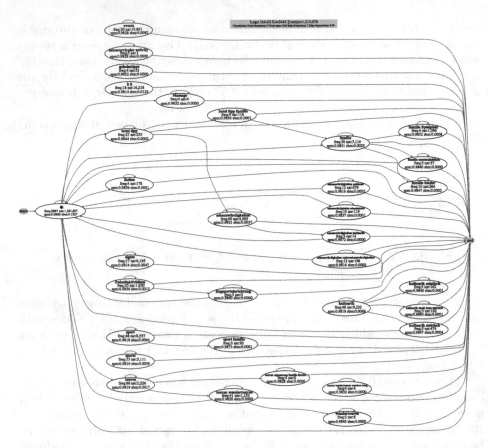

Fig. 4. *oHA* search process model filtered with spm ≥ 0.96, produced by implemented prototype

$P1 = \{\langle start, *(sbm = 0.1527), familie(sbm = 0.0023), familie\,Spielplatz(sbm = 0.0008), end\rangle,$
$\quad \langle start, *(sbm = 0.1527), sport(spm = 0.0064), sport\,familie(sbm = 0.0001), end\rangle,$
$\quad \langle start, *(sbm = 0.1527), touren(spm = 0.0017), touren\,wandertouren(sbm = 0.0009),$
$\quad wandertouren(sbm = 0.0000), end\rangle\}$

$P2 = \{\langle start, *(sbm = 0.1527), hotel\,tipp(sbm = 0.0002), sehenswuerdigkeiten(sbm = 0.0037),$
$\quad end\rangle\}$

$P3 = \{\langle start, *(sbm = 0.1527), hotel\,tipp(sbm = 0.0002), sehenswuerdigkeiten(sbm = 0.0037)$
$\quad sehenswuerdigkeiten\,kulinarik(sbm = 0.0000), end\rangle,$
$\quad \langle start, *(sbm = 0.1527), hotel\,tipp(sbm = 0.0002), hotel\,tipp\,familie(sbm = 0.0001),$
$\quad familie(sbm = 0.0.0023), familie\,kinder(spm = 0.0002), end\rangle\}$

$P4 = \{\langle start, *(sbm = 0.1527), hotel\,tipp(sbm = 0.0002), hotel\,tipp\,familie(sbm = 0.0001), end\rangle\}$

P1 refers to Pattern 1 – Decreasing and is most frequently revealed for the given use case. The sbm results are decreasing along the search path because

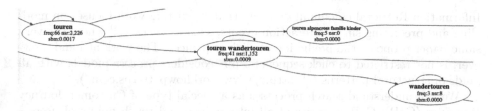

Fig. 5. Search path P1, snippet of search process model, produced by implemented prototype

users refined their search results to find useful results. We illustrate one of the paths as model snippet in Fig. 5.

P2 reflects an increase in the sbm results. Apparently, users tried to broaden their search results because not enough results appeared at the beginning of their search. This pattern appears rarely in the search process model. *P3* shows jumping points (cf. sehenswuerdigkeiten, familie) where users changed their search strategy during the search path. These jumping points can be of interest, e.g., in marketing, by investigating correlations between these jumping points and their previous search terms in their particular paths, for identifying e.g., new user recommendations. *P4* reflects a constant search path. In this example we assume that the users performed the broadening strategy and it was not successful. This pattern appeared only once in the discovered search process model.

Interpretation: The analysis of the search behavior shows that in several search paths users, who are tourists, started with "hotel tipp" which means some advise by the hotel they are staying in. From there, the search continued either with more specialized advises by the hotel ("hotel tipp familie") or by choosing new, probably connected topic such as sights ("sehenswuerdigkeiten"). We can also see that from the more specialized search, users go back to a connected, but more general search term, e.g., from "hotel tipp familie" to "family" (in English "hotel advise family" to "family"). The interpretation could be that users in general try the advises offered by the hotel and from there apply different search strategies (narrowing and/or broadening) along topics they are specifically interested in, e.g., family or sights. Hence, we could suggest to a hotel owner with such paths to further invest in the hotel advises, particularly targeting certain topics such as family. Also, if the system provides an artificial intelligence function for recommendations of search terms, like the present tourism platform does as described before, the system could replace the suggestion "hotel tipp" with "sehenswuerdigkeiten" and "family".

5   Related Work

In web search analysis, e.g., [10], search terms and the number of search results are considered, but not the underlying search process models and the search behavior along paths. This observation is underpinned by current work in the

Information Retrieval community stating that "[e]xisting work focuses on modeling and predicting single interaction events, such as clicks" [2] where the very same paper proposes the prediction of click sequences. The work at hand, however, is not restricted to click sequences, but considers process models with all kinds of structural patterns (cf. http://www.workflowpatterns.com/).

We can understand search processes as a special type of Customer Journey Processes (CJP). CJP comprise of all interactions and touch points of users – such as searches – with a company's information system or (web) platform [5,6]. It seems that currently commercial tools and systems such as Signavio are at the forefront to develop CJP maps and models. CJP mining has been recently discovered as promising in different application domains [6,8]. [1] suggests clustering and merging CJP maps with process trees in order to detect representative CJP models from event logs. If a merge happens will be decided by the analyst. In [4] an alternative method to detect relevant CJP based on Markov models is introduced. [7] presents pre- and post-processing methods, together with a structural path metric in order to detect paths in CJP models. The proposed metric is employed in the work at hand. None of the mentioned approaches addresses the search behavior.

For mining search process models, metrics like the spm can be used for filtering nodes to show only paths of interest for analysts. For example the process mining framework ProM[5] offers several metrics as well as edge and node filtering, particularly in the context of the Fuzzy Miner [3].

6 Discussion and Outlook

This work proposes structural and search behavior metrics for discovering and visually inspecting search process models. This enables the detection and analysis of search behavior along paths and facilitates suggestions for improving the search offer in the sequel. For a data set from the tourism domain, for example, it is possible to discover search paths and to derive that the tourism provider (e.g., a hotel) could improve its search suggestions. The novelty of the approach is to employ data and data values into metrics. Using search results is a first step, particularly suited for search process models, but further data can become relevant in explaining customer behavior, e.g., weather or location. Accordingly, new metrics and enhanced mining, filtering, and inspection techniques become necessary to yield the most valuable insights from the data.

References

1. Bernard, G., Andritsos, P.: CJM-ab: abstracting customer journey maps using process mining. In: CAiSE Forum 2018, pp. 49–56 (2018)
2. Borisov, A., Wardenaar, M., Markov, I., de Rijke, M.: A click sequence model for web search. In: Research & Development in Information Retrieval, pp. 45–54 (2018)

---

[5] http://www.promtools.org/doku.php.

3. Günther, C.W., van der Aalst, W.M.P.: Fuzzy mining – adaptive process simplification based on multi-perspective metrics. In: Alonso, G., Dadam, P., Rosemann, M. (eds.) BPM 2007. LNCS, vol. 4714, pp. 328–343. Springer, Heidelberg (2007). https://doi.org/10.1007/978-3-540-75183-0_24
4. Harbich, M., Bernard, G., Berkes, P., Garbinato, B., Andritsos, P.: Discovering customer journey maps using a mixture of Markov models. In: Symposium on Data-driven Process Discovery and Analysis, pp. 3–7 (2017)
5. Lemon, K.N., Verhoef, P.C.: Understanding customer experience throughout the customer journey. J. Mark. 80(6), 69–96 (2016)
6. Lux, M., Rinderle-Ma, S.: Problems and challenges when implementing a best practice approach for process mining in a tourist information system. In: Business Process Management, Industry Track, pp. 1–12 (2017)
7. Lux, M., Rinderle-Ma, S., Preda, A.: Assessing the quality of search process models. In: Weske, M., Montali, M., Weber, I., vom Brocke, J. (eds.) BPM 2018. LNCS, vol. 11080, pp. 445–461. Springer, Cham (2018). https://doi.org/10.1007/978-3-319-98648-7_26
8. Pmig, Y., Yongil, L.: Customer journey mining. Technical reports, LOEN Entertainment (2018)
9. Richardson, A.: Using customer journey maps to improve customer experience. Harvard Bus. Rev. 15(1), 2–5 (2010)
10. Silverstein, C., Henzinger, M.R., Marais, H., Moricz, M.: Analysis of a very large web search engine query log. SIGIR Forum 33(1), 6–12 (1999)
11. Stelmaszewska, H., Blandford, A.: Patterns of interactions: user behaviour in response to search results. In: JCDL Workshop on Usability of Digital Libraries, pp. 29–32. UCL Interaction Centre (UCLIC) (2002)
12. Sutcliffe, A.G., Ennis, M.: Towards a cognitive theory of information retrieval. Interact. Comput. 10(3), 321–351 (1998)

User-Centered and Privacy-Driven Process Mining System Design for IoT

Judith Michael[1(✉)], Agnes Koschmider[2], Felix Mannhardt[3],
Nathalie Baracaldo[4], and Bernhard Rumpe[1]

[1] Software Engineering, RWTH Aachen University, Aachen, Germany
{michael,rumpe}@se-rwth.de
[2] Karlsruhe Institute of Technology, AIFB, Karlsruhe, Germany
agnes.koschmider@kit.edu
[3] SINTEF Digital, Trondheim, Norway
Felix.Mannhardt@sintef.no
[4] IBM Almaden Research Center, San Jose, USA
baracald@us.ibm.com
http://www.se-rwth.de
http://www.sintef.no

Abstract. Process mining uses event data recorded by information systems to reveal the actual execution of business processes in organizations. By doing this, event logs can expose sensitive information that may be attributed back to individuals (e.g., reveal information on the performance of individual employees). Due to GDPR organizations are obliged to consider privacy throughout the complete development process, which also applies to the design of process mining systems. The aim of this paper is to develop a privacy-preserving system design for process mining. The user-centered view on the system design allows to track who does what, when, why, where and how with personal data. The approach is demonstrated on an IoT manufacturing use case.

Keywords: Privacy-by-design · Process mining · Event log ·
Access control · Meta-model · Privacy preserving system architecture

1 Introduction

The General Data Protection Regulation (GDPR) marks a new era in data privacy. GDPR provides a set of data protection principles, individuals' rights and legal obligations to ensure the protection of personal data of EU citizens. Privacy concerns informal self-determination, which means the ability to decide what information about a person goes where [5]. GDPR imposes organizations to consider privacy throughout the complete development process, which also applies for the design of process mining systems. Process mining uses as input event logs files, which originate from all kinds of systems such as ERP or Internet-of-Things (IoT) systems. To design systems compliant with GDPR, eight privacy design

© Springer Nature Switzerland AG 2019
C. Cappiello and M. Ruiz (Eds.): CAiSE Forum 2019, LNBIP 350, pp. 194–206, 2019.
https://doi.org/10.1007/978-3-030-21297-1_17

patterns have to be considered: minimize, hide, separate, aggregate, inform, control, enforce, and demonstrate [12]. Privacy can be protected, for example, by means of *hide any personal information that is processed from plain view* or *data subjects should have agency over the processing of their personal information*. These privacy design patterns have been acknowledged as useful in order to integrate them into the development processes [7]. They can be considered as requirements for the design of privacy-preserving process mining systems. Whereas process mining does not directly use or require to use personal information - the focus is often more on improving on the organizational level rather than the personal one - event logs can expose sensitive information that may be attributed back to individual persons. For instance, events may contain sensitive information pertaining to preferences of workers. Also the traces, i.e., sequences of activity executions, reveal information on the performance of individual workers, which can constitute personal information that workers may want to protect. Some research has been done on cross-organizational process mining, in which organizations are reluctant to share information [14] and guidelines from a practical viewpoint in a consulting context have been published [19]. So far, however, there has not been research on privacy preservation in the area of process mining.

To fill this gap, this paper aims to develop a user-centered system design, which captures privacy in process mining. The system design is exemplified in the context of IoT manufacturing working tasks. It supports data owners (e.g., workers) to control privacy concerns for sensitive data by means of privacy polices and to monitor their compliance (i.e., is the data captured unauthorized?). In this way, it allows data owners to determine more accurately who can do what with which data and allows them to see which privacy concerns are foreseen in which steps of process mining. The definition of the user-centered privacy system design for process mining requires to understand privacy checkpoints in process mining and how to ensure a user-centered access control to event logs. For this, we define an IoT use case to which we refer throughout the paper.

The remainder of this paper proceeds as follows. The next section summarizes related works and shows that no privacy-preserving meta-model exists for privacy mining. Section 3 discusses terms used as input to define the user-centered privacy system design and presents our IoT use case. Section 4 defines the data model and architecture. Section 5 presents a brief application of the privacy system design in the context of process mining. The paper ends with a summary and an outlook on future work.

2   Related Work

To define the privacy-preserving system design we studied related approaches on (1) privacy-preserving data mining, (2) access control, (3) privacy meta-models and (4) privacy in process mining. Privacy-preserving data mining (PPDM) [2] aims at finding the best suitable privacy preserving technique for the data. The large body of literature on PPDM mainly focus on the hide and aggregate privacy challenges, while privacy concerns of the data provider are mainly disregarded [22]. The privacy-preserving meta-model for event logs as presented in this paper is complementary to PPDM like anonymization measures in order to fulfill compliance with GDPR. With respect to literature on access control, role-based access control (RBAC) and policy-based access control (PBAC) also known as attribute-based access control (ABAC) have been suggested. ABAC grants access to services based on the attributes possessed by a requester. Thus, it replaces the subject (a user) by a set of attributes [21]. PBAC uses digital policies to guide authorization decisions. Such policies can be built with the policy language XACML. In the context of IoT the advantages of ABAC can be exploited: all information within the organization can be accessed in real-time for all types of requests. The system design presented in this paper relies on ABAC and XACML and has been extended for our purpose.

Privacy meta-models can be found in [4,10,11]. Feltus et al. [10] present a model-driven approach for privacy management in business ecosystems. Their privacy meta-model focuses on the privacy in the dynamics of businesses and therefore, only resources, roles and activities are considered for privacy preservation. Grace and Surridge [11] present a formal model of user-centered privacy by using labeled transition systems (LTS) for analysis of a service's behaviour against user preferences. This approach focuses only on data and does not include process mining aspects. In [4], Bergeron proposes a UML profile to model privacy protection for web applications during application design. The restrictions of these privacy meta-models makes them not suitable for our purpose. Therefore, we define a proper meta-model for process mining allowing to consider context information related to environment and location, which is necessary in our IoT use case. Related to event log data, a large body of research exist for security-oriented analysis [20]. For instance, the tool of Stocker and Accorsi [20] allows to configure security concerns (i.e., authentication, binding of duty and separation of duties) when generating synthetic event logs. The literature analysis shows that privacy concerns have been scarcely considered for process mining. Only the work of [16] discusses privacy challenges for process mining, however, without providing a solution how to protect user privacy. To the best of our knowledge, this paper suggests the first system design and privacy-preserving meta-model for process mining.

3　Motivation: Background and Use Scenario

Below, we discuss terms related to the context of privacy and process mining and apply them for the use scenario tracking IoT manufacturing working tasks.

Privacy and Process Mining. The GDPR defines personal data as "any information relating to an identified or identifiable natural person" (referred to as *data provider*) [9]. Privacy protection goes further than security and regulates the authorized access to data based on a lawful basis (e.g., may be bases on consent, but based on legal requirements such as auditing) and organizational measures that should build trust between the individual (i.e., data provider), the entity who process and store the data (referred to as *data controller*) and entities who use or bought the data (referred to as *data consumer*). *Process mining* uses event data recorded by information systems to reveal the actual execution of business processes in organizations. Since most activities in modern organization are supported by technology each process execution leaves behind a digital trace indicating the occurrence and timing of activities in the databases of the company. Process mining takes event logs, records of the sequence of steps, and discovers a de-facto model of the process that can expose performance information, bottlenecks, workarounds, and much more. In this way, events and traces may contain sensitive information pertaining to data provider and being accessible to data controller(s) and data consumer(s). To a certain degree process mining methods already abstract from such privacy related details by deriving a process model that reveals only the observed sequences of activity execution. However, often occurrence frequencies, performance information, and decision rules are discovered in addition to the basic control-flow of the process [18], which may leak additional information from the event log. Furthermore, process mining is often an iterative process in which multiple process models for different subsets of the event log, filtered according to conditions of interest, are discovered and compared [8]. By discovering several process models and slightly varying the filtering condition it is possible to identify workers. Obviously, privacy preservation should be taken into account for process mining.

Use Scenario: Privacy and IoT Manufacturing Tasks. IoT is a domain with a high demand for privacy and security considerations. The large amount of data, that is tracked and analyzed with e.g., learning (AI) software, can originate from internet-enabled machines, working modules labeled with QR-code and workers equipped with wearable such as smart watches, interacting as autonomous agents forming a complex system. In the context of IoT, GDPR relates to privacy compliance of a large number of attributes such as GPS location, working time and salary. From this data, the working practices and performance of workers can be inferred, which may be considered very sensitive information [15].

To understand which privacy concerns may arise in the steps of process mining (i.e., to understand privacy policies between data provider, controller and consumer) we apply the privacy checkpoint diagram proposed by [16] with six stages of data passes for IoT manufacturing working tasks, see Fig. 1.

– *Data source:* given our use case, the sources of data are manufacture information systems, the machine working on, wearables like smart watches, sensors measuring humidity or monitoring malfunctions and (mobile) devices tracking location, identify, etc.
– *Data capture:* data from these data sources is captured when devices and systems log tasks, when recognizing the identity or requesting actions. This stage tracks who does what, when and where (e.g., a worker committed a working task with his smart watch on Nov. 28 at 11:28 h).
– *Primary use:* the data controller (e.g., manager representing a company) determines the purposes for which and the means by which the captured data

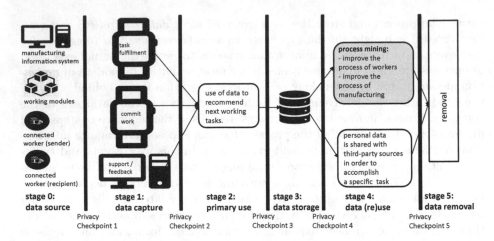

Fig. 1. Identification of data passes and privacy checkpoints for IoT manufacturing working tasks adapted from [16].

is processed. For instance, the captured data can be used for recommending subsequent tasks for workers. In this way, the data controller decides *why* and *how* the personal data should be processed. The privacy concern of the data provider at this stage is to *control* what kind of and how much information other people can obtain from his data [22], while the data controller must ensure an authorized data use.

– *Data storage:* the personal data is stored by the data controller in a database or in event logs.
– *Data (re)use:* at this stage, data from event logs is used for process mining. For instance, the data controller is interested in any compliance violations. Personal data might also be bought by data consumers (e.g., supplier or a quality assurance department, which notifies managers) such as suppliers requiring to demonstrate that the data was retrieved in compliance with GDPR regulations. The duties of the consumer towards the data of providers are specified in a privacy policy and indicate what data is requested and for what purpose and what happens to the personal data once the contract ends.

Although event log analysis becomes relevant at the data (re)use stage, several privacy concerns must be addressed before. Data should not be captured in unauthorized ways (see data capture). Particularly, requirements for event data must be fulfilled in a way that case, timestamp and activity were captured authorized. Also, data should not be processed for unapproved purposes (see primary use), used for unauthorized disposal and violating the policies between data consumers and data controller (see data re(use)). The next section presents a system design supporting these privacy concerns during process mining.

4 User-Centered Privacy-Driven System Design

To ensure user-centered privacy for process mining, the system design relies on privacy policies. First, a context meta-model is introduced, which is used as schema for data storage. Next, the context meta-model is enriched with privacy concepts and process mining concerns captured in a *privacy preserving meta-model*. Lastly, the architectural model is described allowing to monitor the compliance of policies. First, we introduce the context meta-model.

4.1 Context Meta-model

Figure 2 shows the *context meta-model*, which is applied for illustration on the use case of IoT manufacturing working tasks. The context meta-model is defined by four contexts. The **Personal and Social Context** describes all relevant *Persons* (e.g., in the use case of IoT manufacturing working tasks: workers, managers, administration staff, suppliers) referring to their abilities, mental and physical information about persons, tasks or duties. The **Behavior Context** addresses the tasks persons do: steps and goals. The Behavior Context consists of an *Activity* and related *Events*. Activities are part of a *Process* with a certain *Goal* including sub-goals. Goals in our use case are e.g., to produce a certain product, to control a production step or to deliver a component. The **Spatial Context** represents all concepts related to venues like *Departments* (i.e., Factory Buildings) that might differ in *Locations*, within *Areas* and certain *Equipment*, which can be placed in these areas. The **Environmental Context** is highly relevant for our use case, as either the usage of certain *Resources* (device, application, item, fixture) by persons is stored as well as the behaviour of these resources by using its sensor data. *Thing* and *Modeling Element* are the meta-concepts. Also, relationships between different contexts can be modeled like activities and

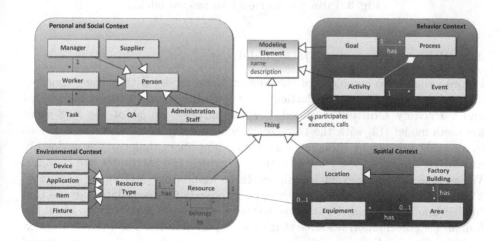

Fig. 2. Context meta-model of the use case

events have calling, executing and participating things (either persons, resources or locations). Resources of a certain resource type (device and fixture) can be placed as equipment in an area. Tasks can be related to certain resources. To define restrictions (e.g. a certain activity can only happen in a certain area) the object constraint language (OCL) has been acknowledged as useful. Note that this is only an excerpt of the context meta-model customized for your use case. A complete version of the context meta-model for AAL is described in [17]. Next, we extend the context meta-model with privacy and process mining concepts (Fig. 3).

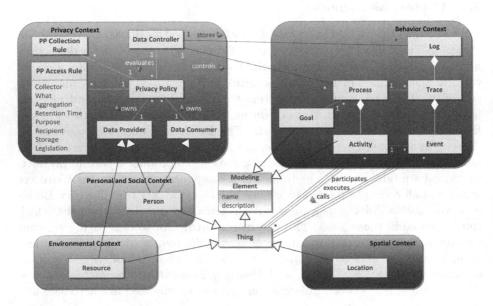

Fig. 3. Privacy meta-model for process mining

4.2   Privacy Preserving Meta-model

Figure 3 shows the extension of the context meta-model with privacy concepts and process mining concerns. Particularly, the **Behavioral Context** is extended and a **Privacy Context** is added. For our purpose, we adopt the XES event log meta-model [13] with the three main concepts *log*, *trace* and *event*. *Events* in an event log can be thought of as unique identifiers that carry a payload of *attributes*, similar to the rows of a table in which the attributes are columns. We assume that each event is assigned three mandatory attributes: `activity`, `time`, and `case`, which fulfills the three requirements for event data. Beyond that further information may be attached to the events of an event log, e.g., about the human (or non-human) resource that executed an activity. The Privacy Context includes *Privacy Policies* with several rules (access and collection rules), owned by *Data Providers* and *Data Consumers*. The *Data Controller* has to compare the policies of data consumers and providers to allow data transmission. In case of policy conflicts, the highest data protection restriction of one or more data providers wins (see Sect. 5 for an example) or legal regulations are superior and force implementation. To allow data providers to specify their privacy concerns, an easy understandable structure for privacy policies is needed. For this, we extend the five privacy elements described in [3] (see Table 1): *What* specifies the set of information (attributes) which will be collected and it ensures to track the connection between data providers and the activation of data source objects (e.g., wearables, devices) in the event log. *Collector* determines who is collecting the data. *Aggregation* is added for process mining purposes and defines the minimum levels of aggregation (e.g., on organizational units and time). The intention of introducing this element is to allow defining the starting point of data (re)use. If aggregation includes a level above 'no limit', anonymity must be ensured on data level. *Retention Time* defines how long the data will be stored within a certain time frame (days, weeks, months, unlimited). *Purpose* outlines a set of operational reasons for data access and storage. It consists of a set of <purpose, level> tuples allowing to specify prohibited purposes (blacklist). Since several data providers should be allowed to specify their privacy preferences and to support the evaluation of privacy policies, we refine the notion of the *Purpose* element through purpose trees [6]. By the use of purpose trees we restrict the access to a certain purpose. In a purpose tree, each node represents a purpose (i.e., attributes defining reasons why such data should be accessed for) and edges represent a hierarchical relationships between them. In our use case, the company or the data controller has to define and maintain the purpose tree. The *Recipient* defines who gets data and is, thus, only relevant for the consumer. *Storage* specifies in which countries the data could be stored. In this

Table 1. Ranges for privacy elements

Privacy element	Data provider	Data consumer
Collector	a set of names or 'any'	single name
What	a list of data attributes	a list of data attributes
Aggregation	levels including time	levels including time
Retention Time	time frame and value	time frame and value
Purpose	'any' or certain purpose, level out of four ordered levels (no collection & no distribution, collection & (no dist. or limited dist. or dist.))	certain purpose, level
Recipient	empty	a set of names
Storage	a defined country, a certain continent, anywhere	country where the requested data will be stored
Legislation	a defined country, a certain continent, anywhere	country of legislation of the consumer

way, the meta-model ensures data sovereignty. *Legislation* defines under which countries legislation data providers are willing to share their data. Both, *access rules* as well as *collection rules* include all of these privacy elements. To allow the *data provider* to see (1) which privacy design strategies are applied on their data and (2) which data was used by which other service including the privacy policy of the data consumer, the next section introduces a privacy preserving system architecture for process mining.

4.3   Architectural Model

The user-centered privacy-driven system relies on the eXtensible Access Control Markup Language (XACML)[1] which we adapted for our purpose. The language allows to evaluate access requests of data consumers according to the rules defined in policies (between e.g., the data provider and data controller) with the notions of:

- *Policy Enforcement Point (PEP):* It is the entry point for access requests. It inspects, requests, generates and sends an authorization request to the Policy Decision Point (PDP) and receives an authorization decision.
- *Policy Decision Point (PDP):* It matches the data provider and data consumer policies and returns an authorization decision.
- *Policy Information Point (PIP):* It acts as a source of data and can preprocess data before it is handed on to the PDP and PEP.
- *Policy Administration Point (PAP):* It allows the policy specification and management for different stakeholders.

Beside these notions the user-centered privacy-driven system consists of an *Information Portal, Data Collection Engine* and *Obligation Engine*, see Fig. 4. The objective of an **Information Portal** is to provide a user friendly representation of stored data, data access attempts, the management of policies and foresee privacy preservation strategies for each stage (see Fig. 1). The objective of the **Data Collection Engine** is to collect data from heterogeneous data sources and to link them to attributes and persons. The **Obligation Engine** is responsible for keeping track of obligation triggers. This system architecture allows to (a) define and manage privacy policies, (b) determine more accurately who can do what with which data, (c) monitor compliance and (d) preview which privacy mechanisms are foreseen in which stages of process mining. Based on this architectural system we can evaluate the access requests as follows. In the set up process (stage 0, see Fig. 1) data controllers define purpose trees (e.g. together with the workers' council or union). Data controllers define privacy policies for data use purposes and data providers and consumers create their access and collection privacy policies in the information portal through the PAP. During stage 1 data is captured when tasks are committed. The *data collection engine* aligns the data to the potential collection policy and the *obligation engine* checks it for

---

[1] http://www.oasis-open.org/committees/xacml/.

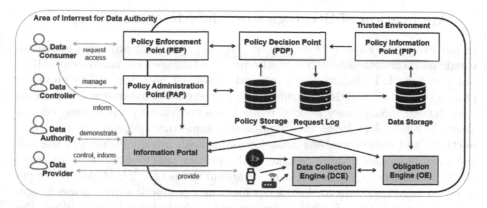

Fig. 4. User-centered privacy-driven system relying on the eXtensible Access Control Markup Language. Information portal, request log, data collection engine and obligation engine were added in order to ensure privacy for process mining.

two issues: (1) whether data collection is allowed and can be directly used in stage 2 for the defined data use purpose, (2) whether this (event) data can be stored or not (conflict resolution), see stage 3. In case of storage approval, personal data is partitioned to reduce data correlations and contention. In stage 4 the data consumer requests a partial access to (event) data and logs through the PEP. The PDP compares each policy element of potential rules of the provider and consumer and decides whether access is granted through the PIP or not. These decisions are stored in a *request log*. According to the concept of user-centered system, which applies for our system design, relevant information (general data and event logs) about a data provider is accessible in the information portal in every stage (see Fig. 1). *Data providers* can read, update and delete privacy policies, track changes in the purpose trees and see which data consumers requested access to their data and to whom it was granted for both, the primary use and data (re)use. They can see in which aggregated representation their data was used. The *data authority* has access to the decisions and request logs as well. He can see all data and communication flows, the security mechanisms for the system and technical information such as encryption methods for data transmission and storage.

To sum up, the context meta-model defines information related to the privacy elements of the privacy preserving meta-model, especially the privacy elements 'What', 'Purpose' and 'Aggregate'. The meta-model is used as foundation to generate the information portal, the decision engine and the obligation engine [1]. The system design is capable to handle the IoT use case and process mining requirements. For instance, the collected data may lead to different fragments of logs having different policies, hence for a particular process mining associated with a given *purpose*, the system filters the collected data and build the log with only acceptable data accordingly.

5   Application of Strategies on the Meta-model

In our example company ManuFuture Ltd, all production processes are monitored based on data collected from the manufacturing execution system (MES) but also from IoT-connected sensors and sensorised operators. Data providers (e.g., an operator) and data consumers (e.g., the quality assurance department) have defined their privacy policies related to a predefined purpose tree, e.g., as shown in Fig. 5. Ann Jones, an operator of ManuFuture Ltd, has a rule for productivity and quality analysis using her data. Each privacy element of the rule is compared to each privacy element of the privacy policy of the data consumer quality assurance (QA) department of ManuFuture Ltd. The QA-department wants to hand over data to the management and production management regularly for the next year. Each privacy element is checked one by each other. Per month in 'Aggregation' is less restrictive that per week, in 'Retention' 1 year is included in unlimited, so the access would be granted to the data consumer. If for example aggregation of the data consumer would be e.g., on each machine or for each day, the access would not have been granted.

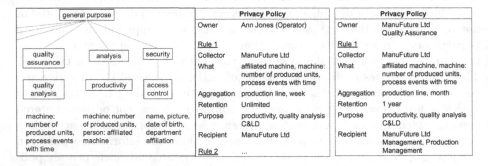

Fig. 5. Definition of a purpose tree and privacy policies for a company aiming to consider privacy.

6   Conclusion and Future Work

Despite the advantage of IoT data for process mining, the increased amount of data brings also with it a high risk that what is disclosed may be private. Privacy cannot longer be neglected or considered as a marginal concern in the design of information systems. Privacy-by-design should be the standard. Relying on this, this paper considered an IoT manufacturing use case and aimed to design a system that preserve privacy for process mining. For this, we adopted an ABAC-based authorization model in order to support the eight privacy design strategies [12] for event logs. Beside the common components our system architecture consists of an information portal, data collection engine and an obligation engine. This allows to specify who does what, when, why, where and how with your own personal data in the IoT context and during process mining.

References

1. Adam, K., et al.: Model-based generation of enterprise information systems. In: EMISA, CEUR Workshop Proceedings, vol. 2097, pp. 75–79 (2018)
2. Agrawal, D., Aggarwal, C.C.: On the design and quantification of privacy preserving data mining algorithms. In: PODS 2001. ACM Press (2001)
3. Allison, D.S., El Yamany, H.F., Capretz, M.: Metamodel for privacy policies within SOA. In: ICSE WS on SE for Secure Systems (2009), pp. 40–46. IEEE (2009)
4. Basso, T., Montecchi, L., Moraes, R., Jino, M., Bondavalli, A.: Towards a UML profile for privacy-aware applications. In: IEEE International Conference on Computer and Information Technology, pp. 371–378 (2015)
5. Bergeron, E.: The difference between security and privacy (2000). https://www.w3.org/P3P/mobile-privacy-ws/papers/zks.html
6. Byun, J.W., Bertino, E., Li, N.: Purpose based access control of complex data for privacy protection. In: 10th ACM Symposium on Access Control Models and Technologies, SACMAT 2005, pp. 102–110. ACM (2005)
7. Colesky, M., Caiza, J.C., Alamo, J.M.D., Hoepman, J.H., Martín, Y.S.: A system of privacy patterns for user control. In: SAC 2018. ACM Press (2018)
8. van Eck, M.L., Lu, X., Leemans, S.J.J., van der Aalst, W.M.P.: PM^2: a process mining project methodology. In: Zdravkovic, J., Kirikova, M., Johannesson, P. (eds.) CAiSE 2015. LNCS, vol. 9097, pp. 297–313. Springer, Cham (2015). https://doi.org/10.1007/978-3-319-19069-3_19
9. Union, E.: Regulation (EU) 2016/679 of the European Parliament and of the Council on the protection of natural persons with regard to the processing of personal data and on the free movement of such data, and repealing Directive 95/46/EC (GDPR). Off. J. Eur. Union L119, 1–88 (2016)
10. Feltus, C., Grandry, E., Kupper, T., Colin, J.N.: Model-driven approach for privacy management in business ecosystem. In: 5th International Conference on Model-Driven Engineering and Software Development, pp. 392–400. INSTICC, SciTePress (2017)
11. Grace, P., Surridge, M.: Towards a model of user-centered privacy preservation. In: International Conference on Availability, Reliability and Security (ARES), p. 91. ACM (2017)
12. Hoepman, J.-H.: Privacy design strategies. In: Cuppens-Boulahia, N., Cuppens, F., Jajodia, S., Abou El Kalam, A., Sans, T. (eds.) SEC 2014. IAICT, vol. 428, pp. 446–459. Springer, Heidelberg (2014). https://doi.org/10.1007/978-3-642-55415-5_38
13. IEEE: Standard for extensible event stream (XES) for achieving interoperability in event logs and event streams. Standard, IEEE (2016)
14. Liu, C., Duan, H., Zeng, Q., Zhou, M., Lu, F., Cheng, J.: Towards comprehensive support for privacy preservation cross-organization business process mining. IEEE Trans. Serv. Comput. (2016). https://ieeexplore.ieee.org/document/7590148
15. Mannhardt, F., Bovo, R., Oliveira, M.F., Julier, S.: A taxonomy for combining activity recognition and process discovery in industrial environments. In: Yin, H., Camacho, D., Novais, P., Tallón-Ballesteros, A.J. (eds.) IDEAL 2018. LNCS, vol. 11315, pp. 84–93. Springer, Cham (2018). https://doi.org/10.1007/978-3-030-03496-2_10
16. Mannhardt, F., Petersen, S., Fradinho Duarte de Oliveira, M.: Privacy challenges for process mining in human-centered industrial environments. In: Intelligent Environments 2018. IEEE Xplore (2018)

17. Michael, J., Steinberger, C.: Context modeling for active assistance. In: ER Forum and the ER Demo Track, CEUR Workshop Proceedings, vol. 1979, pp. 221–234 (2017)
18. Rozinat, A.: Process Mining: Conformance and Extension. Ph.D. thesis, Eindhoven University of Technology, Eindhoven (2010)
19. Rozinat, A., Günther, C.W.: Privacy, Security and Ethics in Process Mining. Technical reports, Fluxicon (2016). https://bit.ly/2QZ9Pxk
20. Stocker, T., Accorsi, R.: Secsy: A security-oriented tool for synthesizing process event logs. In: Proceedings of the BPM Demo Sessions 2014, p. 71 (2014)
21. Wang, L., Wijesekera, D., Jajodia, S.: A logic-based framework for attribute based access control. In: FMSE 2004, pp. 45–55. ACM (2004)
22. Xu, L., Jiang, C., Qian, Y., Ren, Y.: The Conflict between big data and individual privacy. Data Privacy Games, pp. 1–43. Springer, Cham (2018). https://doi.org/10.1007/978-3-319-77965-2_1

ProcessCity

Visualizing Business Processes as City Metaphor

Shinobu Saito[✉] [ID]

Software Innovation Center, NTT CORPORATION, Tokyo, Japan
shinobu.saitou.cm@hco.ntt.co.jp

Abstract. Many organizations are focusing on the digital transformation. To be effective, the organizations need to streamline their own business processes in parallel with digital technology adoption to their businesses. Therefore, one of decisive factors for successful digital transformation is BPM (Business Process Management). Based on data gathered from information systems supporting business processes, the organizations should monitor the business processes on a regular basis, and then update them frequently in order to cope with changes in the business environments. In this paper, we propose ProcessCity, 3D visualization tool, to support the comprehension of complex and large-scale business processes. By analyzing data from the information system related to business processes, ProcessCity visualizes business processes as city metaphor.

Keywords: Business process · Visualization · City metaphor

1 Introduction

Recently, many organizations are focusing on the digital transformation, for example, using digital technologies to transform their existing business processes through automation. To be effective, the organizations need to streamline their own business processes in parallel with digital technologies' adoption. Therefore, we assume that one of decisive factors for successful digital transformation is BPM (Business Process Management). By gathering data from information systems supporting business processes, the organizations should monitor their business processes on a regular basis, and then update them frequently in order to cope with changes in the business environments. However, visual representations by traditional BPM tools is too simple to comprehend the complexity of the business processes.

In this paper, we propose ProcessCity, 3D visualization tool. The tool visualizes business processes as city metaphor in order to support the comprehension of complex and large-scale business processes. Our tool is highly inspired by CodeCity [3] which is a 3D visualization tool for the analysis of software systems. CodeCity represents complex systems (i.e., a set of source codes) as cities. In the cities, classes and package are depicted as buildings and districts. Like software systems, present-day business processes are complex. Therefore, we select city metaphor to visualize business processes.

C. Cappiello and M. Ruiz (Eds.): CAiSE Forum 2019, LNBIP 350, pp. 207–214, 2019.
https://doi.org/10.1007/978-3-030-21297-1_18

2 Approach: From System Data to 2D and Thence to 3D

ProcessCity transforms system data to business processes (2D) and thence to a 3D shape representing them as city metaphor. Figure 1 shows an approach of ProcessCity. We define two steps to realize the transformation. In step 1, the tool identifies business processes as a set of patterns by analyzing an event log and user information. The data is extracted from the system related to the business processes. Then, it visualizes the set as city metaphor in step2. The tool depicts activities as buildings, and swim-lanes as districts. The right side of Fig. 1 shows an example of city overview representing two business process patterns. Based on the analysis result of the event log and user information, the city overview also represents the execution number of activities as the height of the buildings, and the number of users executing the activities as the square sides of buildings.

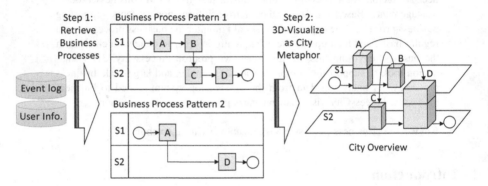

Fig. 1. Overview of approach of ProcessCity.

3 ProcessCity

3.1 Step1: Retrieve Business Processes

Process mining is an approach focused on identifying business processes from the event log collected by information systems [1]. In addition to event log, we use user information to identify business processes that involve multiple organizational entities (i.e., swim lanes). The left side of Fig. 2 contains two tables presenting brief examples of such data. The top side table showing event log comprised four columns: case (i.e., process instance), activity, timestamp, and user ID. The bottom side table shows the user information, which is comprised of two columns: User ID and Organization. The event log shows a list of ten events stemming from three cases (i.e., W_1, W_2, and W_3). For example, the first event for the case W_1 represents that user 001 executed activity A at timestamp TS_1. The table of user information shows a list of four users: 001 to 004. The list describes user IDs and the names of the organizational entities to which the users belong. For example, the first line of the table indicates that user 001 is a member

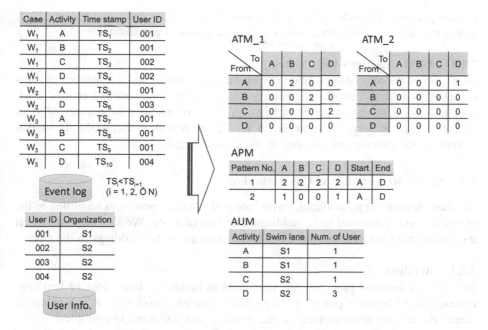

Fig. 2. From system data (Event log and User Info.) to three types of matrices (ATM, APM, and AUM).

of organizational entity S1. We assume that each user belongs to only one organizational entity. In this step, we identify business processes from event log and user information, and then create three types of matrices: ATM (Activity Transition Matrix), APM (Activity - Pattern Matrix), and AUM (Activity - User Matrix).

3.1.1 ATM (Activity Transition Matrix)

We extract the sequence of the given activities in each case from event log. When two sequences are equal, the corresponding cases represent the same business process pattern. For instance, the sequences in case W_1 and W_2 are equal ($A \rightarrow B \rightarrow C \rightarrow D$). So, both case W_1 and W_2 represent the same business process pattern (i.e., pattern 1). Then, for each business process pattern, we create adjacency matrix: ATM. The ATM represents the sequential flow of the business process. The top-right side of Fig. 2 shows ATM_1 and ATM_2 corresponding to pattern 1 and pattern 2, respectively. Two business processes patterns are described in the center of Fig. 1. Each element of ATM denotes a number of the transitions between two activities. For instance, in the ATM_1, the value of the cell in row A and column B is "2". It means that transition from activity A to activity B took place two times.

3.1.2 APM (Activity - Pattern Matrix)

APM shows the number of executions of all activities for each business process pattern. The matrix also contains names of start activity and end activity for each pattern. For instance, the middle-right side of Fig. 2 depicts the APM containing two business process patterns. The value of the cell in row Pattern No. 1 and column A is "2". It means that activity A was executed two times in business process pattern 1.

3.1.3   AUM (Activity - User Matrix)

AUM shows the relationships among swim lanes, activities, and the number of users executing activities. Swim lanes represent names of the organizational entities. Each activity belongs to one of the swim lanes. AUM also indicates the number of users executing each activity. For example, in Fig. 2, the row A in the AUM shows that activity A was executed by one user in the swim lane S1.

3.2   Step2: 3D Visualize as City Metaphor

We map elements (e.g., activities, swim lanes) of business processes identified in the previous step to properties (e.g., buildings, districts) of a city. We also map metrics on the execution of the business processes on dimensions of the buildings in the city.

3.2.1   Buildings

Activities of business processes are visualized as buildings. Each floor of buildings corresponds to business process pattern. When multiple floors exist in a building, it means the activity corresponding to the building was executed in multiple business process patterns. Moreover, the height of each floor depicts the execution number of the activity in the corresponding business process pattern. For example, the left side of Fig. 3 describes the APM. In the column A, the values of row pattern 1 and pattern 2 are "2" and "1", respectively. This means activity A was executed two times in business process pattern 1 and, one time in business process pattern 2. Therefore, as shown in the right side of Fig. 3, the height of the first floor of the building A is 2 [= two times], and that of the second floor of the building A is 1 [= one time]. Tall buildings mean activities were executed with high frequency. Multiple floor buildings mean the corresponding activity is executed in many business process patterns.

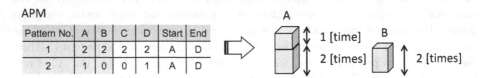

APM

Pattern No.	A	B	C	D	Start	End
1	2	2	2	2	A	D
2	1	0	0	1	A	D

Fig. 3. Mapping number of executions of activities to height of buildings.

3.2.2   Districts, Streets, and Arches

Swim lanes are depicted as the districts of a city. Control flows between activities are depicted as either streets or Arches. When a control flow between two activities which belong to same swim lane, the control flow is depicted as the street between two buildings located at the same district. On the other hand, when a control flow between two activities which belong to different swim lanes each other, the control flow is depicted as the arch between two buildings located at different districts. For instance, the left side of Fig. 4 shows ATM_1 and AUM. The ATM_1 indicates that there are two time transitions both from activity A to activity B and from activity B to activity C. The AUM shows that both activity A and B exist in the same swim lane S1, but activity C exists in the swim lane S2. Therefore, as shown in the right side of Fig. 4, the street from building A to building B is described in the same district S1. On the other hand, the arch is described from building A to building C. Those two buildings are located at district S1 and S2.

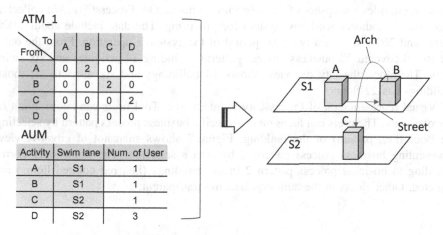

Fig. 4. Mapping control flows to streets or arches.

3.2.3   Square Sides of Buildings

We map the number of users executing activities to the square sides of buildings. The number of users executing an activity is set as the value in square root. Then, the value of the square root is mapped to one square side of the building corresponding to the activity. Figure 5 shows the relationship between AUM and square sides of buildings. In the figure, the AUM shows that activity A and activity D are executed by one user and three users, respectively. Based on these numbers, we map 1 ($=\sqrt{1}$) to the square side of the building A. Similarly, we map $\sqrt{3}$ to that of the building D. Wider buildings mean that a lot of users executed the corresponding activities.

AUM

Activity	Swim lane	Num. of User
A	S1	1
B	S1	1
C	S2	1
D	S2	3

Fig. 5. Mapping number of users executing activities to square sides of buildings.

4   Implementation

ProcessCity is developed using WebGL for visualizing 3D graphics. It also integrates our existing tool [4] which discovers business processes from system data and visualizes them as 2D graphics (BPMN) by GraphViz [2].

4.1   3D Business Processes (City Overview)

Figure 6 provides a snapshot of city overview generated by ProcessCity. We collected data from an industry workflow system for procuring. The data include about 2,000 events and 269 users for a two-year period of the system's operation. From the data, our tool dicovered 22 business process patterns including 14 activities and six swim lanes. Therefore, the city overview shows 14 builidings and six districts. At most, builidings has 22 floors.

Visual representation of ProcessCity is interactive. Tool users can zoom in/out of city overview. The users can focus on one specific business process pattern by selecting the floor (i.e., pattern) of the building. Figure 7 shows snapshot of city overview representing business process pattern 2 by user's selection. The floors only corresponding to business process pattern 2 in the buildings (i.e., red colored floors) are depicted. Other floors in the buildings become transparent.

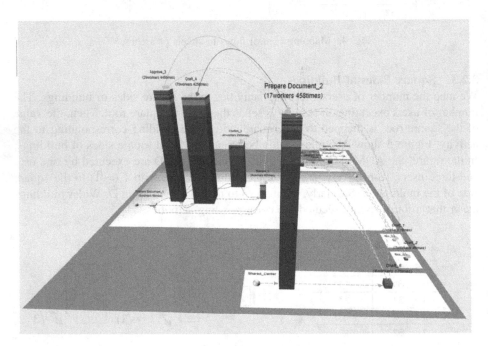

Fig. 6. City overview provided by ProcessCity.

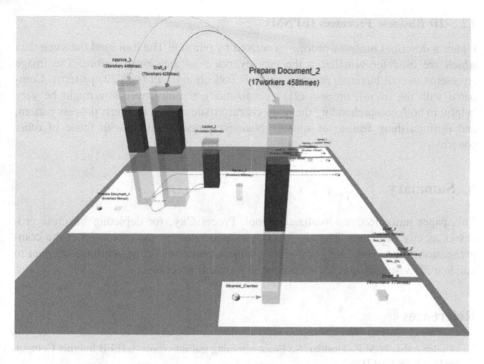

Fig. 7. Only one business process pattern selected in ProcessCity.

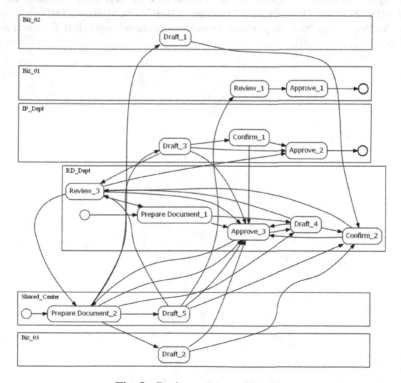

Fig. 8. Business process (BPMN).

4.2   2D Business Processes (BPNM)

Figure 8 describes business process generated by our tool. The tool used the same data which are used for visualizing the city overview as mentioned before. The image represents overall business process which is collection of all (i.e., 22) patterns. Compared with the overall process (2D visualization), the city overview might be very helpful in both comprehending the main characteristic of each business process pattern, and distinguishing feature of specific business process pattern with those of other patterns.

5 Summary

This paper introduced a visualization tool, ProcessCity, for depicting business processes as city metaphor. The city overviews generated by the tool support the comprehension of complex and large-scale business processes. In near future, we plan to validate 3D visualizations for comprehend business processes.

References

1. van der Aalst, W.M.P., Dustdar, S.: Process mining put into context. IEEE Internet Comput. **16**(1), 82–86 (2012)
2. Graphviz: http://www.graphviz.org/
3. Richard, W., Michele, L.: CodeCity: 3D visualization of large-scale software. In: ICSE Companion, Research Demonstration Track, pp. 921–922. ACM Press (2008)
4. Saito, S.: Discovering business processes from user operation history. ISR Technical Report, UCI-ISR-18-1, March 2018

Enhancing Big Data Warehousing for Efficient, Integrated and Advanced Analytics

Visionary Paper

Maribel Yasmina Santos[1]([⊠])(iD), Carlos Costa[1,2](iD), João Galvão[1](iD), Carina Andrade[1](iD), Oscar Pastor[3](iD), and Ana Cristina Marcén[3](iD)

[1] ALGORITMI Research Centre, University of Minho, Guimarães, Portugal
{maribel,carlos.costa,joao.galvao,
carina.andrade}@dsi.uminho.pt
[2] Centre for Computer Graphics - CCG, Guimarães, Portugal
[3] Research Center on Software Production Methods (PROS),
Universitat Politècnica de València, Valencia, Spain
{opastor,acmarcen}@pros.upv.es

Abstract. The existing capacity to collect, store, process and analyze huge amounts of data that is rapidly generated, i.e., Big Data, is characterized by fast technological developments and by a limited set of conceptual advances that guide researchers and practitioners in the implementation of Big Data systems. New data stores or processing tools frequently appear, proposing new (and usually more efficient) ways to store and query data (like SQL-on-Hadoop). Although very relevant, the lack of common methodological guidelines or practices has motivated the implementation of Big Data systems based on use-case driven approaches. This is also the case for one of the most valuable organizational data assets, the Data Warehouse, which needs to be rethought in the way it is designed, modeled, implemented, managed and monitored. This paper addresses some of the research challenges in Big Data Warehousing systems, proposing a vision that looks into: (i) the integration of new business processes and data sources; (ii) the proper way to achieve this integration; (iii) the management of these complex data systems and the enhancement of their performance; (iv) the automation of some of their analytical capabilities with Complex Event Processing and Machine Learning; and, (v) the flexible and highly customizable visualization of their data, providing an advanced decision-making support environment.

Keywords: Big data warehouse · Data governance · Data profiling · Event processing · Performance

1 Introduction

Current advancements in Information Technologies motivated organizations to look towards increased business value and more efficient ways to perform their daily activities. This is usually achieved with data-driven decision-making processes that are

C. Cappiello and M. Ruiz (Eds.): CAiSE Forum 2019, LNBIP 350, pp. 215–226, 2019.
https://doi.org/10.1007/978-3-030-21297-1_19

based in the collection, storage, processing and analysis of huge amounts of data [1]. Also, it is usually associated to characteristics like volume, velocity, variety, variability, veracity and value [2–4], among others, trying to call our attention to the complexity of this area and the difficulties in the integration of such diverse set of data sources, as well as the multiple technologies needed to handle them. Big Data as a research topic is facing several challenges, from the ambiguity and lack of common approaches to the need of significant organizational changes [5], despite some existing efforts of standardizing constructs and logical components of general Big Data systems (e.g., NIST Big Data Reference Architecture [6]). In particular, the research community is looking into the role of a Data Warehouse (DW) in Big Data environments [7], as this data system is usually based on strict relational data models, costly scalability and, in some cases, inefficient performance, opening several opportunities for emerging theories, methodologies, models, or methods for designing and implementing a Big Data Warehouse (BDW) [8]. This can be seen as a flexible, scalable and highly performant system that uses Big Data techniques and technologies to support mixed and complex analytical workloads (e.g., streaming analysis, ad hoc querying, data visualization, data mining, simulations) in several emerging contexts [8]. Although its relevance for supporting advanced analytical processes, research in this area is yet at an early stage, with increased ambiguity in the constructs that can be used, and lacking common approaches.

With the goal of advancing the state-of-the-art and tackle the lack of conceptual guidelines, some of our previous work [8–10] addressed the proposal of models (representations of logical and technological components, data flows, and data structures), methods (structured practices), and instantiations (with demonstration cases based on prototyping and benchmarking) on how to design and implement BDWs. Although filling a major scientific and technical gap, these works were focused on the BDW itself and on its main architectural components, technologies and design patterns, not considering all the additional components, processes and frameworks that must interact with, feed, support (for data analysis and visualization), manage and evaluate this data asset. For advancing data analytics and enhancing the role of the BDW in organizations, this paper presents an overview of the current challenges and some research directions in Big Data Warehousing (BDWing) systems, looking for a continuous practice that allows:

- The integration of new business processes and data sources (*how this integration should be done to provide an integrated view of the organizational business processes and data?*);
- The proper way to achieve this integration, based on adequate data models (*how existing data models should evolve to seamlessly integrate new data sources avoiding uncoordinated data silos?*);
- The management of these complex data systems and the enhancement of their performance (*how can BDWs be monitored in terms of their evolution - business processes and data - and in terms of their performance?*);
- The automation of some of their analytical capabilities (*how can Complex Event Processing and Machine Learning automate and enhance BDWs with advanced real-time events processing?*); and,

- The flexible and highly customizable visualization of their data, providing an advanced decision-making support environment (*how can visualization tools be extended to allow the development of highly interactive and customized data visualizations?*).

Although some of these challenges and open issues may also be relevant for the traditional DW, the complexity associated with the volume, variety and velocity of the data, the variability in data collection and processing, the veracity of the data sources, the complexity of integrating diverse sets of data, the types of analytical workloads (batch, streaming, and interactive), and the diverse and complex technological landscape, impose addressing them with the specificities and needs of Big Data contexts.

This paper is organized as follows. Section 2 presents some background concepts and related work. Section 3 describes the overall framework for advancing BDW research. Section 4 concludes with some highlights of the presented research topics.

2   Background and Related Work

The concept of Data Warehousing (DWing) has a long history, mainly associated to the need to access, analyze and present data to support fact-based analytics [11]. Its aim is to access multiple records at a time. A DW structure is optimized for processing analytical tasks, such as repeatedly queries, reports, Online Analytical Processing – OLAP, data mining or other data science approaches. In a Big Data context, some challenges arise such as inadequate governance of data, lack of skills, cost of implementing new technologies, and difficulties in addressing a modern solution that can ingest and process the ever-increasing amount or types of data [8]. The concept of BDW has been constrained by the fast technological evolution around Big Data, giving short time for developing and maturing research contributions in this area [3]. The BDW can be implemented using two main strategies: (i) the "lift and shift" strategy [12], amplifying the capabilities of relational DWs with Big Data technologies, such as Hadoop or NoSQL databases, proposing particular solutions for specific use cases that may lead to possible uncoordinated data silos [12]; (ii) the "rip and replace" strategy, in which a traditional DW is completely replaced by Big Data technologies [13]. These non-structured practices and guidelines are not sufficient [8], as practitioners and researchers need well-established approaches or guidelines, based on rigorously evaluated models and methods to design and build BDWs [14].

Some existing works explore implementations of DWs on top of NoSQL databases, such as document-oriented [15], column-oriented [16] and graph databases [17], despite the fact that these databases are mainly oriented towards Online Transaction Processing (OLTP) applications [18]. Other works look into storage and processing technologies, discussing SQL-on-Hadoop systems like Hive [19] and Impala [20], or improving these technologies with the use of new storage and processing mechanisms [21]. Moreover, advancements in analytical and integration mechanisms suitable for BDWs are also available [22–24]. In [25], the authors present a framework for evaluating methodologies to design BDWs, defining a set of criteria like application, agility, ontological approach, paradigm, and logical modeling. The authors also divide the methodologies into classes (e.g., automatic, incremental, and non-relational) and define the characteristics being addressed by the methodologies (e.g., value, variety, and velocity).

Taking this into consideration, we have been proposing several prescriptive BDWing contributions grounded on a "rip and replace" strategy and other relevant general contributions in the area of Big Data (e.g., NIST Big Data architecture), to fulfill an emerging gap within the literature, namely the lack of a prescriptive approach to guide practitioners in the design and implementation of BDWs, wherein they can follow rigorous models and methods in real-world projects. Supported by our previous work with: (i) methodological guidelines on the design and implementation of BDWing systems, with proof-of-concepts in the context of Industry 4.0 at Bosch Car Multimedia Braga [9, 10] or Smart Cities [26]; (ii) the extensive evaluation of SQL-on-Hadoop systems for data processing [8, 27–29]; and, (iii) the relevance of extracting value from data, moving from Big Data to Smart Data [30, 31], the next section presents a set of research directions in this field.

3 Big Data Warehousing Systems

Researching in BDWing lacks from reference frameworks and methodological guidelines that help researchers and practitioners in the process of enhancing this valuable data system. Figure 1 depicts the vision proposed in this paper for an integrated BDWing environment supporting the decision-making process. For the current challenges and research directions identified in the introduction of this paper, five main components are here proposed to address them: (i) BDW Entities Resolution, including tasks such as data collection, preparation, enrichment, profiling, and lineage; (ii) BDW Modelling and Implementation; (iii) BDW Management; (iv) BDW Intelligent Event Broker; and, (v) BDW Visualization. Currently, the design and implementation of a BDW is mostly based on use-case driven approaches, preventing a long-term view of the BDW evolution and performance, reason why this proposal looks into a data lifecycle that continuously assists the integration of new data sources, the monitoring of the BDW as a valuable organizational asset, and the enhancement of the decision-making process throughout an innovative and interconnected approach.

3.1 BDW Entities Resolution

The BDW Entities Resolution component addresses the adequate integration of new business processes and data in the BDW, providing a unified and relevant view of the organizational data for decision-making, see Fig. 1. This includes tasks for data sources identification, data understanding, data cleansing, data fusion, data transformation, among many others, with the aim of understanding how new business processes and data can be integrated in the BDW. This is seen as a complex process that is able to deal with the variety of data sources usually available in Big Data contexts, providing adequate and efficient processes to give structure to unstructured or semi-structured data sources (using Data Science techniques and technologies), and to identify relevant entities for analysis, with the Collection, Preparation and Enrichment (CPE) Pipeline, which can be seen as part of a general approach of Big Data management, such as SILE (Search, Identify, Load and Exploitation) proposed in [30], aiming to systematize the search and identification of relevant data to be loaded, analyzed and exploited by a Genomic Information Systems. Although in this case the method is proposed and applied to a specific domain, genomics, the principles are transversal to any application domain: search for relevant data sources; identify relevant datasets; load the relevant data; and, exploit the value of data. From the identification of new business processes

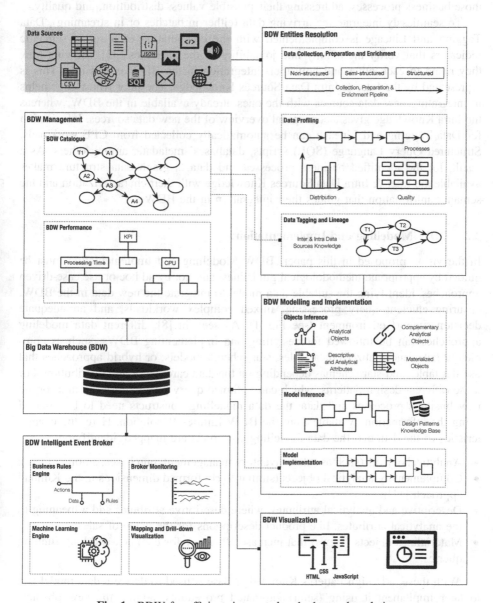

Fig. 1. BDW for efficient, integrated and advanced analytics

and data to their adequate integration in the BDW, there is the need to devise automatic or semi-automatic approaches that are able to take them as input and evaluate how they can be integrated in an already existing data structure, which is highly complex and that needs to comply with demanding workloads and performance issues.

With structured data, Data Profiling characterizes the new business processes (helping in the integration of the new data sources [32] with the already existing data in the BDW), the new data sources, and the attributes that define the events associated to those business processes, addressing their possible values, distribution, and quality.

To seamlessly integrate the arriving data (either in batches or in streaming), Data Tagging and Lineage is complemented with the computation of a set of semantic indicators that verify the affinity and joinability of the attributes [33], showing how they relate to each other and how their integration in the BDW is possible. This is represented by the Inter & Intra Data Sources Knowledge. The Inter Knowledge helps in integrating new data sources with the ones already available in the BDW, whereas the Intra Knowledge gives a conceptual overview of the new data sources. Information for Data Tagging and Lineage can be automatically collected from CPE workloads, Structured Query Language (SQL) scripts, databases' metadata, among others. As a result, for the identified business processes and data, a graph data structure makes available the Inter & Intra Data Sources Knowledge with their characterization and the semantic information that guides their integration in the BDW.

3.2   BDW Modelling and Implementation

In the vision proposed in this paper, BDW Modelling and Implementation must be guided by appropriate methodological guidelines, and not by ad hoc or use case-driven approaches, identifying the suitable data model to integrate the new data in the BDW, ensuring efficient query processing, mixed complex workloads, and an adequate decision support environment (see Fig. 1). As seen in [8], different data modeling approaches can be followed for designing and implementing BDWs, such as completely flat (denormalized) data tables, star schema models, or hybrid approaches that use flat tables and star schemas depending on the data cardinality and distribution. For these different design patterns, which can optimize query processing [27], and for the new business processes and data, the data modelling constructs need to be inferred using the information available from the BDW Entities Resolution. Here, the characteristics of the data and the data modelling constructs are mapped, identifying:

- Analytical objects (such as sales, inventory management, purchases, among others);
- Complementary analytical objects (similar to conformed dimensions in the Kimball approach [11]);
- Descriptive and analytical attributes, where descriptive attributes add a meaning to the analytical attributes, like product descriptions for the value of sales;
- Materialized objects (views) that increase efficiency for complex and long-running queries.

With these, a Design Patterns Knowledge Base is used to derive a data model and to later implement it using (semi)-automated procedures, adding the new physical structures and data to the BDW. This knowledge base stores information about the data modeling design patterns, as well as their performance attending to the characteristics of the data. This way, a data model can be derived, suggesting its implementation by following a specific design pattern. Afterwards, as will be seen in the next subsection, if the volume of data increases, if the data distribution changes, or if performance in query processing is not satisfactory, the BDW Management component can recommend changes to the data model, suggesting the adoption of different design patterns. The model implementation, having the data model and the CPE workloads, can be optimized leveraging agile and performant BDW's updates.

3.3   BDW Management

As the number of business processes and data sources starts to increase in the BDW, there is the need to know which tables and attributes were stored, to which business processes they are related, when they were created or added, and how they are evolving over time, such as how many rows were added, and when were they added. This gives real-time information about the BDW and its evolution. For the adequate BDW Management, the BDW Catalogue (see Fig. 1), a graph-based structure with the BDW's metadata, includes information about the business processes, tables, attributes, loading processes, among others. This structure also complements the semantic knowledge needed for Data Tagging and Lineage in the BDW Entities Resolution, establishing the Inter & Intra Data Sources Knowledge, as it complements the knowledge of the existing data with the one obtained from the new business processes and data sources.

Besides cataloguing the BDW, supporting its governance, it is also relevant to monitor its performance, verifying its efficiency in query processing. This challenge is not seen here as a process of adopting more performant processing tools [28], but as an architectural change in terms of the data models, adjusting the design patterns attending to the characteristics of the available data [8]. This is important to devise strategies for improving the BDW's efficiency. In this case, a recommendation system can analyze the current state of the BDW, using descriptive statistics, affinity measures, joinability measures, metadata, query performance and query repetition, for instance, and propose changes to the BDW data model, through the implementation of additional analytical objects or structures like complementary analytical objects or materialized objects [10], thus increasing the overall efficiency of the system. With this, data models can evolve, changing the previously adopted design patterns, if that is advantageous for the BDW's efficiency. Moreover, the BDW Performance must use a Key Performance Indicators (KPIs) tree that assists this monitoring task, providing a list of objective metrics and the corresponding targets. As the data models evolve, the KPIs can show the impact of those changes in the overall performance of the BDW.

3.4   BDW Intelligent Event Broker

For processing real-time data in the BDW, as a relevant functionality of an analytical system in a Big Data context, there is the need for automated decision-making processes through Complex Event Processing and Machine Learning, adopting innovative ways to process complex events in a streamlined, scalable, analytical and integrated way [34, 35]. The BDW Intelligent Event Broker, see Fig. 1, is a just-in-time data dissemination system using highly flexible business rules and Machine Learning models to handle the event data that is available mainly due to the proliferation of IoT devices. Therefore, there are several contexts in which this system can be used (industry, smart cities, logistics, agriculture, among others), preventing possible problems by using the data produced by several sources and processing it in real-time. The monitoring of a production line is a relevant example where the verification of the rules in a defect product can result in the application of Machine Learning models to predict if the next products will also be defective, and then activating the needed actions. Consequently, for this system, several components are needed, such as the following:

- Business Rules Engine for defining a set of business rules to be applied to the data/events, as well as the actions that must be taken as a consequence of triggering a specific rule. A repository of business rules for managerial actions at different organizational levels (mainly tactical and operational) feeds the Intelligent Event Broker and uses data that arrives to the BDW (in streaming or batch), combining real-time and historical data in the decision-making process;
- Machine Learning Engine for importing previously trained Machine Learning models from a Models Lake, using a Machine Learning as a Service approach, in order to predict future events and, if needed, provide corrective or optimal actions regarding the event;
- Broker Monitoring to automatically track the functioning of the Intelligent Event Broker, by collecting metadata regarding rules, triggers, KPIs, among others. This component is used to monitor the performance of the broker and devise strategies to improve it; and,
- Mapping and Drill-down Visualization to: (i) inspect the rules that have been activated and drill-down into the data that activated those rules; and (ii) visualize KPIs about the broker itself and drill-down into their relationship with the rules, the triggers and the corresponding data.

Considering the analyzed related work [36, 37], some concepts and components here mentioned are widely recognized for this type of system (e.g., rules and triggers). However, these works do not consider: (i) the inclusion of concepts similar to the Machine Learning Models Lake component that can be helpful for patterns discovery in Complex Event Processing systems for Big Data contexts; and, (ii) the relevance of the system monitoring through an innovative visualization platform, as its evolution can quickly become untraceable in Big Data contexts.

3.5   BDW Visualization

Visualization is one of the key components to take advantage of the data made available through the BDW, enhancing decision making with appropriate visual analytics tools. Technological developments in Big Data contexts are mainly driven by open source initiatives, but as the open source Big Data Visualization landscape is still very limited when compared to commercial solutions, practitioners have mainly two alternatives, namely, use open source solutions or custom-made Web visualizations.

In both cases, existing applications usually provide an environment for static and/or more dynamic analyses, with classical or more advanced visualization methods [38], or with the identification of interaction patterns for designing user interfaces oriented towards extracting knowledge from Big Data [39]. In open source tools like Superset (https://superset.incubator.apache.org), base functionalities are provided but improvements are still needed regarding customization. When using commercial solutions, usually including a wide variety of visualization methods and functionalities, there is still the lack of customization and interaction that can be achieved with custom-made Web platforms, like real-time access to data, highly customized events and interactions, or calculations involving multiple sources. Taking this into consideration, there is the need for BDW Visualization (see Fig. 1) platforms oriented towards dashboard development by advanced data analysts and data scientists, providing a way to create custom-made and interactive dashboards using small portions of reusable code that can be easily integrated (like HTML, CSS and JavaScript code), including rich, highly flexible, customizable and interactive charts or other visualization components.

4 Conclusions

This paper highlighted the research topics associated with current challenges and open issues in BDWs as highly flexible, scalable and performant systems for supporting decision-making processes. In this work, some proposals were refined and structured to become a roadmap for the research community for the next years. This vision tries to highlight were value can be added to a BDW, by approaching a fast-changing world that needs to deal with the constant integration of new business processes and data sources, and by understanding the proper way to adjust the BDW and its data model as this evolution occurs. Also, it is crucial to deal with the management of these complex data systems to enhance their performance, as well as addressing real-time analytical capabilities through the use of Complex Event Processing and Machine Learning.

In this paper, all these challenges were instantiated with research areas. For *the integration of new business processes and data sources*, approaches from research areas like Entities Resolution, Data Profiling, Data Tagging, and Data Lineage can be applied to provide information for *the proper way to achieve this integration*, based on appropriate data models, with the attempt to provide a data model in a semi-automated way, based on a Design Patterns Knowledge Base. This type of contribution will help organizations that deal with huge amounts of data arriving from several sources and will help them *to manage these complex data systems and to enhance their performance*, reducing the time needed for tasks such as the BDW management and modeling, allowing their users to focus on retrieving value from data. Moreover, the capability to deal with other contexts, like events and streaming processing, *automating the analytical capabilities of a BDW*, is another way to enhance the BDW and its value.

Currently, streaming data is constantly being produced in different contexts by the several interconnected devices and people within the organizations. Its efficient processing and usage are relevant to promote better decisions for decision makers, or, sometimes, take decisions in an automated way. To accomplish this goal, the Intelligent Event Broker is responsible for the real-time application of business rules and Complex

Event Processing, allowing the identification of events and problems that can be dispatched by several triggers that take semi-automated actions. The Machine Learning component is a core component of the Broker, making available the problems identification and recommendations even before these problems occur, based on the data that arrives to the system. For this kind of system, its complexity needs to be managed, being a monitoring and visualization component proposed to understand and track what happens in the system.

In addition, *the flexible and highly customizable visualization of data*, for extracting value from BDWs, is tightly-coupled with an adequate data visualization mechanism, reason why this work discusses flexible, highly customizable, and interactive visualization mechanisms based on portions of reusable code, which will provide an advanced decision-making support environment based on rich Web-based user interfaces.

Therefore, reference frameworks and methodological guidelines are strictly required in this domain to provide effective solutions intended to manage adequately the studied problem. After analyzing relevant research directions, the paper proposes and introduces a framework that takes into account the most significant aspects of the domain, and that can be used as a starting point to characterize BDWs for efficient, integrated and advanced analytics as expressed in the work title. It is our firm intention to apply, improve and extend it (where necessary) using challenging examples as the Genome Data Science domain and the Industry 4.0 environment with the Bosch Car Multimedia case, in which we already have at the moment some initially, encouraging results.

Acknowledgements. This work has been supported by FCT – *Fundação para a Ciência e Tecnologia*, Projects Scope UID/CEC/00319/2019 and PDE/00040/2013, and the Doctoral scholarships PD/BDE/135100/2017 and PD/BDE/135101/2017. We also thank both the Spanish State Research Agency and the Generalitat Valenciana under the projects DataME TIN2016-80811-P, ACIF/2018/171, and PROMETEO/2018/176. This paper uses icons made by Freepik, from www.flaticon.com.

References

1. Madden, S.: From databases to big data. IEEE Internet Comput. **16**(3), 4–6 (2012)
2. Dumbill, E.: Making sense of big data. Big Data **1**, 1–2 (2013)
3. Gandomi, A., Haider, M.: Beyond the hype: Big data concepts, methods, and analytics. Int. J. Inf. Manag. **35**, 137–144 (2015)
4. Philip Chen, C.L., Zhang, C.-Y.: Data-intensive applications, challenges, techniques and technologies: a survey on big data. Inf. Sci. **275**, 314–347 (2014)
5. Costa, C., Santos, M.Y.: Big data: state-of-the-art concepts, techniques, technologies, modeling approaches and research challenges. IAENG Int. J. Comput. Sci. **44**, 285–301 (2017)
6. NBD-PWG: NIST Big Data Interoperability Framework (2015)
7. Krishnan, K.: Data Warehousing in the Age of Big Data. Elsevier, Burlington (2013)

8. Costa, C., Santos, M.Y.: Evaluating several design patterns and trends in big data warehousing systems. In: Krogstie, J., Reijers, H.A. (eds.) CAiSE 2018. LNCS, vol. 10816, pp. 459–473. Springer, Cham (2018). https://doi.org/10.1007/978-3-319-91563-0_28

9. Santos, M.Y., et al.: A Big Data system supporting Bosch Braga Industry 4.0 strategy. Int. J. Inf. Manag. **37**, 750–760 (2017)

10. Costa, C., Andrade, C., Santos, M.Y.: Big data warehouses for smart industries. In: Sakr, S., Zomaya, A. (eds.) Encyclopedia of Big Data Technologies, pp. 1–11. Springer, Cham (2018). https://doi.org/10.1007/978-3-319-63962-8_204-1

11. Kimball, R., Ross, M.: The Data Warehouse Toolkit: The definitive Guide to Dimensional Modeling. Wiley, Indianapolis (2013)

12. Clegg, D.: Evolving data warehouse and BI architectures: the big data challenge. TDWI Bus. Intell. J. **20**, 19–24 (2015)

13. Russom, P.: Data Warehouse Modernization in the Age of Big Data Analytics (2016)

14. Russom, P.: Evolving Data Warehouse Architectures in the Age of Big Data (2014)

15. Chevalier, M., El Malki, M., Kopliku, A., Teste, O., Tournier, R.: Document-oriented models for data warehouses - NoSQL document-oriented for data warehouses. In: Proceedings of the 18th International Conference on Enterprise Information Systems, Rome, Italy, pp. 142–149 (2016). https://doi.org/10.5220/0005830801420149

16. Chevalier, M., El Malki, M., Kopliku, A., Teste, O., Tournier, R.: Implementing multidimensional data warehouses into NoSQL. In: 17th International Conference on Enterprise Information Systems (ICEIS), Barcelona, Spain (2015)

17. Gröger, C., Schwarz, H., Mitschang, B.: The deep data warehouse: link-based integration and enrichment of warehouse data and unstructured content. In: IEEE 18th International Enterprise Distributed Object Computing Conference (EDOC), pp. 210–217 (2014)

18. Cattell, R.: Scalable SQL and NoSQL data stores. ACM SIGMOD Record. **39**, 12 (2011)

19. Thusoo, A., et al.: Hive-a petabyte scale data warehouse using hadoop. In: 2010 IEEE 26th International Conference on Data Engineering (ICDE), pp. 996–1005. IEEE (2010)

20. Pandis, I.: Impala: a modern, open-source SQL engine for hadoop. In: 7th Biennial Conference on Innovative Data Systems Research (CIDR), p. 10 (2015)

21. Huai, Y., et al.: Major technical advancements in apache hive. In: Proceedings of the 2014 ACM SIGMOD international conference on Management of data - SIGMOD 2014, pp. 1235–1246. ACM Press, Snowbird (2014). https://doi.org/10.1145/2588555.2595630

22. Li, X., Mao, Y.: Real-Time data ETL framework for big real-time data analysis. In: 2015 IEEE International Conference on Information and Automation, pp. 1289–1294. IEEE, Lijiang (2015). https://doi.org/10.1109/ICInfA.2015.7279485

23. Song, J., Guo, C., Wang, Z., Zhang, Y., Yu, G., Pierson, J.-M.: HaoLap: a hadoop based OLAP system for big data. J. Syst. Softw. **102**, 167–181 (2015)

24. Wang, H., et al.: Efficient query processing framework for big data warehouse: an almost join-free approach. Front. Comput. Sci. **9**, 224–236 (2015)

25. Tria, F.D., Lefons, E., Tangorra, F.: A framework for evaluating design methodologies for big data warehouses: measurement of the design process. Int. J. Data Warehouse. Min. **14**(1), 15–39 (2018)

26. Costa, C., Santos, M.Y.: The SusCity big data warehousing approach for smart cities. In: Proceedings of International Database Engineering & Applications Symposium. Bristol, United Kingdom (2017). https://doi.org/10.1145/3105831.3105841

27. Costa, E., Costa, C., Santos, M.Y.: Efficient big data modelling and organization for hadoop hive-based data warehouses. In: Themistocleous, M., Morabito, V. (eds.) EMCIS 2017. LNBIP, vol. 299, pp. 3–16. Springer, Cham (2017). https://doi.org/10.1007/978-3-319-65930-5_1

28. Rodrigues, M., Santos, M.Y., Bernardino, J.: Big data processing tools: an experimental performance evaluation. WIREs Data Min. Knowl. Discov. **9**(2), e1297 (2019)

29. Santos, M.Y., et al.: Evaluating SQL-on-hadoop for big data warehousing on not-so-good hardware. In: Proceedings of International Database Engineering & Applications Symposium (IDEAS 2017), pp. 242–252. ACM Press (2017). https://doi.org/10.1145/3105831. 3105842

30. León Palacio, A., Pastor López, Ó.: Smart data for genomic information systems: the SILE method. Complex Syst. Inf. Model. Q. 1–23 (2018). https://doi.org/10.7250/csimq. 2018-17.01

31. Palacio, A.L., López, Ó.P., Ródenas, J.C.C.: A method to identify relevant genome data: conceptual modeling for the medicine of precision. In: Trujillo, J.C., Davis, K.C., Du, X., Li, Z., Ling, T.W., Li, G., Lee, M.L. (eds.) ER 2018. LNCS, vol. 11157, pp. 597–609. Springer, Cham (2018). https://doi.org/10.1007/978-3-030-00847-5_44

32. Hui, J., Li, L., Zhang, Z.: Integration of big data: a survey. In: Zhou, Q., Gan, Y., Jing, W., Song, X., Wang, Y., Lu, Z. (eds.) ICPCSEE 2018. CCIS, vol. 901, pp. 101–121. Springer, Singapore (2018). https://doi.org/10.1007/978-981-13-2203-7_9

33. Maccioni, A., Torlone, R.: KAYAK: a framework for just-in-time data preparation in a data lake. In: Krogstie, J., Reijers, H.A. (eds.) CAiSE 2018. LNCS, vol. 10816, pp. 474–489. Springer, Cham (2018). https://doi.org/10.1007/978-3-319-91563-0_29

34. Flouris, I., Giatrakos, N., Deligiannakis, A., Garofalakis, M., Kamp, M., Mock, M.: Issues in complex event processing: status and prospects in the Big Data era. J. Syst. Softw. **127**, 217–236 (2017). https://doi.org/10.1016/j.jss.2016.06.011

35. Zhang, P., Shi, X., Khan, S.U.: QuantCloud: enabling big data complex event processing for quantitative finance through a data-driven execution. IEEE Trans. Big Data (2018). https://doi.org/10.1109/TBDATA.2018.2847629

36. Hadar, E.: BIDCEP: a vision of big data complex event processing for near real-time data streaming: position paper, a practitioner view. In: CAiSE 2016 Industry Track, CEUR Workshop Proceedings (2016)

37. Flouris, I., et al.: FERARI: a prototype for complex event processing over streaming multi-cloud platforms. In: Proceedings of the 2016 International Conference on Management of Data - SIGMOD 2016, pp. 2093–2096. ACM Press, San Francisco (2016). https://doi.org/ 10.1145/2882903.2899395

38. Bikakis, N.: Big data visualization tools. In: Sakr, S., Zomaya, A. (eds.) Encyclopedia of Big Data Technologies. Springer, Cham (2018). https://doi.org/10.1007/978-3-319-63962-8_109-1

39. Iñiguez-Jarrín, C., Panach, J.I., Pastor López, O.: Defining interaction design patterns to extract knowledge from big data. In: Krogstie, J., Reijers, H.A. (eds.) CAiSE 2018. LNCS, vol. 10816, pp. 490–504. Springer, Cham (2018). https://doi.org/10.1007/978-3-319-91563-0_30

Business Process Compliance Despite Change: Towards Proposals for a Business Process Adaptation

Tobias Seyffarth[✉], Stephan Kuehnel, and Stefan Sackmann

Martin Luther University Halle-Wittenberg, 06108 Halle (Saale), Germany
{tobias.seyffarth, stephan.kuehnel,
stefan.sackmann}@wiwi.uni-halle.de

Abstract. Business Process Compliance (BPC) denotes the execution of business processes in accordance with applicable compliance requirements. BPC can be satisfied through compliance processes that are integrated into the business process. In addition, compliance requirements place demands against IT components that are sometimes necessary to execute business or compliance processes. Various factors, such as outsourcing or business process reengineering can lead to a change of processes or IT components and thus to a violation of BPC. Consequently, our goal is to provide proposals for a business process adaptation to further ensure BPC. Following the design science research methodology, we developed two artifacts to reach our goal. First, we developed a meta-model that represents the interrelations between alternative compliance process patterns and compliance processes that satisfy the same compliance requirement. Second, we developed a method to automatically put forward proposals for a business process adaptation through the integration of alternative compliance processes to further ensure BPC.

Keywords: Adaptation · Business process compliance · Change · Compliance process · IT component

1 Introduction

Business Process Compliance (BPC) denotes the execution of business processes in accordance with applicable compliance requirements [1]. A compliance requirement is a constraint or assertion that prescribes a desired result or purpose to be achieved by factoring actions or control procedures into processes [2]. In addition to business processes, compliance requirements place demands to components of an information technology (IT) architecture (e.g. software such as a ERP system or hardware such as a physical server) [3]. Further, IT components are sometimes necessary to execute activities of a business process. Thus, there are multilevel interrelations between compliance requirements, business activities, and IT components.

Many factors such as outsourcing decisions, business process reengineering, and new technologies can lead to changing compliance requirements, business activities, or IT components [4, 5]. In dynamic markets the fast adaptation to changing environments is key [6]. Consequently, the fast detection of BPC violations through changes and the

© Springer Nature Switzerland AG 2019
C. Cappiello and M. Ruiz (Eds.): CAiSE Forum 2019, LNBIP 350, pp. 227–239, 2019.
https://doi.org/10.1007/978-3-030-21297-1_20

adaptation of business processes to avoid BPC violations are both important tasks [7]. However, this might be a challenging and time consuming manual task due to many compliance requirements, business process models, and large IT architectures [8].

In the literature various approaches exist to identify impacts on BPC through the respective changes in business processes [4, 5], IT components [3, 9] and even a common change of business processes and IT components [10]. Additionally, there are approaches for an adaptation of business processes to satisfy compliance requirements regarding the control flow of the business process and thus ensuring BPC [11, 12]. Nevertheless, these approaches do not consider IT components for the execution of business activities. So far, there is a lack of an approach to ensure BPC during the design time of business processes despite changes to business processes and IT components. Additionally, to the best of our knowledge, there is no decision support system for the adaptation of business processes to avoid violations of BPC. Thus, we address the following research question: *How can proposals be provided for an adaptation of the business process to further ensure BPC?*

We address this research question by designing and developing two artifacts according to the design science paradigm by Hevner et al. [13]. In this paper we focus on their design and development. The artifacts are each an exaptation that extends known solutions to new problems. Following the problem statement, the developed artifacts address a relevant problem and the required scientific rigor is fulfilled by the usage of existing methodologies of graph search techniques. Finally, we present the following contributions:

- First, we present a meta-model to model alternative compliance processes and their interrelation.
- Second, we present a method to automatically put forward proposals for a business process adaptation through the integration of alternative compliance processes to further ensure BPC.

The remainder of this contribution is structured as follows: In Sect. 2, the preliminaries background of BPC in combination with relevant views on an enterprise architecture, and a motivation scenario are discussed. In Sect. 3, we present a method to put forward proposals for a business process adaptation. In Sect. 4, the related work is discussed and finally, Sect. 5 concludes the contribution.

2 Preliminaries and Motivation Scenario

2.1 Business Process Compliance

As already mentioned, business process compliance (BPC) denotes the execution of business processes in adherence to applicable compliance requirements [1]. In this case, a compliance requirement is a constraint or assertion that results from the interpretation of compliance sources, such as laws, regulations, and standards (e.g. [2]). Various approaches check or ensure BPC. As an example, BPC can be checked after process execution by analyzing log files, or it can be ensured at the time the business processes are designed (e.g., [14]).

In a narrow sense, a business process is simply a sequence of work items (also referred to as business activities). These processes transform one or more kinds of input into output and are aimed at generating value [15]. However, ensuring compliance requires activities that are not merely geared toward pure value generation, but to also meet compliance requirements. The so-called compliance activities are appended to the business process, e.g. at design time or as part of a process redesign [16]. The simple combination of both business and compliance activities increases process complexity and reduces process transparency [17]. For example, with an increasing number of activities in a process model, it becomes increasingly difficult to differentiate between those activities that serve to generate value and thus serve the core business and those that ensure compliance. A promising way to address this difficulty is to separate the view of business and compliance activities or activity sequences [17]. Similar to modular software design, a process graph can thus be built modularly so that it can be separated into exchangeable, functional components [18], i.e., process fragments that serve business goals and those that serve compliance goals (e.g. [19]). Accordingly, we provide the following formal definition of a process graph.

Definition 1 (Process Graph). A process graph G is a 3-tupel $G = (N, E, type)$ [20], where: $N = BA \cup CA \cup C$ is a set of nodes in G, that follow common execution semantics. BA is a set of business activities and CA is a set of compliance activities, where: $BA \cup CA = \emptyset$. C is a set of coordinating nodes and $E \subseteq N \times N$ is a set of edges between nodes representing a control flow such that (N, E) is a connected process graph. The function type : $C \rightarrow \{start, end, split, synchronize, choice, merge\}$ assigns a coordinator type to each coordinating node of G.

A major advantage of a modular process structure is the potential for reusing compliance processes or compliant process fragments to meet compliance requirements in other business processes [12]. In addition, adherence to compliance requirements can be automated and made more flexible through the tool-supported integration of compliance processes into workflows at runtime as shown in [16, 21]. Thus, we define a compliance process as an independent process (part) consisting of compliance-related activities that ensure BPC [22].

Definition 2 (Compliance Process). A compliance process is a subgraph of G and a 3-tupel $CP = (N', E', type')$ if $N' \subseteq CA \cup C$, $E' \subseteq E$ and $type' = type|_{N'}$. $type'$ restricts the function type of G to the set of N'. A compliance fragment CF is a special type of CP with exactly one input and one output node, i.e. CF does not contain coordination nodes of type $\{start, end\}$. Given the business activity $BA_i \in BA$ of process graph G, $Trigger(G, BA_i)$ denotes the compliance process(es) triggered by BA_i.

Although business and compliance objectives seem to sometimes overlap in practice, they can usually be treated and modelled separately, if there is a compliance view of processes (e.g., [12, 17]). A compliance view of processes includes, among other things, the knowledge of relevant compliance requirements that place demands against these process or their single activities [10]. An example is the credit rating before granting a loan.

On the one hand, credit institutions inquire into credit ratings to protect against payment defaults; on the other hand, compliance requirements such as the German

Banking Act stipulate obligations to check creditworthiness. However, the protection against payment defaults is not used to generate value, but to maintain value. Thus, it does not belong to the core business process. A credit rating always pursues a compliance objective, either based on a statutory provision or on an internal need for protection (internal compliance requirement). The credit rating would thus have to be operationalized as a compliance process. Consequently, the idea of modularization is based on the assumption that the amount of business and compliance activities are disjoint, i.e. that an activity meets either a business or a compliance objective.

If the pursuit of a compliance goal only serves value generation, compliance and business activities are difficult to distinguish. This might be the case when complying with requirements constitutes the unique selling proposition of a product or service. However, our approach is limited to cases where modularization is possible.

2.2 Views on Enterprise Architectures

An enterprise architecture is understood as the fundamental organization of a government agency or corporation, either as a whole or together with partners, suppliers and/or customers ('extended enterprise'), or in part (e.g., a division, a department, etc.) as well as the principles governing its design and evolution [23]. In the literature, various sub-architectures of enterprise architectures have been proposed. They include, among other things, a business, process, integration, software, and technology architecture (e.g. [24]). As stated in the introduction, we will focus on three perspectives of an enterprise architecture: (1) business process (2), compliance, and (3) IT architecture. For reasons of simplicity, we refer to a single element within an IT architecture as an IT component that can be either software or hardware-based. The interrelations between the single elements of these perspectives are illustrated in Fig. 1.

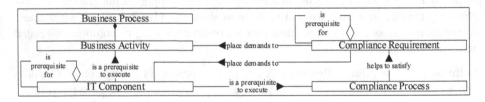

Fig. 1. Considered elements of an enterprise architecture and their interrelations [10]

2.3 Motivation Scenario

The left side of Fig. 2 shows a simplified purchase to pay process including perspectives on compliance requirements, compliance processes, and IT components. Some of the business activities are supported by IT components that are modeled as triangles. We assume that the material management module of an enterprise resource planning system (ERP MM) is a prerequisite for both the business activity 'send purchase requisition' and the compliance process 'check invoice'. Furthermore, a financial module of an ERP system (ERP FI) is a prerequisite for the business activities 'create payment order' and 'execute payment'.

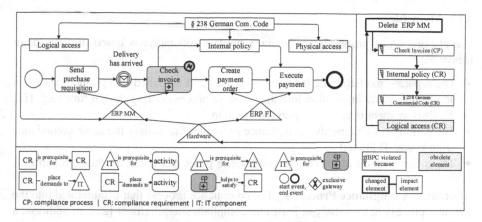

Fig. 2. Purchase-to-pay process (based on [10])

In addition, both business activities and IT components are sometimes affected by compliance requirements. In this example, '§ 238 of the German Commercial Code' demands an accounting obligation for merchants in Germany. It is also related to the proper operation of IT that supports the accounting activities. In this example, the compliance requirements 'physical access' and 'logical access' are prerequisite by '§ 238 of the German Commercial Code'. The compliance requirement 'physical access' requires a regulated access to physical IT components while 'logical access' requires the identification and authentication of users of an application [25]. For simplification, this compliance requirement only place demands on the IT component 'ERP MM'. Furthermore, the compliance requirement 'internal policy' specifies additional requirements that are necessary for the payment of invoices. Finally, the compliance process 'check invoice' helps to satisfy the 'internal policy'.

As shown on the right side of Fig. 2, the compliance process 'check invoice' cannot be executed in the case of deleting 'ERP MM'. Thus, the compliance requirements 'internal policy' and '§ 238 of the German Commercial Code' are violated. Furthermore, the compliance requirement 'logical access' is obsolete. A method and a software prototype to determine the interactions between BPC and business process change have been provided in [10, 26]. In the upcoming section, we propose an approach to put forward proposals for an adaptation of the business process through the integration of alternative compliance processes to further ensure BPC.

3 Towards Proposals for a Business Process Adaptation

In this section we present artifacts to put forward proposals for a business process adaptation to further ensure BPC. First of all, we present the main ideas of our method and show it in a running scenario. Second, we present a meta-model to represent the relations between alternative compliance process and compliance process patterns. Third, we present our method in detail.

3.1 Main Ideas

The elaboration of proposals for business process adaptation is based on three main ideas:

- The separate modelling of business processes and so-called compliance processes and its automatic integration into the business process during design time (e.g. [12, 27, 28]) as mentioned in the previous section;
- The definition of alternative compliance processes that satisfy the same compliance requirement [11]; and
- The differentiation of alternative compliance processes based on their properties.

Alternative Compliance Processes. The compliance process that is integrated into the business process helps satisfy at least one compliance requirement [22]. In addition, a compliance requirement can be satisfied by more than one compliance process, i.e. alternative compliance processes. An example of an alternative compliance processes is the control of the number of bacteria in drinking water. The number of bacteria can be controlled by alternative compliance processes and at different points in the supply process e.g., by analyzing the water sources, the water depots, the hand-over to the consumer, or the consumer him or herself [11].

In case of detecting a violation of BPC due to a changed compliance requirement, business activity, or IT component the business process must be adapted to further ensure BPC. Thus, proposals for the integration of alternative compliance processes into the business process need to be put forward. The bases for these proposals are alternative compliance processes that are separately modelled and stored from the business process.

Properties of a Compliance Process. Each compliance process may have different properties, such as the type of integration into the business process or the type of execution. In [22] we proposed a taxonomy that categorizes properties of compliance processes. In the end, our compliance process taxonomy contains 37 characteristics in 9 dimensions and 3 meta-characteristics.

The meta-characteristic 'Integration Constraint' contains requirements for the integration of a compliance process into a business process. One dimension within these meta-characteristic is the dimension 'Trigger' that indicates the need for the integration of a compliance process into a business process to satisfy a compliance requirement. Another dimension contains further requirements that are necessary for the execution of a compliance process, e.g. the existence of an IT component. The meta-characteristic 'Modeling' includes, in addition to other features, patterns for modelling compliance processes. The meta-characteristic 'Property' contains further properties of a compliance process. These properties may depend on other characteristics of the compliance process taxonomy, such as the type of execution which can either be automatic, IT dependent manual or manual.

3.2   Running Scenario

As explained, the change of a business process or IT component sometimes leads to a violation of BPC. In the motivation example, the removal of the IT component 'ERP MM' leads to the violation of the compliance requirements 'internal policy' and '§ 238 of the German Commercial Code' and thus also leads to a violation of BPC. The reason is the unfeasibility of the compliance process 'check invoice'. In order to avoid this violation, there must be a proposal for a business process adaptation through the integration of an alternative compliance process.

The left side of Fig. 3 shows the interrelation of alternative compliance process patterns and compliance processes that satisfy the compliance requirement 'internal policy'. The right side of Fig. 3 shows the integration of the two alternative compliance processes into the business process. For reasons of simplicity, we do not model the IT components in Fig. 3. As an alternative to checking the invoice, the payment order can also be checked. The annotations at the compliance processes contain their properties derived from the compliance process taxonomy.

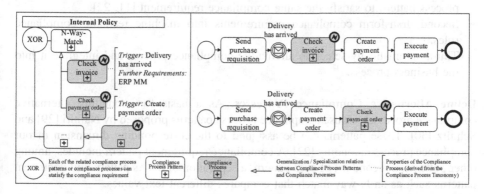

Fig. 3. Model alternative compliance processes and propose an adapted business process

3.3   Meta-model and Method to Put Forward Proposals

In order to understand the following steps of our method, Fig. 4 shows the interrelations between necessary elements. In the following, we briefly define two new elements: the compliance process pattern and the compliance rule.

In general, patterns are high-level domain-specific templates used to represent desired properties and constraints [2]. Following this, we define a compliance process pattern as a process template that contains process elements (e.g. activities, gateways, and connectors) that are necessary to satisfy at least one compliance requirement. Consequently, a compliance process is still necessary to satisfy at least one compliance requirement. Thus, a compliance process is the specialization of the compliance pattern; its properties are derived from the compliance process taxonomy [22]. Further, the compliance requirement and the integration constraint of the compliance process are formalized in a machine readable compliance rule.

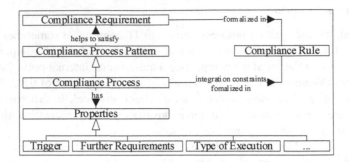

Fig. 4. Modelling alternative compliance processes

Next, we propose a three-step method, in order to put forward proposals for a business process adaptation through the integration of alternative compliance processes:

- First, define alternative compliance processes which are based on a compliance process pattern to satisfy the same compliance requirement [11, 22].
- Second, transform compliance requirements into machine readable compliance rules.
- Third, automatically select an alternative compliance process and integrate it into the business process.

Define Alternative Compliance Processes. As a basis for modelling alternative compliance processes we use compliance process patterns proposed by Namiri [29] and Schultz [30]. These patterns can be assigned to the corresponding dimension of our compliance process taxonomy [22]. A compliance requirement pattern includes, among other patterns, a second set of eyes pattern, a separation of duties pattern and document patterns such as an N-way-match that compares different text values.

In our running scenario, the compliance requirement 'internal policy' can be satisfied by a compliance process pattern 'N-way-match' on a general level. Further, we specialize its level of detail by modelling two alternative compliance processes. One possible specialization is the compliance process 'check invoice'. The trigger to execute this compliance process is the existence of the event 'delivery has arrived'. Further, the compliance process needs the IT component 'ERP MM' to be executed. As already mentioned, the payment order can also be checked as an alternative to the invoice. The trigger for the integration of the corresponding compliance process 'check payment order' is the existence of the business activity 'create payment order'. In contrast to the compliance process 'check invoice', there is no further requirement for the execution of this compliance process.

Transform Compliance Requirements into Compliance Rules. For the automatic selection of an appropriate compliance process, the possibility of its integration into the business process must be examined. Accordingly, a prerequisite for this is the transformation of the compliance requirement into a machine readable compliance rule. Additionally, the compliance rule must be modelled individually for each compliance process. In our case the rule must be able to represent the presence or absence of both business activities and IT components. Thus, the compliance rule must include the control flow and resource perspective of a process. A suitable compliance rule language for this purpose is Linear Temporal Logic (LTL) [31].

Select and Integrate an Alternative Compliance Process. Alternative compliance processes must be selected and integrated to put forward proposals for a business process adaptation. For further explanations, we define the conceptual modelling of compliance requirements and their associated compliance processes, etc., as a directed graph $G = (N, E, F, H, K)$ with its elements $g_i \in G$. In addition, N is a nonempty finite set of nodes, and $e_l \in E$ is a set of directed edges between two nodes $(n_{(i)}, n_{(j)})$. In addition, $f_i \in F$ is the unique identification (id) of the node n_I; $h_i \in H$ is the model type of the node $n_{(i)}$ with $H = \{$Compliance Requirement (CR), Compliance Process Pattern (CPP), Compliance Process (CP)$\}$; and $k_i \in K$ is the machine readable compliance rule of node n_i. Further we limit the allowed edges between the defined node types: $E_r = \{((n_i|h_i = CPP), (n_j|h_j = CR)); ((n_k|h_k = CP), (n_l|h_l = CR)); ((n_m|h_m = CPP), (n_n|h_n = CPP)); ((n_o|h_o = CP), (n_p|h_p = CPP))\}$ with $n_i..n_p \in N$; $h_i..h_p \in H$; and $E_r \subseteq E$.

Basically, the search for alternative compliance processes starts at n_i, which represents the compliance process that is no longer executable. First, we search for sibling nodes of n_i and their existing specializations. The specializations can be found by searching the predecessors of each sibling node of n_i. To check whether these compliance processes can be executed within the business process, each of their compliance rules must be checked against the business process by using graph searching methods (e.g. [32]). If there is no appropriate compliance process, we perform a second search for an appropriate compliance process pattern. Accordingly, we search for successors of n_i that are of the type 'compliance process pattern'.

The search for alternative compliance processes can lead to three results. First, there is one alternative compliance process, which is already the case in the running scenario. Second, there is more than one alternative compliance process. Third, there is no alternative compliance process. We propose a solution for each case. In case of exactly one alternative compliance process the adapted business process is proposed. In case of numerous alternative compliance processes, our method proposes all alternative compliance processes. In these cases, our method will propose more than one adapted business process. In case of no alternative compliance process, our method proposes a generic compliance process pattern, if available. For a first and easy solution, the compliance process pattern is integrated at the place of the original compliance process within the business process.

4 Related Work

In [10, 14] we conducted two structured literature reviews in the field of BPC, business process change and business process adaptation. Despite manual approaches to remodel business processes, there are also methods that automatically adapt business processes to satisfy compliance requirements. The latter approaches can be classified into approaches that (1) change the order of activities, gateways and other flow elements in a business process, and (2) integrate separate modelled compliant process fragments into a business process. However, none of the identified approaches consider IT components as a prerequisite to execute a compliance process and put forward proposals for an adaptation of business processes through (1) alternative compliance processes or (2) compliance process patterns to ensure compliance due to business process change.

Kopp et al. [33] proposed a method that transforms the business process into a well-defined process model that can be used for further automatic compliance checking techniques such as graph searching. Awad et al. [32] developed a method to reorder business activities or change the gateway types within a business process to meet compliance requirements. In addition, Höhn [34] proposed a method to automatically rewrite the business process to enforce obligations.

Schumm et al. [12] proposed a method to integrate separate stored compliant process subgraphs into a business process during their design-time. In [19] they demonstrated their method with a software prototype. Schultz [30] modelled business processes based on log files of an ERP system. Furthermore, he automatically added activities that represent application controls for the business process. Kittel and Sackmann [27, 28] proposed and demonstrated a method with a software prototype to integrate control processes in business processes during their execution.

5 Conclusion

Various factors such as business process reengineering and outsourcing decisions can lead to changing compliance requirements, business processes, compliance processes, and new IT components. Consequently, this can lead to a violation of BPC. In order to avoid such violations, the business process has to be adapted. Thus, we proposed the idea of separate modelling of alternative compliance processes whereby each compliance process has different properties (e.g., manual or automatic execution) and specializes in a specific compliance process pattern. The modelling of the relationships and the search for alternative processes is performed using a graph. In the end, our method proposes adapted business process to further ensure BPC.

Currently, our method considers the control flow and the presence and absence of IT components for the selection and integration of alternative compliance process patterns or compliance processes. Each alternative compliance process pattern and compliance process must be modelled individually. In case of more than one appropriate compliance process there is no criteria for the selection of an alternative compliance process, e.g. by an economic assessment [35].

In a next step, we will demonstrate our method through an extension of our software prototype, BCIT [26]. In addition, the software prototype will be evaluated through the presentation of different scenarios to experts in the field of IT architecture management, business process management and compliance. Additionally, the method can be extended to include, e.g. a data or an organizational perspective on a business process. Further, unsupervised machine learning techniques, such as frequent pattern analysis (e.g., a FP-Growth algorithm) can be used to propose possible alternative compliance processes without explicit prior modelling based on existing business process models that include compliance processes.

References

1. Governatori, G., Sadiq, S.: The Journey to Business Process Compliance. Handbook of Research on Business Process Modeling, pp. 426–454 (2009)
2. Turetken, O., Elgammal, A., van den Heuvel, W.-J., Papazoglou, M.: Enforcing compliance on business processes through the use of patterns. In: 19th ECIS 2011 (2011)
3. Knackstedt, R., Eggert, M., Heddier, M., Chasin, F., Becker, J.: The Relationship of is and Law - The Perspective of and Implications For IS Research. ECIS 2013 Completed Research (2013)
4. Rudzajs, P., Buksa, I.: Business process and regulations: approach to linkage and change management. In: Grabis, J., Kirikova, M. (eds.) BIR 2011. LNBIP, vol. 90, pp. 96–109. Springer, Heidelberg (2011). https://doi.org/10.1007/978-3-642-24511-4_8
5. Fdhila, W., Indiono, C., Rinderle-Ma, S., Reichert, M.: Dealing with change in process choreographies design and implementation of propagation algorithms. Inf. Syst. **49**, 1–24 (2015)
6. Rinderle, S., Reichert, M., Dadam, P.: Correctness criteria for dynamic changes in workflow systems—a survey. Data Knowl. Eng. **50**, 9–34 (2004)
7. Kittel, K.: Agilität von Geschäftsprozessen trotz Compliance. Tagungsband der 11. Internationale Tagung Wirtschaftsinformatik, pp. 967–981 (2013)
8. Elgammal, A., Turetken, O., van den Heuvel, W.-J., Papazoglou, M.: Root-cause analysis of design-time compliance violations on the basis of property patterns. Serv. Oriented Comput. **6470**, 17–31 (2010)
9. Becker, J., Heddier, M., Braeuer, S., Knackstedt, R.: Integrating regulatory requirements into information systems design and implementation. In: Proceedings ICIS 2014 (2014)
10. Seyffarth, T., Kühnel, S., Sackmann, S.: Business Process Compliance and Business Process Change. An Approach to Analyze the Interactions. Business Information Systems. BIS 2018, Lecture Notes in Business Information Processing, pp. 176–189 (2018)
11. Kittel, K., Sackmann, S., Betke, H., Hofmann, M.: Achieving flexible and compliant processes in disaster management. In: 46th Hawaii International Conference on System Sciences (HICSS 2013), pp. 4687–4696 (2013)
12. Schumm, D., Leymann, F., Ma, Z., Scheibler, T., Strauch, S.: Integrating compliance into business processes. process fragments as reusable compliance controls. In: Proceedings of the MKWI 2010 (2010)
13. Hevner, A.R., March, S.T., Park, J., Ram, S.: Design science in information systems research. MIS Quart. **28**, 75–105 (2004)
14. Sackmann, S., Kuehnel, S., Seyffarth, T.: Using business process compliance approaches for compliance management with regard to digitization: evidence from a systematic literature review. In: Weske, M., Montali, M., Weber, I., vom Brocke, J. (eds.) BPM 2018. LNCS, vol. 11080, pp. 409–425. Springer, Cham (2018). https://doi.org/10.1007/978-3-319-98648-7_24
15. Hammer, M., Champy, J.: Reengineering the corporation. a manifesto for business revolution. Harper Business, New York (1993)
16. Kittel, K., Sackmann, S.: Gaining Flexibility and Compliance in Rescue Processes with BPM. Workshops Resilience and IT-Risk in Social Infrastructures (RISI) im Rahmen der 6th International Conference on Availability, Reliability, and Security (2011)

17. Betke, H., Kittel, K., Sackmann, S.: Modeling Controls for Compliance. An Analysis of Business Process Modeling Languages. In: The 27th IEEE International Conference on Advanced Information Networking and Applications Workshops (WAINA-2013), pp. 866–871 (2013)

18. Eberle, H., Unger, T., Leymann, F.: Process fragments. In: Meersman, R., Dillon, T., Herrero, P. (eds.) OTM 2009. LNCS, vol. 5870, pp. 398–405. Springer, Heidelberg (2009). https://doi.org/10.1007/978-3-642-05148-7_29

19. Schumm, D., Turetken, O., Kokash, N., Elgammal, A., Leymann, F., van den Heuvel, W.-J.: Business process compliance through reusable units of compliant processes. In: Daniel, F., Facca, F.M. (eds.) ICWE 2010. LNCS, vol. 6385, pp. 325–337. Springer, Heidelberg (2010). https://doi.org/10.1007/978-3-642-16985-4_29

20. Rastrepkina, M.: Managing variability in process models by structural decomposition. In: Mendling, J., Weidlich, M., Weske, M. (eds.) BPMN 2010. LNBIP, vol. 67, pp. 106–113. Springer, Heidelberg (2010). https://doi.org/10.1007/978-3-642-16298-5_10

21. Kittel, K., Sackmann, S., Göser, K.: Flexibility and Compliance in Workflow Systems. The KitCom Prototype. Tagungsband CAiSE Forum - 25th International Conference on Advanced Information Systems Engineering, 154–160 (2013)

22. Seyffarth, T., Kühnel, S., Sackmann, S.: A Taxonomy of Compliance Processes for Business Process Compliance. 15th International Conference on Business Process Management, Business Process Management Forum (2017)

23. TOGAF (ed.): Content Metamodel. Content Metamodel Vision and Concepts. http://pubs.opengroup.org/architecture/togaf9-doc/arch/

24. Winter, R., Fischer, R.: Essential Layers, Artifacts, and Dependencies of Enterprise Architecture. In: 2006 10th IEEE International Enterprise Distributed Object Computing Conference Workshops (EDOCW 2006), p. 30 (2006)

25. Principles of Proper Accounting When Using Information Technology. IDW AcP FAIT 1 (2002)

26. Seyffarth, T., Raschke, K.: BCIT. A tool for analyzing the interactions between business process compliance and business process change. In: Proceedings of the Dissertation Award and Demonstration, Industrial Track at BPM 2018, pp. 81–85 (2018)

27. Sackmann, S., Kittel, K.: Flexible Workflows and Compliance: A Solvable Contradiction?! In: vom Brocke, J., Schmiedel, T. (eds.) BPM - Driving Innovation in a Digital World. MP, pp. 247–258. Springer, Cham (2015). https://doi.org/10.1007/978-3-319-14430-6_16

28. Kittel, K., Sackmann, S., Göser, K.: Flexibility and Compliance in Workflow Systems. The KitCom Prototype. Tagungsband CAiSE Forum - 25th International Conference on Advanced Information Systems Engineering, pp. 154–160 (2013)

29. Namiri, K., Stojanovic, N.: Using Control Patterns in Business Processes Compliance. WISE 2007 Workshops, pp. 178–190 (2007)

30. Schultz, M.: Enriching Process Models for Business Process Compliance Checking in ERP Environments. Design Science at the Intersection of Physical and Virtual Design 7939, pp. 120–135 (2013)

31. Elgammal, A., Turetken, O., van den Heuvel, W.-J., Papazoglou, M.: Formalizing and appling compliance patterns for business process compliance. Software System Modeling (2014)

32. Awad, A., Smirnov, S., Weske, M.: Resolution of compliance violation in business process models: a planning-based approach. In: Meersman, R., Dillon, T., Herrero, P. (eds.) OTM 2009. LNCS, vol. 5870, pp. 6–23. Springer, Heidelberg (2009). https://doi.org/10.1007/978-3-642-05148-7_4

33. Kopp, O., Leymann, F., Schumm, D., Unger, T.: On BPMN process fragment auto-completion. In: 3rd Central-European Workshop on Services and their Composition, pp. 58–64 (2011)
34. Höhn, S.: Model-based reasoning on the achievement of business goals. In: Proceedings of the 2009 ACM symposium on Applied Computing, pp. 1589–1593 (2009)
35. Kuehnel, S., Zasada, A.: An approach toward the economic assessment of business process compliance. In: Woo, C., Lu, J., Li, Z., Ling, T.W., Li, Guoliang, Lee, MLi (eds.) ER 2018. LNCS, vol. 11158, pp. 228–238. Springer, Cham (2018). https://doi.org/10.1007/978-3-030-01391-2_28

Detecting and Identifying Data Drifts in Process Event Streams Based on Process Histories

Florian Stertz[✉] and Stefanie Rinderle-Ma

Faculty of Computer Science, University of Vienna, Vienna, Austria
{florian.stertz,stefanie.rinderle-ma}@univie.ac.at

Abstract. Volatile environments force companies to adapt their processes, leading to so called concept drifts during run-time. Concept drifts do not only affect the control flow, but also process data. An example are manufacturing processes where a multitude of machining parameters are necessary to drive the production and might be subject to change due to e.g., machine errors. Detecting such data drifts immediately can help to trigger exception handling in time and to avoid gradual deterioration of the process execution quality. This paper provides online algorithms for concept drift detection in process data employing the concept of process histories. The feasibility of the algorithms is shown based on a prototypical implementation and the analysis of a real-world data set from the manufacturing domain.

Keywords: Process technology · Online process mining ·
Concept drifts

1 Introduction

Flexibility and change are still among the most pressing challenges for processes [12]. This holds particularly true for data-driven process executions in volatile environments such as manufacturing processes [11]. Manufacturing processes control and are controlled by a multitude of data, e.g., machining parameters and sensor data that constantly monitor the state of the process and the machines. Changes in these parameters are common due to, for example, environmental changes or errors, and can be of tremendous importance for the quality of the process and the product. Similar requirements hold for patient treatments where shifts in vital parameters have to be detected immediately. Hence it is of great importance to be able to detect changes in the data attributes of processes, specifically during run-time, i.e., based on process event streams.

This necessitates making a next step in detecting and evaluating so called concept drifts [6]. So far concept drift refers to changes in the control flow of the process that are discovered based on process execution logs. In [14], we have provided algorithms for detecting and representing concept drifts in control

© Springer Nature Switzerland AG 2019
C. Cappiello and M. Ruiz (Eds.): CAiSE Forum 2019, LNBIP 350, pp. 240–252, 2019.
https://doi.org/10.1007/978-3-030-21297-1_21

flow from *event streams*. This work aims at detecting changes in process data, called data drift in the following, from process event streams at run-time. This is necessary as detecting data drifts from process execution logs ex-post might be too late in order to take necessary actions in many cases.

Generally, data drifts can be categorised following the same guidelines gathered from [6]: data drifts can have recurring effects as well as incremental effects or just reflect sudden changes in the business process logic. As said before, data drifts are also to be detected during run-time and not ex post.

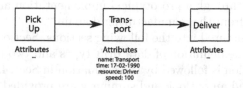

Fig. 1. Process model with data attributes of event `Transportation`

Figure 1 shows a process example from the logistics domain. A product is picked up by a delivery service, transported and delivered to the customer. The data attributes for the event `transportation` are timestamp, name of the event, resource that is executing this event, and average speed. Suddenly this attribute of newer events changes as the driver is now driving significantly slower on average. The reason for this can be manifold, like a construction site on the road, or even a construction site on a different road, which causes the normal route to be jammed. The control flow of this process is not changed, but the data attributes show a drift in the execution of the process, a data drift. Detecting such drifts early helps tremendously in finding errors and bottlenecks that suddenly occur. A data drift could also reflect the natural evolution of a process, e.g, instead of only doctors, nurses administer drugs as well, due to a legislation change. This would be reflected in a new organisational role for this event.

Similarly to control flow drifts [6], data drifts can have different effects, i.e., recurring as well as incremental effects or they just reflect sudden changes in the business process logic. Moreover, data drifts must be detected during run-time and not ex post for many application domains where immediate action is required. Finally, data-intense processes are often emitting a huge amount of events in high frequency. All these challenges will be tackled along the following research questions: **RQ1** How to detect data drifts from process event streams online, i,e., during run-time? and **RQ2** Which types of data drifts can be identified from event streams? How to define and identify them?

Note that the problem is two-fold as reflected by the research questions: In RQ1 it is detected that a data drift has just happened. RQ2 and RQ3 aim at identifying the type of the data drift, e.g., recurring. For addressing RQ1, the already established concept of `process histories` [14], is extended to store information on process data attributes and to allow the detection of data drifts. These drifts are identified using outlier detection on the values of a data attribute. The approach can independent of the contol flow of the process if instead of a model, only event attribute pairs are saved. This would yield the disadantage of not seeing the data drifts as the evolution of a process without the process history. RQ2 yields a formal definition for the data drift types. RQ3 is tackled by an algorithm that determines the type of a data drift based on process histories. Summarizing, this paper provides definitions for extended process histories and data drifts as well as two algorithms. One of them synthesizes the extended process history in order to detect the data drift and the other one determines its type. The definitions and algorithms form the conceptual artefacts of this paper. They are evaluated through a prototypical implementation and application to a real-world data set from the manufacturing domain.

The paper is structured into the following sections. Section 2 provides fundamentals. In Sect. 3 the definition of data drift types and two new algorithms are presented. This section is followed by the evaluation in Sect. 4. In Sect. 2, related work is discussed and an outlook and summary are provided in Sect. 5.

2   Fundamentals and Related Work

We recap the fundamentals on process mining and event streams, especially events containing data attributes using related work. Process histories, previously defined in [14], are extended to comprehend viable data attributes into the process history and to detect new types of drift, so called data drifts.

Process mining covers three tasks [3]: process discovery, the mining of a process model based on a process execution log, process conformance checking, which calculates the fitness of a process instance to a process model, and process enhancement, which allows to improve already discovered models. A process execution log consists of a `log` root node. A log may contain an arbitrary number of process instances, so called `traces` and these traces have an arbitrary number of activities, so called `events`. Process execution logs use the XES format [1].

The main contribution of this work focuses on events and their data attributes. Common attributes would be the point of time when an event has been executed, a organisational resource that has executed the event, or other arbitrary data attributes, e.g., the cost of an activity.

Process mining is usually applied ex post. This means that process models are discovered offline after their execution and storage in a process execution log, like the α-miner [10], which transfroms a directly follows translation [15] out of the log into a Petri Net. To negate this disadvantage, so called online process mining algorithms [14,15] have been developed. The main difference is the input data. While the offline algorithms use a process execution log file, online algorithms use an `event stream` as input.

An event stream represents a continuous flow of sequentially processes events and can be used to discover process models [7,15] as well to synthesise **process histories** [14]. A process history contains every viable business process model, that has been detected using an event stream. A viable model is defined, if it fits the currently relevant traces significantly better than the old model. To calculate the viability of process models, conformance checking techniques are applied. So far, only control flow drifts are captured in a process history, in fact data attributes are rarely considered except some exceptions like the decision mining algorithm [13]. In order to enable the detection of data drifts, we define the data-extended process history as follows.

Definition 1 (Data-extended Process History). *Let P be a process and ES the corresponding process event stream. A data-extended process history $H_P :=< M_0, M_1, ..., M_{n-1}, M_n, .. >$ is a list of viable process models $M_n, n \in \mathbb{N}$ that have been discovered for P from ES with M_n being the current model for P. $M \in H_P$ is defined as*

$$M :=< E, < (e_0, A_0^c), \ldots, (e_k, A_k^c) >>, e_i \in E \ with$$

- *$E \subseteq ES$ is the set of all events in M;*
- *$e_i \in E : e_i = (l_{e_i}, A_i)$, i.e., an event stores its label l_{e_i} and the set of data attributes A_i;*
- *For e_i, $A_i^c \subseteq A_i$ denotes the sub set of attributes from A_i that have caused the data drift.*

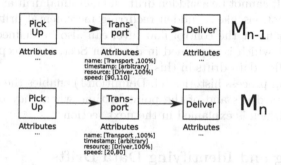

Fig. 2. Process History showing a data drift in the attribute speed.

Figure 2 shows the extended process history for the example of Fig. 1. The control flow of the models M_n and M_{n-1} is not changed, but still a new model has been detected because of a data drift in the event Transport. As can be seen, the lower bound for the average speed in M_{n-1} equals 90 and the upper bound equals 110. A number of outliers have been detected, e.g, $40, 40, 40, 40, 50, 50, 50, 60, 60, 60, 60, 50, 50$, and 50. This results in the new lower bound 20 and the upper bound 80. The data extension does not interrupt the detection of control flow drifts as presented in [14]. The process history is used in Algorithm 1 in Sect. 3 to detect data drifts and append new process models that show no difference at the control flow, but at the data level.

For the algorithm the data structure trace_map is used. A trace_map represents key value pairs as a hash-map. Hereby, the trace id, e.g., "Process instance 1" is used as a key. Using such unique identifiers bears advantages regarding the look up time of certain values. The corresponding value would be the trace, that has been detected in the event stream. In addition, the data attributes are now stored as well for each event in the trace_map. In the following algorithms, this map is synthesised using an event stream. This stream has the advantage that every time an event is detected, it is processed immediately, so all the data elements of this event will be saved in the trace_map. To detect the currently relevant traces in an event stream, the sliding window approach is used. This means that only k traces are considered for the detection of drifts. If a new trace is detected and there are already k traces in the trace_map, the oldest trace is removed and the new trace is stored.

Concept/Data Drifts: [5] differentiates four types of concept drifts at control flow level. ① are incremental drifts, which consist of small changes to the business process model, like a new event or a removed event. ② are recurring drifts, which show typical seasonal effects, like in a hotel for example. The business process logic differs from winter to summer and alternates back to winter. ③ are gradual drifts, that represent a change in the business process logic, where process instances of the old logic are still being executed. ④ are sudden drifts, which are the direct opposite to ③, i.e., no process instances of the old logic are still being executed.

A concept drift cannot be a sudden drift and a gradual drift at the same time. All other combinations like a sudden recurring incremental drift, are possible. These concept drifts at the control flow level can also be defined and detected at the data level, which is explained in detail in Sect. 3. Concept drifts on the data level are called data drifts in this work.

The concept of process histories (cf. Definition 1) enables the detection of all four types of data drifts and of the point in time when they occurred in the process history, which is explained in the next section.

3   Detecting and Identifying Data Drifts

In this section, the synthesis of data-extended process histories as basis for detecting and identifying data drifts is elaborated.

3.1   Detecting Data Drifts

Assume a data-extended process history $H_P = < M_0, ..., M_n >$ as defined in Definition 1 with most current process model M_n and the corresponding trace_map. Following [14] the core idea of detecting drifts is to synthesize a new viable process model M_{n+1} in the data-extended process history in case changes to the data attributes have happened. The difference between M_n and M_{n+1} yields the data drift and its type. As basis, for each new event in the stream, the data attributes are checked for changes. In this work, changes in data attributes are detected based on outlier detection in the data attribute values. For this statistical methods will be used. However, it is not feasible to compare every new event to all previous events in all traces as this might be too complex and might lead to misleading results in terms of the drifts. Imagine that a change happened in one event and later the inverse change occurs. Considering all traces this change would not be detected as a drift. Hence, it is feasible to restrict the set of considered events and traces. In [14], the idea of using a sliding window on the traces has been proven promising and hence this concept will be applied for the synthesis of data-extended process histories in the following as well.

Algorithm 1 implements the core ideas of using a sliding window on the traces and outlier detection on the data attributes. As input an event stream, ES, a window limit k and the thresholds ϕ and κ are required. The thresholds are described in detail in the following paragraphs. The algorithm is used while synthesising a process history. A data drift is detected after the detection of a control flow drift; algorithms for detecting control flow drifts are provided in, e.g., [14]. At the beginning of Algorithm 1, process history H_P is an empty list and does not contain any process models. Also the trace_map which is used in the detection of data drifts does not contain any items in the beginning.

The sliding window technique, allows to identify currently significant traces for the detection of new viable models, where k is the maximal number of traces stored in the trace_map. The data extension uses the same window for detecting drifts in the data elements. Since outliers shall be detected, a certain amount of values for a specific data element, respectively a certain number of an events, needs to be detected for statistical analysis. The minimum number of events, κ, is user defined and a value between 0 and k, since it is, except for a loop, impossible to have more events stored, than there are traces in the trace_map.

After the event has been stored in the trace_map, the algorithm tries to detect a data drift. A whole new range of drift types is possible if a concept drift and a data drift occur simultaneously, which require a definition and an algorithm to be detected. This approach is beyond the scope of this paper.

If the process history contains at least one model, a copy of the current model and its events with attributes is created. At the start the list_of_data_drifts is an empty list and contains pairs of the drifting attribute and its corresponding event. If the current model of the process history contains the currently processed event, an iteration over the data attributes of this event starts. In this iteration, a denotes a data attribute of currently processed event e. The next expression checks, if a is an outlier to e of the current model.

For the outlier detection following methods are used. If the data attribute a contains continuous data, the data could be transformed into a normal distribution [8] and a range is calculated. We are using the box plot approach, since it is very distribution independent. The whiskers, here used as lower and upper bounds of limits for outlier detection, are placed at 1.5 times of the interquartile range below the first quartile and 1.5 times of the interquartile range above the third quartile. The implementation currently only supports continuous data. If the data attribute a does not contain continuous data, we use the likelihood. If for example, only 3 equally common values have been detected in the last model for this attribute in 50 events, and a new value occurs, its likelihood is lower than all of the known values. On the other hand, if there are 50 different values for one attribute in 50 events, it could be deduced that this attribute is arbitrary. A user input, defining the maximum distance between the new likelihood and the average likehood of choices, is used as threshold, to detect outliers for this. If this attribute is not in the last known model for event e, the outlier function automatically returns true.

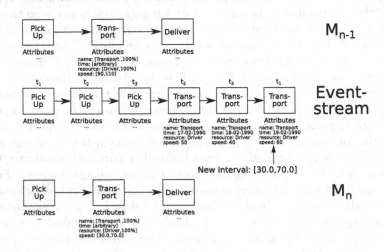

Fig. 3. Synthesising a process history with $\kappa = 1$ and $\phi = 1$

In the next step an empty list list_a is created and the variable as is initialised with 0. This variable counts how often event e is found in the trace_map containing a. The algorithm searches every trace in the trace_map. If an event is found that equals e and also has the same attribute a as an outlier, this attribute is added to the list.

If the number of occurrences for attribute a in the trace_map (as) is smaller than κ, a data drift has been detected. Apparently this data attribute is not used often enough to retrieve significant information and is removed from the new model. The pair e, a is appended to the list_of_data_drifts

Otherwise, the new range or likelihoods will be calculated using only the information of outlying attribute values. It is then counted how often an attribute of the trace_map fits the new properties and is divided by the number of events e. This yields a score value, which represents the percentage of fitting attributes for the new properties. If this score is greater or equal than ϕ, the new properties are added to the new model and the pair e, a is appended to the list_of_data_drifts. The threshold ϕ is in $[0, 1]$, where 0 would be everything and 1 would be only considering scores, where 100% of the attributes match the new properties as a data drift. Afterwards, Algorithm 2 is executed, to detect the type of the data drift.

Figure 3, shows how an outlier is detected for the running example Fig. 1 and how and when a new model is appended. The range from 90 to 110 has been

Input: Event Stream ES (a series of events)
    k (Limit for number of trace_map items)
    κ (Threshold for number of an attribute for consideration, [0,k])
    ϕ (Threshold for distinction of a new viable data range [0,1])
Result: **Process History** H_P (contains all viable process models in chronological order.)
H_P = [ ], trace_map<trace_id,trace> = 0
for e in ES **do**
    if *trace_map contains_key e.trace_id* **then**
      | trace_map['e.trace_id'].append(e)
    else
      if *trace_map.size* ≥ k **then**
        | trace_map.delete_oldest
      trace_map.insert(e.trace_id,e)
    detect_concept_drifts_based_on_workflow_drifts();
    if $|H_P| \neq 0$ **then**
      New_Model = H_P.last, list_of_data_drifts = [ ]
      if $H_P.last.contains(e)$ **then**
        for a in e **do**
          if *outlier($H_P.last[e],a$)* **then**
            list_a = [ ], as = 0
            for t in trace_map.values **do**
              for ev in t **do**
                if ev == e and ev contains a **then**
                  | as+=1;
                if *ev == e and outlier($H_P.last[e],ev.a$)* **then**
                  | list_a.append(ev.a);
            if *as < κ* **then**
              if *New_Model[e] contains a* **then**
                | New_Model[e].remove(a);
                | list_of_data_drifts.append({e,a});
              break;
            else
              e_size = 0; fitting_e = 0; properties = calc_properties(list_a);
              for t in trace_map.values **do**
                for ev in t **do**
                  if ev==e **then**
                  e_size+=1;
                  if *!outlier(properties,ev.a)* **then**
                    | fitting_e+=1;
             score = fitting_e / e_size;
             if *score* ≥ ϕ **then**
               New_Model[e].a.properties = properties;
               list_of_data_drifts.append({e,a});
      if *|list_of_data_drifts| >0* **then**
      | H_P.append(New_Model)

Algorithm 1: Algorithm to synthesise a process history

detected earlier. In the event stream three new traces are occuring, each of them having an outlier in the event `Transport`. With a sliding window size of 3, only outliers are in consideration for new models. Each time an outlier is detected, a new range is calculated if there are more or equal κ outlier in the sliding window. When the third outlier is detected, this requirement is met and the new range from 30 to 70 is calculated. Each of the currently viewed speed values are fitting this range. A new model is appended to the process history.

3.2   Data Drift Identification

Algorithm 1 detects data drifts in an event stream and creates new models for the process history. Every time a new process model is appended to the process history a data drift is detected. The four types of data drifts, in relation to a process history, can be defined formally as follows:

Definition 2 (Data Drift Types). *Let U be a given set of unfinished traces. Moreover let H be a process history for a process P containing only data drifts, which can be easily filtered by checking if the list of data drifts in a Model M is $\neq \emptyset$. Let $H_{dd} \subseteq H$ be the models of the process history containing data drifts and for $M_n =<E, <(e_0, A_0^c), ..., (e_k, A_k^c)>> \in H_{dd}$ let $M_n.drifts :=<(e_0, A_0^c), ..., (e_k, A_k^c)>$ yield the list of event attribute pairs, containing the attributes which have shown the data drift. Let $\phi \in [0,1]$, $\sigma \in [0,1]$ be thresholds, the function outlier, defined for a model and a data attribute, yielding true or false and the function similarity, defined for two attributes of an event, ranging from 0 to 1. The following drift types are defined as follows:*

- *Incremental Drift if $|H| \geq 2 \wedge \exists (e, A) \in M_n.drifts, (A \not\subseteq M_{n-1}[e] \wedge A \subset M_n[e]) \vee (A \not\subseteq M_n[e] \wedge A \subset M_{n-1})$*
- *Recurring Drift if $|H| \geq 3 \wedge \exists m \in \mathbb{N}, 2 \leq m \leq n, M_{n-m} \forall (\{e, A\} \in M_n.drifts,$*
  $similarity(M_n[e].A, M_{n-m}[e].A) \geq \sigma$
- *Gradual Drift if $|H| \geq 2 \wedge \exists t \in U, \{e, A\} \in M_n.drifts, \neg outlier$*
  $(M_{n-1}, t[e].A))$
- *Sudden Drift if $\neg GradualDrift$*

As a fitness function the same technique as in [14] using conformance checking with only considering moves in the log [2] is used. The similarity function checks if the statistical properties are alike. For example, if the intervals have a tremendous overlap or the distribution of likelihoods is similar.

It should be noted, that in this definition of data drift types, only the sudden and the gradual drift are distinct. It is possible for a data drift to be an incremental drift and recurring drift at the same time, e.g., a new data attribute has been detected in comparison to the last model, but this data attribute is also available and similar to an even older model. In the following, Algorithm 2, is explained in detail and shows how to answer RQ3.

As input parameters a list of unfinished traces U for M_0, M_{n-1}, a process history H_P and σ are required. σ describes the threshold for determining if two statistical properties are alike and ranges from 0 to 1, where 0 determines any 2 properties as equal and 1 determines only exactly equal properties to be similar.

If there is only one process model in the new process history no data drift had happened. The first distinction is made between a gradual drift and a sudden drift. It has to be either of them, so if it is a gradual drift, it cannot be a sudden drift and vice versa. For this, the algorithm iterates over the list_of_data_drifts of the current model. If there is a trace out of U for which its attributes and events match an entry in the list and is not an outlier, if compared to the second to last model, M_{n-1}, a gradual drift is detected, because there are still unfinished traces, that corresponds to the older model. The outlier function is the same, like in Algorithm 1. The third position in the return vector is set to 1, which signals a

Input: Traces u (list of unfinished traces), H (Process History),
  ϵ (maximum error between similar statistical properties.)
Result: **type_vector[0,0,0,0]** (**Positions represent Drifts [Inc,Rec,Grad,Sudden], 1**
  represents this type of drift occurred.)
res = [0,0,0,0];
if $|H| \leq 1$ **then**
  | return "Error: No drift"
// M is an abstraction to directly access the models of H
for e,a in M.list_of_data_drifts **do**
  | **for** t in U **do**
  | | **if** !outlier(M_{n-1},t[e].a) **then**
  | | | res[2] = 1 //Gradual Drift
  | | | break;
if res[2]$\neq$ 1 **then**
  | res[3]=1; // Sudden Drift
for e,a in M_n.list_of_drift_events **do**
  | **if** (!(M_{n-1}[e].contains a) **then**
  | | res[0]=1; // Incremental Drift
  | **if** (!(M_n[e].contains a) **then**
  | | res[0]=1; // Incremental Drift
if $|H| \geq 3$ **then**
  | **for** m in (M_0,M_{n-2}) **do**
  | | bool found = false;
  | | **for** e,a in M_n.list_of_drift_events **do**
  | | | **if** similarity(M_n[e].a,m[e].a) $< \epsilon$ **then**
  | | | | found = true;
  | | | | break;
  | | **if** found **then**
  | | | res[1]=1; // Recurring drift;
return res;

Algorithm 2: Algorithm to identify data drift.

detected gradual drift. Likewise it can be determined if it is not a gradual drift, a sudden drift is detected.

In the next step, the list_of_drift_events is again iterated. If an attribute is not found in the older model M_{n-1} or if an attribute is not found in the current model M_n, it can be deduced that the attribute has been added or removed respectively. This indicates an incremental drift, represented by a change the value of the first element to 1 of the return vector.

If there are at least 3 process models in the history, a recurring drift can be detected. If there is at least one model from M_0 to M_{n-2} where all attributes of the list_of_data_drifts are similar, a recurring drift is detected. The resulting vector is returned at the end containing the information on which data drift could been detected. In the next section, the two algorithms are evaluated on a real life log, using a log from the manufacturing domain.

4   Evaluation

For evaluating the approach, a prototypical implementation in Ruby [9] is used and applied on a real world process execution log from the manufacturing domain. The underlying process executes the manufacturing of small metal parts for different machines.

Algorithms 1 and 2, are integrated into the algorithms presented in [14], however the work at hand is completely independent of the existing work. The steps creating the trace_map and using a sliding window have been merged from the algorithm from [14] into Algorithms 1 and 2 to save computation time.

The log files from the real world example are stored in XES format and consist of 10 process instances containing 40436 events in total, but instead of being serialised in XML, the log files are serialised in YAML [4]. There is no information lost while transforming XML into YAML and vice versa. The process execution log has been transformed into an event stream. The models in the process history have been discovered, using the approach in [14].

For this evaluation we pick the event "AXIS/Z/aaTorque" and look at the data attribute "value". This event appears 4415 times in the log files in total and is numeric. The only available non-numeric data attributes in this log file, reflect either an enumeration, where only specific values are allowed or an arbitrary value, which lets us only detect the moment this attribute has been detected often enough to be in the process history, κ times.

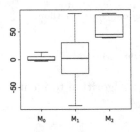

Fig. 4. Results reflecting the range of the torque value

The event "AXIS/Z/aaTorque" describes the positioning of the machine part in the z axis. With the sliding window k set to 200 and κ to 100, the first boxplot, seen in Fig. 4 (M_0), has been detected. For the outlier detection, the length of the whiskers, the interval $[-11.05, 15.28]$ has been calculated. Using 0.9 for the threshold ϕ, 2 data drifts have been detected, at the 123rd and 3187th time the event appeared in the event stream, shifting the boxplot to Fig. 4 (M_1) and (M_2) with the new intervals $[-105.10, 38.75]$ and $[-20.28, 89.99]$, two significant changes in the business process logic. This could be caused by a different part being produced in the machine using different values, or the replacement of a part of the machine where the new part is using new parameters.

Using a less strict drift detection threshold ϕ with 0.8, 8 drifts have been detected. The ranges of the intervals differ greatly, where only the fourth drift, when the event appeared for the 1795th time and the last drift, when the event appeared for the 2800th time could be suggested as a recurring drift. The intervals $[-105.10, 38.75]$ and $[-117.42, 91.08]$ overlap about 68%. Since there is always the same number of data attributes in the event, caused be the process execution engine which saved these logs, the only incremental drift is always the first on at the κth time the event occurs, since in the previous model the data attribute is absent. All of these drifts are gradual drifts, because the drift never occurred in the last appearance of an event of a process instance.

This evaluation was carried out with a proof of concept implementation to visualise and present data drifts in a data attribute of an event and the determination of its type. This procedure can be reproduced with any number of attributes of events, yielding a new model with adjusted statistical properties for the drifting attributes.

5 Summary and Outlook

This work introduces an extension to process histories to include data attributes and to detect and identify data drifts from event streams. Data drifts are part of the evolution of business process, therefore a data drift can be categorised into the four categories of concept drifts., i.e., incremental, recurring, gradual, and sudden. All four types can be detected and are formally defined. Two new algorithms have been presented. The first one synthesises a process history with data attributes. The other one allows to determine the type of data drift. The evaluation shows promising results. Based on a prototypical implementation and a real-world data set from the manufacturing domain it is possible to detect data drifts. The future work includes a more user friendly implementation of the algorithms and testing the algorithms on more data sets.

Acknowledgment. This work has been partly funded by the Vienna Science and Technology Fund (WWTF) through project ICT15-072 and by the Austrian Research Promotion Agency (FFG) via the "Austrian Competence Center for Digital Production" (CDP) under the contract number 854187.

References

1. IEEE standard for extensible event stream (XES) for achieving interoperability in event logs and event streams. IEEE Std 1849–2016, pp. 1–50, November 2016
2. Van der Aalst, W., Adriansyah, A., van Dongen, B.: Replaying history on process models for conformance checking and performance analysis. Wiley Interdisciplinary Reviews: Data Mining and Knowledge Discovery **2**(2), 182–192 (2012)
3. van der Aalst, W.M.P.: Process Mining - Data Science in Action, 2nd edn. Springer, Heidelberg (2016). https://doi.org/10.1007/978-3-662-49851-4
4. Ben-Kiki, O., Evans, C., Ingerson, B.: Yaml ain't markup language (yaml^{TM}) version 1.1. yaml.org, Technical Report, p. 23 (2005)
5. Bose, R.P.J.C., van der Aalst, W.M.P., Žliobaitė, I., Pechenizkiy, M.: Handling concept drift in process mining. In: Mouratidis, H., Rolland, C. (eds.) CAiSE 2011. LNCS, vol. 6741, pp. 391–405. Springer, Heidelberg (2011). https://doi.org/10. 1007/978-3-642-21640-4_30
6. Bose, R.J.C., Van Der Aalst, W.M., Zliobaite, I., Pechenizkiy, M.: Dealing with concept drifts in process mining. IEEE Trans. Neural Netw. Learn. Syst. **25**(1), 154–171 (2014)
7. Burattin, A., Sperduti, A., van der Aalst, W.M.: Heuristics miners for streaming event data. arXiv preprint arXiv:1212.6383 (2012)

8. Chen, S.S., Gopinath, R.A.: Gaussianization. In: Advances in Neural Information Processing Systems, pp. 423–429 (2001)
9. Matsumoto, Y., Ishituka, K.: Ruby programming language (2002)
10. Alves de Medeiros, A., Van Dongen, B., Van Der Aalst, W., Weijters, A.: Process mining: Extending the alpha-algorithm to mine short loops. Technical report, BETA Working Paper Series (2004)
11. Pauker, F., Mangler, J., Rinderle-Ma, S., Pollak, C.: centurio.work - modular secure manufacturing orchestration. In: BPM Industry Track, pp. 164–171 (2018)
12. Reichert, M., Weber, B.: Enabling Flexibility in Process-Aware Information Systems - Challenges, Methods, Technologies. Springer, Heidelberg (2012). https://doi.org/10.1007/978-3-642-30409-5
13. Rozinat, A., Aalst, W.M.P.: Decision mining in business processes. Beta, Research School for Operations Management and Logistics (2006)
14. Stertz, F., Rinderle-Ma, S.: Process histories-detecting and representing concept drifts based on event streams. In: CoopIS, pp. 318–335 (2018)
15. van Zelst, S.J., van Dongen, B.F., van der Aalst, W.M.: Event stream-based process discovery using abstract representations. Knowl. Inf. Syst. **54**(2), 407–435 (2018)

How Complex Does Compliance Get?

Andrea Zasada[(✉)]

University of Rostock, Rostock, Germany
andrea.zasada@uni-rostock.de

Abstract. Metrics have been applied in software engineering to manage the complexity of program code. This paper explores a new application area of the classic software engineering metrics to determine the complexity of compliance rules in business processes. Despite the critical voices noting the rather weak theoretical foundation, metrics provide effective measures for overlooking the concepts that may drive the complexity of a program. Their scope, scalability, and perceived ease of use do not diffuse these doubts, but provide ample reasons to believe that there is more to complexity analysis than numbers, and that a better methodological approach can help to reveal their true potential. Utilizing this potential would be of great importance, not only for establishing effective and efficient compliance management, but also for providing innovative solutions to digitalization trends and increasing data stacks. While some extant work has shown the applicability of software metrics for analyzing the complexity of process models, metrics have not been applied so far to manage the complexity of compliance rules. The approach presented in this paper provides an integrated view on the complexity of compliance rules that are modeled with conceptually different compliance languages. To this end, we review and discuss the literature on software metrics to derive the definitions needed to compute the complexity of compliance rules, and to refurbish the methodological foundation of software engineering metrics.

Keywords: Complexity metrics · Compliance rules · Business process ·
Model complexity · Compliance modeling

1 Introduction

Compliance modeling is hard work. Not only do we encounter numerous regulations that need to be interpreted and applied to the respective field of business, but compliance management has arrived at a point where it is essential to prove its efficiency and prepare for emerging problems in process modeling, such as the challenges of big data [1]. While quality attributes and the comprehension of a business process model have been studied, for instance in [23, 27], similar evaluations are novel to compliance research. Existing studies focus on the expressiveness of the language [16, 20], whereas user evaluations and formal analysis addressing the manageability or comprehension of compliance rules are missing. Reasoning about the suitability of a language, however, requires both the expressiveness and complexity of a language to be managed [18]. While expressiveness is mostly positively associated with the representational capability of a language [28], from a practical point of view models that are too complex

© Springer Nature Switzerland AG 2019
C. Cappiello and M. Ruiz (Eds.): CAiSE Forum 2019, LNBIP 350, pp. 253–265, 2019.
https://doi.org/10.1007/978-3-030-21297-1_22

can create various problems for the process modeler, like the increasing amount of time consumed in reading and writing a model [26], or the increasing risks of modeling errors [22].

To contribute to the ease of use of current and future compliance modeling languages, this paper tackles the practical complexity of compliance rule formalizations and derives complexity measures for language constructs used in a concrete model. In contrast, theoretical complexity refers to the number of language constructs specified by a whole language [9]. All in all, we adopt three complexity metrics, and alter the determinants of the metrics to the format of compliance rules. This is a necessary and important step, since compliance rules are usually represented by much smaller units than any software module. The findings can be used (a) to analyze and compare the complexity of different compliance languages based on the modeling result; and (b) to achieve a better alignment between the expressiveness of compliance languages and their complexity.

To this end, we adopt the metrics proposed by Halstead [14], Henry and Kafura [17], as well as Cardoso [3]. The complexity measures are illustrated by calculating the complexity of example rules that are modeled with three conceptually different compliance languages; that is, Compliance Request Language (CRL), the declarative modeling language Declare, and Process Compliance Language (PCL). By choosing a rather heterogeneous sample, we ensure that the derived complexity measures capture various language aspects, and that the procedure can be easily transferred to other languages.

The remainder of this paper is structured into four sections. In Sect. 2, some of the most commonly used software metrics are discussed. Section 3 presents the example rules that will illustrate the application of the metrics in Sect. 4. Section 5 summarizes the contributions and limitations of this work.

2   Complexity Metrics

A software metric is basically a mathematical function which expresses a certain property of the software by a numerical value [2]. This number is interpreted with respect to relevant benchmarks and serves for the evaluation of program code regarding its textual or structural complexity. Metrics can be a useful tool to detect and predict modeling errors, improve programming productivity, and ensure overall software quality [22]. The most prominent examples are Halstead's complexity, McCabe's cyclomatic complexity, Henry and Kafura's information flow and lines of code (LOC) [19].

Halstead [14] defines several metrics for calculating the effort it takes to read and write a program. In their basic configuration, the metrics define different functions to estimate the vocabulary, length, volume, and difficulty of a program. Vocabulary and length are determined by a simple operand and operator count [5]. The results are reused in the following functions. The problem with this approach is that the metrics have been developed without a proper formal foundation [29]. That is, differences between programming languages have not been accounted for and may lead to wrong interpretations. Besides, Halstead's metrics concentrate on lexical complexity. Consequently, concepts implicating a direction, or other structural relationships, are more difficult to map.

For measuring the complexity of a graph, McCabe [21] provides an interesting solution. He suggests computing the number of independent paths in a program. The nodes of a graph are assigned to specific code sequences. A link in terms of a directed edge between two nodes persists if the second code sequence can be executed directly after the first one [12]. Because of these rudimentary assignments, the metric can serve as an indicator for the structuredness of a program. More recently, Cardoso [3] developed a metric to analyze the control flow complexity of business processes. Using McCabe's instrument, the metric describes the control flow based on the decision types in a model. In contrast to McCabe, this metric tackles the semantic difference between nodes.

More simple structures can be measured by LOC [11]. Its calculation is based on counting the number of semicolons, which equates to the number of physical source lines of code, excluding comments and blank lines. LOC serves as input for the information flow metric of Henry and Kafura [17]. The metric calculates the data flow as incoming and outgoing data calls with respect to LOC. The criticism has been made that the function yields a complexity value of zero if one of the data parameters is missing [29]. To capture typical program structures, like segmentation into lines or the nesting of code, LOC has been modified repeatedly [12]. However, it is this focus on high-level structures which makes LOC overall less attractive for mapping compliance details.

As the discussion shows, the translation of process elements into mathematical functions is not free of information losses, not to mention that the different process aspects are quite difficult to combine in one metric. Beyond this background, there are at least two motivations to check the applicability of different metrics rather than to adopt a single metric. First, the expressiveness of the individual metric depends on the combination of factors that can be captured, but, as we can see from the degree of specialization, there is not one solution fitting all process dimensions. Furthermore, the conceptual difference between the investigation subjects; that is, the compliance approaches themselves, hinders the comparability of the languages if no formal foundation is provided. To close this gap, we explore the applicability of three metrics for estimating the complexity of compliance rules for different compliance languages. The choice among Halstead's, Henry and Kafura's, and Cardoso's metrics has been influenced by the quality and quantity of the concepts that can be expressed.

3   Example Rules

In this section, we will provide examples to illustrate the different calculation methods of the metrics. Table 1 shows four requirements describing basic airport security procedures [10]. The first and last requirements relate to the control flow; that is, the order (R4) and occurrence (R1) of activities. R2 and R3 depict a permission and an authorization. The formalized compliance rules are given in Tables 2 through 4.

As Table 2 shows, CRL provides four patterns to formalize the given requirements [8]. Two of them, the *Exists* and *Precedes* patterns, are very common among pattern-based approaches [25]. The first pattern specifies that a task has to occur at least once in a process model (R1), while the second pattern defines a relation between two tasks so

Table 1. Example requirements (adopted from [10], Annex I)

ID	Requirement	Section
R1	All originating, transfer and transit passengers and their cabin baggage shall be screened	4.1.1 (a)
R2	Transit passengers and their cabin baggage may be exempted from screening, if: (a) they remain on board the aircraft	4.1.3 (a)
R3	Persons […] shall have successfully completed a background check before either a crew identification card or an airport identification card authorising unescorted access to security restricted areas is issued to them	1.2.4
R4	All hold baggage shall be screened prior to being loaded onto an aircraft	5.1.1

that the second task is released, if the first task becomes true (R4). In R3, we model a condition on a task that needs to be fulfilled before the next task can be performed. However, the deployed *Frees* pattern cannot capture how the decision is made for one of the ID cards. R2 cannot be modeled unequivocally either, because there is no direct support of the concept of permissions in temporal logics [13]. To compensate for this deficit, we modeled this requirement with the *Substitute* pattern.

Table 2. Formalized compliance rules in *CRL*

ID	Compliance rule
R1	Pattern: (ScreenPassenger *And* ScreenCabinBaggage) *Exists* LTL: F(ScreenPassenger $\wedge$ ScreenCabinBaggage)
R2	Pattern: (PassengerRemainOnBoard *And* CabinBaggageRemainOnBoard) *Substitute* Screening LTL: G(¬Screening) $\rightarrow$ F(PassengerRemainOnBoard $\wedge$ CabinBaggageRemainOnBoard)
R3	Pattern: BackgroundCheck = 'Successful' *Frees* (IssueCrewID *Or* IssueGroundStaffID) LTL: BackgroundCheck = 'Successful' R(IssueCrewID $\vee$ IssueGroundStaffID)
R4	Pattern: ScreenHoldBaggage *Precedes* LoadHoldBaggage LTL: ¬LoadHoldBaggage W ScreenHoldBaggage

Temporal operators: F = final, G = global, W = weak until, R = release; Logical operators: $\wedge$ and, $\vee$ or, ¬ not.

Table 3 shows the rule mapping for Declare. Similar to CRL, each visual pattern of Declare owns a formal representation in temporal logic. Both languages share a large set of control flow patterns inspired by Dwyer's property patterns [6]. In contrast to CRL, we modeled R3 by a combination of a *Branched_Existence* pattern and an *Exclusive_1_Of_2* pattern [24] to express the link from the background check to the decision between two different ID cards. Similar to CRL, R3 cannot be modeled without information loss. The biggest semantic difference, though, can be observed for the permission (R2). For Declare, we decided to use the *Not_Response* pattern which resembles a negated *LeadsTo* pattern of CRL. Obviously, the semantics is not the same

Table 3. Formalized compliance rules in *Declare*

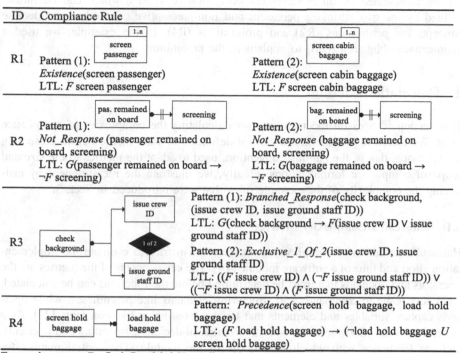

ID	Compliance Rule
R1	Pattern (1): [1..n screen passenger] *Existence*(screen passenger) LTL: *F* screen passenger	Pattern (2): [1..n screen cabin baggage] *Existence*(screen cabin baggage) LTL: *F* screen cabin baggage
R2	Pattern (1): [pas. remained on board ⊣⊢ screening] *Not_Response* (passenger remained on board, screening) LTL: *G*(passenger remained on board → ¬*F* screening)	Pattern (2): [bag. remained on board ⊣⊢ screening] *Not_Response* (baggage remained on board, screening) LTL: *G*(baggage remained on board → ¬*F* screening)
R3	[check background → issue crew ID / 1 of 2 / issue ground staff ID] Pattern (1): *Branched_Response*(check background, (issue crew ID, issue ground staff ID)) LTL: *G*(check background → *F*(issue crew ID ∨ issue ground staff ID)) Pattern (2): *Exclusive_1_Of_2*(issue crew ID, issue ground staff ID) LTL: ((*F* issue crew ID) ∧ (¬*F* issue ground staff ID)) ∨ ((¬*F* issue crew ID) ∧ (*F* issue ground staff ID))
R4	[screen hold baggage →• load hold baggage] Pattern: *Precedence*(screen hold baggage, load hold baggage) LTL: (*F* load hold baggage) → (¬load hold baggage *U* screen hold baggage)

Temporal operators: F = final, G = global, U = until; Logical operators: ∧ and, ∨ or, ¬ not.

as for the *Substitute* pattern of CRL, but none of the other Declare patterns seems to have a better fit.

The last table in this section presents the deontic modalities that we need to capture the normative meanings of the legal requirements. Compared to CRL and Declare, PCL does not struggle with interpretation of the requirements, because it depends on a

Table 4. Formalized compliance rules in *PCL*

ID	Compliance rule
R1	NewPassenger ⇒ [*OAPNP*] ScreenPassenger, ScreenCabinBaggage
R2	TransitPassenger, RemainOnBoard ⇒ [*P*] NoScreening CabinLuggage, RemainOnBoard ⇒ [*P*] NoScreening
R3	CabinCrew, BackgroundCheckSuccessful ⇒ [*OAPNP*] IssueIDCard GroundStaff, BackgroundCheckSuccessful ⇒ [*OAPNP*] IssueIDCard
R4	LoadHoldBaggage ⇒ [*OAPNP*] ScreenHoldBaggage **Alternatively** ¬ScreenedHoldBaggage ⇒ [*OM*] ¬LoadHoldBaggage

Obligation operators: OAPNP = achievement, persistent, non-preemptive, OM = maintenance, P = permission; Logical operator: ¬ not.

different conceptual angle than temporal logics [15]. The requirements R1, R3, and R4 can be represented by an achievement obligation (OAPNP), which can be further defined by the two attributes persistent and non-preemptive. The other two deontic concepts are permissions (R2) and prohibitions (R4). In the example, we used a maintenance obligation (OM) to implement the prohibition.

4   Calculation Method

This section focuses on the measures for calculating the complexity of compliance rules. We therefore provide first a general definition of each metric before presenting the approach, that is, the naming convention, used to adapt the metrics to the size and scope of compliance formalizations. Finally, we illustrate the measurement by estimating the complexity of the example rules that were introduced in Sect. 3.

4.1   Halstead's Complexity Metrics

Halstead's definition of complexity comprises six metrics to estimate the implementation effort and time of a software module [14]. The key concepts of the metrics are the operators and operands that must be determined before the functions can be calculated. Operators relate to commands and structuring elements like parentheses, while operands capture variables and elements that have a fixed value like constants [22]. As a general rule, the effort increases with the number of decidable operators and operands, and the frequency with which they occur in the module. The central metrics for measuring complexity (and time in seconds) are presented below:

$$\textbf{Vocabulary}\, n = n_1 + n_2 \tag{1}$$

$$\textbf{Length}\, N = N_1 + N_2 \tag{2}$$

$$\textbf{Volume}\, V = N \cdot \log_2(n) \tag{3}$$

$$\textbf{Difficulty}\, D = \frac{n_1}{2} \cdot \frac{N_2}{n_2} \tag{4}$$

$$\textbf{Effort}\, E = D \cdot V \tag{5}$$

$$\textbf{Time}\, T = \frac{E}{18} \tag{6}$$

where n_1 (n_2) is the number of unique operators (operands) and N_1 (N_2) is the total number of operators (operands). The metrics can be extended by functions for, for example, program level (L) or number of delivered bugs (B) [12], which are indicators for the error-proneness of a program.

To transfer these metrics to all three compliance languages, we developed the scheme in Table 5. The definitions for the operator and operand count are designed to capture the typical elements of compliance rules. To arrive at this point, we reviewed the documentation of the three selected languages regarding recurring elements, such as patterns, nodes, and edges for the visual language; and respective patterns, modalities, and logical expressions for the other two languages. Thereafter, we applied the metrics to our example rules and recorded the results.[1]

Table 5. Definitions for the operator and operand count

Type	n_1	n_2
Flow object	{pattern, modality}	{activity, event, gateway}
Connecting object	{and, or, not, else, parentheses, sequence flow, message flow}	n.a.
Process constraint	n.a.	{data, resource, time}

Notes: Pattern, modality etc. *types* are counted per rule. Parentheses are counted as pair. Brackets of modalities are not counted. Sequence flow and data flow edges can be specified by different arrow types.

Table 6 shows how the metrics are calculated for CRL. Overall, the requirements R2 and R3 seem to be more complex due to the repetition of operands (i.e., task descriptions) and logical connections. This is supported by the results for CRL (E_{CRL} = 33.94), Declare (E_{DEC} = 48.10), and also PCL (E_{PCL} = 102.02/107.85). Compared to PCL (V_{PCL} = 17.55/18.97; D_{PCL} = 5/5.25), we found that the rules modeled with CRL (V_{CRL} = 10.31; D_{CRL} = 2.88) and Declare (V_{DEC} = 12.23; D_{DEC} = 3) diverge in volume and difficulty, possibly, because the rule length is considerably higher.

Another difference results from the semantic expressiveness of the languages. In contrast to CRL and PCL, Declare is restricted to control flow rules. Hence, data constraints could neither be modeled nor considered in the metrics. However, the

Table 6. Metrics calculation for *CRL*

ID	n_1	n_2	n	N_1	N_2	N	V	D	E	T
R1	3	1	4	3	2	5	10	3	30	1.67
R2	3	1	4	3	3	6	12	4.50$_{max}$	54$_{max}$	3
R3	3	2	5	3	4	7	16.25$_{max}$	3	48.76	2.71
R4	1	1	2	1	2	3	3$_{min}$	1$_{min}$	3$_{min}$	0.17
Σ	10	5	15	10	11	21	41.25	11.50	135.76	339.40
Mean	2.50	1.25	3.75	2.50	2.50	5.25	10.31	2.88	33.94	1.89

Operators (n_1): pattern, parentheses, and, or; operands (n_2): activity, data.

---

[1] A complete documentation of all metric calculations can be retrieved from http://win-dl.informatik. uni-rostock.de/190101_metrics_calculation.pdf.

calculation shows a relatively high effort for Declare, although it deploys almost the same patterns as CRL. This might be the case because we had to repeat certain patterns to model more complex rules. The last metric measures the implementation time. It has to be interpreted bearing in mind ($T_{CRL} = 1.89$; $T_{DEC} = 2.67$; $T_{PCL} = 5.67/5.99$) that the number 18 is an approximation for program code.

4.2   Henry and Kafura's Information Flow Metric

Henry and Kafura define a complexity value which attempts to measure how simple the connections between software modules are [17]. Connections are defined as channels or information flows whereby one module can pass information to the other [5]. The data exchange is restricted by the flow type. Local flows may either be direct, if module A passes parameters to B, or indirect, if A returns a value to B or module C calls A and B, and the result value is passed from A to B. Global flows indicate that A writes to a data structure and B reads from that data structure. The connections between modules, named coupling, is also known in the process domain, where it is used to locate design and implementation weaknesses.

The concrete metric is composed of two channels (fan_{in} and fan_{out}), describing the information flow between modules, and a weighing factor (length). The fan_{in} (fan_{out}) of module A is defined as the number of local flows into (from) module A plus the number of data structures from which module A retrieves (updates) information. Thus, the complexity value (C_v) can be described by the function:

$$\textbf{Complexity } C_v = length \cdot (fan_{in} \cdot fan_{out})^2$$

where the length is measured by LOC (or cyclomatic complexity). That means the complexity depends on the procedure code (module size) as well as the complexity of the procedure's connections to its environment.

Like Halstead's complexity, information complexity is a software-specific measure that needs to be adapted to compliance languages. To this end, we propose to distinguish the presentation mode, i.e., textual or visual; see Table 7. LOC is reinterpreted to the number of patterns or modalities that are used to express one requirement. In the case of LTL, we counted the temporal operators. Another interpretation can be found in [30]. Fan_{in} and fan_{out} can be simply mapped to the inputs and outputs of activities. To avoid a zero value, we set the base of each $fan_{in} = fan_{out} = 1$. Moreover, we found that the measure is not sensitive to text-based languages. Consequently, the metric can only serve as a weak indicator for the complexity of compliance rules.

Table 7. Definitions for LOC and information flow

Mode	LOC	fan_{in}	fan_{out}
Textual	{pattern, modality, temporal operator}	{and-split, or-split}	{and-join, or-join}
Visual		{ingoing edges}	{outgoing edges}

The complexity of the example rules is calculated as Table 8 illustrates. The complexity values for Declare ($C_{v\ DEC} = 28$) and PCL ($C_{v\ PCL} = 28.25$) are almost identical, whereas CRL yields the lowest complexity ($C_{v\ CRL} = 3.25$). In contrast to Halstead's metrics, R2 and R3 do not result in higher complexity. Due to the lack of split and join connectors in CRL and PCL expressions, we decided to count the logical connector "and" as fan_{in} and "or" as fan_{out}. Structuring elements such as parentheses could not be mapped to the metric. Overall, the calculation suffers from the uneven differentiation of inputs and outputs, which explains the low complexity of CRL.

Table 8. Metrics calculation for *Declare*

ID	LOC	fan_{in}	fan_{out}	$C_{v\ DEC}$
R1	2	2	1	8
R2	2	2	1	8
R3	2	1	2	8
R4	1	2	1	4_{min}
$\sum$	1.75	1.75	1.25	7
Mean	7	7	5	28

4.3 Cardoso's Control Flow Metric

Cardoso defines process complexity as the degree to which a process model is difficult to analyze, understand, or explain [4]. He assumes that complexity depends on the elements that are used to describe the logical structure of a process. These can be divided into activities and transitions. Activities are represented using circles and transitions using arrows. The focus lies on the transitions, which indicate the possible execution states of a process. A new state results from the execution of an activity. An activity with more than one outgoing transition can be classified as xor-split, or-split, or and-split. The metric counts the present split constructs of the process. The absolute control flow complexity is then calculated as the sum of all split constructs:

$$\text{Complexity } CFC_{abs}(P) = \sum_{i \in \{XOR-splits\ of\ P\}} CFC_{XOR-split}(i)$$
$$+ \sum_{j \in \{OR-splits\ of\ P\}} CFC_{OR-split}(j)$$
$$+ \sum_{k \in \{AND-splits\ of\ P\}} CFC_{AND-split}(k)$$

where CFC_{abs} is the absolute complexity of process P, and the or-split is determined by CFCOR-split (activity$i$) = $2^n - 1$ with n = fan_{out} of the split. The or-split is set to a higher level because it generates a greater number of states. The relative control flow complexity CFC_{rel} (P) can be calculated from CFC_{abs} (P) divided by the number of distinct xor-or-and-splits of the process [3].

For the calculation of the complexity, we adopt the definitions in Table 9. Or-splits are not specified, because compliance rules typically imply an exclusive choice. Since the metric is based on output flows, the different split types can be determined

Table 9. Definitions for the splits of the control flow

Mode	xor-split	or-split	and-split
Textual	{or, ∨}	–	{and, comma, ∧}
Visual	{or}	–	{and}

unambiguously. However, in comparison to information flow complexity, the CFC metric does not provide a measure for the internal complexity of a module.

Table 10 shows the metrics calculation for PCL. The numbers indicate a difference between the absolute complexity of both CRL ($CFC_{abs\ CRL}$ (P) = 3) and Declare ($CFC_{abs\ DEC}$ (P) = 2) compared to PCL ($CFC_{abs\ PCL}$ (P) = 7). The relative complexity shows a similar picture ($CFC_{rel\ CRL}$ (P) = 1.50; $CFC_{rel\ DEC}$ (P) = 1; $CFC_{rel\ PCL}$ (P) = 3.50). R2 and R3 exceed the complexity of the other rules, especially because some rules have a zero value due to the patterns that do not use split connectors. PCL, on the other hand, deploys two modalities with a pair of and-splits which increases the complexity considerably. In this regard, the metric provides only limited access to the control flow complexity of compliance rules.

Table 10. Metrics calculation for *PCL*

ID	xor-split	and-split	$CFC_{abs\ PCL}$	$CFC_{rel\ PCL}$
R1	0	1	1	1
R2	1	2	3	1.50
R3	1	2	3	1.50
R4	0	0	0_{min}	0_{min}
∑	2	5	7	3.50
Mean	0.50	1.25	1.75	1.00

5 Contributions and Limitations

In this paper, we were able to address a part of the problem of the complexity of compliance rule formalizations. The excerpt that we used to develop and demonstrate our approach is complete, since "Any 'real' complexity is irrelevant, as we never interact with the total systems, only certain aspects of them at any one time" [7]. We focused on typical process elements that are used in compliance rule languages to model legal requirements. To assess the complexity of the regulatory expressions, we employed software metrics, and derived definitions for the application of the metrics' instruments. One main contribution is therefore, an overview of common software metrics, as well as a practical application of complexity metrics to simplify the selection and use of approved tools of another domain. In this regard, we found that Halstead's metrics were most flexible in adopting the features of compliance languages.

Nevertheless, there are certain limitations to this work. Since the focus has been on the knowledge transfer and differentiation problem, we concentrated our endeavors on a small but concise sample. Therefore, we can answer questions regarding how complex compliance rules are, but not what high complexity is. This is because there exist benchmarks for programs but not for compliance rules. That means, as of now, that it can only be said whether a formalization is complex in comparison to another formulation. In order to learn more about the practical complexity of compliance modeling languages, and process constraints in general, it is necessary to expand the sample in terms of requirements and compliance languages. A case study approach might be best suited in this regard.

Finally, there are several possibilities for extending this work. Most important in our view is to include more specific concepts in complexity discussion and measurement, such as similarity, cohesion and so forth. Besides, there is no better way to show how complex a language can get, than to determine its theoretical complexity as well. Another aspect is the human factor in compliance modeling. Many times it has been argued that automation is a desired feature to detect compliance violations, but this addresses mainly run time and post execution compliance. A major problem of organizations is the amount of information that is exchanged and that the individual must process. Thus, we need more information on the cognitive complexity of compliance to improve the design process and to make it cost- and time-efficient. Usability studies deploying cognitive theories in a context of information overload, complexity, and mental effort may be intriguing approaches to that problem.

References

1. Antoniou, G., et al.: Legal reasoning and big data: opportunities and challenges. In: 17th Workshop Proceedings of MIning and REasoning with Legal texts (MIREL), 17 September 2018, Luxembourg (2018)
2. Boehm, B.W., Brown, J.R.; Liplow, L.: Quantitative evaluation of software quality. In: Proceedings of 2nd International Conference on Software Engineering (ICSE), pp. 592–605 (1976)
3. Cardoso, J.: Business process control-flow complexity: metric, evaluation, and validation. Int. J. Web Serv. Res. 5(2), 49–76 (2008)
4. Cardoso, J.: Control-flow complexity measurement of processes and Weyuker's properties. In: 6th Proceedings of International Enformatika Conference, 23 December 2005, Warsaw, Poland, 213–218 (2005)
5. Curtis, B., Sheppard, S.B., Milliman, P., Borst, M.A., Love, T.: Measuring the psychological complexity of software maintenance tasks with the Halstead and McCabe metrics. IEEE Trans. Soft. Eng. 2, 96–104 (1979)
6. Dwyer, M.B., Avrunin, G.S., Corbett, J.C.: Patterns in property specifications for finite-state verification. In: Proceedings of the International Conference on Software Engineering, pp. 411–420 (1999)
7. Edmonds, B.: What is complexity? The philosophy of complexity per se with application to some examples in evolution. In: The evolution of complexity, pp. 1–17. Kluwer, Dordrecht (1999)
8. Elgammal, A., Turetken, O., van den Heuvel, W.J., Papazoglou, M.: Formalizing and appling compliance patterns for business process compliance. Softw. Syst. Model. 15, 119–146 (2016)

9. Erickson, J., Siau, K.: Theoretical and practical complexity of modeling methods. Commun. ACM **50**(8), 46–51 (2007)
10. EUR-Lex: Regulation (EC) No 300/2008 of the European Parliament and of the Council of 11 March 2008 on common rules in the field of civil aviation security and repealing Regulation (EC) No 2320/2002
11. Fenton, N.E.: Quantitative analysis of faults and failures in a complex software system. IEEE Trans. Softw. Eng. **26**, 797–814 (2000)
12. Ferrer, J., Chicano, F., Alba, E.: Estimating software testing complexity. Inf. Softw. Technol. **55**(12), 2125–2139 (2013)
13. Governatori, G., Hashmi, M.: No time for compliance. In: 19th IEEE Proceedings of International Enterprise Distributed Object Computing Conference (EDOC), 21–25 September 2015 (2015)
14. Halstead, M.H.: Elements of Software Science Operating and Programming Systems. Series, vol. 7. Elsevier, New York (1977)
15. Hashmi, M., Governatori, G., Wynn, M.T.: Normative requirements for regulatory compliance: an abstract formal framework. Inf. Syst. Front. **18**(3), 429–455 (2016)
16. Hashmi, M., Governatori, G.: Norms modeling constructs of business process compliance management frameworks: a conceptual evaluation. Artif. Intell. Law **26**(3), 1–55 (2017)
17. Henry, S., Kafura, D.: Software structure metrics based on information flow. IEEE Trans. Softw. Eng. **7**(5), 510–518 (1981)
18. Kiepuszewski, B.: Expressiveness and Suitability of Languages for Control Flow Modelling in Workflows. PhD Thesis, Queensland University of Technology, Brisbane (2003)
19. Kitchenham, B.: What's up with software metrics? - a preliminary mapping study. J. Syst. Softw. **83**(1), 37–51 (2010)
20. Knuplesch, D., Reichert, M.: A visual language for modeling multiple perspectives of business process compliance rules. Softw. Syst. Model. **1701**(3), 52–55 (2016)
21. McCabe, T.J.: A complexity measure. IEEE Trans. Softw. Eng. **SE-2**, 308–320 (1976)
22. Mendling, J.: Detection and prediction of errors in EPC business process models. PhD Thesis, Vienna University of Economics and Business, Vienna (2007)
23. Moreno-Montes De Oca, I., Snoeck, M., Reijers, H.A., Rodríguez-Morffi, A.: A systematic literature review of studies on business process modeling quality. Inf. Softw. Technol. **58**, 187–205 (2015)
24. Pesic, M.: Constraint-based workflow management systems: shifting control to users, PhD Thesis, Eindhoven University of Technology, Eindhoven (2008)
25. Ramezani, E., Fahland, D., van der Aalst, Wil M.P.: Where did i misbehave? Diagnostic information in compliance checking. In: Barros, A., Gal, A., Kindler, E. (eds.) BPM 2012. LNCS, vol. 7481, pp. 262–278. Springer, Heidelberg (2012). https://doi.org/10.1007/978-3-642-32885-5_21
26. Recker, J., Dreiling, A.: Does it matter which process modelling language we teach or use? An experimental study on understanding process modelling languages without formal education. In: 18th Proceedings of Australasian Conference on Information Systems (ACIS), 5–7 December 2007, Toowoomba, Australian (2007)
27. Recker, J., Reijers, H.A., van de Wouw, S.G.: Process model comprehension: the effects of cognitive abilities, learning style, and strategy. Commun. Assoc. Inf. Syst. **34**, 199–222 (2014)

28. Recker, J.: Opportunities and constraints: the current struggle with BPMN. Bus. Process Manag. J. **16**(1), 181–201 (2010)
29. Shepperd, M., Ince, D.C.: A critique of three metrics. J. Syst. Softw. **26**(3), 197–210 (1994)
30. Vanderfeesten, I., Cardoso, J., Reijers, H.A., Van Der Aalst, W.M.P.: Quality metrics for business process models. In: BPM and Workflow Handbook, vol. 144, no. 3, pp. 1–12 (2006)

Author Index

Printed in the United States
By Bookmasters